Rendering with MicroStation

Jerry Flynn

Bentley Institute Press

Exton, PA
2005

Rendering with MicroStation

First Edition

Copyright © 2005 Bentley Systems, Incorporated. All Rights Reserved.

Bentley, "B" Bentley logo, Bentley Institute Press, and MicroStation are either registered or unregistered trademarks or servicemarks of Bentley Systems, Incorporated or one of its direct or indirect wholly-owned subsidiaries. Other brands and product names are trademarks of their respective owners.

Publisher does not warrant or guarantee any of the products described herein or perform any independent analysis in connection with any of the product information contained herein. Publisher does not assume, and expressly disclaims, any obligation to obtain and include information other than that provided to it by the manufacturer.

The reader is expressly warned to consider and adopt all safety precautions that might be indicated by the activities herein and to avoid all potential hazards. By following the instructions contained herein, the reader willingly assumes all risks in connection with such instructions.

The publisher makes no representation or warranties of any kind, including but not limited to, the warranties of fitness for particular purpose of merchantability, nor are any such representations implied with respect to the material set forth herein, and the publisher takes no responsibility with respect to such material. The publisher shall not be liable for any special, consequential, or exemplary damages resulting, in whole or part, from the readers' use of, or reliance upon, this material.

ISBN Number: 0-9714141-7-3

Library of Congress Control Number: 2005932494

Published by:
Bentley Institute Press
Bentley Systems, Incorporated
685 Stockton Drive
Exton, PA 19341
www.bentley.com

Bentley Institute Press

Printed in the U.S.A.

Foreword

Ray Bentley of Bentley Systems, Inc.

Great visualization happens when you combine inspiration with good tools and the knowledge to use those tools. You bring inspiration to your work every day, and MicroStation has all the tools necessary to generate excellent 3D renderings of your designs – renderings that help you communicate intent, describe impact and demonstrate advantages.

The release of "Rendering with MicroStation" brings the required knowledge right to your fingertips. Authored by Jerry Flynn, the world's leading MicroStation visualization expert and evangelist, this book is a product of the years that Jerry has spent practicing great visualization and sharing his knowledge with MicroStation users around the world.

I first met Jerry Flynn in the late 1980s. Back then the visualization tools in MicroStation were very primitive, but Jerry was already creating inspired, compelling renderings. Since then, Jerry has remained a visionary for visualization in MicroStation and has helped guide the evolution of its rendering tools. And over the years, he's helped hundreds of firms and thousands of AEC professionals bring their designs to color and life from within the design program.

In truth, visualization was formerly an expensive, specialized, and often outsourced portion of the design flow. Companies sometimes would spend six figures acquiring the talent and tools to make renderings from MicroStation files. Today, visualization is in the mainstream and a common part of the design team's work. No longer the stuff of Hollywood movie magic and high-end gaming elite, excellent visualization in AEC is within reach of every MicroStation user today. This book just further proves it.

I am grateful for Jerry's enthusiasm and expertise, and with the guidance this book provides, I know you will be too.

Brian Parker of Cooper Carry, Architects

"AT LAST Jerry Flynn's vast rendering knowledge has been put to paper!

This book is a MUST HAVE for anyone, at any skill level, who is rendering and visualizing in MicroStation. Beginners will be led step by step through basic rendering techniques and onward to advanced visualization procedures... Pros will love having the book on the shelf as a reference and reminder guide for all those steps and settings we often forget. THANKS Jerry, and Bentley, for creating a training/reference book for the 3D masses!"

Contents

Chapter 1: Introduction to 3D Space 1
Opening MicroStation 1
   3D Space...1
   The 3D Design Cube 2
   Standard 3D Views..3
View Rotation 5
   Rotating a View with Dynamics.............................8
   Rotating a View by 3 Points 10
   Rotating Relative to a View or Drawing 13
View Volume...13
View Control Tool Box 15
   Display Depth and Active Depth 15
   Clip Volume and Clip Mask 18
   Displaysets 22
Rendering Tools tool box 24
Review Questions 25
Chapter Summary...25

Chapter 2: Camera Setups and Navigation 27
View Cameras 27
Perspective in a View 28
   The Change View Perspective Tool 28
Camera Settings Tool...31
The Define Camera Tool 36
   Camera View Projections 37
   Working with the Define Camera Tool....................42

v

| Contents |

    Camera Actions. 49
        Controlling Movement with the Pointer. 50
        Additional Define Camera Tool Settings 51
        Precision Settings 52
        Pan 53
        Pan Horizontal 57
        Pan Vertical 59
        Roll Camera 61
        Dolly/Elevate 63
        Dolly 65
        Lens Focal Length 67
        Lens View Angle 70
        Pan/Dolly 71
    Navigate Camera. 74
        Navigate Camera Advanced Mode. 78
    Review Questions 81
    Chapter Summary. 82

Chapter 3: Rendering Options and Settings 83
Gamma Correction for Photorealistic Rendering 83
Wiremesh, Hidden Line, and Filled Hidden Line 84
Constant, Smooth, and Phong 86
Photorealistic Ray Tracing 89
    Render and Ray Trace Settings. 91
    Photorealistic Rendering Workflow 91
Stereo Renderings. 99
Rendering Settings 99
    Miscellaneous Settings 100
    Distance Cueing Settings 112
View Attributes. 114
Rendering View Attributes 115
Working with Fog and Depth Cueing. 117
    Controlling Fog and Depth Cueing 117
Ray Tracing Dialog Box 122
    Real World Lighting 125
    Antialiasing Settings 126
    Advanced Rendering Settings 129
    Adjusting Ray Trace settings 131
Environment Mapping 133
Fresnel Effects 137
Render All Objects 138
Rendering Setup dialog box 139
Review Questions 143
Chapter Summary. 144

| Contents | vii

Chapter 4: Global and Source Lighting 144
Global Lighting 145
    Global Lighting Types 146
    Add Sky Light to All Solar and Distant Lights 157
    Approximate Ground Reflection for Sky Light 159
Light Ring and Solar Cluster 161
Source Lighting 163
Define Light Tool 165
    Light Source Types 168
Predefined Light Sources 171
    Creating Predefined Light Sources 171
Placing Lights 172
    Creating a Sky Opening 174
    Placing Point Lights 177
    Placing Spot Lights 180
    Creating Area Lights 185
    Attenuation 187
Review Questions 190
Chapter Summary 190

Chapter 5: Introduction to Materials 191
MicroStation's Color Table 192
Assigning Materials 194
Attaching Materials 197
Modifying Materials Using Query 198
Removing Assigned or Attached Materials 199
Working with Solids 202
Render Ready Cells 204
Review Questions 209
Chapter Summary 209

Chapter 6: Defining and Applying Materials 211
The Material Editor 211
    Assigning Materials by Level and Color 213
    Removing Material Assignments 216
    Materials attached as attributes 217
    Creating New Materials 221
    Pattern Mapping Modes 225
    Preview Material 225
Material Editor Advanced Mode 227
    The Advanced Options 228
Creating Photorealistic Materials 229
    Working from Existing Materials 230
    Using Transparent Background 233

| Contents |

    Creating More Materials 235
        Blending Texture with Base Color 240
        Using Bump Mapping 241
    Applying Materials. 244
        Dynamic Map Adjust. 251
        Rendering the Scene. 253
    Review Questions 254
    Chapter Summary. 254

Chapter 7: Advanced Materials 255

    Procedural Textures. 255
        Working with Procedural Textures 256
    Gradient Maps. 265
    Using ArchVision RPC files 271
        ArchVision Content Manager 271
        The RPC Tool Box 271
        Placing RPCs 272
        Editing RPCs 277
    Review Questions 278
    Chapter Summary. 279

Chapter 8: Facet Smoothing and Elevation Draping 281

    Surface Normals 281
    Facet Smoothing. 283
    Elevation Draping. 286
    Review Questions 289
    Chapter Summary. 289

Chapter 9: Exterior Rendering 291

    Daytime Lighting Setup. 291
        Using Sky Light. 294
        Using Light Ring and Solar Cluster 296
    Adding Background Images 298
    Applying Fog to Add Realism. 300
    Defining and Using Sky Cylinders. 302
    Adding Sky background with Environment Mapping 306
        Visible Environment Maps 307
    Nighttime or Dusk-to-Dawn Rendering. 311
        Sunset Rendering Setup. 311
        Dusk or twilight rendering 312
        Nighttime Rendering Setup. 315
        Nighttime Particle Traced Rendering 317
    Review Questions 320
    Chapter Summary. 320

| Contents |

Chapter 10: Interior Spaces and Global Illumination 321
Radiosity..321
    Radiosity and Lighting...322
    How radiosity solutions are generated 323
    Sky Openings and Radiosity 326
    Refining Radiosity Settings 330
Particle Tracing..335
    Particle Tracing Compared 335
How Particle Tracing works 341
    The Particle Shooting Phase 341
    Display Phase..342
    Disk Space Requirements for Particle Tracing..................342
    Meshing Settings..343
    Saving Particle Traced Solutions 345
IES Lighting..349
    Lighting Considerations for Photorealism 349
    Lighting Solution Considerations.............................352
Review Questions 354
Chapter Summary...354

Chapter 11: Photomatching 355
Match Design Geometry to a Raster Reference 355
Making Adjustments with the Photomatch Tool....................359
Displaying the Proposed Geometry................................362
Photomatch Using a Civil Engineering Example....................364
    Final Photomatch Render 368
Review Questions 370
Chapter Summary...370

Chapter 12: Generating Output 371
Saving Images to Disk 371
Banded Rendering 373
    Creating a Rendered Image Using the Banded Method 374
    Using Multiple Computers to Compute a Single Image..........375
Creating Panoramas..377
    Viewing the Panorama..381
Image Objects 382
    Creating an Image Object Panorama.........................383
Saving Multiple Images 385
3D Content in PDF Files 389
    Adding 3D Content from Design Models......................390
    Interacting with 3D Content in Adobe Reader 392
    3D Content Tool Bar in Adobe Reader 7.0....................394
    Items Added to the Right-Click Menu 396

Contents

Review Questions 397
Chapter Summary 397

Appendix: Rendering Glossary 399

Index 405

Exercises

1-1:	Review view orientations	3
1-2:	Rotate the Front view	5
1-3:	Center the active depth before rotating the view 6	
1-4:	Use the Rotate View tool's graphics	6
1-5:	Rotate views to standard view orientations	8
1-6:	Dynamic rotation options	8
1-7:	Rotate View 1 to align a plane in the design with view X-Y plane	10
1-8:	Rotate a view -90° about the x-axis	12
1-9:	Rotate a view -90° about the y-axis	12
1-10:	Change display depth in the Front view	16
1-11:	Change display depth in the Top view	17
1-12:	Apply a clip volume	18
1-13:	Move a clip volume	19
1-14:	Clear a clip volume	20
1-15:	Work with clip volumes and clip masks	21
1-16:	Use displaysets	23
1-17:	Select a different displayset	23
2-1:	Dynamically setting perspective for a view	28
2-2:	Set perspective with Dynamic Display disabled	29
2-3:	Toggle perspective display in two views	30
2-4:	Set up a camera view	31
2-5:	Set up a camera view using 3D data points	33
2-6:	Activate a view for Define Camera	36
2-7:	Change the view projection of the camera view	37
2-8:	Change projection to parallel	38

| Exercises |

2-9:	Set up a camera view with the Define Camera tool	43
2-10:	Interactively modify the eye point of a view cone	45
2-11:	Locate the eye point or target with precision inputs	47
2-12:	Move the view cone	48
2-13:	Select another view to be the camera view	49
2-14:	Pan the camera relative to the target	53
2-15:	Precisely pan the camera	55
2-16:	Rotate the camera in 5° increments about the target	56
2-17:	Pan the camera horizontally relative to the target	57
2-18:	Pan the camera vertically relative to the target	59
2-19:	Roll the camera	61
2-20:	Roll the camera in 5° steps	62
2-21:	Dolly/elevate the camera	63
2-22:	Dolly/elevate the camera in 10 unit steps	65
2-23:	Dolly the camera	65
2-24:	Dolly the camera in 10 unit steps	67
2-25:	Change the lens focal length of the camera view	68
2-26:	Change the lens focal length by varying the eye-to-target distance in 100 unit steps	69
2-27:	Change the lens view angle of the camera view	70
2-28:	Change the lens view angle in 10° steps	71
2-29:	Use the Pan/Dolly setting	72
2-30:	Pan/dolly the camera in steps of 10 units distance or 5° rotation	73
2-31:	Use Navigate Camera	76
2-32:	Navigate the camera using the mouse	78
3-1:	Compare the line rendering modes	85
3-2:	Compare the basic shading modes	87
3-3:	Use ray tracing	92
3-4:	Add environment maps	93
3-5:	Additional rendering options	95
3-6:	Render the element having a bump map material	96
3-7:	Control the number of reflections	97
3-8:	Turn on Visible Environment	98
3-9:	Stereo 3D	99
3-10:	Effect of stroke tolerance on rendering	100
3-11:	Stroke Tolerance and view dependency	101
3-12:	Use antialiasing	104
3-13:	Phong Shadow settings	107
3-14:	Phong Shadow Tolerance	108
3-15:	Use Multilevel Texture Interpolation	110
3-16:	Render with distance cueing	113
3-17:	Control fog	117
3-18:	Perform more adjustments to distance cueing	119
3-19:	Depth cueing	121
3-20:	Adjust basic settings for ray tracing	131

3-21:	Enable shadows, transparency, and reflection 132
3-22:	Increase the Transparency setting 133
3-23:	Set up environment maps for model 134
3-24:	Turn on Visible Environment 136
3-25:	Fresnel effects 137
3-26:	Render All Objects 138
3-27:	Create a Rendering Settings Setup 141
4-1:	Review the effect of global lighting 146
4-2:	Adjust ambient light settings 147
4-3:	Change material definitions by switching palettes 149
4-4:	View the effect of ambient lighting on materials 150
4-5:	Adjust the Flashbulb settings 151
4-6:	Ray trace the current solution with Flashbulb lighting 152
4-7:	Enable and configure solar lighting 155
4-8:	Turn on Solar Shadows 156
4-9:	Render with solar lighting and shadows 159
4-10:	Add sky light to reduce starkness of Solar shadows 160
4-11:	Use Light Ring 162
4-12:	Place a Distant Source light 172
4-13:	Add sky light to the distant light source 174
4-14:	Create a Sky Opening 174
4-15:	Place Point Lights 177
4-16:	Reduce the intensity of the Distant light 179
4-17:	Place spot lights 180
4-18:	Edit already placed lights 184
4-19:	Create area lights 186
4-20:	Attenuation of source lights 187
4-21:	Turn on attenuation for each light source 189
5-1:	Render with MicroStation's color table 192
5-2:	Attach a different color table 193
5-3:	Assign materials based on level and color 194
5-4:	Effect on material of changing element color 196
5-5:	Attach material to one of the columns 197
5-6:	Change the level/color of the right column 198
5-7:	Use Query Material to check materials and assignments 199
5-8:	Remove material 200
5-9:	Attach materials to solids 202
5-10:	Attach materials to faces of a SmartSolid 203
5-11:	Use render ready cells 205
6-1:	Tour the MicroStation Material Editor 212
6-2:	Assign materials by level and color 214
6-3:	Remove a single material assignment 216
6-4:	Remove multiple material assignments 217
6-5:	Check for missing materials 218
6-6:	Create a new palette and add/load an existing palette 219

| Exercises |

6-7:	Copy the required materials to the new palette	220
6-8:	Unload the original material palette	221
6-9:	Rename the default material	222
6-10:	Adjust the new material's properties	222
6-11:	Add a pattern map to the material definition	223
6-12:	Preview the floor material	226
6-13:	Assign the floor material	226
6-14:	Explore the Material Editor's Advanced Mode	227
6-15:	Create the ceiling material	230
6-16:	Create a second ceiling material	232
6-17:	Create main wall material	232
6-18:	Create stair railing material	234
6-19:	Create pendant lamp finish material	235
6-20:	Create the stair material	236
6-21:	Create the pendant lamp bowl material	237
6-22:	Create rug material	238
6-23:	Create window sill material	238
6-24:	Create window pane material	239
6-25:	Create window frame material	239
6-26:	Create trim material	240
6-27:	Create the base for the stair top rail material	240
6-28:	Edit material main wall to include a bump map	242
6-29:	Create second material for walls	243
6-30:	Decorative bump for Tiffany lamp	244
6-31:	Turn off display of the referenced elements	245
6-32:	Attach ceiling material to the face of a solid	246
6-33:	Assign materials stair top rail and stair railing	247
6-34:	Assign the trim material	247
6-35:	Assign the wall materials	248
6-36:	Assign further materials	248
6-37:	Assign a material to an element in a cell	249
6-38:	Assign materials to the pendant light	250
6-39:	Dynamically adjust texture map	252
6-40:	Render the scene	253
7-1:	Select a procedural texture	256
7-2:	Set the parameters for the Stone procedural texture	259
7-3:	Create a wood procedural texture	261
7-4:	Procedural texture clouds	262
7-5:	Work with settings for procedural texture Clouds	263
7-6:	Work with linear gradient maps	266
7-7:	Inspect the gradient material settings	267
7-8:	Use radial gradients	269
7-9:	Inspect the radial gradient settings	270
7-10:	Place an RPC	273
7-11:	Place a second RPC	274

| Rendering with MicroStation | xv

7-12: Render another view 276
7-13: Edit RPC 277
8-1: Attach facet smoothing to a DTM 284
8-2: Attach all the polygons for smoothing 285
8-3: Get information for material map 286
8-4: Create the elevation drape material 287
8-5: Assign the elevation drape material 288
9-1: Check the global lighting 292
9-2: Adding Sky Light 294
9-3: Add distant lights to fill in shadows 297
9-4: Add background images 298
9-5: Apply fog 300
9-6: Adjust the values for fog 301
9-7: Create a new material for the sky cylinder 302
9-8: Define the new material 303
9-9: Apply the material to the cylinder 305
9-10: Select Environment Maps 307
9-11: Environment maps seen through a cube 309
9-12: Sunset rendering setup 311
9-13: Twilight setup 313
9-14: Nighttime setup 316
9-15: Particle trace exterior night scene 318
9-16: Display Illuminance of view 319
10-1: Create a sky opening 326
10-2: Create a radiosity solution 327
10-3: Adjust the radiosity settings for a better result 329
10-4: Refining settings for final radiosity solution 330
10-5: Use Ray Trace Direct Illumination 331
10-6: Create a more complete solution 332
10-7: Save the radiosity solution 333
10-8: Loading a radiosity solution from a file 334
10-9: First look at particle tracing 336
10-10: Add particles to the solution 337
10-11: Turn on Ray Trace Direct Illumination 338
10-12: Fine-tune the lighting 340
10-13: Save a particle traced solution to disk 346
10-14: Retrieve a particle traced database and render other views 346
10-15: View an IES lighting photometric web and its data file 350
10-16: Render with IES lighting 351
11-1: Set up the initial camera view size 356
11-2: Attach a background image to the resized view 358
11-3: Use the camera tools to align the geometry to the photograph 358
11-4: Use Photomatch 360
11-5: Display the proposed geometry and render the view 362
11-6: Photomatch model 1 363

| Exercises |

11-7: Photomatch model 2 364
11-8: Photomatch survey points 364
11-9: Fine-tune the photomatch by adding additional points 367
11-10: Ray trace the final civil photomatch 369
11-11: Modify the Solar lighting to match the photograph 369
12-1: Save an image file to disk 372
12-2: Save an image in bands 374
12-3: Network distributed image creation 375
12-4: Save a panorama image file 380
12-5: View the saved panorama 382
12-6: Save an image object 384
12-7: Save multiple images 385
12-8: Finalize the list and execute the script 389
12-9: 3D in PDF from a design model 390
12-10: View PDF with 3D content in Acrobat 7.0 392

Introduction

This book assumes you know nothing about rendering. It starts out slowly, covering the important basics, and then progresses to more advanced topics. The concepts in this book are laid out in order of importance, beginning with three basic requirements for rendering, *Cameras*, *Lights*, and *Materials*.

While it is intended for users that are beginners in rendering, through to intermediate, it covers many advanced topics also. Even an expert could learn many valuable tips and tricks to improve his or her renderings. This book requires a prerequisite knowledge of MicroStation 3D.

It is my belief that if you cannot master MicroStation's camera tools, you will have great difficulty taking that all-important picture of your finished project. This very important topic is covered in detail in Chapter 2.

A great deal of time is devoted to lighting, which comes in second on my list but may, in fact, be the single most important aspect of the rendering process. You should be able to make a 3D scene look good even if all your materials happen to be cardboard. Setting up the right lighting can make or break a rendering. Therefore, considerable content is devoted to this subject.

| Introduction |

For truly photorealistic results, you will learn to master MicroStation's Material Editor and how to attach and apply these materials to a variety of 3D models, including civil, architectural, and industrial design.

Navigating through a myriad of rendering dialog boxes and settings, you will learn what these settings are and how they affect each rendering mode. Through exercises you will be able to see the effects a setting can have on your renderings. You will learn specialized procedures, such as using ArchVision® RPC™ files to add realPeople™ and realTrees™ to your 3D scenes. You will learn how to plot 3D content to Adobe® PDFs and to navigate a PDF, containing 3D content, using Adobe® Reader® 7.0.

Advanced rendering methods, particle tracing and radiosity, are covered in detail using several hands-on exercises. You will learn how to use multiple computers across a network to render a single high-resolution image in a fraction of the time normally required. You will learn all about generating image output from still images to panorama virtual reality images and image objects.

This book uses hands-on exercises to reinforce the topics covered.

Included with the book is a CD with a workspace containing all the models and materials used in the course. Bonus materials on the CD include a complete image library of textures, skies, environment boxes, and bump maps. Also included are several sample RPC content files, provided courtesy of ArchVision, Inc.

EXTRACTING THE DATA SETS

Before doing any exercises, you need to extract the data sets from the accompanying CD. The CD contains the Workspace you will be using for all the exercises, including design files, palettes, materials, and image library.

Extract all the files from the *RWM.zip* file into the folder where MicroStation in installed on your computer. By default, MicroStation is installed in *\Program Files\Bentley* folder, but this could be different on your computer.

Extract the files using the folder names. Select to overwrite the existing files since the Workspace folder already exists.

| MySELECT CD | xix

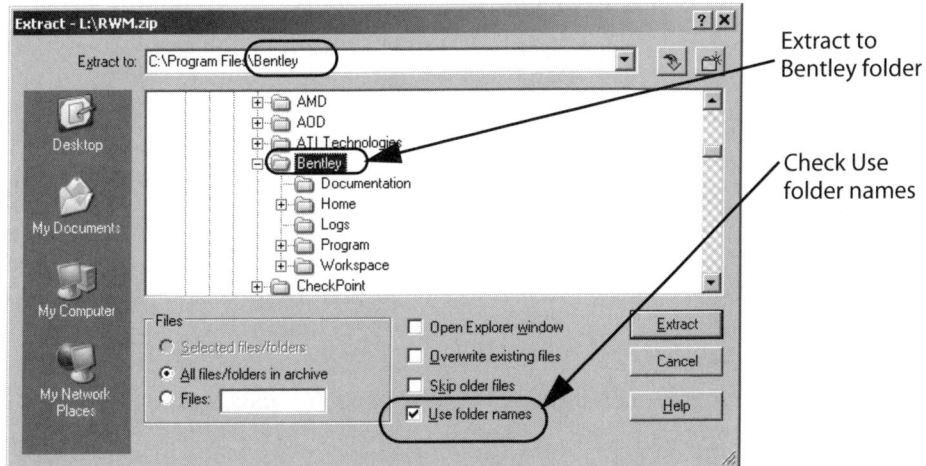

MYSELECT CD

Bentley SELECT Subscribers can order the data set and supporting files through the MySELECT CD program. MySELECT CD allows you to select the Bentley software or documents you need and have a CD delivered to your door.

To become a Bentley SELECT Subscriber, go to *http://www.selectservices.bentley.com*. Bentley SELECT is a subscription program that features product upgrades and updates.

ABOUT THE AUTHOR

Jerry Flynn is a visualization specialist at Bentley Systems. He has more than 17 years of visualization experience, and over 24 years of experience working with 3D computer models.

As a design engineer with Planning Research Corporation (PRC), at the Kennedy Space Center, Jerry designed launch support equipment and access platforms for the Space Shuttle. Using a highly accurate 3D computer model of the Space Shuttle's outer mold lines, Jerry was able to design critical access equipment and verify the designs on the computer prior to fabrication. In his own words "I was hooked on 3D" from that point, in 1981, on.

| Introduction |

When the design and construction phase for the Shuttle facilities ended in 1987, Jerry left PRC and went to work for McDonnell Douglas Space Systems. At that time McDonnell Douglas provided all support and processing of flight hardware in preparation for launch of the Space Shuttle. As a senior design engineer at McDonnell Douglas, Jerry brought his experience in 3D computer graphics to an even higher level. Using MicroStation, version 2.01.3, and an 8 MHz 286 PC, he created the first accurate 3D models of a processing facility and the Magellan spacecraft. These models then were used to perform access studies and fit checks, far in advance of the spacecraft's actual arrival at the Kennedy Space Center. This effort proved to NASA that computer modeling would be a tremendous time saver over existing methods.

From Jerry's pioneering efforts, a new Visualization Group was born. This group performed complex tasks and expanded their responsibilities to include conceptual design and advanced studies for future missions to the moon, Mars, and beyond. This group now has more than 11 full-time employees dedicated to various visualization tasks.

During his time at McDonnell Douglas, Jerry won 14 Golden Mouse awards in InterGraph's computer art competition and a Best in Application, from Kodak, during the 1991 SIGGRAPH convention. The Design Visualization Group that Jerry was instrumental in forming won the Silver Eagle award in 1993, the highest award achievable at the Space Systems division.

Jerry Flynn departed McDonnell Douglas in November of 1994 to join Bentley Systems. He was responsible for much of the animation and graphics used on the Discovery CD-ROMs to launch MicroStation 95, GeoGraphics, Modeler, and TriForma. He continues to work closely with development on improving and adding new visualization features to MicroStation. He also played a major role in the development of "Model City Philadelphia" a virtual reality model of Philadelphia, which was shown at AEC Systems and SIGGRAPH in 1997.

Jerry is the author of the Bentley Institute's "Animating with MicroStation" and "Rendering for Building Design" courses and provides 3D and visualization training for users in the US and sites around the world. Jerry Flynn also supports Bentley's Professional Services Group. In this capacity, he provides professional consulting and services, including onsite training, 3D modeling, animation, rendering, multimedia, and video editing services.

| Acknowledgments | xxi

Jerry Flynn's graphics have been on the covers of 16 MicroStation books. He has been the creator of seven MicroStation Manager covers, and his photorealistic images have made the covers of *Road & Bridges, Computer Aided Engineering* and *Computer Graphics World* magazines. He is responsible for the "Orbiter, Oldhotel, Livroom and Lobby" example DGN files that were shipped with MicroStation. He was instrumental in the development of the texture library that is delivered with MicroStation.

Acknowledgments

I would like thank several people for their help in turning what was originally planned as a new Bentley Institute course into a complete published book. It is a much-needed self-study guide and classroom workbook which now, for the first time, is available to all users, with or without an instructor.

I would like to sincerely thank David Wilkinson for being a contributing editor and for being one of only a handful of visualization experts within Bentley's ranks capable of ensuring that this book is ready to put into the hands of any MicroStation 3D user. Without David's help, this book would not have made it to fruition.

A huge thanks to Ray Bentley, my long-time friend and someone who shares the passion for visualization and for being instrumental in assuring that MicroStation's visualization capabilities are among the best in the world. Even before I joined Bentley, while at McDonnell Douglas Space Systems, Ray was there to help in a crunch. I remember at the time you could not put a hole in a surface. The workaround was to split the surface along the hole centers. This looked okay when rendered, but it seemed odd not to have this modeling ability. I called Ray and explained what we needed. The very next day we had a tool to test. You will all know this as the Group Hole tool.

Thanks to Peter Segal, Bentley's lead visualization developer. Without Pete's help I could never have become an expert at visualizing with MicroStation. Kudos to the entire visualization development team, which includes Pete Segal, David Zareski, Paul Chater, and Dennis Bragg. They have provided help and guidance in one way or another over my last ten years with Bentley.

Visualization requires a 3D model, and I must say I have built many over the years. Some of these have been fairly complex and, at times, pushed

| Introduction |

the limits of MicroStation's modeling tools, sometimes even requiring a nonexistent tool or command. When this occurred, I could always count on Brien Bastings or Lu Han to make it happen, providing either the tools, methods, or both, to accomplish the task at hand.

I would like to thank the following content contributors:

- Peter Yeh and the South Carolina Department of Transportation's Roadway design team for providing the photomatch data set used as a civil example in Chapter 11.

- Randall Stevens and Archvision for providing example "Rich Photorealistic Content" (RPC) files included on the accompanying CD-ROM. Additional information can be obtained at *www.archvision.com*.

- Pjer Zanchi with OnyxTree for providing OnyxTree Garden Suite, including the newly released OnyxFlower for those times you really need a 3D tree to get under in a scene. Examples can be seen in *Villa.dgn* or by visiting their website, *www.onyxtree. com*.

- Sebastion Volkamer at *www.vb-visual.com* for providing "VBexteriors 3D Plants" used in *SB Motors landscape.dgn* and also *main st trees.dgn*. The best example can be seen in *environment map2.dgn* which references the *main st trees.dgn*. The trees are mixed in with some RPC trees, but it will be pretty obvious which ones are VB, as they appear much more detailed in the wireframe view.

I would like to thank the Bentley Institute Press Team: Gilda Cellini, Frank Conforti, Charley Ferrucci, Lissa Jennings, Drew Knox, Carol Leyba, Maureen Rhoads, and Chris Rogers, without which this book would have never gotten off the ground.

1 Introduction to 3D Space

Before you can render 3D models, you must be familiar with the viewing tools that are part of the MicroStation design environment. These tools allow you to visualize the model from any plane or an in isometric view. These tools allow you to rotate, clip, and mask the views.

OPENING MICROSTATION

When you open MicroStation to do the first exercise, open the program from the menu or shortcut rather than double-click on the design file name. When the MicroStation Manager dialog box opens (as shown in the illustration on the next page), select the following:

User: Rendering with MicroStation
Project: Render

3D Space

You live in a three-dimensional world in which you can move and look in any direction. Likewise, in a 3D model, you can move the eye point and change the viewing direction, to view your design from any direction. MicroStation's 3D view control tools let you view a design from any location within the design cube. For quick setup, there are a number of standard views that you can use. You can rotate the view in any direction or add perspective using camera view. Once you have the view set up,

| Chapter 1: Introduction to 3D Space |

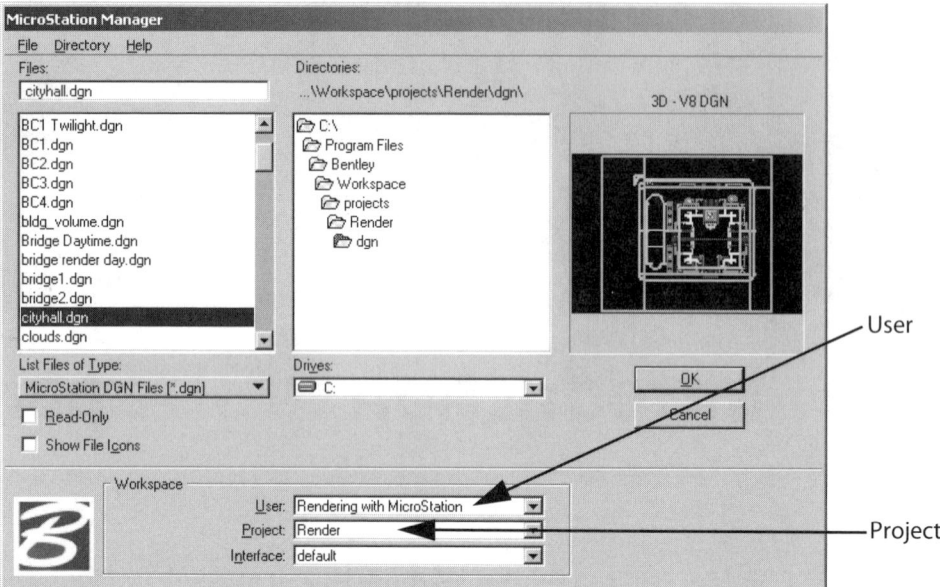

you can produce photorealistic images, walkthroughs, or animations of the finished construction before it is built.

The 3D Design Cube

In a 3D model, you work within a design cube, which differs from the 2D model design plane as follows:

2D design plane coordinates are expressed in the form (x,y).

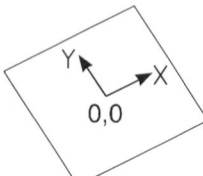

3D design cube coordinates are expressed in the form (x,y,z).

In the 3D seed files provided with MicroStation, the Global Origin is located at the exact center of the design cube and assigned the coordinates (0,0,0).

In 3D models, the coordinate system often is called the Rectangular or Cartesian coordinates system.

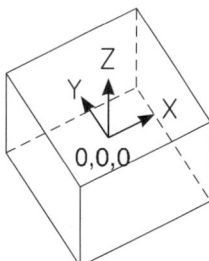

| Opening MicroStation | 3

Standard 3D Views

MicroStation provides eight standard views: Top, Front, Right, Isometric, Bottom, Back, Left, and Right Isometric. The standard view names describe the orientation of the design cube in the view, relative to the viewer.

- Top and Bottom: Displays the design cube as viewed from the top or bottom, respectively. The X-Y plane is parallel to the screen, and you view the design along the z-axis.

- Front and Back: Displays the design cube from the front or back, respectively. The X-Z plane is parallel to the screen, and you view the design along the y-axis.

- Right and Left: Displays the design cube from the right or left, respectively. The Y-Z plane is parallel to the screen, and you view the design along the x-axis.

- Isometric and Right Isometric: Displays the design cube equally inclined from all three axes. You view the design from the top left front corner to the bottom right back corner of the design cube (Isometric) or from the top right front corner to the bottom left back corner (Right Isometric).

NOTE: *Only in the Top view are the design file's axes aligned exactly with the view (or screen).*

✔ **Exercise 1-1: Review view orientations**

1 Open ***Nebula.dgn*** (Default model).

This model is of a conceptual sports car (model courtesy of Charles Wood).

2 Open the View Control tool box by selecting Tools >View Control.

NOTE: *View controls also are located on the view control tool bar associated with each view. You can add or remove tools from this tool bar by using the right-click menu.*

This model has been saved with four views open, displaying the Top, Isometric, Front, and Right views of the design. This is unlike 2D where you would have separate models for various elevations of the design. Each view in this 3D model displays the same design, but from different directions.

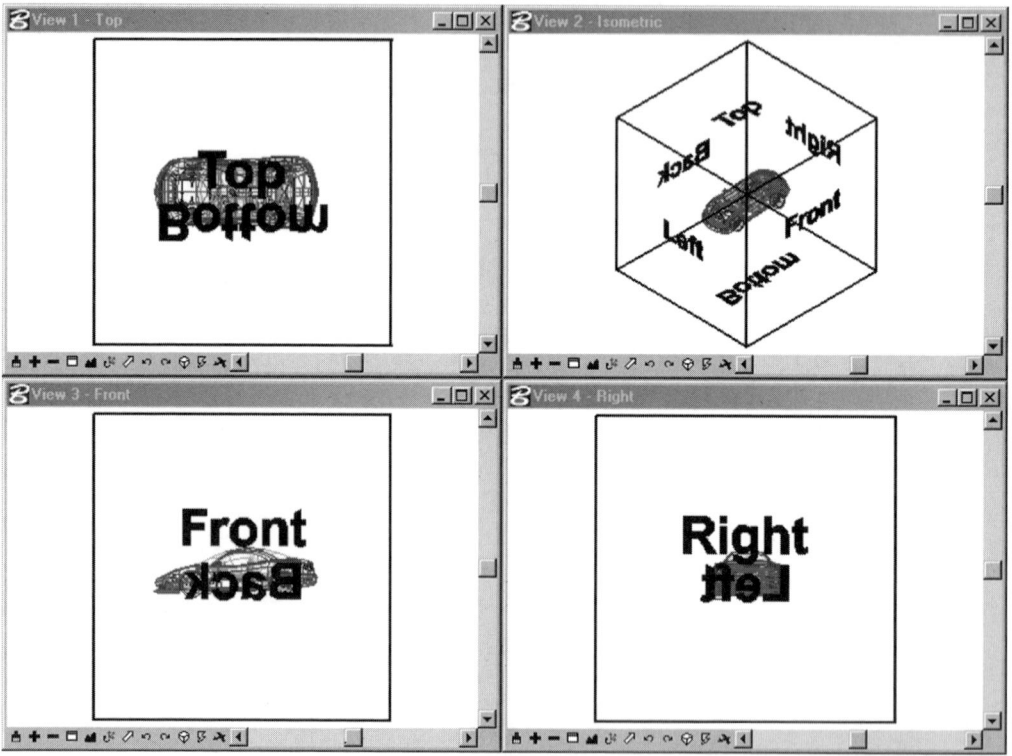

Looking at the Isometric view, you can see a cube around the car. The faces of the cube contain text describing the location of each face. That is, the top face is labeled Top, the right face is labeled Right, and so on. Currently the view display is wireframe, the default. With wireframe display, you see the edges of surfaces and you can see through the 3D model. In the Top view, not only can you see the word Top on the top face, but you also see the word Bottom, which is on the bottom face of the cube. Of the four views, the Isometric view (View 2) gives you the best idea of what the design looks like. Later, you will see that the Isometric view, generally, is the easiest of the standard views to work with in 3D space.

| View Rotation | 5

NOTE: *Whenever a standard view displays, the view title bar displays its name.*

Standard views can be very useful in orienting yourself in a 3D model, but they are not the only rotations that you can use.

VIEW ROTATION

In 2D models, you work in an X-Y plane and, where necessary, you can rotate the view. Visually, on the screen, this is like rotating the X-Y plane about a perpendicular or z-axis. When you are working in a 3D model, you can rotate the view about any of the three axes (x-, y-, or z-axis). Again, visually on screen, it is like rotating the design cube.

✔ **Exercise 1-2: Rotate the Front view**

1   Continuing in *Nebula.dgn*, in View 3 (Front), select Rotate View with the following tool settings.

    Method: Dynamic
    Dynamic Display: Enabled

2   Enter a data point near the center of View 3 by clicking only once. Do not hold the data button down.

3   Move the screen pointer to rotate the model interactively, but *do not* enter a data point.

    As you rotate View 3, the image appears to rotate off the screen. This is due to the fact you are rotating about a point based on the current active depth for the view you chose to rotate. In this instance, the active depth is well behind the design model in the view.

4   Reset to return the view to its previous condition.

    Entering a data point would have actually rotated the view. If you had rotated the view, you could use the View Previous control (from either the view border or the View Control tool box) to return the view to its previous state.

The Set Active Depth tool is used to graphically set a view's active depth. This is the plane, parallel to the screen in a view, on which data points

Chapter 1: Introduction to 3D Space

are entered by default. The active depth's value is measured along the view's z-axis.

When rotating a view, to get the desired result you may need to redefine the active depth for the view. Alternatively, you can snap to a piece of geometry to indicate the point about which you want to rotate. A third option for fitting a view is to select the Center Active Depth option to center the active depth in the view.

Exercise 1-3: Center the active depth before rotating the view

1   Continuing in *Nebula.dgn*, in View 3 (Front), select the Fit View tool, with the following tool settings:

    Expand Clipping Planes: Enabled
    Center Active Depth: Enabled
    Center Camera: Enabled

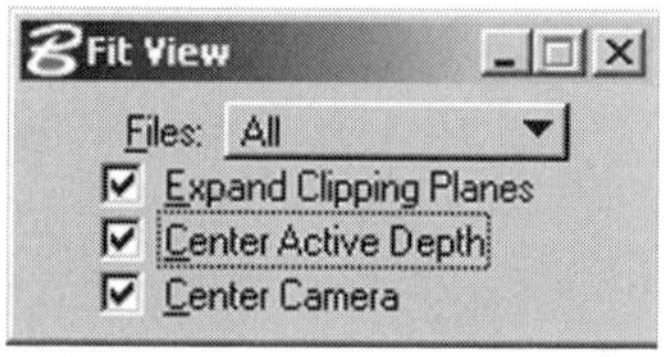

2   Enter a data point in View 3.

3   Select Rotate View.

4   Enter a data point near the center of the view.

5   Move the pointer to interactively rotate the model.

    The view is now rotating about the center of the design geometry as a result of enabling Center Active Depth in the Fit View tool settings.

6   Enter a data point to complete the rotation.

Next you will turn off the construction elements that were placed in the design file to help you visualize the 3D cubic space. In this exercise you will be using the Rotate View tools graphics as a visual aid while rotating the view.

Exercise 1-4: Use the Rotate View tool's graphics

1   Continuing in *Nebula.dgn*, from the main menu select Settings > View Attributes.

    You can also click the Bentley B at the top of View 3 and select View Attributes from the menu, or use the keyboard shortcut <Ctrl B> to open the View Attributes dialog box.

| View Rotation |

2 In the View Attributes dialog box, set the following:

   View Number: 2
   Constructions: Disabled

3 Click Apply.

4 Click on the Rotate View icon in the view border of View 2 and, in the tool settings, turn off Dynamic Display.

5 Enter a data point in View 2.

   A cube graphic appears. The bold outline represents the orientation of the front plane of the design cube, to provide a visual reference when rotating the view.

6 Move the pointer to rotate the cube graphic.

   As you rotate the cube graphic, the view of the model remains stationary.

7 Enter another data point to complete the rotation.

   The view updates to display a new orientation. Note that only the eye point of the viewer has changed. The design model has not been rotated or moved.

At any time, you can return a view to one of the standard view orientations.

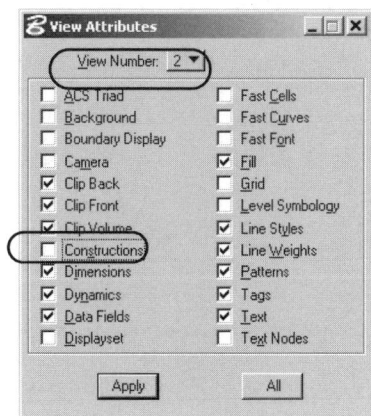

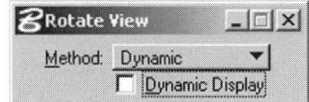

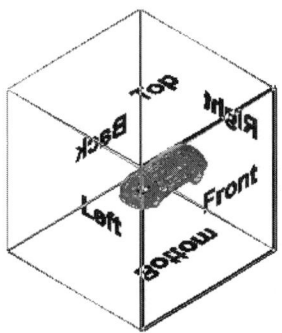

Cube graphic with a bold outline representing the front plane orientation of the design cube.

8 | Chapter 1: Introduction to 3D Space |

✔ **Exercise 1-5: Rotate views to standard view orientations**

1. Continuing in *Nebula.dgn*, in View 2, select Rotate View with the following tool setting:

   Method: Isometric

2. Enter a data point in View 2.

   View 2 returns to an Isometric view orientation.

   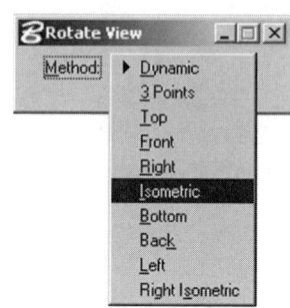

   Similarly, you can rotate any view to a standard view orientation.

3. With Rotate View still active, change the Method to Bottom in the tool settings.

4. Enter a data point in View 1, which is a Top view.

   View 1 updates to display the model from the bottom. Note the word Bottom is in the correct orientation and Top now is reversed.

Rotating a View with Dynamics

On a modern computer, most models can be rotated dynamically. That is to say, the view updates constantly as you change its rotation. Furthermore, you can enable graphics acceleration and perform the operation much more smoothly, taking advantage of your graphics card's graphics processing unit (GPU). Graphics acceleration can be used with wireframe and hidden line display modes, as well as with constant or smooth shaded display.

✔ **Exercise 1-6: Dynamic rotation options**

1. Continuing in *Nebula.dgn,* select Settings > Level > Display. Turn off level *design cube* and fit View 2.

2. Close the Level Display dialog box.

| View Rotation | 9

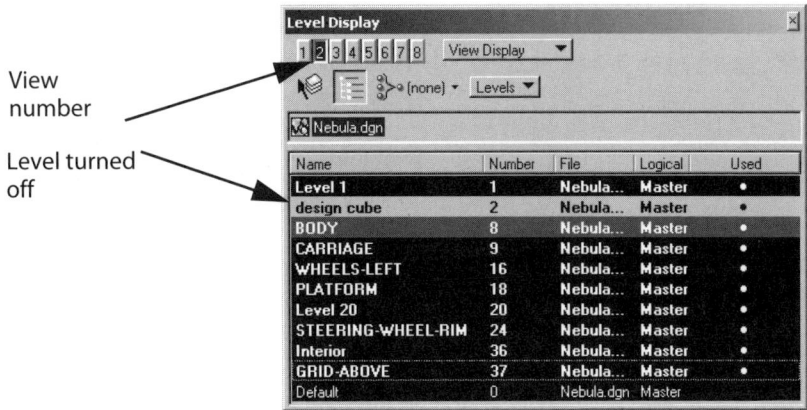

View number

Level turned off

3 From the view border, select the view rotation tool and set:

Method: Dynamic
Dynamic Display: Enabled

4 Enter a data point in View 2 and rotate it by moving the cursor in the view.

Notice how the display appears to flash until you stop moving your cursor. This is due to the view constantly being updated.

5 Select the Change View Display Mode tool in the view border of View 2, and set the following:

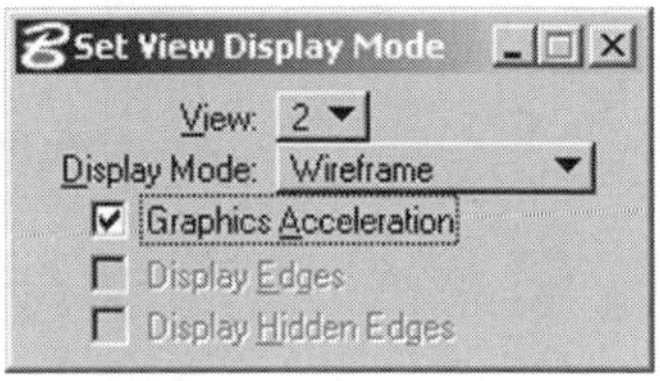

View: 2
Display Mode: Wireframe
Graphics Acceleration: Enabled.

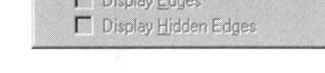

6 Select the Rotate View tool and enter a data point in View 2.

7 Move your cursor in View 2 to dynamically rotate the view using graphics acceleration.

Notice how the view smoothly rotates without the flashing that was present prior to enabling graphics acceleration.

8 Select the Change View Display Mode tool in the view border of View 2.

9 In the tool settings, set Display Mode to Smooth, leaving Graphics Acceleration enabled.

Results of smooth rendering with graphics acceleration.

10 Again use the Rotate View tool to rotate View 2.

Notice how the view can be smoothly rotated even while appearing in smooth rendering mode. Again, there is none of the flashing that was present prior to enabling graphics acceleration.

Rotating a View by 3 Points

In a situation where a face of your model does not coincide with any of the orthogonal views, you may use another view rotation setting to rotate the view to align with a face of the model. That is, the view will be rotated so that the defined face is parallel to the screen.

To define a plane requires a minimum of three points, so rotating a view to have a particular plane parallel to the screen requires you to define three points. The first two points define the x-axis, and the third defines the direction of the y-axis relative to the x-axis.

✔ **Exercise 1-7: Rotate View 1 to align a plane in the design with view X-Y plane**

1 Open model *3pts*, in DGN file *equip_bldg.dgn*, by selecting File > Models.

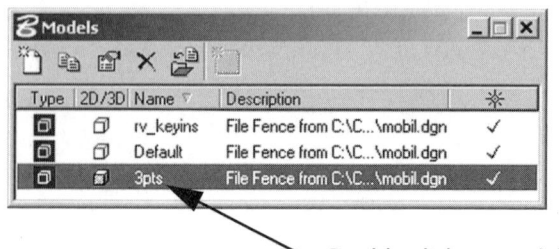

Double-click on model to switch

| View Rotation | 11

The model has four standard views open: Top, Front, Right and Iso. Notice that the building model is not aligned with the xy-axis of the Top view.

2 In View 1, select Rotate View with the following tool setting:

Method: 3 Points

3 Snap to the lower left corner of the large square that the building is sitting on and accept with a data point.

This locates the first point on the x-axis for the proposed view.

4 Snap to the lower right corner and accept with a data point.

This determines the direction of the x-axis for the proposed view. As the pointer is moved, graphics display the plane that is being defined.

5 Snap to the upper left corner of the green square and accept with a data point.

This defines the direction of the y-axis of the rotated view. The graphics displaying the plane now appear aligned with the view's xy-axis.

Before *(left)* and after *(right)* rotation by 3 points.

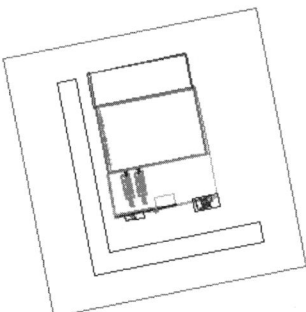
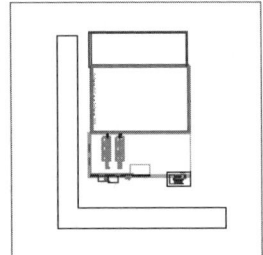

Using the Rotate 3Pts method, you can rotate any view so that any plane in the design is aligned exactly to a view.

NOTE: *You can also rotate views using key-ins, as you will see in the following section.*

View rotation key-ins

Using key-ins you can rotate any view about its x-, y-, or z- axis. The Key-in is **rv=x,y,z** where x, y, and z are the angles, in degrees, that you

| Chapter 1: Introduction to 3D Space |

want to use to rotate the view about its x-, y-, or z-axis, respectively. In the following exercise, you will see where these key-ins are particularly useful. The model is a copy of that used in the previous exercise and has a rotated view, showing the plan view of the design, from which you will create orthogonal front and right elevations. If the model had been aligned with the design file axes, you could have used the standard views.

✔ **Exercise 1-8: Rotate a view -90° about the x-axis**

1   Open model *rv_keyins*, in *equip_bldg.dgn*.

   This model contains the rotated view (View 1) from the previous exercise.

2   Use the Copy View tool from the View Control tool box to copy the rotated View 1 to View 3.

   Remember to read the prompts for the tool if you are unfamiliar with its usage.

   Now you can rotate the copied view to provide an orthogonal front view of the building model.

3   Open the Key-in window (Utilities > Key-in).

4   In the Key-in input field, enter **rv=-90**.

5   Enter a data point in View 3.

   The view is rotated about its x-axis and is aligned with View 1, providing you with an orthogonally aligned front view of this building model.

   NOTE: *The rotate view key-in uses the right-hand "screw" rule. To check the direction of rotation, first hold your right hand up and align your outstretched thumb pointing along the positive direction of the view axis about which you want the rotation. Your curled fingers then indicate the positive rotation direction for view rotation.*

✔ **Exercise 1-9: Rotate a view -90° about the y-axis**

1   Continuing in model *rv_keyins*, use the Copy View tool to copy the rotated View 3 to View 4.

| View Volume | **13**

2   In the Key-in window, enter rv=,-90

   This is the same as keying in rv=0,-90 (the 0 is assumed if no figure is given), or 0 about the x-axis and 90° about the y-axis.

3   Enter a data point in View 4.

   The view is rotated about the y-axis of the view and appears aligned with View 3, effectively giving you an orthogonally aligned right view of this building model.

Rotating Relative to a View or Drawing

Whenever you look at a MicroStation view on your screen, the axes for the view are always orientated as follows.

- X — horizontal, positive from left to right of screen
- Y — vertical, positive from bottom to top of screen
- Z — perpendicular, positive toward you (the viewer)

Often these axes are referred to as the *relative axes*, meaning that they are relative to the view or screen. Within the view, however, the design file axes can be oriented in any direction, depending on how the view has been rotated.

Remember, when you rotate a view, you are rotating the view about the design cube. Visually, on screen, it appears that you are rotating the design cube and its contents relative to the view or screen. If you could physically walk around a model in the real world, you could view it from any direction. With MicroStation, you rotate the view camera around the "world" of the design (the design cube) to view a model from other directions.

Using the Change View Rotation tool, which is in the 3D View Control tool box, you have the option of rotating the view relative to either the view axes or the design axes. To open the 3D View Control tool box, select Tools > Tool Boxes and turn on 3D View Control in the Tool Boxes tool box.

VIEW VOLUME

Each MicroStation view window lets you look at any portion of the model. In a 2D model, each view window displays an area of the design plane. In a 3D model, each view window displays a volume of the design cube, often referred to as the *view volume* or *display volume*.

Each view window has a display area (as in 2D) and a display depth (the third dimension). This display depth is limited by front and back clipping planes. Any element not contained within the front and back clipping planes of the view will not display in that view. Many first-time users of MicroStation 3D think that they have accidentally deleted elements, as zooming in or out does not make them visible. In fact, the elements are simply outside the range of the display depth for the view in which they are looking.

The view volume is defined by the size of the view (window area), the front clipping plane, and the back clipping plane (defining the display depth).

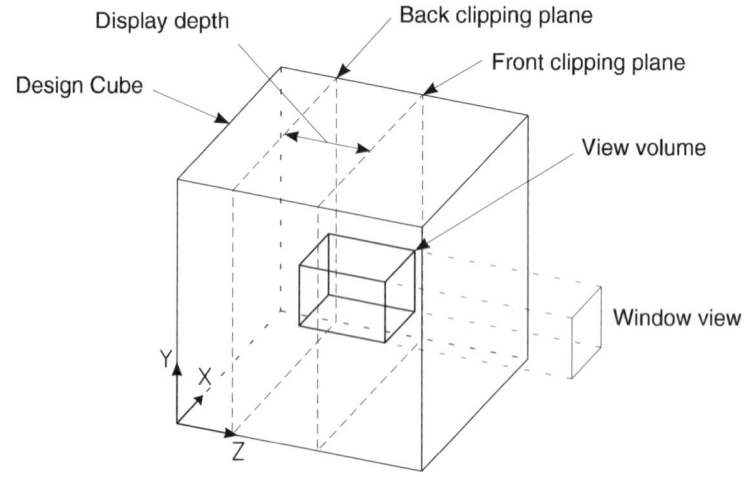

View volume with the front and back clipping planes.

Nothing is visible in front of the front clipping plane, and nothing is visible behind the back clipping plane. Only elements or parts of elements in between the clipping planes are visible. Just as Window Area lets you select a discrete area of a view, Display Depth lets you select a discrete slice or depth of a view.

NOTE: *You can enable or disable the front and/or back clipping planes via the Clip Front and Clip Back settings in the View Attributes dialog box.*

| View Control Tool Box | **15**

VIEW CONTROL TOOL BOX

You have already used tools from the View Control tool box. This next section will provide you with explanations of some of the view control tools that are specific to working in a MicroStation 3D model. Selecting Tools > View Control opens the View Control tool box which includes several view manipulation tools.

To	Select in the View Control tool box
Change the magnification of a view volume	Zoom In/Out
Change the perspective angle of a view (covered later in this course)	Change View Perspective
Set a view's display depth graphically	Set Display Depth
Set a view's active depth by placing a data point	Set Active Depth
Show the display depth setting for a view(s)	Show Display Depth
Show the Active Depth setting for a view(s)	Show Active Depth
Rotate a view	Rotate View
Create a camera view (covered later in this course)	Camera Settings
Render a view(s), the fence contents, or an element(s) (covered later in this course)	Render
Apply Clip Volume to a view	Clip Volume
Mask the display of elements in a view that are located within the region of a clipping element.	Clip Mask

Display Depth and Active Depth

Each MicroStation 3D view has both a display depth and an active depth. In each view, the display depth defines how much of the overall depth of the view is displayed. It is controlled by the location of front and back clipping planes. These planes are always parallel to the view (your screen) with the front clipping plane nearest to you and the back clipping plane farthest from you in the view.

Between these clipping planes is another plane, set to the active depth of the view. The active depth defines the depth at which data points are placed by default. That is, if you place data points in a view without first snapping to another element, they assume the Z value of the active depth plane. The active depth plane is always located within the display depth of a view.

Both display depth and active depth can be affected by the Fit View control.

✔ Exercise 1-10: Change display depth in the Front view

1 Open model *Depth*, in *bldg_volume.dgn*.

NOTE: *Right-clicking anywhere along the lower edge of Primary Tools will produce a menu that lets you add the Models tool to the Primary Tools tool bar.*

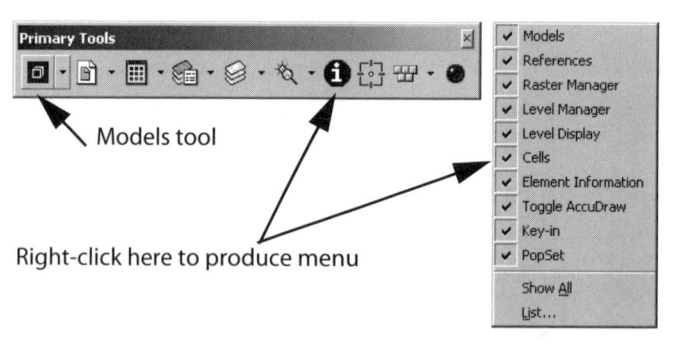

2 In the View Control tool box, select Set Display Depth.

The status bar prompts Set Display Depth > Select view for display depth.

3 Enter a data point in View 3 - Front to set it as the view in which to change the display depth.

As you set the clipping planes, in the following steps, notice the dynamic box which is a graphical representation of the changing display depth for the selected view.

4 In View 2, snap to the red dashed line at the base of the building model and accept with a data point to define the front clipping plane.

5 Still in View 2, snap to the blue dashed line at the base of the building model and accept with a data point to define the back clipping plane.

| View Control Tool Box | **17**

This causes View 3 to update with the new display depth setting.

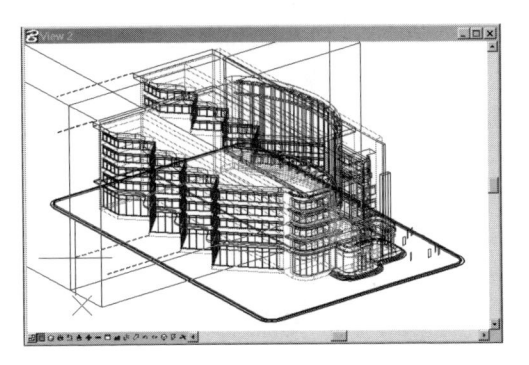

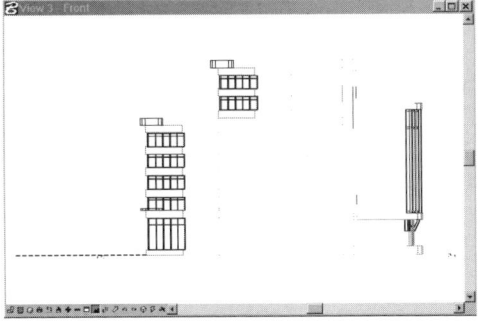

Defining display depth in View 2 *(left)*, and results applied to View 3 *(right)*.

You changed or limited what you see in the Front View by using the Set Display Depth tool. In the next exercise, you will change the display depth of the Top view.

✔ Exercise 1-11: Change display depth in the Top view

1. Continuing in model ***Depth***, select Set Display Depth.
2. Select View 1-Top by entering a data point on View 1.
3. In View 2, snap to the red dashed line at the top and back of the building and accept with a data point.
4. Snap to the blue dashed line at the top and back of the building and accept with a data point.

   View 1 updates to show the adjusted display depth.

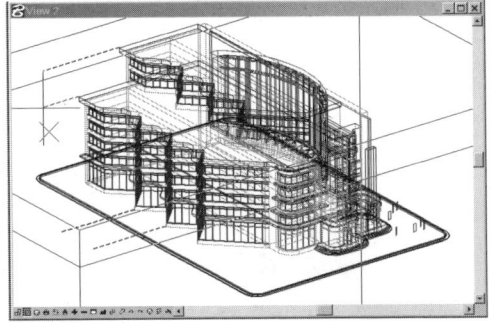

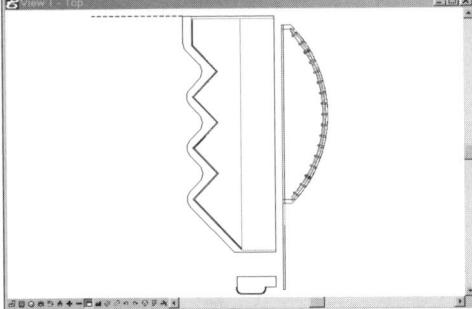

Defining display depth in View 2 *(left)* and results applied to Top View 1 *(right)*.

| Chapter 1: Introduction to 3D Space |

NOTE: *Display depth defines the depth (that is the Z dimension) of the volume of the design cube that you can see in a view. Active depth is the default depth on which graphically entered points fall.*

Clip Volume and Clip Mask

The Clip Volume tool is used to limit the displayed volume for a view. This is very useful for working within a limited volume of a design without being hindered by geometry outside the volume of interest. When a clip volume is applied to a view, only elements that are located within the clip volume will display, or can be snapped to, in that view. The Clip Mask tool works in the opposite way to the Clip Volume tool in that the elements within the defined mask are excluded from a view. You can use a clip mask in conjunction with clip volume to exclude from view a region within a defined clip volume. Unlike the clipping planes described in the previous section, a clipped volume is oriented with the drawing plane and not the view.

Other operations, such as view rotation, fence processing, hidden line removal, and rendering, also honor the clip volume. They ignore any elements that are not displayed within the defined volume for the view.

Clipping elements may consist of any solid (spheres excluded) or closed extrusion, cylinders, or closed planar elements (shapes, circles, ellipses, complex shapes, grouped holes). Where a planar element is chosen, the clipping volume is generated by sweeping the planar element through the entire model. Planar elements may be selected in any view, because the sweep direction is orthogonal to the plane of the element.

If you later modify a planar element that was used to apply a clip volume, then the clip volume is modified also. If you delete the element used to apply a clip volume, the clipped volume extents are removed.

NOTE: *Once a clip volume has been applied to a view, you can turn it on and off via the Clip Volume check box in the View Attributes dialog box (Settings > View Attributes).*

✔ Exercise 1-12: Apply a clip volume

1. Open model **Volume**, in **bldg_volume.dgn**.
2. In the View Control tool box, select the Clip Volume tool.

| View Control Tool Box | **19**

3 In the Clip Volume settings window, select the Apply Clip Volume By Element icon with Display Clip Element disabled.

4 Select the 3D solid in View 2 - Isometric.

You are given the option to select a view.

5 Enter a data point in View 2.

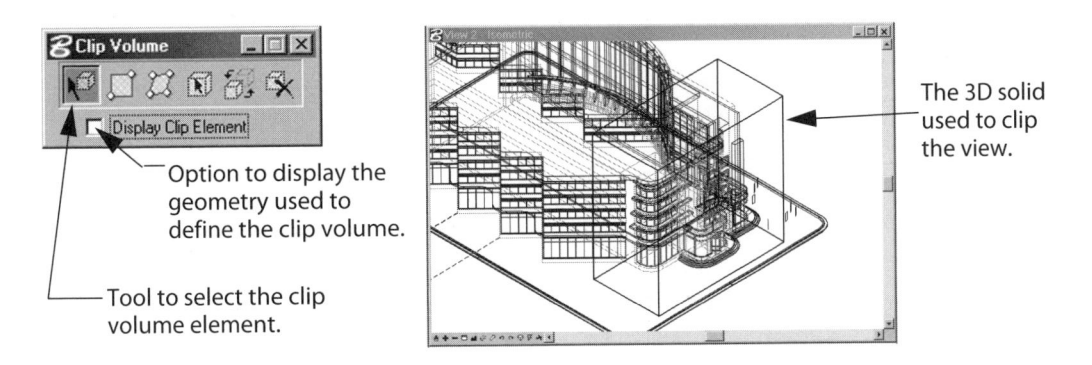

Option to display the geometry used to define the clip volume.

Tool to select the clip volume element.

The 3D solid used to clip the view.

6 Continue, entering further data points in Views 1, 3, and 4 to apply the clip volume to these views also.

In the previous exercise, when you created the clip volume, the Display Clip Element setting was disabled, so that the clip element did not remain displayed with the clip volume. If you want to manipulate the clip volume, first you need to turn on the display of the clipping element as shown in the following exercise.

✔ **Exercise 1-13: Move a clip volume**

1 Continuing in model *Volume*, with the Clip Volume tool active, verify that AccuDraw also is active.

2 In the Clip Volume tool settings, click the Show or Hide Clip Volume Element icon.

3 Select any view.

The clipping element appears in each view.

| Chapter 1: Introduction to 3D Space |

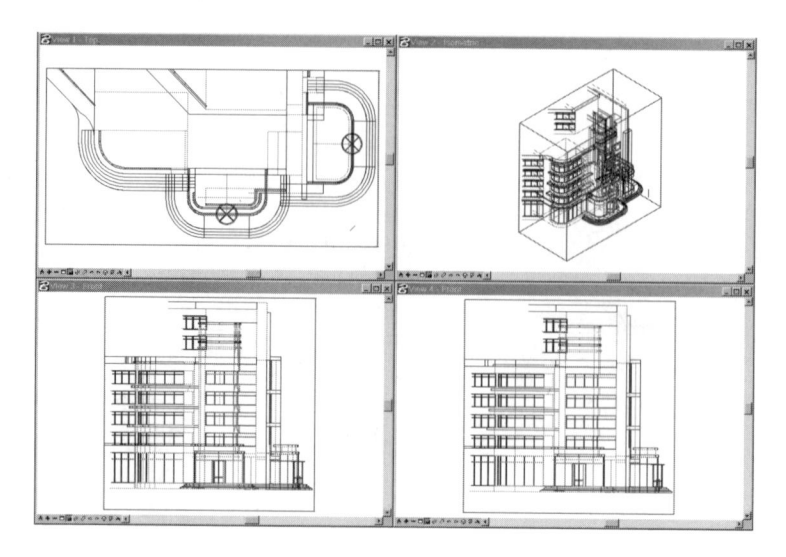

4   From MicroStation's Main tool palette, select the Move Element tool.

5   Snap to the clipping element you used to define the clip volume in View 1 - Top and enter a data point.

6   Use AccuDraw to move the clip volume element 25 units north, in the Y direction of View 1.

Observe the effect that moving the clipping element has on the open views. In each view, the clipping volume has been redefined to the new location of the clipping element.

7   Move the element back to previous position.

You can use undo for this.

Where you want to clear the clip volume, but keep the clipping element, you can use the Clear Clip Volume tool.

✔ Exercise 1-14: Clear a clip volume

1   Continuing in model *Volume*, select the Clip Volume tool.

2   In the tool settings, click the Clear Clip Volume tool.

3   Enter a data point in each view to clear the current clip volume.

NOTE: *In addition to using Clear Clip Volume, the clip volume can be removed by deleting the object that was used to define it. Additionally,*

| View Control Tool Box | 21

Clip Volume is a view attribute that can be toggled on a per view basis via the View Attributes dialog box.

As well as 3D solids (other than spheres), you can use polygons to create both clip volumes and clip masks.

✔ **Exercise 1-15: Work with clip volumes and clip masks**

1. Continuing in model **Volume**, select Rotate View.

2. Set Method to Right Isometric and enter a data point in View 2.

3. Fit View 2 to display all the geometry.

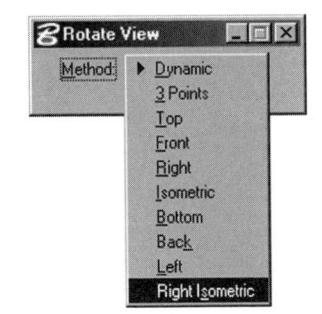

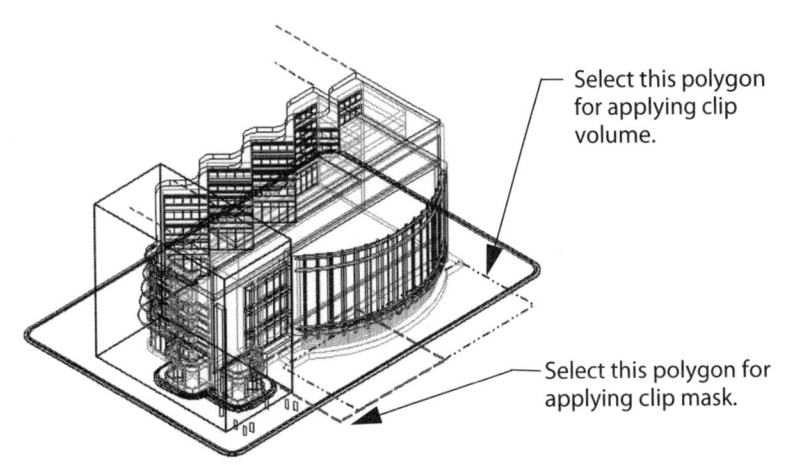

Select this polygon for applying clip volume.

Select this polygon for applying clip mask.

4. Select the Clip Volume tool and, in its tool settings, click Apply Clip Volume By Element.

5. Enter a data point in View 2 over the cyan-colored polygon to apply a clip volume to the view.

   The view is updated and contains only those elements that were included within the (extruded) polygon used to define clip volume.

6. Select the Render tool with the following settings:

   Target: View
   Render Mode: Ray Trace

| Chapter 1: Introduction to 3D Space |

7. Enter a data point in View 2.

8. Select the Clip Mask tool and, in its tool settings, click Apply Clip Mask By Element.

9. Snap to and accept the red polygon that includes half of the curved windows in the building model. This can be selected in any view.

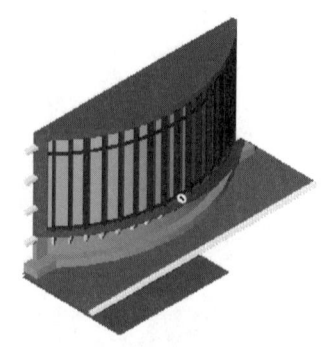

Model after volume clipping has been applied and rendered.

10. Enter a data point in View 2 to apply the clip mask to the view.

The clip mask is applied. Only the geometry that is in the clipped volume is displayed, not that in the mask volume.

11. Again render View 2 with the mode set to Ray Trace.

12. Select the Clip Volume tool and, with Clear Clip Volume selected, enter a data point in View 2 to clear the current clip volume.

13. Select the Clip Mask tool and, with Clear Clip Mask selected, enter a data point in View 2 to clear the current clip mask.

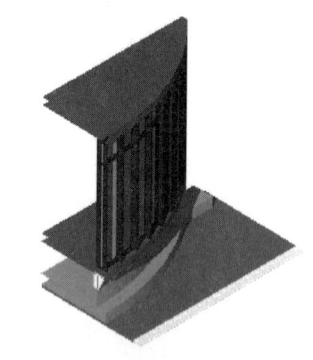

Model after the clip mask has been applied.

Displaysets

In addition to the Clip Volume and Clip Mask tools, you can restrict the display to objects that you select with the Element Selection tool. You can name this selection set and then recall it at a later time using displaysets. You can display these in any view by enabling the view attribute. All elements in a current selection set can be added to a displayset.

✔ Exercise 1-16: Use displaysets

1. Open model *Displayset*, in **bldg_volume.dgn**.
2. Open the View Attributes dialog box (Settings > View Attributes) and set the following:

   View Number: 2
   Displayset: Enabled

3. Click Apply.

   View 2's title changes to indicate that the displayset attribute is set for the view.

4. Select Utilities > Named Groups.
5. In the Named Groups dialog box, select the named group *Curved Windows*.
6. Click on Select Elements in Named Group to put the elements from the named group into a selection set.
7. Select Put Elements into the Displayset.

   The displayset appears in View 2, since you enabled the view attribute for this view.

   You have not deleted any elements, but are limiting what will display in that view.

8. Fit View 2.
9. Render with mode Ray Trace.

   Notice that only the elements that are in the displayset are rendered.

Where multiple display sets are present, you can change from one to another as follows.

✔ Exercise 1-17: Select a different displayset

1. Continue in model *Displayset*.
2. In the Named Groups dialog box, select the named group *Main Entrance*.
3. Click on Select Elements in Named Group.

| Chapter 1: Introduction to 3D Space |

4 Select Put Elements into the Displayset.

5 Fit View 2.

6 Render View 2 with mode Ray Trace.

Displaysets are an easy way for you to isolate elements from multiple levels for the purpose of rendering or viewing.

> **NOTE:** *Press <Shift> and right-click in any view to produce a menu that lets you manipulate many view parameters in addition to displaysets. You can save selection sets easily from this menu and recall them at anytime from the same menu. The downside to this method over using named groups is that you are only provided with 10 numerical registers in which to store and recall the information from this simple menu.*

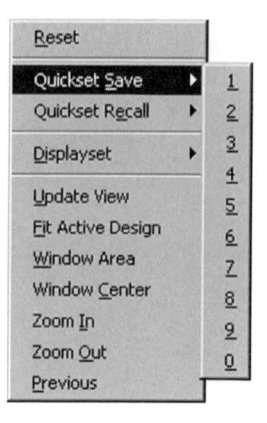

Menu produced by shift+ right-clicking in any view window.

RENDERING TOOLS TOOL BOX

As you work your way through this manual, you will be introduced to the tools in the Rendering Tools tool box. This tool box contains all the tools for setting up a view for rendering. The tool box is accessed by selecting Tools > Visualization > Rendering.

To	Select in the Rendering Tools tool box
Create or modify a light source.	Define Light
Open the Global Lighting dialog box to: Turn on/off Ambient, Flashbulb, or Solar lighting, or Add Skylight to Solar and Distant lights.	Global Lighting
Set up the virtual view camera.	Define Camera
Apply, modify, or identify an existing material definition to an element(s), or Preview the application of a material definition, or Remove a previously applied material definition.	Apply Material

| Review Questions | 25

To	Select in the Rendering Tools tool box
Open the Material Editor dialog box to: Create or modify a material definition, or Create a material palette file.	Define Materials
Interactively adjust the size, position, and orientation of a pattern/bump map.	Dynamically Adjust Map
Render views, fence contents, or individual elements.	Render
Display the amount of light reaching the point indicated by the pointer.	Query Illumination
Improve the rendered quality of discrete polygons	Facet Smoothing
Match the view perspective to that of a photograph.	Photomatch
Change the size of a view window to match another view window, or to match a standard format	View Size

REVIEW QUESTIONS

1 How many standard views does MicroStation provide?

2 Which standard view has both the design and view axes aligned?

3 Is active depth measured along a view's x-, y-, or z-axis?

4 How many points are required to rotate a view by points?

5 Which view control tool controls how much you see in a view: active depth or view depth?

6 Can you use both Clip Volume and Clip Mask together in the same view?

7 What view attribute lets you display only elements that are selected?

CHAPTER SUMMARY

In this chapter you have learned about MicroStation's 3D design cube and its standard views. You learned how to rotate a view with and without dynamics. You have gained knowledge of the display depth and active depth tools and how to apply them to a view. You learned also how to work with the clip volume and clip mask tools and how displaysets can be utilized with rendering. Finally, the Rendering Tools tool box was introduced.

2 Camera Setups and Navigation

You learned how to view a model by rotating views and by modifying the view display depths. As well, you discovered how to restrict what is displayed in a view via volume clipping/masking and how you can use displaysets to display only selected elements.

This chapter presents MicroStation's camera tools and settings, including the Define Camera tool, which has a comprehensive set of options for setting up a camera view for rendering. Additionally, the Change View Perspective tool lets you quickly add perspective to a view, and the Camera Settings tool has several options for setting up a camera view.

VIEW CAMERAS

Each of the eight views available in a MicroStation model shows the design from some point in the design cube. This is similar to having up to eight cameras that you can position anywhere in the model. By default, the viewing mode is parallel projection. That is, unlike real life, there is no perspective to indicate those parts of the design that are closer to you than others in the view. MicroStation, however, does have tools that let you display views in a more natural manner, with perspective.

Perspective in a View

When viewing a design in wireframe mode, often it is difficult to ascertain the orientation with respect to the design. Adding perspective to one or more views adds a feeling of depth and thereby improves spatial orientation as you view a model. You can use a view camera to add perspective to a view (which you will discover later), or you can use the Change View Perspective tool.

The Change View Perspective Tool

Using the Change View Perspective tool, you can dynamically set the degree of perspective applied to each view. When you define a view's perspective, a camera automatically is defined and enabled for the target view. To set the perspective, you can work with a cube graphic, or else interactively with the model.

✔ **Exercise 2-1: Dynamically setting perspective for a view**

1. Open model *Cam_01*, in *cityhall.dgn*.

2. In the View Control tool box, or in the view border, select the Change View Perspective tool with the following tool setting:

   Dynamic Display: Enabled

3. Enter a data point at the center of View 2.

4. Slowly move the pointer away from the first data point, in any direction.

   As you move farther away from the first data point, observe how the model changes perspective. Moving farther away increases perspective, while moving back toward the first data point location decreases perspective.

5. When you are satisfied with the amount of perspective, enter a data point to accept.

When working with large complicated models, where screen updates are slower, it may be more convenient to work with the cube graphic when setting perspective.

| Perspective in a View | 29

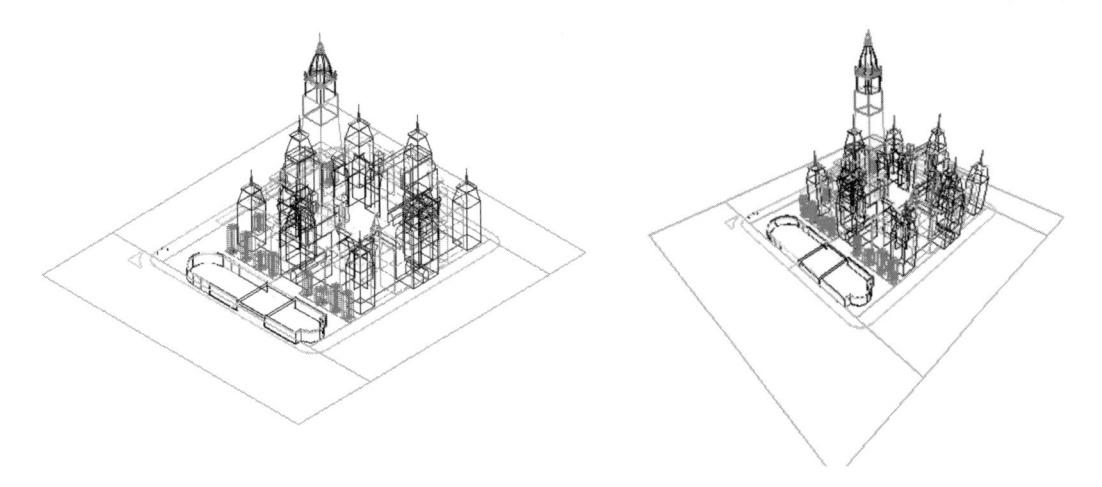

View before *(left)* and after *(right)* applying perspective.

✔ Exercise 2-2: Set perspective with Dynamic Display disabled

1. Continuing in model ***Cam_01***, with the Change View Perspective tool active, turn off Dynamic Display in the tool settings.

2. Enter a data point at the center of View 1.

   A cube graphic appears, showing the view orientation and perspective. A heavy line weight indicates the front face of the cube.

3. Slowly move the pointer away from the first data point, toward the bottom of the view.

   As you move farther away from the first data point, notice that a second cube graphic shows how the perspective would be changed. Moving farther away increases perspective, while moving back toward the first data point decreases perspective.

4. When you are satisfied with the amount of perspective, enter a data point to set it.

When you have set perspective in a view, this setting remains in effect until you change it back again. Try this for yourself, using the Rotate View tool to rotate the perspective views. With the perspective set, the orientation of the model is much easier to work out.

| Chapter 2: Camera Setups and Navigation |

Toggling perspective

When you set perspective in a view, you are creating a camera view. This is a view like you would see through a camera viewfinder. Having set the perspective in a view, you can toggle it on or off using the Camera settings. To disable perspective, simply turn off the view camera. This lets you retain your perspective setting for future use, which you can reinstate simply by turning on the camera for the view.

NOTE: *You can also turn off perspective by selecting the Change View Perspective tool and entering two data points near the center of the view.*

Exercise 2-3: Toggle perspective display in two views

1. Continuing in model *Cam_01*, in the View Control tool box, select Camera Settings, with the following tool setting:

   Camera Settings: Off

2. Enter data points in Views 1 and 2.

   The views are returned to the default parallel projection.

   Similarly, you can turn on the view camera, and so return to the previously defined perspective setting.

3. Select Camera Settings with the following tool setting:

   Camera Settings: On

4. Enter data points in Views 1 and 2.

   Views 1 and 2 again are displayed with perspective.

   NOTE: *You can turn the view camera on or off by choosing Settings > Camera > On or Settings > Camera > Off from the MicroStation tool bar.*

When you use the Change View Perspective tool, in effect you are creating a camera view, using the existing view eye point and target point. In the following sections, you will learn how to use the camera tools.

Camera Settings Tool

When you use the Camera Settings tool, you have options that let you set both the camera position and its target point, or you can move the target or camera positions individually. In the next exercise, you will set up an initial camera view using data points that rely on the active depth of the view to determine the z depth.

✔ **Exercise 2-4: Set up a camera view**

    1 Open model *Cam_02*, in *cityhall.dgn*.

    2 Select Tools > Visualization > Rendering.

    3 Dock this tool box, as you will be using these tools often throughout the rest of this course.

    4 Fit View 2.

    5 Select Render with the following tool setting:

        Target: View
        Render Mode: Ray Trace

    6 Enter a data point in View 2, the Isometric view.

Rendered Isometric view of the cityhall model.

| Chapter 2: Camera Setups and Navigation |

7   In the View Control tool box, select Camera Settings with the following settings:

   Camera Settings: Set Up
   Image Plane Orientation: Perpendicular

   This sets the image plane perpendicular to the direction of the camera, as it would be in a normal camera.

   You are prompted to select a view.

8   Enter a data point in the Isometric view to define it as the camera view.

   You are prompted to Define Camera Target Point. At the same time, the camera settings for the Angle, Focal Length, and Standard Lens become active.

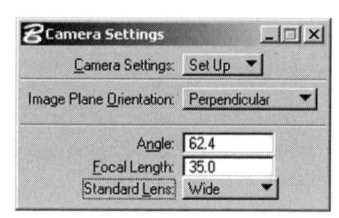

9   From the Standard Lens option menu, select Wide.

10 In the Top view, without snapping to an element, enter a data point at location 1, which is under the main tower.

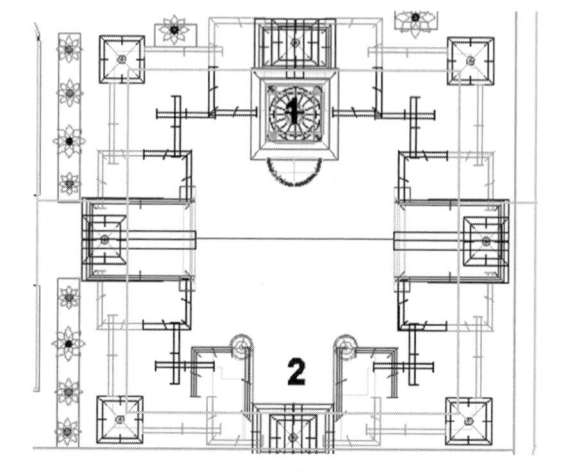

Top view of model showing location points 1 and 2.

A graphic appears in each view, displaying the view cone for the camera view. The screen pointer controls the apex of the view cone, which is the camera location.

You are prompted to Define Camera Position.

11 In the Top view, without snapping to an element, enter a data point at location 2.

   View 2 - Isometric updates to display the camera view.

12 Use the Render tool to ray trace the camera view.

In the previous exercise, you used data points in the Top view to define the camera target point and the camera position. You defined the horizontal positions (x and y values) with data points, while the active depth of the view determined the height, or z value. Where you want to specify different z values for these positions, you can use 3D data points to define both the target and camera positions.

3D data points are entered by holding down the <Alt> key as you press the data button. They let you define the target and camera positions interactively, by eye. To do this, you must have at least two orthogonal views open, such as the Top and Front views. Each 3D data point requires two inputs in order to define the x, y, and z values. This may sound complicated, but you will see that 3D data points are easy to use.

✔ Exercise 2-5: Set up a camera view using 3D data points

1 Continuing in model *cam_02*, in the View Control tool box, select the Camera Settings tool with the following tool settings:

Camera Settings: Set Up
Image Plane Orientation: Perpendicular

2 Enter a data point in View 2 to define it as the camera view.

3 Hold down the <Alt> key and enter a data point in the Top view at location 1 to define the x, y values of the data point.

| Chapter 2: Camera Setups and Navigation |

Borelines appear in each view, showing the location of the data point in the horizontal plane of the Top view. They show the x, y position of the data point that you entered in the Top view. In the Front and Right views, you are looking along the x, y plane. This lets you specify a z value anywhere along the boreline.

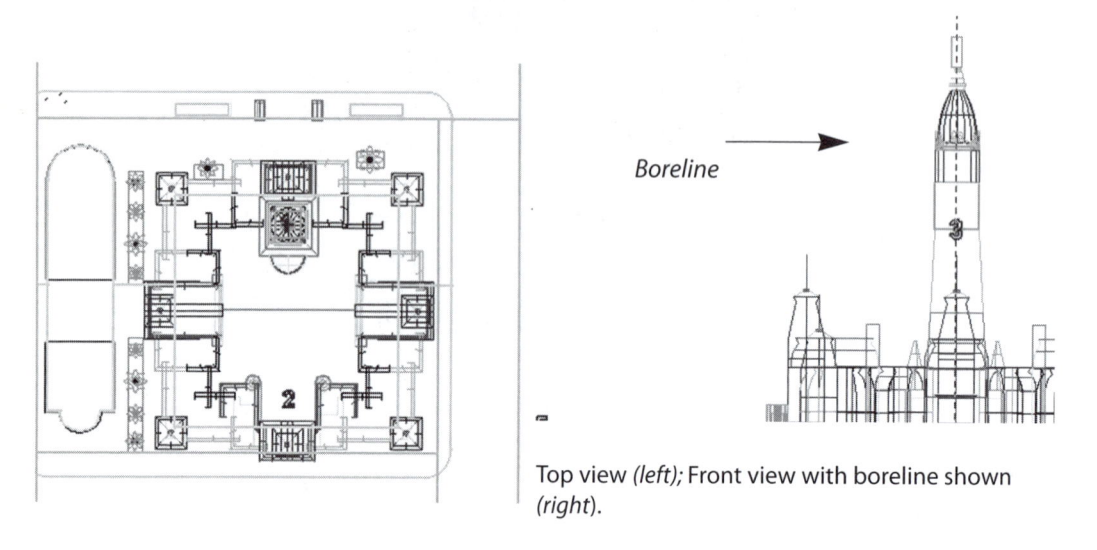

Top view *(left)*; Front view with boreline shown *(right)*.

4   Move the pointer into the Front view and enter a second data point along the boreline about halfway up the building at location 3 (do not snap to any element) to set the z value of the data point.

A graphic appears in each view, displaying the view cone for the camera view. The pointer controls the apex of the view cone, which is the camera location.

NOTE: *In V7 and earlier versions of MicroStation, the data point entered along the boreline required you to enter a 3D data point as well. In V8, once the boreline is visible, the second point can just be a regular data point.*

5   Move the pointer into the Top view, hold down the <Alt> key, and enter a data point at location 4 to set the x, y values.

Again, borelines appear in the other views. The apex of the camera view cone is attached to the boreline.

| Camera Settings Tool | 35

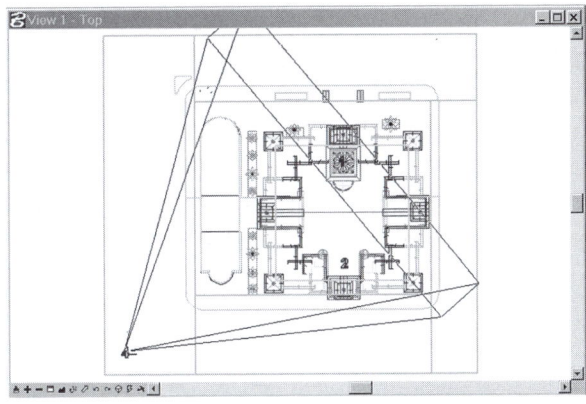

Top *(top)* and Front *(bottom)* views with dynamics indicating the camera cone.

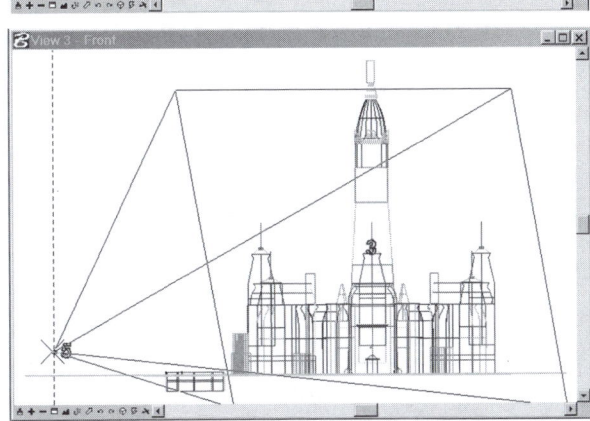

6 Move the pointer into the Front view and enter a data point just above ground level, at location 5, to set the z value.

View 2 updates to display the newly defined camera view.

7 Use the Render tool to ray trace the camera view.

NOTE: *When working with 3D data points, you do not have to start in the Top view. You could start in the Front view, setting the x, z values first, before moving to the Top view to set the remaining y value.*

You can use the Camera Settings tool, with the Camera Settings option set to Move, or Target, to move the camera view eye point or target point, respectively. That is, you can move the eye point, while the target point remains stationary, and vice-versa. These manipulations, however, are more simply performed with the Define Camera tool, which you also can use to set up a camera view.

THE DEFINE CAMERA TOOL

When working with camera views, the Define Camera tool, in the Rendering Tools box, provides a simple tool for manipulating them. Using similar terminology to that used in the movie industry, it lets you orient, pan, roll, or dolly the camera. It is easy to imagine a real camera and its movements using these tools. For example, when you pan horizontally to the left, objects on your screen move to the right as you would expect.

With the Define Camera tool, you can set up a view for rendering by graphically manipulating the dynamically displayed view cone. Alternatively, you can use this same tool for specific manipulations, and its tool settings for precision inputs.

When you use the Define Camera tool for the first time in a design, you are prompted to choose an active view. This view becomes the camera view. If Display View Cone is enabled in the tool settings, then view cones appear in the other open views. These show the viewing extents of the camera view. The shape and features of the view cone will depend on the Projection setting that is active at the time.

✔ **Exercise 2-6: Activate a view for Define Camera**

1 Continuing in model *cam_02*, in the Rendering Tools tool box, select the Define Camera tool.

2 Check in the tool settings that Display View Cone is enabled.

3 Enter a data point in View 2 to make it the active view.

After entering the data point, you will see a new camera cone graphic with several weighted points, or handles.

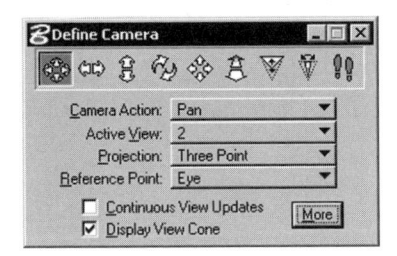

4 Fit Views 1, 3, and 4.

Notice that the fitted views now include the camera cone, and that the target point and eye point handles are where you positioned them in the previous exercise. Shortly, you will see that these points can be selected and manipulated on screen.

Camera View Projections

You have a choice of four different camera view projections in MicroStation. The standard projection is parallel, and this projection is used most during the design phase. Parallel projection is orthogonal, having no perspective.

- Parallel — default MicroStation (no perspective).
- One Point — for dimensionally correct sectional perspectives.
- Two Point — for architectural use where vertical edges are required to stay vertical.
- Three Point — for conventional perspectives.

Choosing any of these options changes the projection in the camera view accordingly. Similarly, the view cone updates with the new viewing parameters. You may change the view projection at any time.

In the next exercise you will switch between the camera perspective options and see their effect on the view.

✔ **Exercise 2-7: Change the view projection of the camera view**

1 Open model *Cam_03*, in *cityhall.dgn*.

The Define Camera tool still should be active from the previous exercise, with its Active View set to 2.

2 In the tool settings, check that Projection is set to Three Point.

The view looks natural, as three point projection gives you the same perspective you would get when using a real camera.

3 In the tool settings, set Projection to Two Point.

The results are immediately applied to the active view.

Results of applying three point projection *(left)* and two point projection *(right)*

Notice that after applying two point projection to View 2, all vertical edges are perfectly straight (vertical). In two point projection, the image plane is kept vertical but is oriented in the horizontal direction of the view. In this way, you get perspective while keeping all vertical edges completely vertical in the image.

Parallel projection

MicroStation's standard viewing projection is parallel. This projection is most commonly used during the design process. Here, the view cone is rectangular in shape.

Exercise 2-8: Change projection to parallel

1 Continuing in model *Cam_03*, select Rotate View with Method set to Isometric.

2 Enter a data point in View 2.

3 Select the Define Camera tool.

The camera tool still is active for View 2 from the previous exercises.

4 In the tool settings, change Projection to Parallel.

Switching to Parallel projection turns off the camera and any perspective for the view.

5 Fit all views.

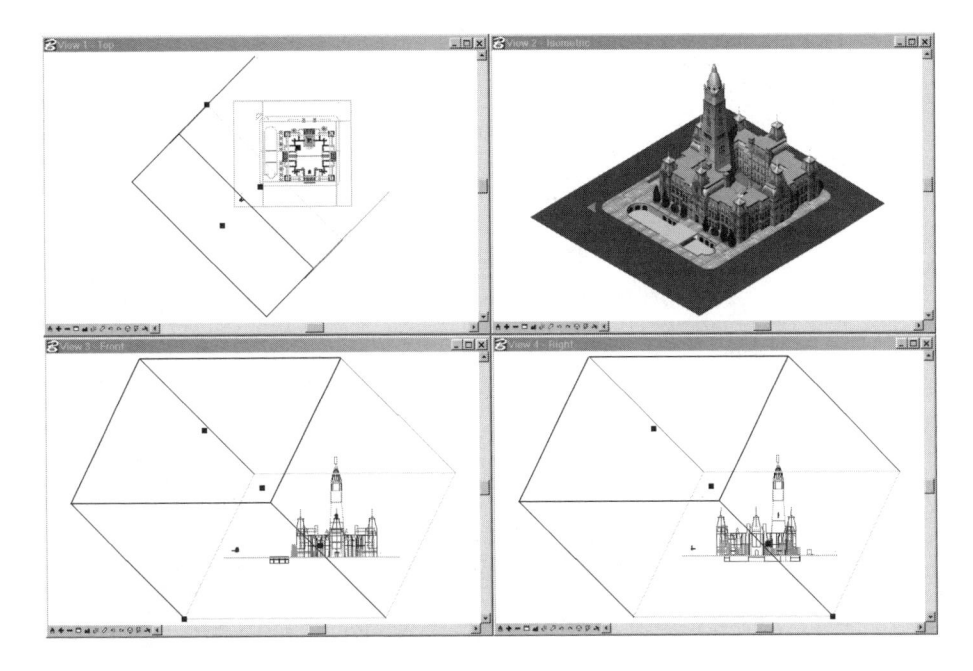

One point projection

Working like a bellows camera, one point projection orients the image plane completely independently of the view direction. This requires the addition of an extra handle oriented normal to the image plane. This handle controls the direction of the image plane.

One point projection allows the image plane to be manipulated independently from the viewing direction.

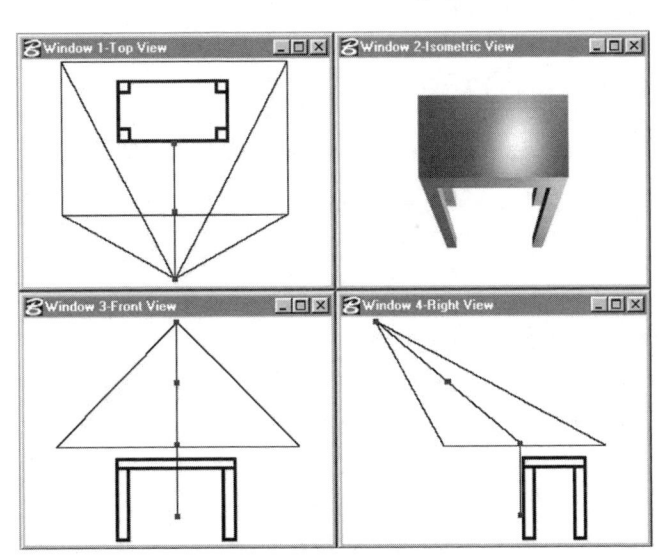

An advantage of one point projection is that dimensional correctness can be achieved for a view that has perspective. For instance, if you have the image plane parallel to a plane of the model, then the dimensions of the model in that plane are to scale. This enables you to create an image that has both depth and dimensional correctness in the selected plane.

Once the camera and target locations have been set, you use the plane handle to orient the image plane to be parallel to the required face. This can be done graphically, or via settings in the Camera Orientation settings fields.

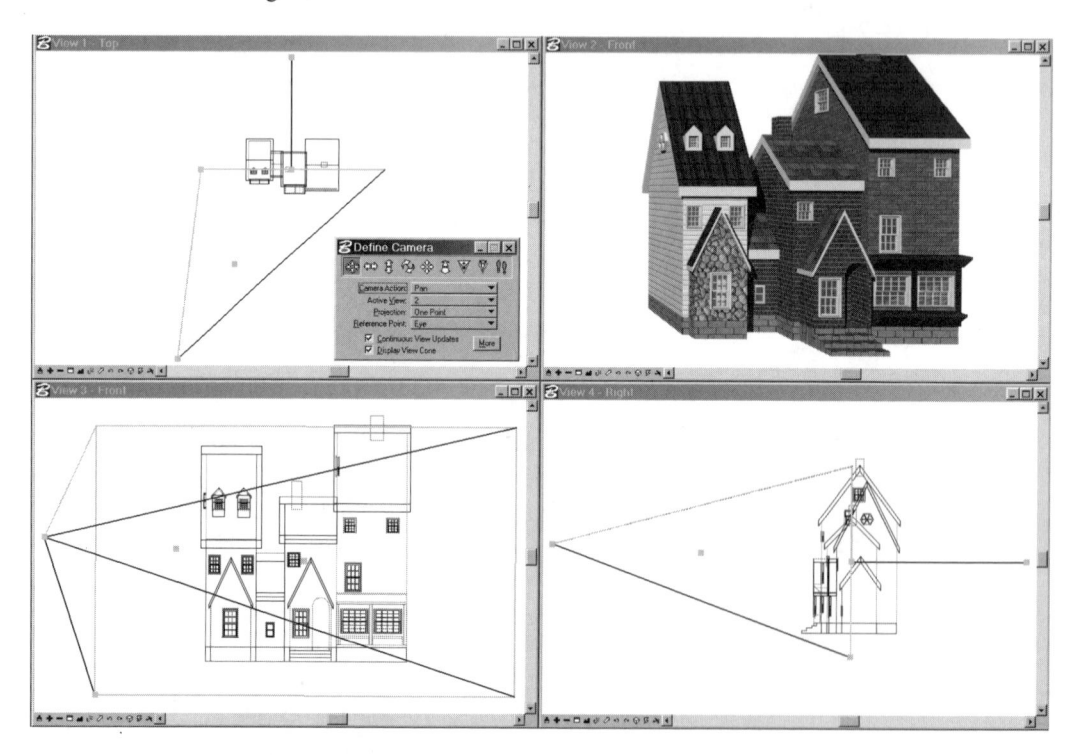

One point projection allows the image plane to be manipulated independently from the viewing direction.

Two point projection

This is most commonly used for architectural renderings where vertical edges are required to be aligned vertical to the image, even in the perspective views. This is a somewhat artificial constraint, but one that is easily handled by MicroStation.

| The Define Camera Tool | 41

Using two point projection, the image plane is kept vertical, but oriented in the horizontal direction of the view. In this way, you get perspective while keeping all vertical edges completely vertical in the image.

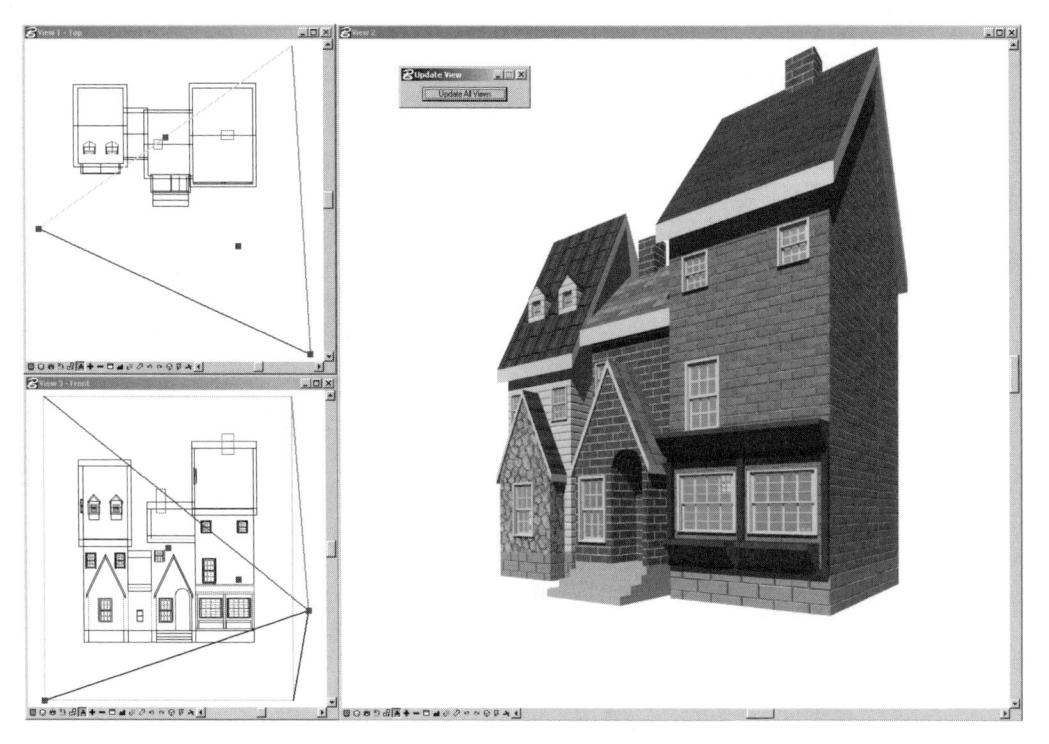

Two point projection can be used to ensure that vertical edges remain vertical in a perspective view.

Three point projection

Three point projection is the most natural projection and is used for conventional images. In this projection, the image plane is normal to the direction of the view, as in a conventional camera.

> **NOTE:** *Using wide-angle camera lenses with focal lengths 28 to 35 mm (view angle 62.4 to 74.3) often will leave you with views that appear distorted. The wider the camera angle, the more extreme the perspective and perceived distortion. A normal lens of 50 mm with a view angle of 46 degrees is close to that of the human eye, and provides the most natural look with three point perspective.*

Use the wider-angle lenses with caution and consider using two point perspective where these lenses are needed.

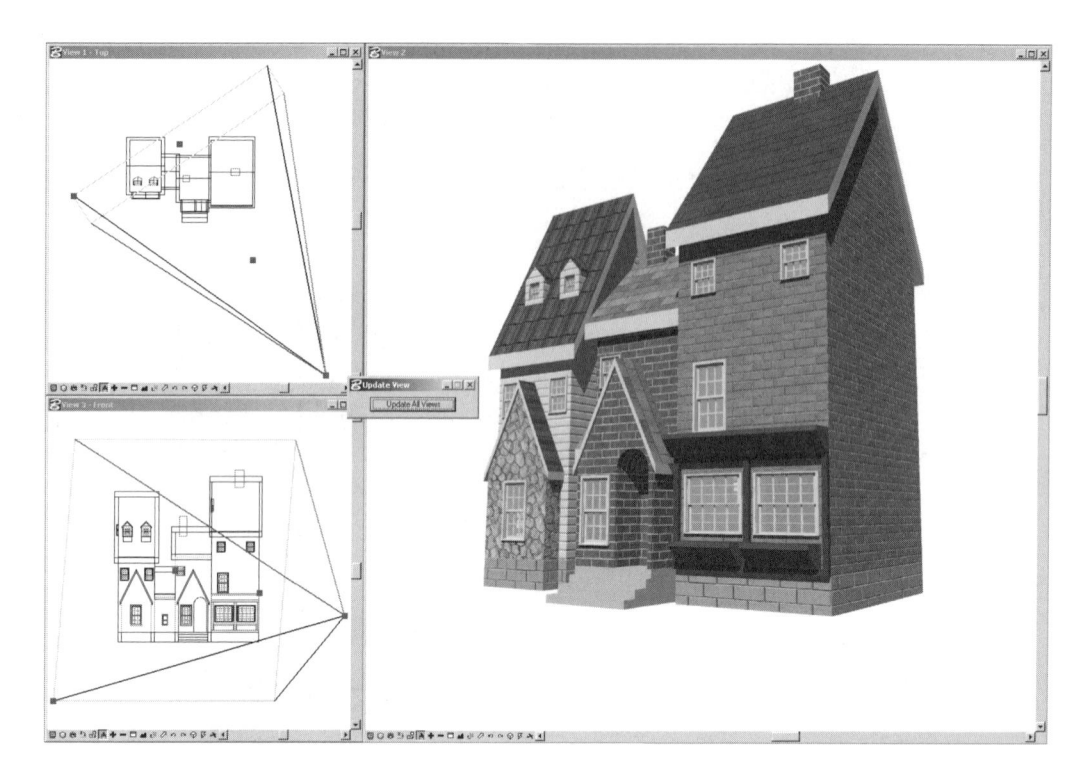

Three point projection provides a view as would be seen through a standard camera.

Working with the Define Camera Tool

When a camera view is defined, you can control the orientation of its view cone by positioning the handles dynamically, or by entering values in the Define Camera tool settings. In earlier exercises, you used the Camera Settings tool to set up the camera view. The Define Camera tool also lets you define a camera view and, using the same tool, you can manipulate the camera.

NOTE: *To display the view cone, you must ensure that Display View Cone is enabled.*

In the following exercises you will use Define Camera to turn on the camera for a view, switch the view from parallel (orthogonal projection) to three point projection, and then manipulate the camera.

| The Define Camera Tool | 43

✔ Exercise 2-9: Set up a camera view with the Define Camera tool

1 Open *surveyors office.dgn* (model Default).

2 In the Rendering Tools tool box, select the Define Camera tool with the following setting:

   Display View Cone: Enabled

3 Enter a data point in View 2 to activate the camera for the view.

4 Fit all views.

   Since View 2 was an isometric view with no camera perspective, the display of the camera view cone is a rectangular block (orthogonal view) rather than a pyramid shape.

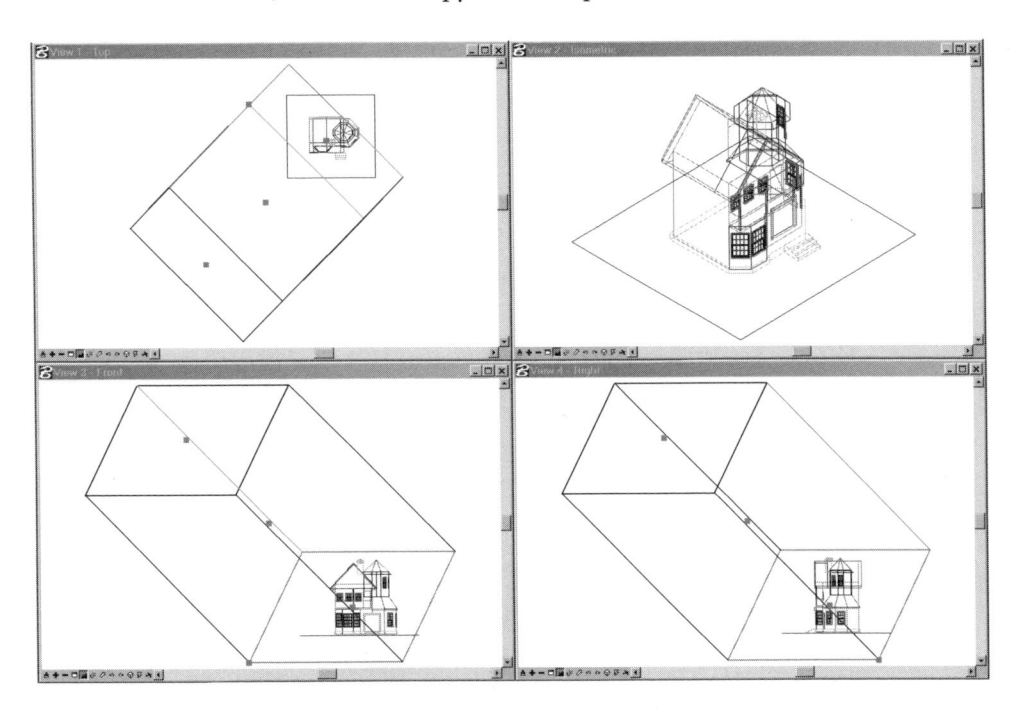

Display of camera views as orthogonal projection without perspective.

5 Again select the Define Camera tool.

6 In the tool settings, change Projection from Parallel to Three Point.

7 Fit Views 1, 3, and 4, which are displaying the camera view cone.

By changing projection from Parallel (orthogonal) to Three Point, you have enabled the camera in View 2, and the camera view cone displays in the other views.

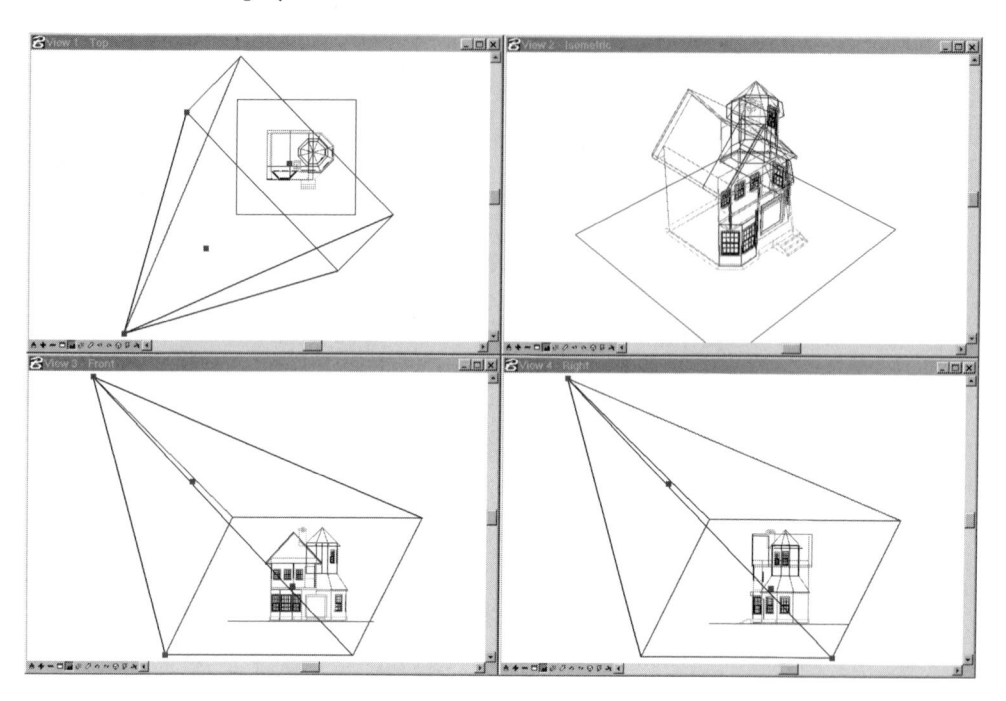

NOTE: *Fitting a view while the Define Camera tool is active will fit the entire camera cone as well.*

NOTE: *If you change the design cube's global origin while the view cone is displayed, it is recommended that you select another tool (not a view control) and then reselect Define Camera before proceeding with camera manipulation.*

View cone color coding

To assist you in relating the view cone to the camera view, it is color coded. In the view cone geometry,

- the red line is the top left corner of the camera view,
- the green line is the top right corner, and
- the two blue lines are the lower corners of the camera view.

| The Define Camera Tool | 45

View cone handles

You can use the view cone handles to interactively modify the viewing parameters. When the Continuous View Updates option is enabled, the camera view updates dynamically, as you modify the view cone.

Here are some additional considerations when modifying a view cone:

- Moving the eye point handle does not affect the position of the target handle, and vice-versa.
- Moving the center handle moves the whole view cone.
- Moving the image plane handle of the one point projection view cone lets you rotate the image plane independent of the eye and target points.

In the next exercise you will interactively manipulate the camera view cone using the Define Camera tool.

Exercise 2-10: Interactively modify the eye point of a view cone

1. Continuing in *surveyors office.dgn*, select the Define Camera tool with the following settings:

   Continuous View Updates: Enabled
   Display View Cone: Enabled

2. Select the eye point handle with a data point.

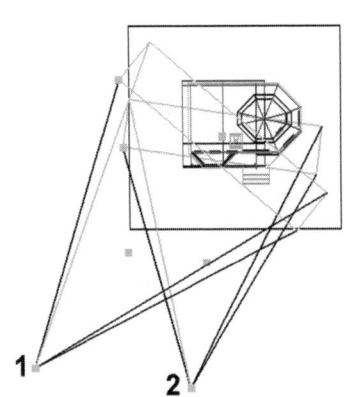

3. Use the Top view to move the handle downward and to the right (such as shown in the diagram at left, moving from point 1 to point 2). Notice that the camera view updates interactively as you move the handle

4. Enter a data point to fix the new position.

   NOTE: *Pressing reset instead of a data point in this last step would have released the handle and returned the view cone to its original position.*

With Continuous View Updates enabled, you are able to monitor changes to the camera view as you manipulate the view cone.

Rendered images showing the model before *(left)* and after *(right)* moving the camera eye point.

Moving the eye point in this manner leaves the target at its current location. Similarly, you can reposition the target, leaving the eye point at its current location.

NOTE: *You can also use the click and drag method to move the handles. To use this method, hold down the data button as you move the handle. Releasing the data button sets the view to the new position. With this method, pressing reset does not return the view to its original position.*

Precision placement of view cone handles

When you know the exact coordinates for the location at which you want to place the eye point or target, you can use precision inputs. That is, you can specify the coordinates for both.

In this next exercise, you will modify the camera target and eye point by entering these positions as x, y, and z coordinates. This lets you, for example, place the eye point or camera precisely at the height of a person walking by the design.

In the following exercise, you will be setting up the camera to take some pictures of the surveyors office as it would be seen from a pedestrian's view.

| The Define Camera Tool | **47**

✔ Exercise 2-11: Locate the eye point or target with precision inputs

1. Continue in *surveyors office.dgn*, with the Define Camera tool still active.

2. Click More in the tool settings.

   The tool settings expand to display additional options.

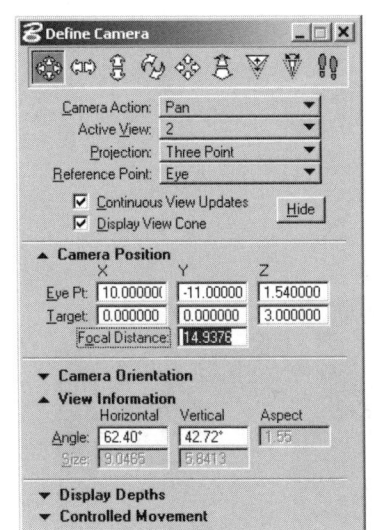

3. If necessary, click the down arrow for Camera Position to display its settings.

   Coordinate input fields appear for Eye Pt and Target.

4. In the Eye Pt field enter 10,-11,1.54, as shown at left.

   The units are in meters; the center of the polygon representing the house is located at 0,0,0. This would put the eye height at 1.54 meters above the ground level or roughly 5 ft.

5. In the Target field, enter 0,0,3.

   The camera view updates with the new viewing parameters. In other views, the view cone moves to reflect the new values.

6. In the View Information field, set the Angle to 62.4.

   This view angle will provide you the equivalent view as a lens having a Focal Length of 35 mm.

7. Ray trace the camera view.

   In addition to the eye point and target handles, there is a third handle located at the center of the view cone. This center handle lets you interactively move the whole view cone.

The result of precision inputs used to exactly locate the camera position, via its eye point and target.

In the next exercise, you will be moving the camera closer to the building by moving the camera cone and maintaining the eye height and target height from the previous exercise.

| Chapter 2: Camera Setups and Navigation |

✔ Exercise 2-12: Move the view cone

1. Continuing in *surveyors office.dgn*, select the Define Camera tool with Display View Cone enabled.

2. Fit the Top view (View 1) to display the entire view cone.

3. Again select the Define Camera tool and, in the Top view, use a data point to select the center handle of the view cone.

4. Still in the Top view, move the view cone closer to the building.

5. Enter a data point to accept the new location.

   The camera view displays the new viewing parameters.

6. Ray trace the camera view.

Moving the view cone *(left)* and the rendered camera view *(right)*.

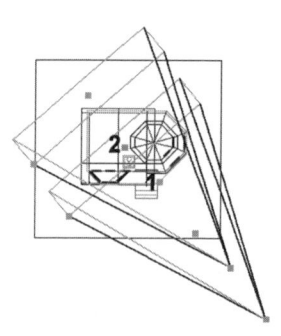

All modifications to the view cone, in any view, adjust the viewing parameters of the camera view, which is selected when you first select the Define Camera tool. At any time, you can change the camera view to another of MicroStation's views. Where the view selected is not open at the time, then it is opened and its parameters appear in the Define Camera tool settings.

NOTE: *The results of moving the camera will vary and may not look exactly like those shown in the documentation or from student to student. What is important at this point is to understand the operation of the Define Camera tool.*

| Camera Actions | 49

✔ Exercise 2-13: Select another view to be the camera view

1. Continuing in *surveyors office.dgn*, select the Define Camera tool.
2. In the tool settings, set:

   Active View: 5

   The selected view opens and the view cones update to display its view projection parameters.

CAMERA ACTIONS

Modifying the view cone graphically is a quick way to set up a view for rendering. For more precise manipulation, however, you can select from the Define Camera tool's Camera Action options. These let you quickly and precisely adjust a view with controlled movement of the view cone:

- relative to the pointer movement in the camera view.
- with Controlled Movement, so that each data point moves, rolls, or rotates the view cone by a defined distance or angle.
- as defined by key-ins in the relative settings fields.

The following table describes each of the Camera Actions options.

To	In the tool bar, select:
Move the camera or the target radially (horizontally or vertically) relative to each other	Pan
Move the camera or the target radially (horizontally) relative to each other	Pan Horizontal
Move the camera or the target radially (vertically) relative to each other	Pan Vertical
Roll or tilt the camera	Roll
Move the camera horizontally or vertically	Dolly/Elevate
Move the camera in, out or sideways	Dolly
Change the Lens Focal Length	Lens Focal Length

To	In the tool bar, select:
Change the Lens Viewing Angle	Lens View Angle
Walk through the view	Pan/Dolly

Controlling Movement with the Pointer

For manipulation of the active or camera view, using controlled movement, the screen is sectioned off.

Controlled movement

For manipulations that allow movement horizontally and vertically, the middle section is the origin, and clicking in any other section produces movement in the direction as shown.

Screen partitioning for controlled movement horizontally and vertically.

Clicking in any of these sections produces movement as shown.

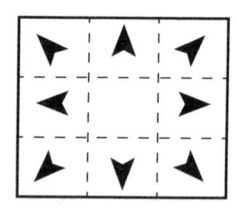

Graphic representing screen areas.

Where movements are restricted to the horizontal or vertical direction only, the center strip (horizontally or vertically, respectively) becomes the origin. Here, clicking in the sections on either side of the origin strip produces the desired movement.

Screen partitioning for controlled movement horizontally or vertically.

Movements are as shown for horizontal *(left)*, and vertical *(right)*.

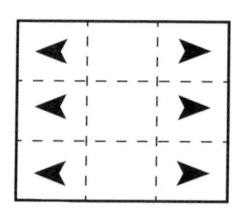

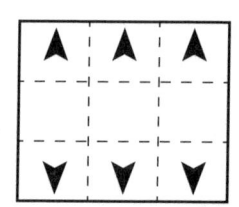

| Camera Actions | 51

Continuous view updates

When this option is enabled, the camera view updates dynamically as the pointer is moved. The origin point for camera control is the first data point in the camera view. The screen sectioning just described is about this first data point location. Movement of the pointer from this data point produces the relative movement in the camera.

Additional Define Camera Tool Settings

Settings that can be used in conjunction with the action buttons let you control the positioning and movement of the camera. You can display just those tool settings that you require. Using the More/Hide button, you then can quickly display or dismiss the settings as necessary.

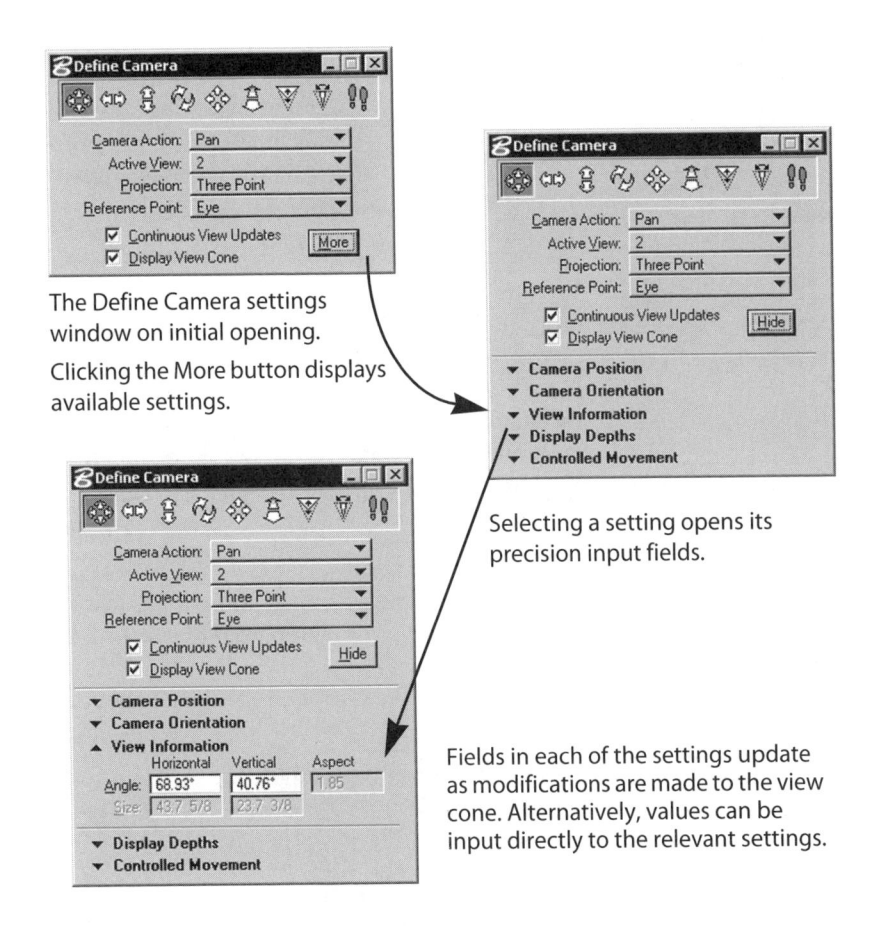

The Define Camera settings window on initial opening.

Clicking the More button displays available settings.

Selecting a setting opens its precision input fields.

Fields in each of the settings update as modifications are made to the view cone. Alternatively, values can be input directly to the relevant settings.

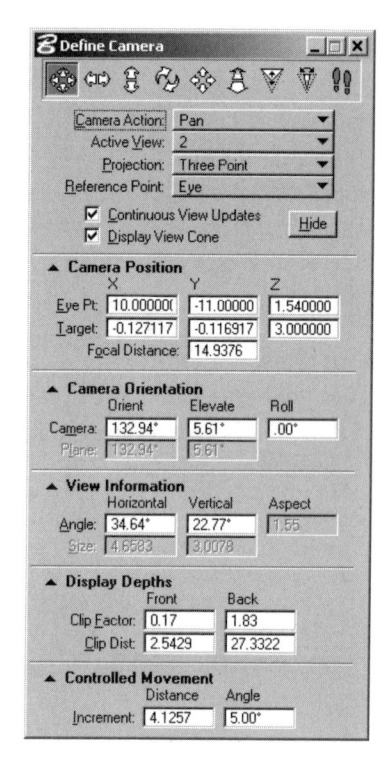

Precision Settings

The tool settings apply to the viewing parameters of the active or camera view. You can change this view's parameters by keying in values to the various fields. When you make changes to the view interactively, values in these fields update automatically. Interactive adjustments can be made via the view cone, or directly in the camera view using one of the Camera Action settings.

Listed in the following table are the settings that are accessible from the Define Camera tool dialog box.

The Define Camera settings window showing all settings input fields

Tool Setting	Effect
Camera Position	Sets the location of the camera and target: Eye Pt. — x, y, and z coordinate values for the eye point, or camera position. Target — x, y, and z coordinate values for the target of the camera. Focal Distance — Resets the distance to target from eye, useful when using the Depth of Field option with Antialiased Ray Traced rendering.
Camera Orientation	Sets the camera and image plane orientation. **Camera**: Defines the camera location Orient — Horizontal angle, measured from the positive (design file) X direction. Elevate — Vertical angle, measured from the positive (design file) X direction. Roll — Angle that camera is rotated, measured about the z-axis of the camera view. **Plane (One Point projection only)**: Defines the image plane orientation Orient — Horizontal angle, of the image plane's normal, measured from the positive (design file) X direction. Elevate — Vertical angle, of the image plane's normal, measured from the positive (design file) X direction.

| Camera Actions |

Tool Setting	Effect
View Information	Sets the viewing angles and aspect ratio: **Angle:** Horizontal — Horizontal view angle. Changing this value automatically adjusts the Vertical, relative to the view aspect ratio. Vertical — Vertical view angle. Changing this value automatically adjusts the Horizontal, relative to the view aspect ratio. Aspect — Ratio of the width/height of the camera view. **Size:** Horizontal — Horizontal dimension, in working units, of the camera view. Vertical — Vertical dimension, in working units, of the camera view.
Display Depths	Sets the clipping planes for the camera view. **Clip Factor:** Front — Sets the front clipping plane at the percentage distance from the eye to target (normally between 0 and 1). Back — Sets the back clipping plane to be a factor of the eye-to-target distance (normally greater than 1). Clip Dist. — Display only, showing distances from the eye point to the front and back clipping planes.
Controlled Movement	Sets incremental limits, Distance and Angle, for controlled movement of the camera, target, or view cone. The maximum Distance increment is one-half the distance from the eye to the target. The maximum Angle increment is 45°.

Pan

Pan is used to modify the view (cone) by revolving either the Camera about the target (horizontally or vertically), or vice-versa. With Reference Point set to Eye, the target is rotated about the eye point (camera). When it is set to Target, the eye point (camera) is rotated about the target.

✔ **Exercise 2-14: Pan the camera relative to the target**

1. Open model *Pan_01*, in *village home.dgn*.
2. Select the Define Camera tool.
3. Select View 2 as the active view and set the following tool settings:

    Camera Action: Pan
    Projection: Three Point
    Reference Point: Target

Chapter 2: Camera Setups and Navigation

Continuous View Updates: Enabled
Display View Cone: Enabled

NOTE: *Camera action can be set using the icon bar or selecting from the Camera Action options.*

4 Enter a data point in View 2.

5 Move the pointer left/right or up/down to rotate the camera about the target, in the direction of the pointer, relative to the initial data point in the view.

As the pointer moves, the camera view updates dynamically, as does the view cone in other open views.

6 Enter a data point to accept the new view orientation, or Reset to return the view to its original rotation.

With Reference Point set to Target:

Moving the screen pointer horizontally or vertically, in the camera view (View2), rotates the camera horizontally (Top view) or vertically (Front view), about the target.

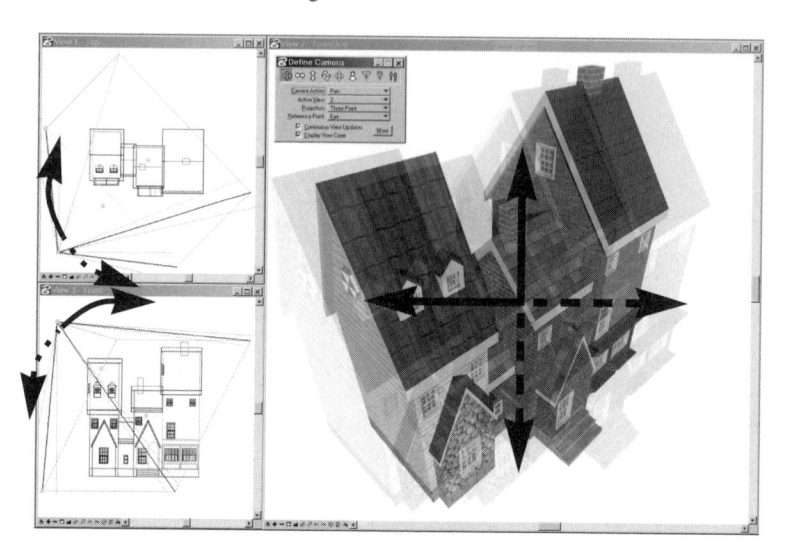

7 Similarly, you can rotate the target about the eye point by selecting Eye as the reference point.

| Camera Actions | 55

With Reference Point set to Eye:

Moving the screen pointer horizontally or vertically, in the camera view (View 2), rotates the Target horizontally (Top view) or vertically (Front view), about the eye point (camera).

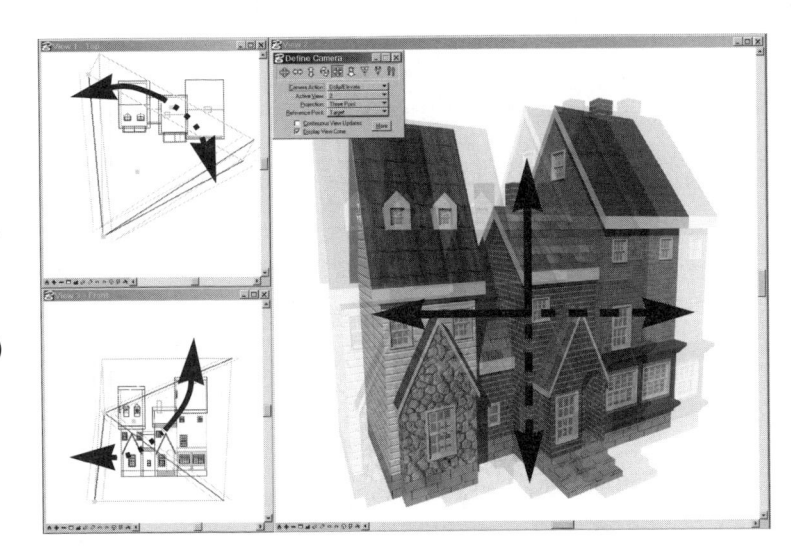

Pan Camera precision inputs

Using the precision input fields in the Define Camera tool settings, you can enter exact values for Pan settings.

✔ Exercise 2-15: Precisely pan the camera

1 Open model *Pan_02*, in *village home.dgn*.

2 Select the Define Camera tool, with the following settings:

Camera Action: Pan
Active View: 2
Projection: Three Point
Reference Point: Target
Continuous View Updates: Disabled

3 Click More.

4 Open the Camera Orientation settings.

5 In the Orient field, enter 60.

6 In the Elevate field, enter 10.

The camera view updates to reflect the new values, as does the view cone graphics in other view.

Rendered images of View 2 before *(left)* and after *(right)* changing camera orientation.

NOTE: *Any manipulation of the view cone automatically updates values in the precision input fields.*

Pan with controlled movement

As well as interactive control of the view cone, you can specify a controlled movement. Here, you enter data points at the left/right or top/bottom section of the camera view to rotate the camera or target by the specified value. For Pan, the relevant setting is Angle.

In this next exercise, you will adjust the controlled movement step sizes and then use this information to rotate the camera around a target.

✔ Exercise 2-16: Rotate the camera in 5° increments about the target

1. Continuing in model **Pan_02**, select the Define Camera tool with the settings as selected in the previous exercise.

2. In the tool settings, open the Controlled Movement settings.

   The Controlled Movement settings appear, with fields for increments in Distance and Angle.

| Camera Actions | **57**

3 In the Angle field, enter 5.

4 In the camera view, enter a data point in the top/bottom or left/right section of the view.

The camera rotates 5° horizontally or vertically, from the center of the view, in the direction of the data point.

5 Enter further data points to rotate the camera (eye point) in 5° increments about the target, either horizontally or vertically, in the direction indicated by the pointer.

Similarly, by setting Reference Point to Eye, you can incrementally rotate the target about the camera (eye point).

Pan Horizontal

This setting provides the horizontal component of the Pan camera setting. It lets you rotate the eye point (camera) in the horizontal direction only about the target, and vice-versa. With Reference Point set to Eye, the target rotates horizontally about the eye point. Set to Target, the eye point rotates horizontally about the target.

✔ Exercise 2-17: Pan the camera horizontally relative to the target

1 Open model *Pan_03*, in *village home.dgn*.

2 Select the Define Camera tool with the following settings:

Camera Action: Pan Horizontal
Active View: 2
Projection: Three Point
Reference Point: Target
Continuous View Updates: Enabled
Display View Cone: Enabled

3 With the pointer in the camera view, enter a data point.

4 Move the pointer left or right to rotate the camera about the target, in the same direction, relative to the initial data point.

As the pointer moves, the camera view updates dynamically, as does the view cone in other open views.

5 Accept the new view orientation.

With Reference Point set to Target:

Moving the screen pointer horizontally, in the camera view (View 2), rotates the camera horizontally about the target (Top view).

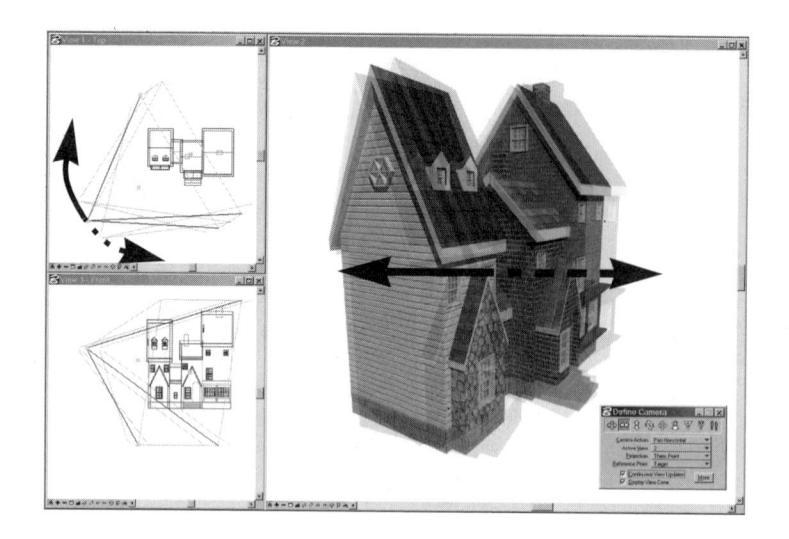

Similarly, you can rotate the target horizontally about the eye point by selecting Eye as the reference point.

With Reference Point set to Eye:

Moving the screen pointer horizontally, in the camera view (View 2), rotates the target horizontally about the eye point, (Top view).

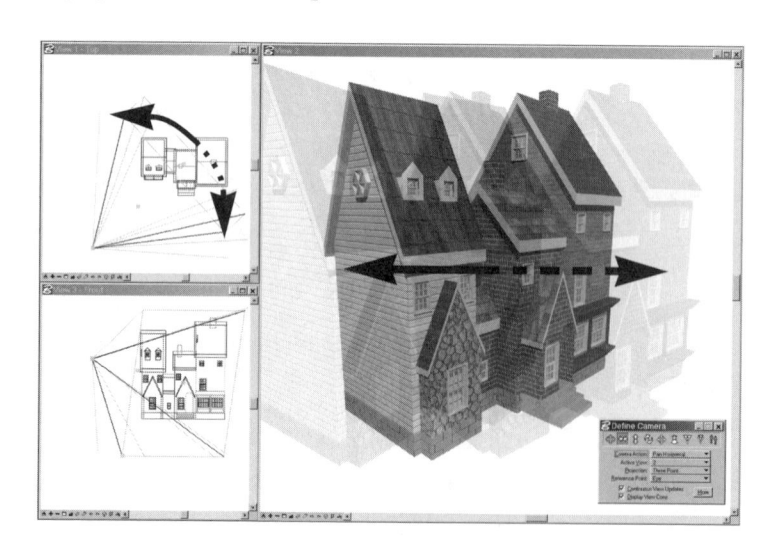

Pan Horizontal precision inputs

Using the precision input fields in the Define Camera tool settings, you can enter an exact value for the Pan Horizontal setting. This works similar to the Pan function, except that only the Orient field is relevant. If in Pan Horizontal mode, the Elevate and Roll options are not used when moving the camera by entering data points in the view.

| Camera Actions |

With Controlled Movement set to Increment Angle by 5.0° and Continuous View Updates off, entering a data point in Camera view will rotate to the left or right depending on which side of the view you enter the data point. This rotation will be in the specified 5.0° increments.

Pan Horizontal with controlled movement

You can restrict rotations to a preset amount by setting the Angle field to the amount of rotation in degrees you want to see per click or data point. This works similar to that of the Pan function, except that rotation is horizontal only. Acceptable values for Controlled Movement Angle are from 0.01 to 45.

Pan Vertical

This setting gives you the vertical component of the Pan camera setting. It lets you rotate the eye point (camera) vertically about the target, and vice-versa. With Reference Point set to Eye, the target rotates vertically about the eye point. Set to Target, the eye point rotates vertically about the target.

✔ Exercise 2-18: Pan the camera vertically relative to the target

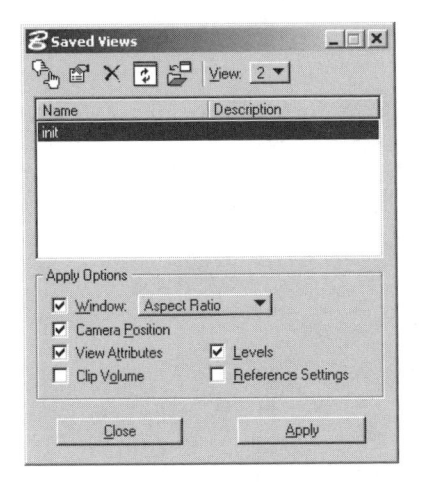

1   Continuing in model *Pan_03*, open the Utilities > Saved Views dialog and apply the saved view *init* to View 2.

2   Select the Define Camera tool with the following settings:

Camera Action: Pan Vertical
Active View: 2
Projection: Three Point
Reference Point: Target
Continuous View Updates: Enabled
Display View Cone: Enabled

3   With the pointer in the camera view, enter a data point.

4   Move the pointer up or down to rotate the camera in the same direction, relative to the initial data point.

| Chapter 2: Camera Setups and Navigation |

As the pointer moves, the camera view updates dynamically, as does the view cone in other open views.

5 Accept the new view orientation

With Reference Point set to Target:

Moving the screen pointer vertically, in the camera view (View 2), rotates the camera vertically about the target (Front view).

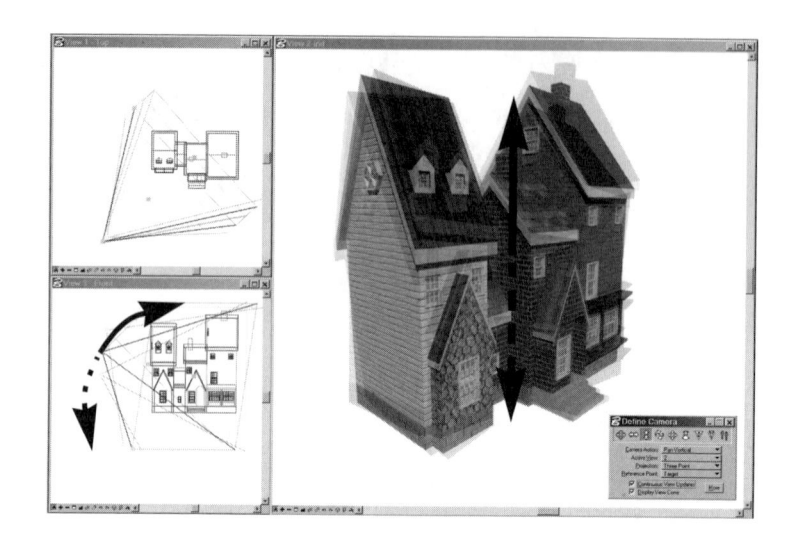

Similarly, you can rotate the target about the eye point by selecting Eye as the reference point.

With Reference Point set to Eye:

Moving the screen pointer vertically, in the camera view (View 2), rotates the target vertically about the eye point (Front view).

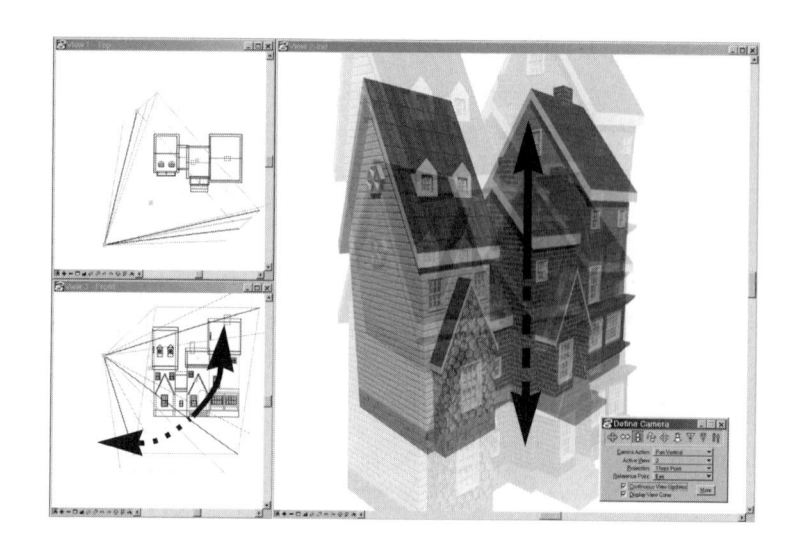

| Camera Actions | 61

Pan Vertical precision inputs

Using the precision input fields in the Define Camera tool settings, you can enter an exact value for the Elevate setting. This works similar to the Pan function, except that the Elevate field is the only field that is relevant to the possible movement.

Pan Vertical with controlled movement

You can restrict rotations to a preset amount. This works similar to the Pan function. except that rotation is vertical only.

Roll Camera

This tool is used to roll, or rotate, the camera about the z-axis of the camera view. For this setting, there is no difference when Reference Point is set to Eye or Target.

✔ **Exercise 2-19: Roll the camera**

1   Open model *Roll_01*, in *village home.dgn*.

2   Select the Define Camera tool with the following settings:

Camera Action: Roll
Active View: 2
Projection: Three Point
Continuous View Updates: Enabled
Display View Cone: Enabled

3   With the pointer in the camera view, enter a data point.

4   Move the pointer upward relative to the initial data point to roll the camera clockwise, downward to roll the camera counterclockwise, and then around the view to continue the rotation.

As the pointer moves, the camera view updates dynamically, as does the view cone in other open views.

5   Accept the new view orientation.

| Chapter 2: Camera Setups and Navigation |

The Roll setting lets you rotate the camera about the z-axis of the camera view.

Moving the pointer upward rolls the camera counterclockwise.

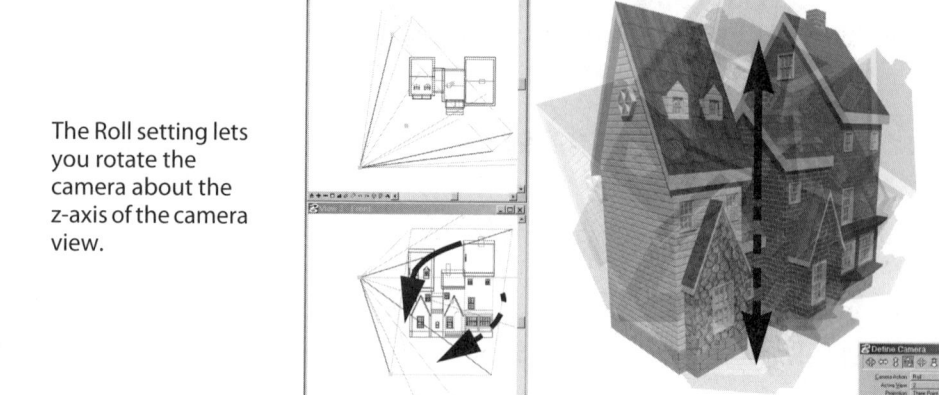

Moving the pointer downward rolls the camera clockwise.

Roll Camera precision input

You can control the Roll angle of the camera with the Roll value in the Camera Orientation portion of the tool settings. When a value is entered in the Roll field, the view updates with the camera roll angle set to the new value.

> **NOTE:** *Any roll manipulation of the view cone automatically updates the roll value in this field.*

Roll Camera with controlled movement

You can roll the camera in predefined steps using this setting.

✔ Exercise 2-20: Roll the camera in 5° steps

1 Continuing in model **Roll_01**, apply the saved view *start* to View 2.

2 Select the Define Camera tool with the following settings:

Camera Action: Roll
Continuous View Updates: Disabled

3 If necessary, click More to reveal the precision settings options.

4 Open the Controlled Movement settings.

| Camera Actions | 63

5   If necessary, in the Angle field, enter 5 (this should be the current setting from a previous exercise).

6   In View 2, enter a data point in the top or bottom section of the view.

    The camera is rolled 5° either clockwise, or counterclockwise, depending on the direction of the data point up or down from the center of the view.

7   Further data points rotate the camera in 5° increments about the z-axis of the camera view.

8   In the Camera Orientation section of the Define Camera dialog, enter a zero in the Roll field to remove roll.

Dolly/Elevate

Dolly/Elevate is used to move the camera view cone linearly in a horizontal or vertical direction. This lets you move the camera sideways or vertically relative to the camera view. The action is similar to moving the view cone using its middle handle.

Moving the whole view cone in this manner keeps the camera and target points in the same positions relative to each other. It makes no difference whether Eye or Target is set as the reference point.

✔ Exercise 2-21: Dolly/elevate the camera

1   Open model *Dolly_01*, in *village home.dgn*.

2   Select the Define Camera tool with the following settings:

    Camera Action: Dolly/Elevate
    Active View: 2
    Projection: Three Point
    Continuous View Updates: Enabled
    Display View Cone: Enabled

3   With the pointer in the camera view, enter a data point.

4   Move the pointer up/down or left/right to move the camera vertically or horizontally in the direction of the pointer relative to the initial data point.

    As the pointer moves, the camera view updates dynamically, as does the view cone in other open views.

64 | Chapter 2: Camera Setups and Navigation |

5 Accept the new view orientation.

Moving the pointer horizontally in the camera view (View 2) moves the view cone horizontally (Top view).

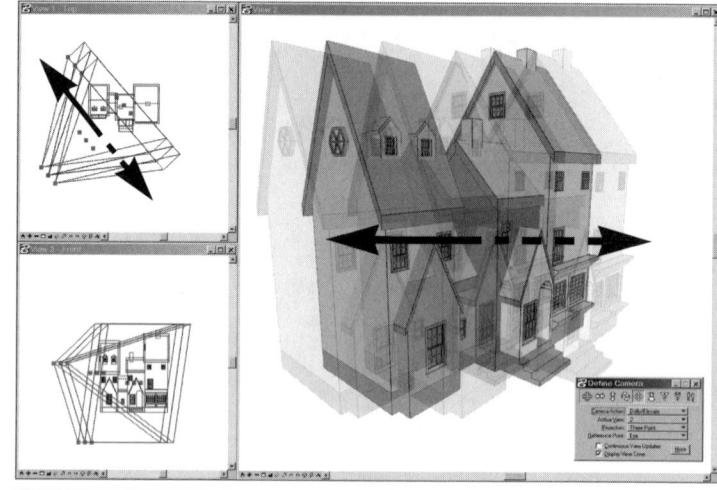

Moving the pointer vertically in the camera view (View 2) moves the view cone vertically (Front view).

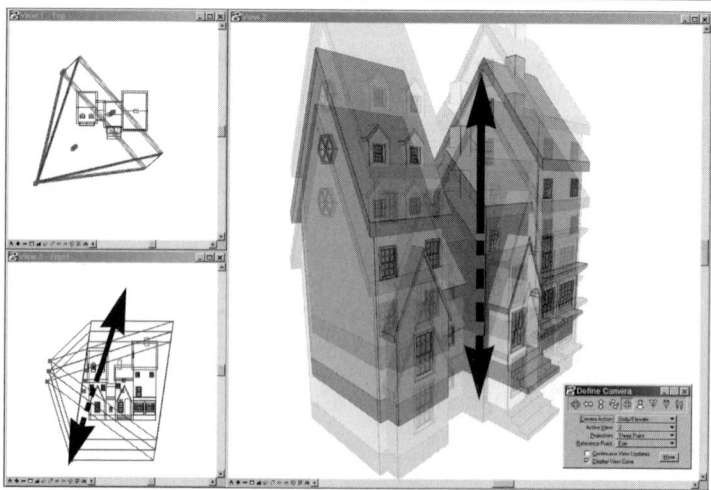

Dolly/Elevate camera precision input

As you move the camera in the camera view, the Eye Pt and Target fields adjust automatically to reflect their new positions. To control the movement of the camera, you should use the Controlled Movement settings.

Dolly/Elevate camera with controlled movement

You can move the camera in predefined steps using this setting. For these movements, the Distance value of the Controlled Movement Increment fields controls movement.

| Camera Actions | **65**

✔ Exercise 2-22: Dolly/elevate the camera in 10 unit steps

1 Continuing in model *Dolly_01*, apply the saved view *Begin* to View 2.

2 Select Define Camera with the following tool settings:

   Camera Action: Dolly/Elevate
   Active View: 2
   Projection: Three Point
   Continuous View Updates: Disabled

3 If necessary, click More, and then open the Controlled Movement section.

4 In the Distance field of the Controlled Movement section, enter 10.

5 In the camera view, enter a data point in the top, bottom, left, or right of the view.

   The camera is moved 10 units in the direction of the data point. This has the effect of moving the model in the opposite direction on the screen.

   Further data points move the camera in 10 unit increments.

Dolly

Similar to the Dolly/Elevate camera setting, with Dolly you can move the camera view cone directly into or out from the view. You can also move it sideways. This is similar to moving the view cone using its center handle.

Moving the whole view cone in this manner keeps the camera and target points in the same positions relative to each other. It makes no difference whether Eye or Target is set as the reference point.

✔ Exercise 2-23: Dolly the camera

1 Continuing in model *Dolly_01*, apply the saved view *Begin* to View 2.

2 Select the Define Camera tool with the following settings:

| Chapter 2: Camera Setups and Navigation |

Camera Action: Dolly
Continuous View Updates: Enabled

3 With the pointer in the camera view, enter a data point.

4 Move the pointer:

- Up or down to move the camera in or out of the view, respectively.

- Left or right to pan the camera horizontally (in the direction of the pointer from the initial data point).

As the pointer moves, the camera view updates dynamically, as does the view cone in other open views.

5 Accept the new view orientation.

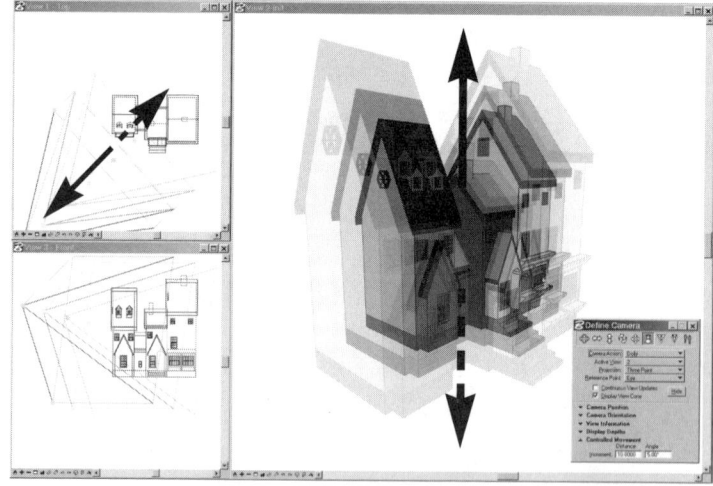

Moving the pointer vertically, in the camera view (View 2), moves the view cone in or out of the view.

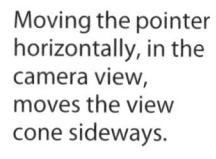

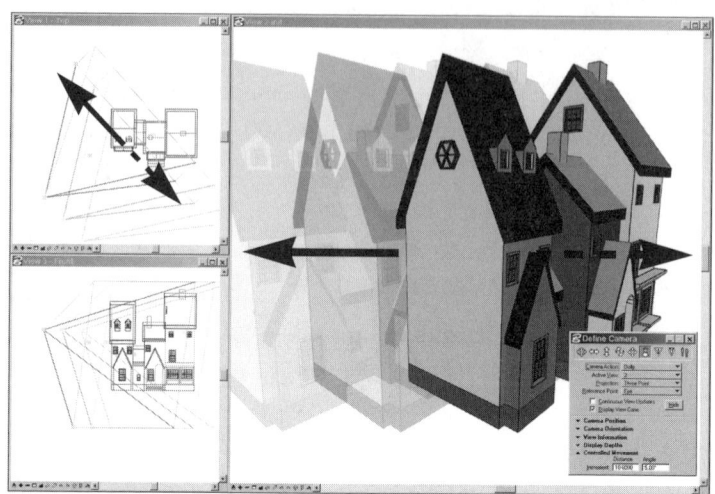

Moving the pointer horizontally, in the camera view, moves the view cone sideways.

| Camera Actions | **67**

Dolly camera precision input

As you dolly the camera in the camera view, the Eye Point and Target fields adjust automatically to reflect their new positions. To control the movement of the dolly setting, you should use the Controlled Movement settings.

Dolly camera with controlled movement

You can dolly the camera in predefined steps using this setting. For dollying operations, the Distance value of the Controlled Movement Increment fields controls movement.

✔ **Exercise 2-24: Dolly the camera in 10 unit steps**

1. Continuing in model **Dolly_01**, apply the saved view *Begin* to View 2.

2. Select Define Camera with the following tool settings:

   Camera Action: Dolly
   Projection: Three Point
   Continuous View Updates: Disabled

3. Check that the Distance field in the Controlled Movement section is set to 10 (this value was used in a previous exercise).

4. In the camera view, enter a data point in the top, bottom, left, or right of the view.

   The camera is dollied 10 units in the direction determined by the location of the data point.

   Further data points dolly the camera in 10 unit increments.

Lens Focal Length

This setting is used to manipulate the focal length of the camera lens of the camera view. It is done by changing the distance between the target and the eye point (camera). You can move the camera closer to or away from the fixed target, interactively or with controlled movement. Whether the camera or the target moves, movement is controlled by the setting for Reference Point. When it is set to Eye, the target moves relative to a fixed camera. Set to Target, the camera moves relative to a fixed target.

✔ Exercise 2-25: Change the lens focal length of the camera view

1. Open model *Lens_01*, in *village home.dgn*.
2. Select the Define Camera tool with the following settings:

   Camera Action: Lens Focal Length
   Active View: 2
   Projection: Three Point
   Continuous View Updates: Enabled
   Display View Cone: Enabled

3. With the pointer in the camera view, enter a data point.
4. Move the pointer:

   ▶ Up to reduce the focal length.

   ▶ Down to increase focal length.

   As the pointer moves, the camera view updates dynamically, as does the view cone in other open views.

5. Accept the new view settings.

Lens Focal Length precision input

As you change the lens focal length in the camera view, either the Eye Point or Target field adjusts automatically to reflect the new position—that is, the one that is not selected as the (fixed) reference point (Target or Eye) changes. To control the increment movements for focal length settings you can change the Controlled Movement settings to the required values.

Lens Focal Length with controlled movement

In the next exercise you will be changing the focal length in predefined steps. To do this, you will use the Distance value of the Controlled Movement Increment fields.

| Camera Actions | 69

With Reference Point set to Target, the camera moves, while the target remains fixed.

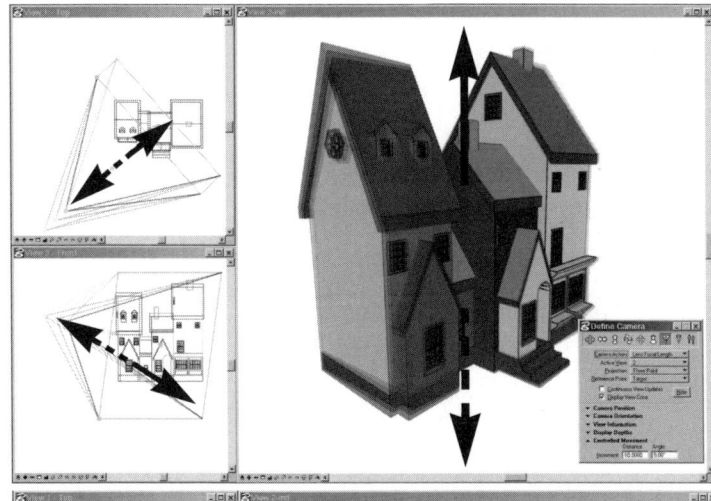

With Reference Point set to Eye, the target moves, while the camera remains fixed.

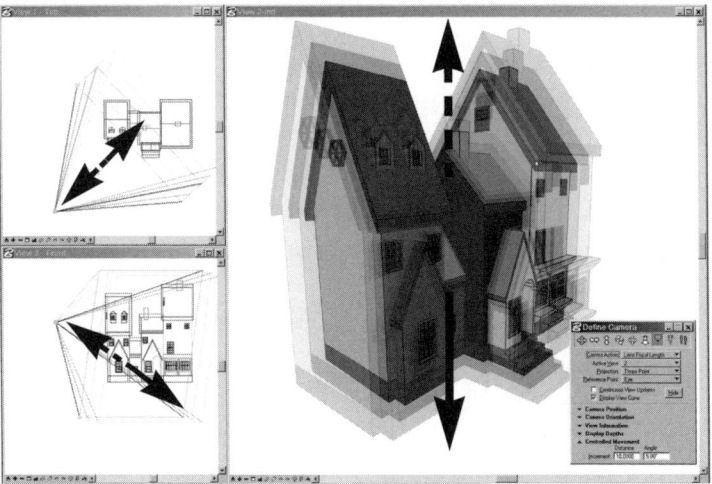

✔ **Exercise 2-26: Change the lens focal length by varying the eye-to-target distance in 100 unit steps**

1 Continuing in model *Lens_01*, apply the saved view *Origin* to View 2.

2 Select the Define Camera tool with the following settings:

Camera Action: Lens Focal Length
Active View: 2
Projection: Three Point
Continuous View Updates: Disabled

3 In the Distance field of the Controlled Movement section, enter 100.

4 In the camera view, enter a data point in the top or bottom of the view.

The distance between the eye point (camera) and target is increased, or reduced, by 100 units. If the data point is in the top half of the view, it is reduced, and vice-versa.

Further data points change the distance in 100 unit increments.

Lens View Angle

This setting is used to change the camera lens viewing angle. This can be performed interactively, or in defined steps using Controlled Movement. The lens view angle is made up of horizontal and vertical viewing angles. These are related by the aspect ratio of the camera view. This would be same as zooming in or out with a camera's lens. Both target and eye positions remain fixed regardless of reference point choice, as only the view angle changes.

✔ Exercise 2-27: Change the lens view angle of the camera view

1 Continuing in model *Lens_01*, apply the saved view *Origin* to View 2.

2 Select the Define Camera tool with the following settings:

Camera Action: Lens View Angle
Active View: 2
Projection: Three Point
Reference Point: Eye
Continuous View Updates: Enabled
Display View Cone: Enabled

3 With the pointer in the camera view, enter a data point.

4 Move the pointer:

▶ Up to increase the view angle.

▶ Down to decrease the view angle.

As the pointer moves, the camera view updates dynamically, as does the view cone in other open views.

5 Accept the new view settings.

View Angle precision input

You can control the view angle with precision inputs. In the View Information section of the Define Camera settings window are input fields for Horizontal and Vertical view angles. These are related by the Aspect setting. When you enter a value for one, the value in the other changes accordingly.

Lens View Angle with controlled movement

When adjusting the lens view angle interactively, you can use the Controlled Movement settings to restrict the changes to a defined amount.

✔ **Exercise 2-28: Change the lens view angle in 10° steps**

1 Continuing in model *Lens_01*, apply the saved view *Origin* to View 2.

2 Select the Define Camera tool with the following settings:

Camera Action: Lens View Angle
Active View: 2
Projection: Three Point
Continuous View Updates: Disabled

3 In the Angle field of the Controlled Movement section, enter 10.

4 In the camera view, enter a data point in the top or bottom of the view.

The lens view angle is increased by 10° if the data point is in the top half of the view and decreased by 10° if the data point is in the lower half of the view.

Further data points change the focal length in 10° increments.

Pan/Dolly

This setting is useful for walking through a model, in particular when the movement is on a plane, as in walking around the floor of a building. It lets you rotate the camera and to move forward or backward along the z-axis of the camera view.

How the camera rotates is determined by the Reference Point setting. A natural method is to have Reference set to Eye, which causes the camera to rotate about the eye point when you move the pointer left or right. This lets you, in effect, turn your head (that is, the camera) by moving the pointer in the direction that you wish to look. When Reference is set to Target, the camera rotates around the target when you move the pointer left or right in the camera view.

✔ Exercise 2-29: Use the Pan/Dolly setting

1. Open model *PanDolly*, in *village home.dgn*.

2. Select the Define Camera tool with the following settings:

   Camera Action: Pan/Dolly
   Active View: 2
   Projection: Three Point
   Reference Point: Eye
   Continuous View Updates: Enabled
   Display View Cone: Enabled

3. With the pointer in the camera view, enter a data point.

4. Move the pointer:

   ▶ Up to move forward.

   ▶ Down to move back.

   ▶ Left to look left.

   ▶ Right to look right.

   As the pointer moves, the camera view updates dynamically, as does the view cone in other open views.

5. Accept the new view orientation.

Pan/Dolly precision input

As the camera is moved, the settings for the Camera Position update, as does the Orient Angle value in the Camera Orientation section. To simply control the movement of the camera you should use the Controlled Movement settings.

| Camera Actions | 73

Using the Pan/Dolly setting to "walk through" a model.

Pointer movement up or down moves the camera forward or back.

Pointer movement left or right turns the camera.

(Shown with Reference Point set to Eye.)

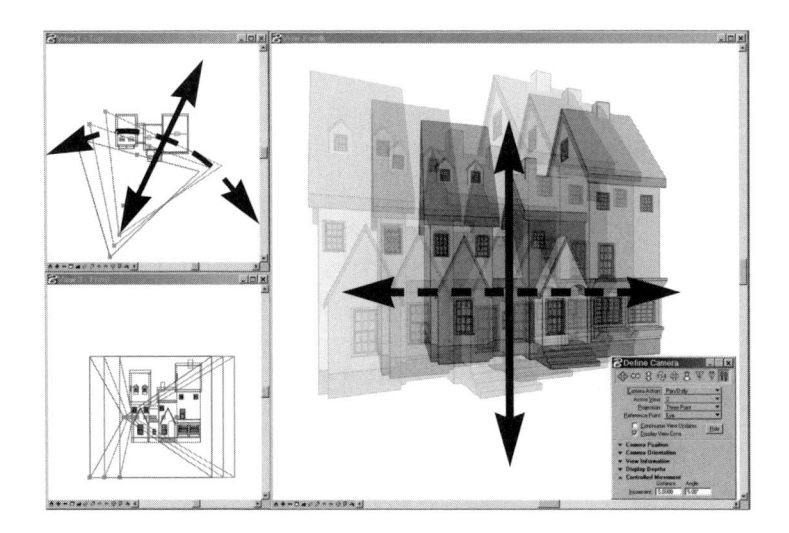

Pan/Dolly with controlled movement

You can control the distance that the camera moves forward or backward, and the angle that the camera turns left or right.

✔ Exercise 2-30: Pan/dolly the camera in steps of 10 units distance or 5° rotation

1. Continuing in model *PanDolly*, apply the saved view *View_01* to View 2.

2. Select Define Camera with the following tool settings:

    Camera Action: Pan/Dolly
    Active View: 2
    Projection: Three Point
    Continuous View Updates: Disabled

3. In the Controlled Movement settings, set Distance to 10 and Angle to 5.

4. In the camera view enter a data point in the top, bottom, left, or right of the view.

    The camera is dollied 10 units, or rotated 5°, depending on the position of the data point.

Further data points pan or dolly the camera in 5°, or 10 unit increments, respectively.

NAVIGATE CAMERA

In addition to the Define Camera tool options, the Navigate Camera view control also lets you move through a model. In the following section, you will learn how to move through a design using the keyboard and/or mouse. You will do this using the Navigate Camera view control, which can be found in the 3D View borders.

3D View border with Navigate Camera selected.

When initially selected, the tool is in Basic Mode. This mode lets you move through a design immediately, using the default settings. Navigate Camera also supports an Advanced mode in which you can configure the default navigation options to suit your own specific needs.

Basic Mode tool settings are:

- Active View — Sets the view in which to navigate the camera. If you try to navigate in a view that does not have a camera enabled, a warning message displays. Once you dismiss the message, the camera is enabled in parallel projection for that view.

- Mode — Lets you choose between Basic (default key maps) and Advanced (allows custom key maps).

- Mouse Control — If on, lets you use the mouse to navigate (as well as keyboard keys).

When you click Show Settings, additional settings are displayed:

- Display View Cone — Lets you display the camera view cone in all other views. This is useful for orientation in the design file.

| Navigate Camera |

- Distance — Lets you set the default distance moved for each key press, or for relative movement of the mouse when Mouse Control is on.

- Degrees — Lets you set the default angle that the camera turns for each key press, or for relative movement of the mouse when Mouse Control is on.

The following table shows you the default navigation keys and what they do. Notice that you can use the arrow keys, or you can use alpha keys on either the left or right side of the keyboard.

Key	Key alone	<Shift>+Key	<Ctrl>+Key	<Ctrl-Shift>+Key
Left arrow, <A> or <J>	Turn left	Roll left	Move left	Move left
Right arrow, <D> or <L>	Turn right	Roll right	Move right	Move right
Up arrow, <W> or <I>	Move forward	Tilt up	Move forward	Move up
Down arrow, <S> or <K>	Move back	Tilt down	Move back	Move down

Other keys let you change the default settings as follows:

- \+ increases Distance settings by 10%

- \- decreases Distance settings by 10%

- [increases Degrees settings by 10%

-] decreases Degrees settings by 10%

Pressing the Home key, <Q>, or <U> resets the camera's roll, elevation, and orientation. For example, pressing the Home key on your keyboard

- Once — Sets the camera's tilt angle back to zero degrees (roll).

- Twice — Sets the roll, then sets the camera's elevation angle, back to zero degrees (camera is horizontal to the ground).

- Three times — Sets the roll, then sets the elevation angle, then sets the camera's orientation angle, back to zero degrees (camera points in the direction of the positive x-axis).

| Chapter 2: Camera Setups and Navigation |

When using the mouse to navigate, the following table shows the effects of moving the mouse left/right or forward/back.

Mouse Movement	Mouse alone	<Shift>+ Mouse	<Ctrl> + Mouse	<Ctrl-Shift> + Mouse
Left	Turn left	Roll left	Move left	Move left
Right	Turn right	Roll right	Move right	Move right
Forward	Tilt up	Tilt up	Move forward	Move up
Back	Tilt down	Tilt down	Move back	Move down

✔ Exercise 2-31: Use Navigate Camera

1. Open *Longbeach.dgn* (model Default).
2. Open View 8.
3. In View 8, select Navigate Camera.
4. Click the downward arrow in the lower left corner of the tool settings.

   Additional settings appear.

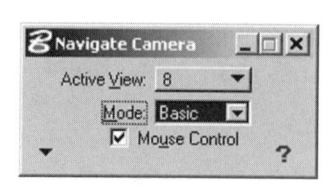

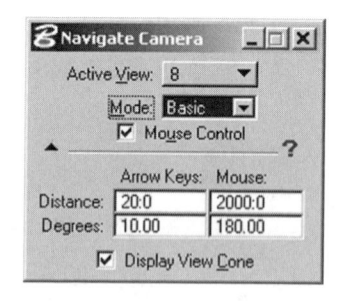

5. Ensure that Mouse Control and Display View Cone are enabled.

   This model has been saved with a camera view set up in View 8. Note that the camera view cone is present in the other open views. This helps you work out where the camera is located and where it is aimed.

6. Press the up arrow key several times.

   Observe how the camera moves forward in the camera view. This can be verified in the Top and Right views where you can see the camera view cone move forward.

   Each key press moves the camera forward by the amount specified in the Distance field for Arrow Keys, in the tool settings.

| Navigate Camera |

7 Press the down arrow key several times.

Observe how the camera now moves backward, again by the specified distance for each key press.

8 Press the right arrow key several times to pan the camera to the right. Check in the other views to see that the camera view cone has panned right.

Each key press pans the camera by the amount specified in the Degrees field for Arrow Keys.

9 Press the left arrow key several times to pan the camera back to the left.

You can use your mouse to perform these same tasks. To navigate with the mouse, enter a data point in the camera view and then move the mouse to manipulate the camera. When you have finished, you place a second data point to accept the new camera position, or Reset to return the camera to its original position. Various key and mouse movement combinations are required to perform different tasks.

To	Mouse action
Move forward	Hold down the <Ctrl> key as you move the mouse forward
Move back	Hold down the <Ctrl> key as you move the mouse back
Move left	Hold down the <Ctrl> key as you move the mouse left
Move right	Hold down the <Ctrl> key as you move the mouse right
Pan right	Move the mouse to the right (without holding down a key)
Pan left	Move the mouse to the left (without holding down a key)

You may accidentally move the mouse slightly up or down as you are panning left or right. This tilts the mouse up or down, respectively. Don't worry if this happens, as you can easily correct it. After you have positioned the camera, you can press the Home key twice to zero the roll and elevation.

✔ **Exercise 2-32: Navigate the camera using the mouse**

1. Continuing in *Longbeach.dgn*, with the Navigate Camera view control still active, enter a data point in View 2.

2. Hold the <Ctrl> key and move the mouse forward.

   Observe how the view camera moves forward. You can use the other views to check the position of the camera.

   The sensitivity of the mouse movement is controlled by the Distance field for Mouse value. Input a higher/lower value to increase/decrease the amount of movement, respectively.

3. Hold the <Ctrl> key and move the mouse backward to move the camera back, or left/right to move the camera left/right.

4. Release the <Ctrl> key and move the mouse left/right/forward/back to pan the camera left/right/up/down, respectively.

5. Enter a data point to accept the new orientation of the camera.

   Your view will appear slightly skewed.

6. Press the Home key on your keyboard twice.

   This zeroes out the roll and elevation.

7. Practice using both the key controls and the mouse to navigate around the model.

   Remember that you can place the camera anywhere in the design cube, pointing in any direction.

Navigate Camera Advanced Mode

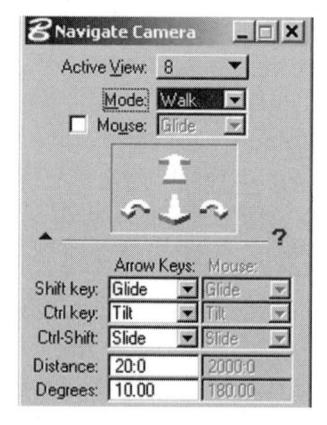

This mode allows the use of custom keymaps. The navigation option that you choose from this location in the settings window only applies to the keyboard. As you switch among navigation mode options, notice the navigation graphic changes.

Navigate Camera in Advanced mode.

| Navigate Camera |

Fly — Move forward/back, turn left/right:

- Up arrow, or moving the mouse forward — Moves the camera forward along the current angle of the camera. For example, if the camera is pointed at an upward angle, you will move forward and upward along that angle.

- Down arrow, or moving the mouse backward — Moves the camera backward at the current angle of the camera. For example, if camera is pointed at an upward angle, you will move backward and downward along that angle.

- Left/right arrow, or moving the mouse to the left/right — Same as Turn.

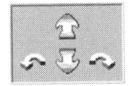

Turn — Turn about camera axes:

- Up arrow, or moving the mouse forward — Turns the camera upward, perpendicular to the ground (as if standing still and turning your head toward the sky).

- Down arrow, or moving the mouse backward — Turns the camera downward, perpendicular to the ground (as if standing still and turning your head toward the ground).

- Left arrow, or moving the mouse to the left — Turns the camera to the left parallel to the ground (as if standing still and turning your head toward the left).

- Right arrow, or moving the mouse to the right — Turns the camera to the right parallel to the ground (as if standing still and turning your head toward the right).

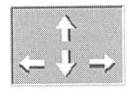

Slide — Move up/down/left/right in camera plane:

- Up arrow, or moving the mouse forward — Moves the camera up, perpendicular to the ground (as if you were looking straight out of a glass elevator that was going up).

- Down arrow, or moving the mouse backward — Moves the camera down, perpendicular to the ground (as if you were looking straight out of a glass elevator that was going down).

- Left arrow, or moving the mouse to the left — Moves the camera left, parallel to the ground (as if you were looking straight out of the window of a train moving in the direction of your left shoulder).

- ▸ Right arrow, or moving the mouse to the right — Moves the camera right, parallel to the ground (as if you were looking straight out of the window of a train moving in the direction of your right shoulder).

Glide — Move forward/back/left/right in camera plane:

- ▸ Up/down arrow, or moving the mouse forward/backward — Same as Fly.

- ▸ Left/right arrow, or moving the mouse to the left/right — Same as Slide.

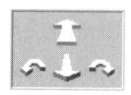

Walk — Move forward/back at current height, left/right swivel:

- ▸ Up arrow, or moving the mouse forward — Moves the camera forward, parallel to the ground (as if walking into the design).

- ▸ Down arrow, or moving the mouse backward — Moves the camera backward, parallel to the ground (as if walking away from the design).

- ▸ Left/right arrow, or moving the mouse to the left/right — Same as Swivel.

Swivel — Turn about design axes:

- ▸ Up/down arrow, or moving the mouse forward/backward — Similar to Turn, except that the camera turns up or down perpendicular to the tilt of the camera, and stops when it points straight up or straight down.

- ▸ Left arrow, or moving the mouse to the left — Turns (swivels) the camera to the left, parallel to the tilt of the camera.

- ▸ Right arrow, or moving the mouse to the right — Turns (swivels) the camera to the right, parallel to the tilt of the camera.

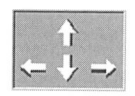

Float — Move up/down/left/right in design plane:

- ▸ Up/down arrow, or moving the mouse forward/backward — Similar to Slide, except that the camera moves up or down perpendicular to the tilt of the camera.

| Review Questions | **81**

- Left/right arrow, or moving the mouse to the left/right — Similar to Slide, except that the camera moves to the left or right parallel to the tilt of the camera.

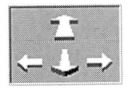

Dolly — Move forward/back/left/right at current height:

- Up/down arrow, or moving the mouse forward/backward — Same as Walk.

- Left/right arrow, or moving the mouse to the left/right — Same as Float.

Tilt — Tilt camera about camera axes:

- Up/down arrow, or moving the mouse forward/backward — Same as Turn.

- Left arrow, or moving the mouse to the left — Tilts the camera to the left (as if standing still and leaning your head toward your left shoulder).

- Right arrow, or moving the mouse to the right — Tilts the camera to the right (as if standing still and leaning your head toward your right shoulder).

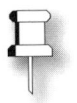

NOTE: *Once you get that perfect camera view setup, you should use the Saved Views dialog box (Utilities > Saved Views) to name and save the view for future recall.*

REVIEW QUESTIONS

1. By default, what kind of view mode projection does MicroStation use?
2. What view attribute turns perspective on or off?
3. When you use the Define Camera tool for the first time in a design, what are you prompted to choose?
4. What are the four different camera view projections?
5. Which projection makes the vertical edges appear straight?
6. What projection provides the most natural image, like that of a conventional camera?

7 Which camera lens provides a viewing angle closest to the human eye: 35 mm, 50 mm, or 85 mm?

8 Which camera tool is used to move the camera view cone linearly in a horizontal or vertical direction?

CHAPTER SUMMARY

In this chapter you have learned how to add perspective to a view and how to set up a camera using the Camera Settings tool. Using 3D data points you learned how to quickly set up an initial camera, then using the Define Camera tools how to modify the perspective in the view and manipulate the camera target, location, and lens angle to suit your taste. In addition you learned how to use the Navigate Camera tool to navigate a camera through a 3D scene.

3 Rendering Options and Settings

MicroStation offers a variety of rendering options, ranging from the simplest wireframe image to photorealistic images.

This chapter presents an overview of MicroStation's hidden line and rendering options. In addition, you will be introduced to tool boxes and settings that have an effect on your renderings. The Constant, Smooth, Phong, and Ray Trace routines are presented and their settings explained. The importance of Antialiasing, Environment Mapping, Fresnel Effects, and Render All Objects options are reviewed. The use of the Depth of Field tool to achieve photographic-quality renderings is presented along with other tools including Distance Cueing and Fog and Depth Cueing effects.

GAMMA CORRECTION FOR PHOTOREALISTIC RENDERING

Gamma correction is used to compensate for the fact that monitors and printers don't have the same visual response as the human eye, and serves to bring out more detail in darker areas of images. Typically, the gamma correction for a standard monitor (CRT) should be set to 1.8 to

2.5, while for an LCD display, it can be left at 1.0. In MicroStation, you can set the gamma correction value for your display in the View Options category of the Preferences dialog box (select Workspace > Preferences). An exact figure is not critical, but a good starting value to experiment with is 2.0.

Similarly, when you save an image from MicroStation, you have the option of applying gamma correction to it. This may be to accommodate a printer to produce hard-copy output that more closely represents what is seen on the screen. As a rule, to avoid "tying" your image to one particular display/printing device, it is better to save images with a neutral gamma value (1.0) and let other software, or printing device software, that you use add the gamma correction that they require. Each display/printing device can have different characteristics such that the correct gamma correction for one device may not be correct for another. Once gamma correction has been saved with an image, changing the gamma value will not let you return the image exactly to its original state (with gamma correction of 1.0).

Typically, printers tend to darken images more than display monitors, so a higher value may be required if you intend to print the finished image. Where required, gamma correction can be performed on the saved image, after rendering, using the MicroStation image display utility (select Utilities > Image > Display) or other imaging software.

If your renderings differ substantially from those depicted in this book, you may need to adjust your gamma correction.

WIREMESH, HIDDEN LINE, AND FILLED HIDDEN LINE

To begin, you will look at the wireframe routines. Wireframes have been in existence for many years and are still useful today for reviewing 3D models. The first of these, Wiremesh, is similar to wireframe display. All elements are transparent and do not obscure other elements. Hidden lines are not removed. Wiremesh differs from Wireframe display in that curved surfaces are represented by a polygonal mesh. This can increase the realism of curved surfaces, although it may also increase the amount of clutter as more lines are displayed for surfaces that normally would be hidden. Both Hidden Line and Filled Hidden Line display only those surfaces that would be visible in real life.

| Wiremesh, Hidden Line, and Filled Hidden Line | 85

✔ Exercise 3-1: Compare the line rendering modes

1. Open model *Default* in *no2_pencil.dgn*.

   The design file has six views defined to allow easy comparison among the different rendering modes.

2. In the Rendering Tools tool box, select the Render tool with the following settings:

   Target: View
   Render Mode: Wiremesh

3. Enter a data point in View 3.

Wireframe *(left)* and Wiremesh *(right)*.

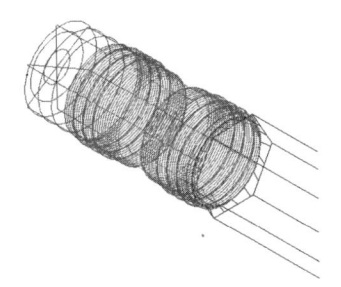

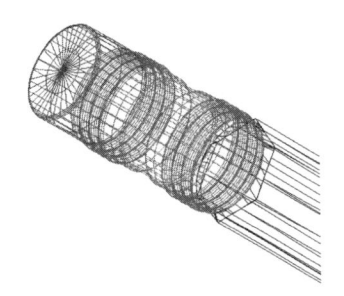

Note the difference in appearance between the default Wireframe display in View 2 and the Wiremesh display in View 3. Wiremesh is similar to Wireframe but with more lines and/or triangles to better display surfaces.

4. In the Render tool settings, set:

   Render Mode: Hidden Line.

5. Enter a data point in View 4.

   View 4 updates with hidden lines removed.

Wiremesh *(left)* and Hidden Line *(right)*.

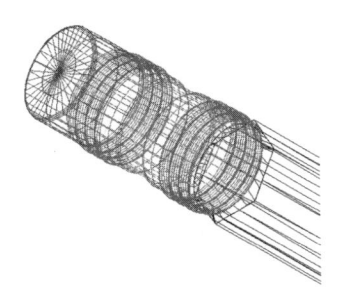

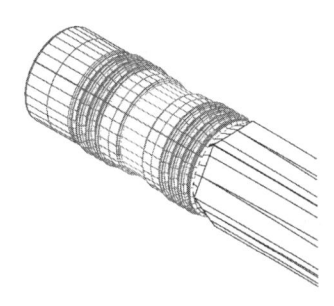

In Hidden Line mode, the display shows only those parts of elements that actually would be visible. Lines hidden behind objects are removed. Hidden line is also considered to be a polygon display where each element is first decomposed into polygons (in memory) prior to the final display. Due to these calculations, hidden line display takes more CPU time to generate than wireframe or wiremesh display. This is more evident with larger designs.

6 In the Render tool settings, set:

Render Mode: Filled Hidden Line.

7 Enter a data point in View 5.

View 5 updates as Filled Hidden Line.

Hidden Line *(left)* and Filled Hidden Line *(right)*.

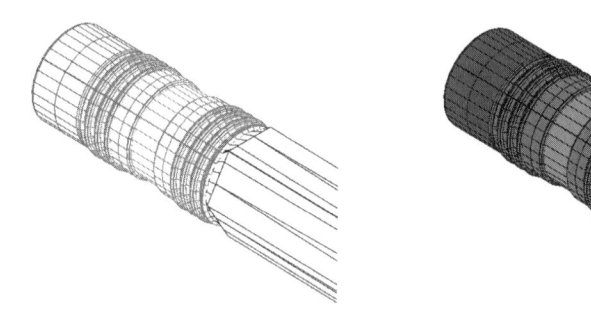

Filled Hidden Line is similar to Hidden Line display except that, in addition to removing the hidden lines, the polygons are filled with the color of the rendered element. This creates a cartoon-like appearance in the resulting rendered image. This mode also is referred to as *filled polygon display*.

CONSTANT, SMOOTH, AND PHONG

This next set of rendering modes are commonly known as *shaded image renderers*. Instead of simply removing the hidden lines, these rendering methods apply a more realistic variable shading to each element. The amount of shading and its final appearance depends on the type of shaded rendering you choose.

Although the newer ray trace rendering technologies have overshadowed these older shading techniques, there still may be times that you will find a use for them. For instance, if you are using an OpenGL en-

| Constant, Smooth, and Phong |

abled video system, the graphic acceleration can handle only those rendering modes up through Smooth (Gouraud shading).

In the following exercise, you will contrast the different shaded rendering methods and their effect on the final image quality. The model used in the exercise already has materials assigned to the elements. Later, you will learn about materials and how to create them and apply them. For now, we will concentrate on the rendering modes.

✔ Exercise 3-2: Compare the basic shading modes

1. Open DGN file *ring.dgn*.

   The model displays six views, five of which are identical.

2. Select the Render tool, with the following tool setting:

   Render Mode: Constant

3. Enter a data point in View 1.

   The view updates with an image generated using the Constant rendering method.

   With constant shading, surfaces are displayed as one or more polygons. Each polygon is filled with a single constant color. The color for each polygon is determined by the material definition of the surface and the lighting applied. With this form of shading, curved surfaces are decomposed into a mesh of polygons, and have a decidedly tiled appearance.

4. In the Render tool settings, set:

   Render Mode: Smooth

5. Enter a data point in View 2.

   The view updates with an image generated by the Smooth rendering method.

   Smooth shading, like constant shading, displays surfaces as one or more polygons. In smooth shaded models, however, the appearance of curved surfaces is more realistic than in constant shaded models. With smooth shading, colors are calculated at the vertices of the polygons and then blended across each polygon's surface. This gives curved surfaces a smooth appearance, eliminating the tiled effect associated with the Constant rendering method.

Constant *(left)* and Smooth *(right)* render modes.

6 In the Render tool settings, set:

Render Mode: Phong

7 Enter a data point in View 3.

The view updates to display an image rendered using the Phong shader.

Smooth *(left)* and Phong *(right)* rendering modes compared. In the Phong image, notice shadows and bump mapped engraving.

Phong shading differs from constant shading and smooth (Gouraud) shading in that the color of each individual pixel is computed separately. This is extremely useful when higher quality results are more important than the time it takes to generate the image.

Phong shaded images have a much more realistic appearance than either constant or smooth rendered images. This is especially true if the light source for the image is close to the object, such as a spotlight on a wall. Additionally, phong shading can include other effects in its calculations.

| Photorealistic Ray Tracing |

These include shadows, bump maps, material transparency, and distance cueing. You will learn about materials, lights, bump maps, and the like, later in the course.

PHOTOREALISTIC RAY TRACING

Where phong rendered images still are not realistic enough for your needs, you will need to use a more sophisticated rendering method, such as Ray Trace. Along with Radiosity and Particle Tracing, this type of rendering is extremely computation intensive. Typically, rendering times are at a magnitude greater than that associated with Phong rendering. The payoff, however, is extremely realistic images which, when set up properly, can result in images indistinguishable from a real-world photograph. This is possible, in part, because ray tracing, radiosity solving, and particle tracing all take into account all lighting sources including the reflection and the refraction of light. In addition, radiosity and particle tracing also can calculate diffuse reflections. Furthermore, particle tracing is able to produce caustics such as reflected light, and refraction.

Ray Tracing

Ray tracing is a photorealistic rendering technique in which an image is generated by simulating the specular reflection of light rays around a 3D model or scene. In theory, these rays are generated from the various light sources found in the 3D model which then bounce off objects in the model until they either exit into space or else intersect with the eye point of the view. When they intersect with the view eye point, they appear in the final image.

It was found, however, that because most of these light rays bounce off into space, never to be seen, it is more efficient, computationally, to trace the light path in reverse—that is, to trace the light path from the view's eye point back to the light source, bouncing off the various 3D objects in transit between the two ends of the ray (eye point, light source). This is done for each pixel associated with the view and greatly reduces computational overhead. The system computes only those rays of light that are actually seen by the view, ignoring those that have no impact on the final results of the process.

One thing that ray tracing does not do is display diffuse reflections. Diffuse reflections are those reflections that are a bit fuzzy in appearance as a result of the texture of the material assigned to a given object in the design. Ray tracing can, however, be used in conjunction with radiosity or particle tracing solutions to produce the specular highlights and reflections that these processes do not display. Both Radiosity and Particle Tracing have an option for ray tracing the final display.

Tracing a ray involves testing all objects in a scene for intersection with that ray. For these initial rays, often referred to as *primary rays* or *eye rays*, the nearest intersection along each ray must be computed. The entire design must be examined to find the nearest of all the intersections along the ray. Hidden surface removal is also performed by this procedure.

Once it is determined which rays are visible, the illumination and shading of the visible objects is computed. The illustration below shows the various rays that must be computed during ray tracing:

1 — Primary or eye ray.

2 — Reflected ray.

3 — Shadow ray, which is traced to the light source, checks for any obstructions to the light.

4 — Transmitted ray.

5 — Secondary reflected ray.

6 — Secondary transmitted ray.

Tracing a ray from the camera (eye) position.

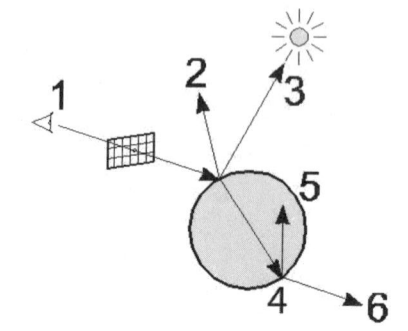

NOTE: *There are significant differences in how transparency is rendered in phong rendering versus the true transparency of ray tracing. For example, in the exercise model, the rubies in the ring used a material optimized for phong's limited transparency. In the exercise following shortly, the model includes a similar ring, but this time the ruby material in the gems has been created specifically with ray tracing in mind.*

| Photorealistic Ray Tracing | 91

Render and Ray Trace Settings

When you ray trace a view, a rendering database or solution is created in memory. This solution consists of the model's geometry decomposed into triangles and includes the material information. The process of creating the rendering solution can take a considerable amount of time. Being able to redisplay a previously generated solution in any view can be a huge time saver, particularly for rendering large projects.

MicroStation always retains the solution in memory unless you indicate that you want to Create a New Solution.

Create New Solution.

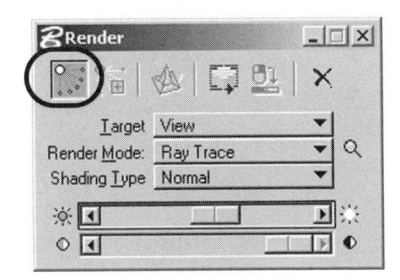

This lets you redisplay or render the current solution in any view without having to do any preprocessing.

Display current solution in any view.

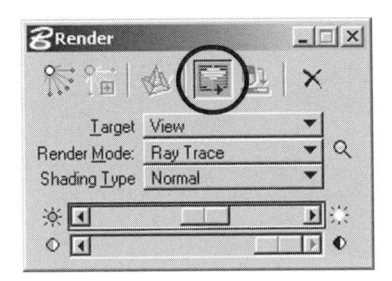

Photorealistic Rendering Workflow

For all photorealistic rendering modes, you now have the choice of Creating a New Solution or Displaying the Current Solution (if any) in any view. In addition, particle tracing and radiosity add the option of Adding to the Current Solution (if any).

For particle tracing, when you click any of the icons contained within the Render tool settings, this specifies the Action that will appear in the Particle Tracing dialog box. For Ray Trace, Radiosity, and Particle Trace

| Chapter 3: Rendering Options and Settings |

render modes, the Render tool dialog box includes a Settings button that opens the settings dialog box for the currently selected render mode. Where required, you can clear the current solution by clicking the Clear Solution icon on the Render tool dialog box (to free up the associated memory).

In the following exercises, you will discover some of the features of ray tracing.

✔ Exercise 3-3: Use ray tracing

1 Open the file *ring raytrace.dgn*.

2 Select the Render tool with the following setting:

Render Mode: Ray Trace

The tool settings change when Ray Trace, Radiosity, or Particle Trace is selected. This is necessary to show additional settings and options.

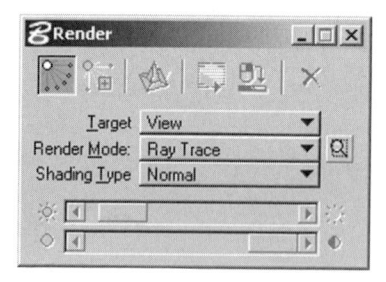

3 Enter a data point in View 1.

The view is rendered using the Ray Trace rendering technique.

Rings ray traced. If you are viewing this in color, notice the colored shadows.

If you are viewing this in color, notice the color of the shadows cast by the gems. Notice also that you see relatively few reflections in the ray traced image. Since the rings and the polygon they are sitting on (the marble surface) are the only objects in the model, there are very few surfaces

| Photorealistic Ray Tracing | 93

from which to reflect. The most significant reflection, in this case, is the background color (black). This can be seen clearly reflected in the gems.

In the real world, the rings would be in an environment filled with other objects which add to the number of reflections captured in the surfaces of the rings. With ray tracing, a clever way to add additional reflections and realism without having to model a real world environment, is to use an environment map.

Environment Maps

You can add more realism to your Ray Traced renderings through the use of a feature called *environment mapping*. An environment map is simply a set of images used to enclose your model in an imaginary cube. The imagery in an environment map is used in the computation of the rays for additional reflections, resulting in a more realistic final appearance. Environment maps are assigned from the Apply Material tool dialog box. Later in this course, you will learn more about the Apply Material tool. For now, we will use only the Environment Maps option.

✔ **Exercise 3-4: Add environment maps**

1 Continuing in *ring raytrace.dgn*, select the Apply Material tool from the Rendering Tools tool box.

In the Assign Material dialog box, click the Environment Maps icon.

The Environment Maps dialog box opens.

2 Click the Browse For File icon for the Front map (until maps are defined, this is the only browse icon that is enabled).

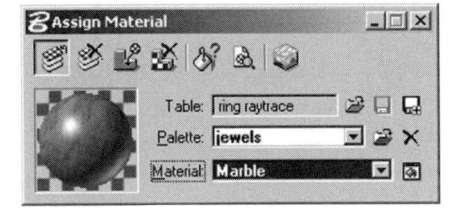

The Select Environment Map [All] dialog box opens.

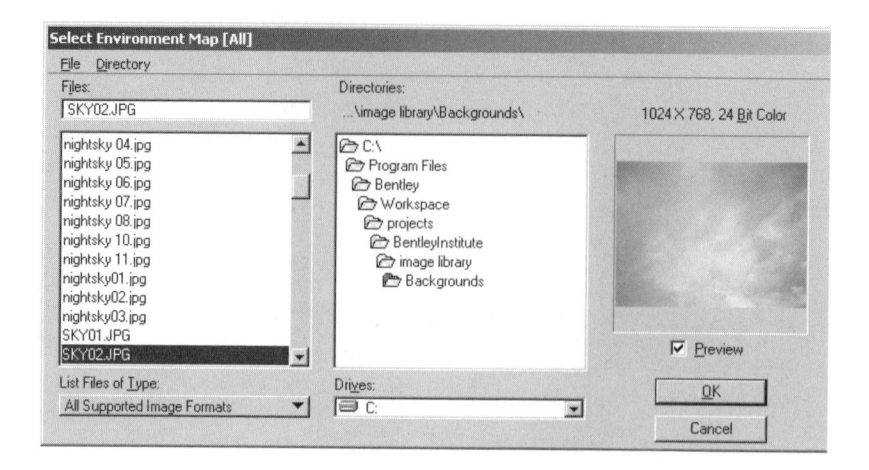

| Chapter 3: Rendering Options and Settings |

3 Select *SKY02.jpg* from the course *\Image Library\Backgrounds* folder.

4 Click OK.

The file name appears for each of the environment maps. That is, it will be used for each face of the environment cube.

5 In the Environment Maps dialog box, click OK.

6 Select the Render tool with the following setting:

Render Mode: Ray Trace

7 Click the Settings icon in the Render tool dialog box.

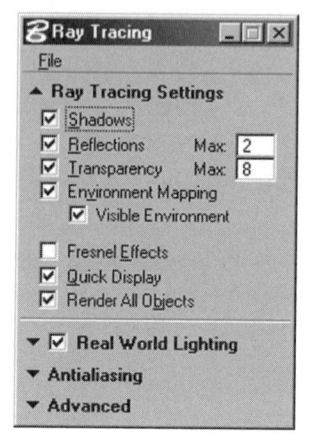

The Ray Tracing settings appear. Environment Mapping already is enabled as a result of defining the environment maps in the previous step.

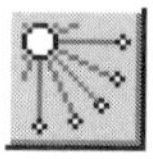

8 In the Render tool dialog box, click Create New Solution.

9 Enter a data point in View 2.

View 2 is ray traced. Note the effects of the environment map on the new ray traced image. This is particularly evident in the gems.

| Photorealistic Ray Tracing |

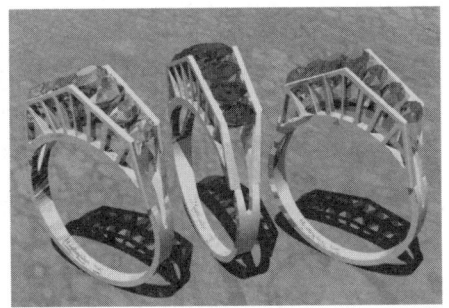

Rings ray traced without *(left)* and with *(right)* environment mapping.

Comparing the two views, the one using environment maps, View 2, has a more realistic appearance. The gold in the rings is brighter and the gems have a more brilliant appearance. Looking closer at the tops of the gems, you can readily see the difference between the black background reflection in View 1 and the effect of the (sky image) environment maps reflected in View 2.

✔ Exercise 3-5: Additional rendering options

1. Continuing in ***ring raytrace.dgn***, in the Ray Tracing dialog box, turn on Quick Display.

2. Enter a data point in View 3.

    Notice how the image is ray traced in four passes, each pass further refining the image. This is a great time saver when tweaking materials and checking lighting. Often you can tell if a pattern map is applied wrongly or the lighting is not what you want in the first pass without having to wait for the entire image to process. This can save time when initially setting up a model and adjusting settings.

3. In the Render tool dialog box, change the Target from View to Fence.

    NOTE: *Using the Target option to ray trace only a portion of a design can save considerable time in a large design where you are interested in rendering only a portion of the view.*

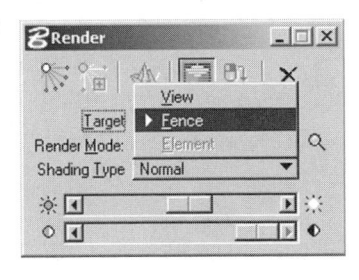

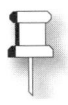

    NOTE: *The Element option for Target is grayed out as it is available for use only with the older rendering techniques such as phong.*

| Chapter 3: Rendering Options and Settings |

4 Place a fence around a portion of the rings in View 4.

5 Ray Trace View 4 with the current solution.

Only the area within the fence is ray traced.

Next you will use phong shading to see how the Target mode works when set to Element.

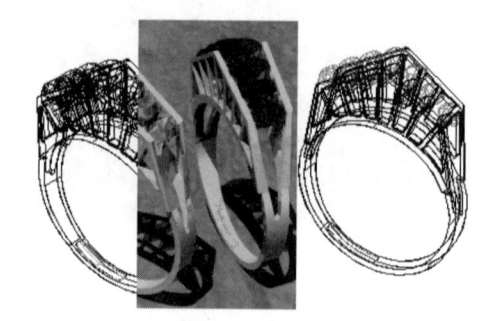

Image with fenced area rendered.

✔ Exercise 3-6: Render the element having a bump map material

1 Continuing in *ring raytrace.dgn*, select Render with the following tool settings:.

Render Mode: Phong
Target: Element
Shading Type: Normal

2 In View 6, identify the Bspline surface.

3 Accept with a data point.

The element is rendered, leaving the rest of the view in wireframe mode.

As you can see, rendering a single element is convenient for test rendering of specific elements in a model.

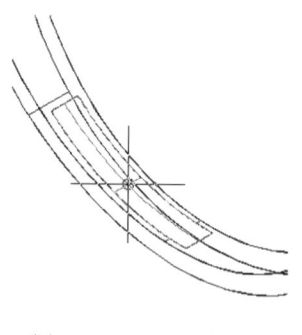

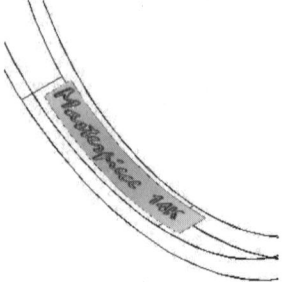

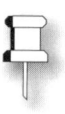

NOTE: *This is especially true if the element you want to check was placed last in the model. With phong rendering, elements are processed in the order in which they were placed in the design. If you processed the entire image, you would have to wait until the end of the*

| Photorealistic Ray Tracing | 97

rendering operation before you see rendering's effect on the new element. Using the Fence or Element target option lets you selectively check parts of an image and reduce processing time.

Ray Trace reflections

By default, the value for the maximum number of reflections is set to 2 in the Ray Tracing dialog box. This means that you will see a reflection of the first reflection only. Further reflections of this first reflection are ignored. In the case of a diamond, the property that makes them appear brilliant is the inner reflections off the faceted surfaces. By increasing the default reflection from 2 to something like 32, you can make an object such as a diamond look much more realistic. Where the extra reflections are not important, you should leave the value set lower to reduce processing time.

In the following exercise, you will see how the number of reflections can improve the appearance of a diamond ring model.

✔ Exercise 3-7: Control the number of reflections

1 Open DGN file *diamond ring.dgn*.

Use the Render tool to ray trace View 1.

This model of a diamond ring has environment maps enabled, but still the diamonds lack sparkle due to the default Max value of 2 for reflections.

2 If necessary, in the Render tool dialog box, click the Open Ray Trace settings dialog icon.

The Ray Tracing dialog box opens.

3 Change the value of Reflections Max from 2 to 32.

4 Use the Render tool to Ray Trace View 2 with the current solution.

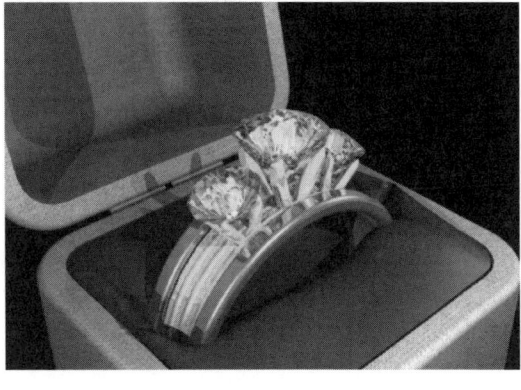

| Chapter 3: Rendering Options and Settings |

The diamonds now sparkle more like the real thing. Increasing the number of reflections has improved the quality of the image.

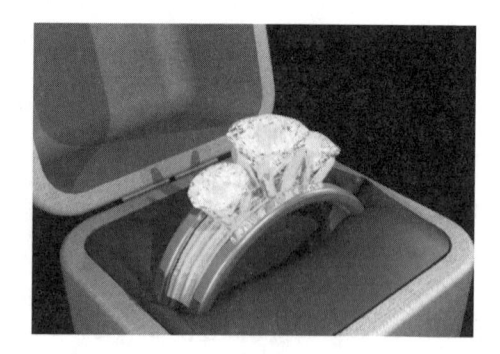

Visible Environment

You have used environment maps to improve the appearance of reflections in an image. In the previous exercise, it was noticeable that the environment maps were reflected in the diamonds of the ring. The background of the image, however, still looked out of place. In situations like this, you can turn on Visible Environment, in which case the environment maps will be seen rather than the background color of the view. The Visible Environment option is available only when Environment Maps have been applied and Environment Mapping also is enabled in the Ray Tracing dialog box.

✔ Exercise 3-8: Turn on Visible Environment

1. Continuing in *diamond ring.dgn*, in the Ray Tracing dialog box, turn on Visible Environment.

2. Use the Render tool to ray trace View 3 with the current solution.

Instead of seeing a black background, the image now displays the environment map image behind the subject of the view.

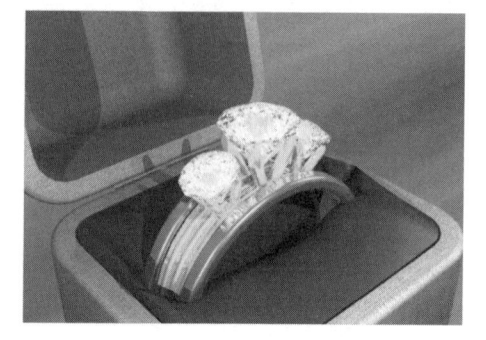

STEREO RENDERINGS

MicroStation can render and display stereo anaglyph images, although 3D glasses are required to properly see the final result in stereo. The only major drawback to this type of stereo viewing is that the image colors are altered by the red and blue lenses needed to visualize the 3D stereo effect. The advantages to this type of stereo viewing is that you can visualize the results on a monitor, projection screen, or a print using inexpensive glasses.

The next exercise requires a pair of anaglyph red/blue 3D glasses to view the rendered image in stereo.

✔ Exercise 3-9: Stereo 3D

1   Continuing in *diamond ring.dgn*, in the Ray Tracing dialog box, turn off Visible Environment.

2   In the Render dialog box, change the Shading Type to Stereo.

3   Use the Render tool to ray trace View 4 with the current solution.

The view will render twice before the final image is combined and displayed. You will need a pair of anaglyph 3D glasses to properly view the resulting image.

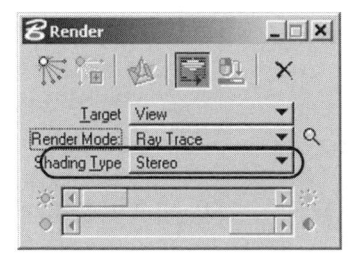

NOTE: *All render modes and hidden line routines will display as stereo when the Shading Type is set to Stereo, except for Wiremesh.*

RENDERING SETTINGS

Rendering is controlled by a number of settings, some of which you have already seen and worked with. The various settings that affect the rendering process are located in the Rendering Settings dialog box (Settings > Rendering > General).

Miscellaneous Settings

Settings in this group control the accuracy and appearance of the rendered images.

Stroke Tolerance

Stroke Tolerance is a very important setting as it affects both rendering time and image quality, where curved surfaces are involved. All rendering and hidden line routines are affected by this setting.

When a 3D design is rendered, it is divided into polygons (in memory), with curved surfaces being represented by a polygon mesh. Stroke tolerance determines the size of these polygons, which directly affects the accuracy of curved surfaces displayed in the shaded image. This is most apparent at the edges of curved objects.

Stroke tolerance is the maximum distance (in pixels) that a surface can deviate from the polygons used to render it. Stroke Tolerance can be from 0.001 through 1000.00, with smaller settings providing more accurate representations of curved surfaces, but at the cost of longer rendering times. For most rendering, the default of 0.500 provides excellent results. For some images, however, you may need to use a smaller setting.

• •

✔ **Exercise 3-10: Effect of stroke tolerance on rendering**

1. Open DGN file *divetime.dgn*.

2. Select Settings > Rendering > General.

    The Rendering Settings dialog box appears.

3. Change the Stroke Tolerance setting to 5.0.

4. Select Render with the following tool setting:

    Render Mode: Hidden Line

5. Enter a data point in View 1.

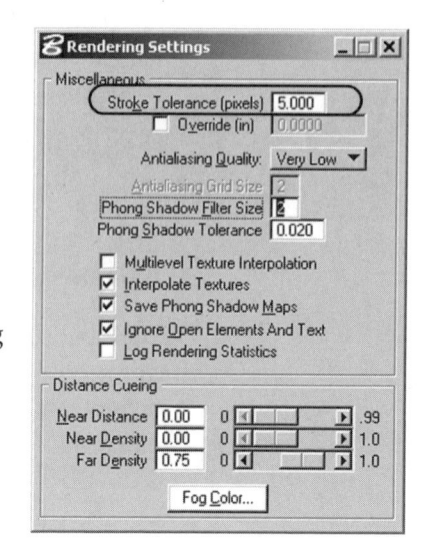

| Rendering Settings | **101**

Look closely at the polygon mesh for the button on the side of the watch in the model.

6 In the Rendering Settings dialog box, change the Stroke Tolerance to 0.5.

7 Enter a data point in View 2.

8 Now, change the Stroke Tolerance to 0.1.

9 Enter a data point in View 3.

If you now look closely at each of the hidden line views, you will notice that the polygon mesh becomes progressively smaller from View 1 through View 3.

From left to right: Stoke Tolerance set to 5.0, 0.5, and 0.1.

Stroke Tolerance and view dependency

Because the Stroke Tolerance setting is a view-dependent setting, it can produce undesirable results in certain cases. Take the situation where you ray trace a camera view that has perspective, and where curved surfaces are very small relative to the rendered view. If you then use the same solution to ray trace another view, where the same curved surfaces are more prominent, they may appear faceted.

In the next exercise, you will see clearly this effect. You will ray trace a view of the model and then ray trace a close-up view, with this same solution in memory.

✔ **Exercise 3-11: Stroke Tolerance and view dependency**

1 Continuing in *divetime.dgn*, change the Stroke Tolerance to 0.5.

This is the default value.

2 Change the Render Mode to Ray Trace.

3 Select Create New Solution and enter a data point in View 4.

The view is rendered and a rendering database, or solution, is created based on the camera perspective for View 4.

4 Select Ray Trace Current Solution (in any view) and enter a data point in View 1.

This renders the view based on the default stroke tolerance of 0.5 using the rendering database created by rendering the perspective camera view (View 4).

You can see that the button does not look good in the close up. This is because the rendering solution was created from View 4 where the curved surfaces were seen from a greater distance and the resolution of the geometry, in pixels, was less than adequate to correctly render the close up detail in View 1.

5 Select Create New Solution and enter a data point in View 2.

Comparing View 1 and View 2, the results are completely different even though you used the same stroke tolerance. By creating a solution in View 4 with perspective and being farther away from the curved surfaces, a deviation of 0.5 pixels is magnified when that same solution is displayed in the close-up view as in View 2.

6 Change the Stroke Tolerance to 0.1.

7 Select Create New Solution and enter a data point in the camera view, View 4.

You have just created a new rendering database based on the same camera view as before, but with a smaller, more precise stroke tolerance.

8 Select Ray Trace Current Solution (in any view) and enter a data point in View 3.

View 3 is ray traced using the view-dependent solution created from perspective View 4, but this time using a more precise stroke tolerance. It is a big improvement over the image in View 1.

NOTE: *The camera automatically is turned off when creating animations or a lighting solution based on particle tracing or radiosity, to help avoid insufficient stroking of curved surfaces.*

| Rendering Settings | 103

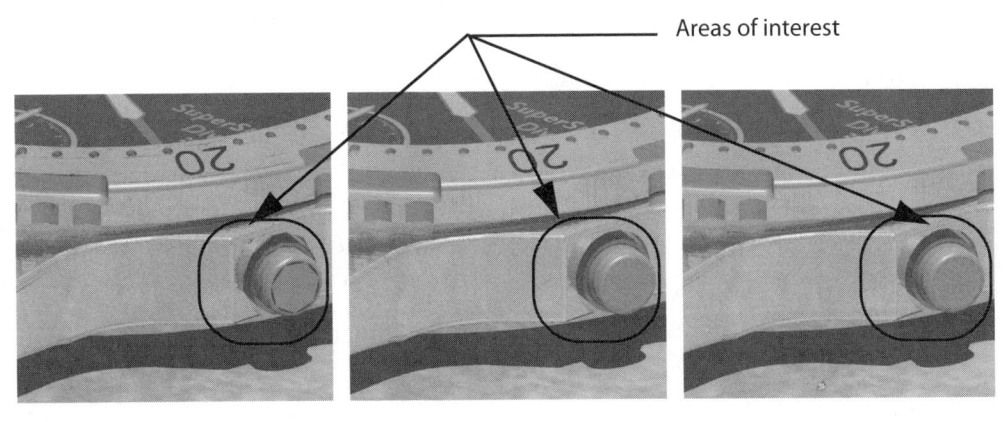

Areas of interest

Stroke Tolerance 0.5 with rendering database created from camera view in View 4.

Stroke Tolerance 0.5, View 2 rendered with rendering database created in same view.

Stroke Tolerance 0.1 with rendering database created by rendering View 4.

NOTE: *For ray tracing, you should consider creating the rendering database from a non-camera view when you intend to reuse the solution for other views. In addition, for Render all Objects, a Ray Tracing setting should be enabled as well if you intend to reuse the solution for other views. This topic will be covered in detail a little later on in this chapter.*

(Stroke Tolerance) Override

This setting lets you override the stroke tolerance setting. When you turn on Override, the associated value is the maximum distance (in master units) that a surface can deviate from the polygons used to render it. This is very useful when you are creating a view-independent solution, such as ray tracing an animation with Render All Objects enabled, or generating a radiosity or particle tracing solution.

For example, there are certain times when a view is set up so that the camera is temporarily disabled, such as during the creation of the rendering database. With the camera turned off, the design would appear very small within the view. Under these circumstances, the solution could appear extremely rough. You can overcome this by setting the Stroke Tolerance Override in working units.

NOTE: *The Override setting works only with Radiosity and Particle Tracing or when Ray Tracing using the Animator with Render All Objects enabled. Even when enabled, it is ignored for ray tracing* unless using the Animator, and all other rendering routines other than Particle Tracing and Radiosity.

Antialiasing

Antialiasing reduces the jagged edges that are particularly noticeable on low resolution displays. The additional time required for antialiasing is especially worthwhile when saving images for presentation, publication, or animated sequences.

When a design is rendered with antialiasing in Constant, Smooth, or Phong render mode, the image is rendered in several passes. In each pass the image is shifted slightly in the X and Y directions. Each of the resulting images is averaged to create a single antialiased image. The number of passes in each direction is determined by the antialiasing grid. If set to 2, for example, the system will antialias on a 2 x 2 grid using four passes. If set to 3, it will use nine passes. The higher grid size values result in more passes, producing higher quality images. This value is set automatically when you choose an antialiasing quality setting and is not editable unless you select Custom.

Antialiasing Quality

This setting is used to set the grid size used during antialiasing calculations for all but ray tracing, which uses sampling to determine antialiasing quality (set in the Ray Tracing dialog box). Choosing from any of the preset options automatically sets the values for the Antialiasing Grid Size, and the values for Min and Max Samples for Ray Tracing. Selecting Custom lets you manually edit the Antialiasing Grid Size value (and the Min/Max Samples settings in the Ray Tracing dialog box).

✔ Exercise 3-12: Use antialiasing

1. Open model **AAlias**, in *no2_pencil.dgn*.

2. From the main menu, select Settings > Rendering > General to open the Rendering General Settings dialog box and review the Antialiasing Quality setting, leaving it at Medium.

3. Select the Render tool with the following settings:

   Render Mode: Phong
   Shading Type: Normal

| Rendering Settings | 105

4 Enter a data point in View 1.

The view is rendered with normal shading, no antialiasing.

5 Set Shading Type to Antialias.

6 Enter a data point in View 2.

The view is phong rendered in nine passes since the current antialiasing setting is set for Medium, or a grid size of 3. You can see the reduction of the jagged edges along the diagonal in the antialiased view.

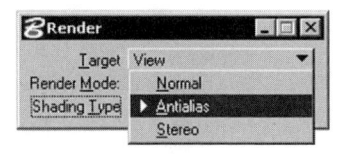

Render dialog, Render Mode options.

Phong rendering Normal *(top)* and Antialiased *(bottom)*.

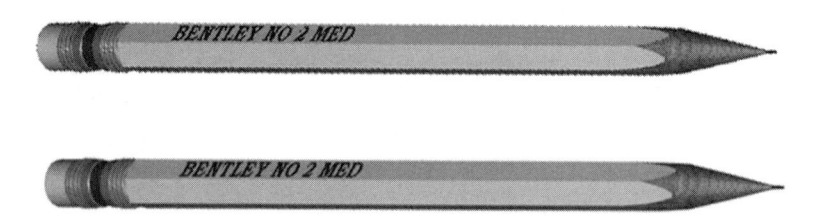

NOTE: *It is pretty obvious that the antialiased image looks much better than the non-antialiased image. Antialiasing can greatly increase the time to render a view nine times longer in this example. Antialiasing is not necessary for adjusting materials or lighting — so most of the time you will render screen views without it. However, when you save an image to a file, you will certainly want to enable antialiasing for a high-quality final image.*

Phong shadows

Phong rendering mode can generate shadows. These are generated as shadow maps, the accuracy of which is determined by settings in the Rendering Settings dialog box. In addition, phong-produced solar shadow resolution is determined by the Solar Shadow Resolution setting found in the Global Lighting dialog box.

Solar Shadow Resolution

This sets the resolution of the shadow map generated for the solar light with Phong rendering. The lower the value, the less resolute the solar

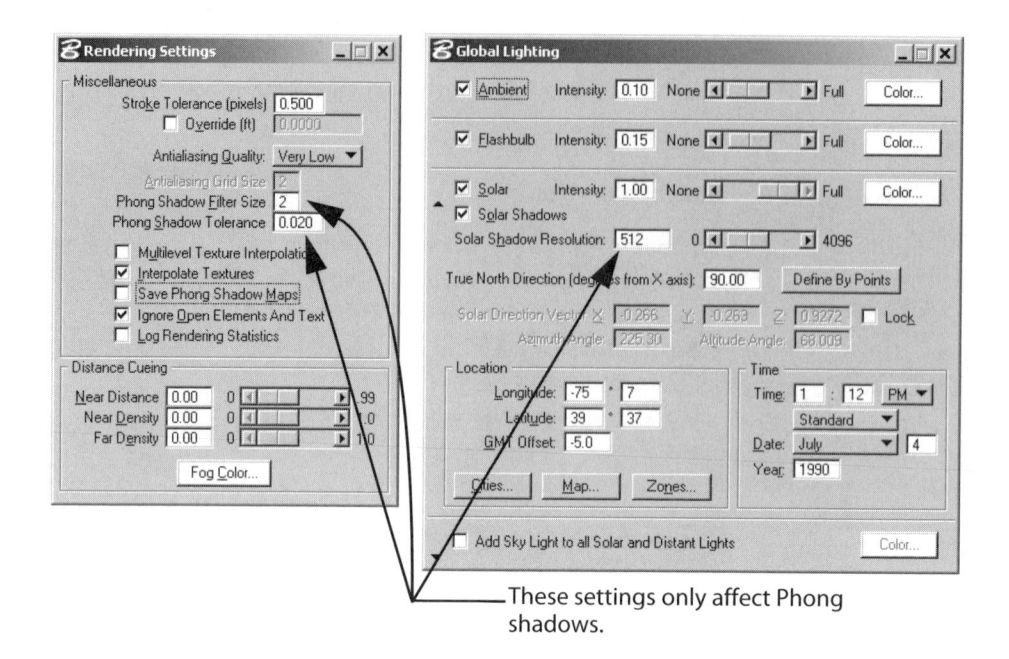

[Screenshot of Rendering Settings and Global Lighting dialog boxes with annotation: "These settings only affect Phong shadows." pointing to Phong Shadow Filter Size and Phong Shadow Tolerance fields.]

shadows will be, and processing time will be reduced. When Save Phong Shadow Maps is enabled, the size of file created will be larger or smaller based on this setting, high values producing larger files.

Phong Shadow Filter Size

With allowable values from 0 to 15, this setting determines the softness of shadows. Larger values produce softer shadows. The value describes the number of adjacent pixels to look at in the shadow map. A value of 0 or 1 produces hard shadows. A value of 2 or 3 produces softer shadows.

Phong Shadow Tolerance

This setting determines how close objects must be together to cast shadows on each other, and is used to prevent surfaces from casting shadows on themselves. The default value, 0.02, usually is sufficient to prevent self-shadowing. Large phong shadow tolerance values can cause inaccurate shadow generation. Through experimentation I have found that a phong shadow tolerance of 0.008 produces more accurate phong shadows than the default. However, anything lower than this will leave you at risk of producing self-shadowing — a real problem as you will soon see.

| Rendering Settings |　　　　　　　　　　　　　　　　　　　　　　　　**107**

✔ **Exercise 3-13: Phong Shadow settings**

1. Open design file *ring.dgn*.

2. Open the Rendering Settings dialog box and check that the current Phong Shadow settings are:

   Phong Shadow Filter Size: 2
   Phong Shadow Tolerance: 0.020

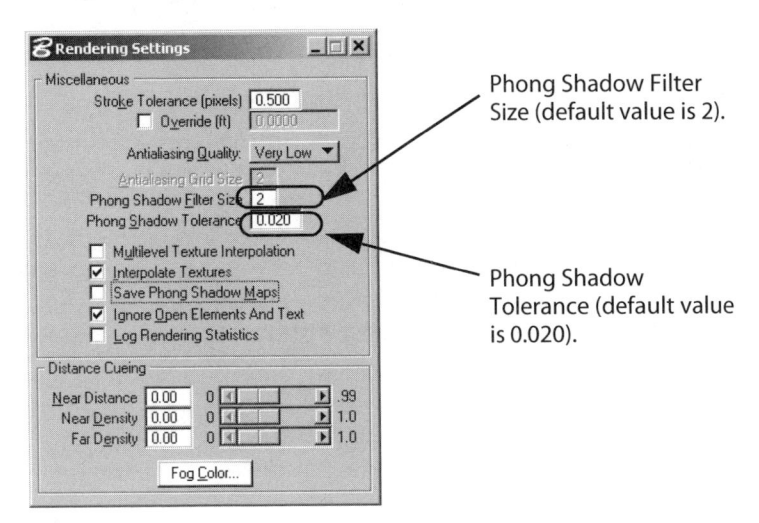

   Phong Shadow Filter Size (default value is 2).

   Phong Shadow Tolerance (default value is 0.020).

3. Select the Render tool with the following settings:

   Target: View
   Render Mode: Phong

4. Enter a data point in View 1.

5. Change the Phong Shadow Filter Size from 2 to 0.

6. Enter a data point in View 2.

7. Compare the two views.

   Notice that the shadows are much sharper in View 2, but appear harsh and unrealistic.

8. Now change the Shadow Filter Size to 15 and phong render View 3.

   The shadows in this case are quite indistinct and blurred.

| Chapter 3: Rendering Options and Settings |

Shadow Filter Size default 2 *(left)*, 0 *(center)*, and 15 *(right)*.

Notice how the shadows with lower shadow filter sizes make the ring appear to be floating a little off the surface. To fix this you could lower the phong shadow tolerance.

✔ Exercise 3-14: Phong Shadow Tolerance

1 Continue in *ring.dgn*.

2 In the Rendering Settings dialog box, change the Phong Shadow Filter Size back to 2.0, the default setting.

3 Change the Phong Shadow Tolerance from the default of 0.020 to 0.008.

4 Phong render View 4.

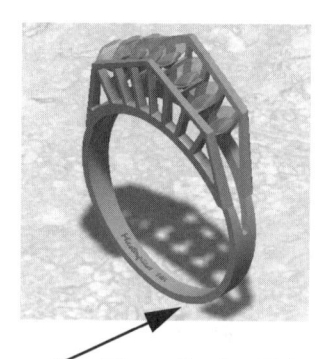

Phong Shadow Tolerance of 0.020: the ring appears to be floating above the surface.

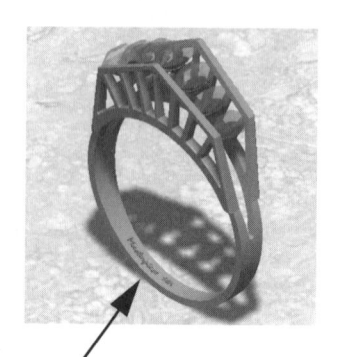

Phong Shadow Tolerance of 0.008: the ring appears to be on the surface.

| Rendering Settings |

NOTE: *If the shadow tolerance setting is too large, objects may not cast shadows on other objects that are too close. If the setting is too small, objects might shadow themselves, causing a rippled appearance across the surface.*

Examples: Shadow Tolerance of 0.000 *(left)* with self-shadowing occurring; and set to 0.008 *(right)*.

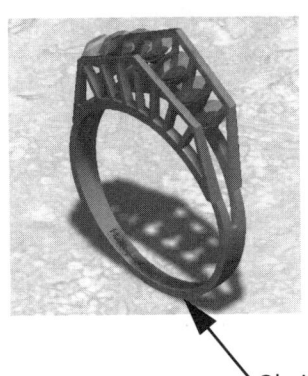

Obvious self-shadowing here

NOTE: *With Save Phong Shadow Maps enabled, in the Rendering Settings dialog box, shadow files will be saved to your hard disk. Phong rendering large files with many shadow-casting lights could eventually take up considerable disk space. Occasionally, you will want to delete these files. You can do this manually, or you can delete the shadow maps for the current design using the Define Light tool. This tool is covered in a later chapter.*

Shadow map files have the extension *.lgt* and, by default, are located in the same folder as the design file. You can, however, specify a different storage location for them with the configuration variable MS_SHADOWMAP (Workspace > Configuration > Rendering/Images > Shadow Maps).

Interpolate Textures

Surface color is extracted from the pattern image by interpolating between the two closest pixels. In most cases, this produces the best results, although it may be undesirable in certain instances.

Multilevel texture interpolation

This is a texture mapping option for Phong and Ray Traced rendering that provides less noisy images and smoother animations. When this option is enabled, each texture map and bump map is prefiltered into a se-

| Chapter 3: Rendering Options and Settings |

ries of successively lower resolution maps when it is referenced for the first time.

When a pixel from the texture map is needed, pixels from the two pre-filtered images of the size closest to the needed size are interpolated to determine a pixel value. This provides a less noisy appearance when the texture is scaled down, and a much smoother transition of pixel values as the size of the texture changes on screen during an animation.

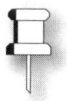

NOTE: *Multilevel Texture Interpolation requires that Interpolate Textures be enabled. When it is disabled, Multilevel Texture Interpolation is disabled, even if checked in the Rendering Settings dialog box.*

✔ Exercise 3-15: Use Multilevel Texture Interpolation

1 Open *BC1.dgn*.

2 From the main menu, select Setting > Rendering > General to open the Rendering Settings dialog box and set the following:

Interpolate Textures: Enabled
Multilevel Texture Interpolation: Disabled

3 Select the Render tool with the following setting:

Render Mode: Ray Trace

4 Enter a data point in View 5 to ray trace the view without multilevel texture interpolation.

5 In the Rendering Settings dialog box, enable Multilevel Texture Interpolation.

6 In the Render dialog box, select Ray Trace Current Solution (in any view).

7 Enter a data point in View 6.

The view is ray traced using current solution and multilevel texture interpolation.

Notice that the textures appear less noisy and smoother in the second image that has Multilevel Texture Interpolation enabled.

| Rendering Settings | 111

(Left) Without Multilevel Texture Interpolation; and *(right)* with Multilevel Texture Interpolation enabled.

Ignore Open Elements And Text

This setting restricts rendering processes to only those elements that include an area component. Surfaces and all closed elements, such as shapes, ellipses, and complex shapes, fall into this element category. Conversely, all open elements, such as lines, arcs, text, and points, are not rendered and, therefore, do not display in the rendered images.

Typically, you would want to ignore open elements and text in a rendered image. However, in the following example, you could depict the wires leading from this transformer model with line strings. Rather than having to model the wires as surfaces, you could simply render the linear elements.

23 Kv circuit breaker model, with open elements rendered *(left)* and open elements ignored *(right)*.

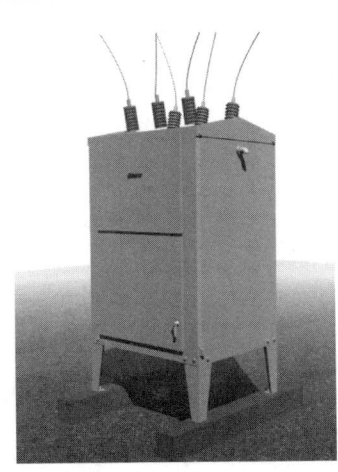

Log Rendering Statistics

If enabled, an ASCII text file is created in the same directory that you configure for saved image output. This can be set to any folder you choose via the Image Output configuration variable in the Rendering/Images category of the Configuration dialog box.

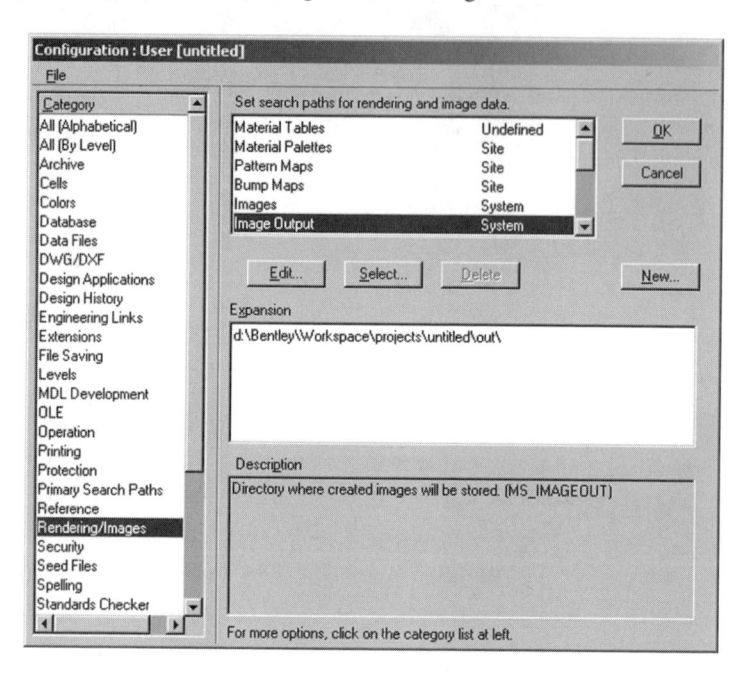

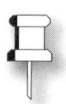

NOTE: *By selecting the appropriate configuration variable in the Configuration dialog box, you can change the paths for most rendering-related directories.*

Distance Cueing Settings

This is a Rendering View Attribute that can be set for any view. Here, you can control the extent of the distance cueing effect. Distance Cueing settings consist of three sliders with a range from zero to 1.0 which, in turn, adjust the following settings:

- Near Distance – Sets the distance at which fading begins, specified as a proportion of the distance from the front to the back clipping plane. For example, if set to 0.25, there is no fading in the nearest 25% of the view's volume.

- Near Density – Sets the fog intensity at the Near Distance.

| Rendering Settings | **113**

▸ Far Density – Sets the fog intensity at the back clipping plane defined for the view.

The fog color also can be changed by clicking Fog Color and defining the new color in the Modify Fog Color dialog box.

✔ Exercise 3-16: Render with distance cueing

1 Open model *Fog*, in *Longbeach.dgn*.

Views 1 and 2 are set up with similar camera views. View 1 has no Distance Cueing applied, while View 2 has Distance Cueing enabled with Fog applied.

2 Open the Rendering Settings dialog box and check the Distance Cueing settings.

The current settings show Near Distance to be 0.30. This means there is no fog for the first 30% of distance from camera, or eye point, to the back clipping plane defined for the view.

3 Select the Render tool with the following setting:

Render Mode: Ray Trace

4 Enter a data point in View 1.

View 1 is ray traced without fog, and Distance Cueing is not enabled.

Ray traced View 1 without fog.

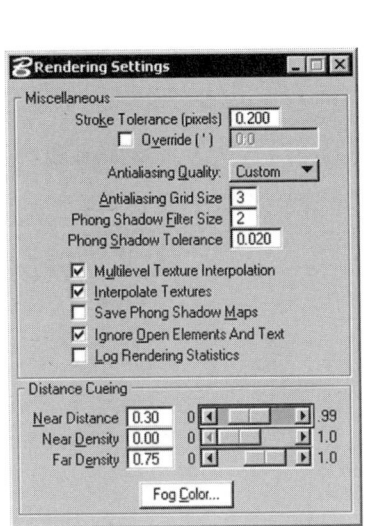

| Chapter 3: Rendering Options and Settings |

5   Select Ray Trace current solution (in any view).

6   Enter a data point in View 2.

The view is ray traced with Distance Cueing and Fog enabled. Note the appearance of the background in each of the views just rendered.

Ray traced View 2 with fog.

VIEW ATTRIBUTES

Several settings in the View Attributes dialog box affect the display of rendered images. For example, you can use View Attribute settings to affect whether and how certain types and classes of elements display. Changes take effect when you click Apply (for the view shown in View Number) or All (to apply to all views).

The view attributes that affect the rendering process are as follows.

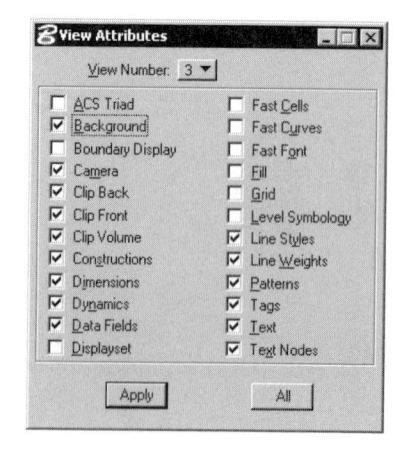

Background

If checked and a background image is defined, the background image will be displayed. If unchecked, a background image will not be displayed even if defined.

Camera

If checked, the view will have camera perspective. If unchecked, the view will be orthogonal.

Clip Back, Clip Front, and Clip Volume

If checked, these features are applied to the view. If unchecked, these view options are disabled.

Constructions

This setting is particularly important to rendering. As a rule, constructions should be turned off in rendered views. MicroStation lights, for example, are made of construction elements and can cast unwanted shadows.

Displayset

This determines whether or not elements in a displayset are displayed in a view. If a displayset is present and this attribute is enabled, only those elements in the current displayset are visible.

RENDERING VIEW ATTRIBUTES

Several rendering settings are controlled in the Rendering View Attributes dialog box, which is opened by selecting Settings > Rendering > View Attributes.

View Number

This sets the view for which rendering view attribute settings are displayed.

Delayed Display

If on, rendering is not displayed as it is performed. Instead, the entire rendered image is displayed only at the conclusion of the rendering process.

- ▶ Advantages: Faster rendering, particularly with slow display hardware. Also, if the display is not true color, delayed images use a superior dithering process, resulting in a much better image on a 16-color display, and a subtle improvement on a 256-color display.

- ▶ Disadvantages: More memory (4 bytes per pixel) is required for delayed display. If antialiasing or transparency is performed, this will require more memory again. Delayed display gives no visual indication that rendering is in progress.

Pattern/Bump Maps

If on, Pattern/Bump maps are displayed in the view.

Shadows

If on, Shadows in phong shaded models are displayed in the view.

> **NOTE:** *For shadows to be generated in a ray traced image, the Shadows option must be enabled in the Ray Tracing dialog box.*

Transparency

If on, materials that have a Transmit value greater than 0 are displayed with a translucent appearance. With phong rendering, transparent objects are updated last when rendering the view.

> **NOTE:** *For transparent surfaces to display in ray traced images, Transparency must also be enabled in the Ray Tracing dialog box.*

Display

This controls whether the contents of a view are continuously rendered and, if so, how the view is rendered.

Distance Cueing

In nature, when you view a landscape, distant objects often fade off into the darkness or fog. Distance cueing simulates atmospheric fading in computer generated images. You can choose from:

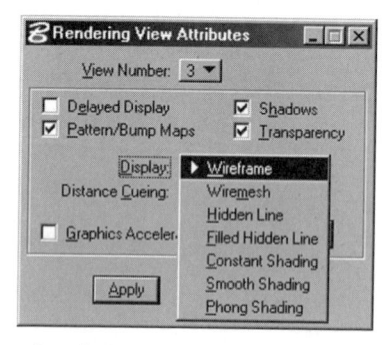

Rendering View Attributes with Display options

- None — No atmospheric fading is produced.

- Depth Cueing — Surfaces in the shaded image fade into darkness (black) as their distance from the eye increases.

- Fog — Surfaces in the shaded image fade into fogginess as their distance from the eye increases.

You can also specify the color of the fog and where the atmospheric fading starts to take effect. This lets you produce images with a realistic atmospheric haze.

| Working with Fog and Depth Cueing | **117**

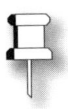

> **NOTE:** *Near Distance, Near Density, Far Density, and Fog Color are set in the Rendering Settings box and also in the Rendering category in the Design File Settings box.*

Graphics Acceleration

If on, MicroStation will take advantage of the graphics hardware present in your system. Graphics Acceleration uses OpenGL to communicate with the graphics card. Graphics Acceleration is available only for Wireframe, Wiremesh, Hidden Line, and Constant and Smooth shading (not Phong). Graphics Acceleration also can be used without the aid of special graphics hardware.

WORKING WITH FOG AND DEPTH CUEING

In an earlier exercise, you saw the effect of having fog defined for a view. Here, you will learn more about controlling both fog and depth cueing.

Controlling Fog and Depth Cueing

In the next exercise, you will see how easy it is to control both fog and depth cueing by changing the front and back clipping planes of the view.

✔ **Exercise 3-17: Control fog**

1. Open **BC1 distance cue.dgn**.

2. Open the Rendering Settings dialog box: Settings > Rendering > General. If necessary, set the following:

   Near Distance: 0.20
   Near Density: 0.00
   Far Density: 0.65

   You will be using the row of red construction lines in the Top view as reference markers to set the display depth. By using these reference points, you will be setting each view's display depth to progressively shorten the depth of the camera for Views 3, 5, and 6. This moves the Far Density (back clipping plane) and greatly affects the rendered result. Initially, you will see all the street lights and trees.

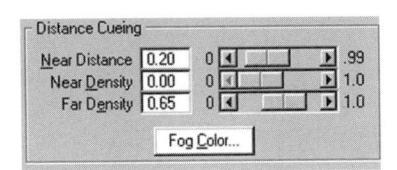

| Chapter 3: Rendering Options and Settings |

Then, as you progressively move the back clipping plane toward the camera, the farthest street lights and trees will be left in the fog.

3   Ray trace View 2.

The rendered view appears to get more foggy the deeper into it you look. Because the back clipping plane is set beyond the most distant street lights and trees, you can still see all of the street lights and trees in the scene even though it is foggy.

4   In the View Control tool box, select the Set Display Depth tool.

5   Enter a data point in View 3.

This indicates that you intend to set the display depth for View 3.

A dynamic view cone appears in each view, and you are also prompted to define the front clipping plane.

6   In View 1 - Top, enter a data point near or behind the apex of the camera cone.

This sets the front clipping plane. You now are prompted to define the back clipping plane.

7   In View 1, snap to the top of the right-hand vertical red line and enter a data point.

This sets the back clipping plane.

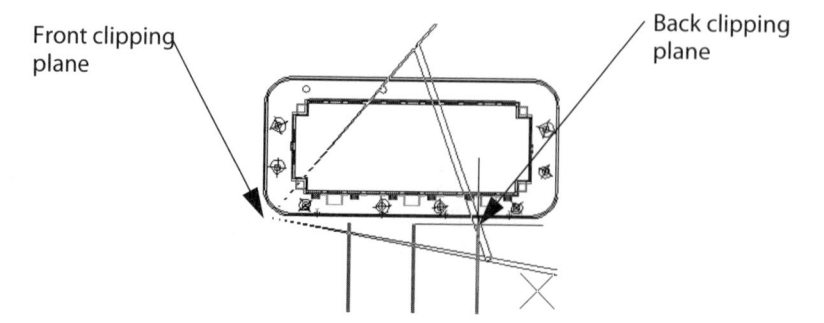

8   Select the Render tool, and click the ray trace current solution (in any view) icon.

9   Enter a data point in View 3 to ray trace the view with fog and a redefined back clipping plane.

Comparing Views 2 and 3, you can see that, after moving the back clipping plane forward, the most distant street lights now disappear into the fog.

| Working with Fog and Depth Cueing | 119

(Left) The display depth sets the clipping plane back beyond the far street light.
(Right) The clipping plane is moved between the third and fourth street lights.

✔ **Exercise 3-18: Perform more adjustments to distance cueing**

1. Continuing in *BC1 distance cue.dgn*, select the Set Display Depth tool.

2. Enter a data point in View 5.

3. In View 1 - Top, enter a data point near or behind the apex of the camera cone.

    This sets the front clipping plane. You now are prompted to define the back clipping plane.

4. In the Top View, snap to the top of the center vertical red line and enter a data point.

    This sets the back clipping plane.

5. Select the Render tool and click the Ray Trace current solution (in any view) icon.

6. Enter a data point in View 5 to ray trace the view with fog and with the redefined back clipping plane.

    The view is ray traced with new display depth settings. As you can see, more street lights and trees have disappeared into the fog.

7. Select the Set Display Depth tool.

8. Enter a data point in View 6.

9. Use View 1 to set the display depth as before, but use the top of the left vertical red line to set the back clipping plane.

10 Ray trace View 6 using the current solution.

11 Compare the rendered views.

You can see that changing the display depth also changes the effects of distance cueing. This applies to both fog and depth cueing, which you will look at next.

Comparison of the effects on fog by changing the back clipping planes.

View 2

View 3

View 5

View 6

NOTE: *In the previous exercises, the Far Density was set to 0.65 for a more dramatic effect and also to aid in visualizing the effects of moving the back clipping plane. In reality, you would use a much lower number to add a hint of atmospheric effects to your renderings. Adding a little fog to a rendered view reduces that "too perfect" appearance often seen in computer generated images.*

Depth Cueing

Another option for distance cueing is Depth Cueing. Similar to fog, with Depth Cueing applied to a view, the objects appear to fade into darkness (black) as their distance from the eye point increases.

| Working with Fog and Depth Cueing | 121

✔ Exercise 3-19: Depth cueing

1 Continuing in *BC1 distance cue.dgn*, open the Rendering View Attributes dialog box, Settings > Rendering > View Attributes and set the following:

View Number: 2
Distance Cueing: Depth Cueing

2 Click Apply.

3 Repeat for Views 3, 5, and 6.

Now you will be able to compare the camera views using depth cueing rather than fog.

4 Open the Rendering Settings dialog box, if not already open, and change Far Density from 0.65 to 0.85.

5 Ray trace Views 2, 3, 5, and 6 using the current solution.

Comparison of the effects on depth cueing by changing the back clipping planes.

View 2

View 3

View 5

View 6

| Chapter 3: Rendering Options and Settings |

RAY TRACING DIALOG BOX

You have worked with settings from the Ray Tracing dialog box in previous exercises. The following describes all the settings located in this dialog box.

The Ray Tracing dialog box is used to adjust all Ray Tracing settings. To open the Ray Tracing dialog box, select Settings > Rendering > Ray Tracing, or, with Ray Trace as the render mode, click the Open Ray Tracing settings dialog icon in the Render dialog box.

> DIALOG RAYTRACE

Ray Tracing Settings

This contains general ray tracing settings.

Shadows

If on, shadows are rendered for each light that has shadows enabled. If off, no shadows are rendered for any lights.

> RAYTRACE SHADOWS
> RAYTRACE SET SHADOWS ON
> RAYTRACE SET SHADOWS OFF

Reflections

If on, reflections are rendered for any elements that have their Reflect material attribute set to a value greater than 0. If off, no reflections are rendered for any elements.

> RAYTRACE REFLECTIONS
> RAYTRACE SET REFLECTIONS ON
> RAYTRACE SET REFLECTIONS OFF

(Reflections) Max

The Max field to the right of the Reflections field sets how many reflections can be generated per ray if Reflections is on. This can be any integer from 0 to 999.

> RAYTRACE SET MAXREFLECTIONS <value>

Transparency

If on, transparency is rendered in a view that has its Transparency attribute on (Settings > Rendering > View Attributes) and transmitted rays are computed for any elements whose Transparency material setting is greater than 0.

If off, transparency is not rendered for any element. This also applies to elements that have patterns with transparent backgrounds assigned to them.

> RAYTRACE TRANSPARENCY
> RAYTRACE SET TRANSPARENCY ON
> RAYTRACE SET TRANSPARENCY OFF

NOTE: *Transmit is set for a material in the Define Materials dialog box.*

(Transparency) Max

The Max field to the right of the Transparency field sets how many transmitted rays can be generated per ray if Transparency is on. This can be any integer from 0 to 999.

> RAYTRACE SET MAXTRANSPARENCY <value>

Environment Mapping

If on, environment maps are used for any element that is reflective or transparent when no element is seen in the transmitted or reflected direction.

If off, no environment maps are used for any elements.

> RAYTRACE ENVIRONMENT
> RAYTRACE SET ENVIRONMENT ON
> RAYTRACE SET ENVIRONMENT OFF

Visible Environment

If on, the defined environment can be seen, wherever the view background color would have been visible, without the need to look through transparent objects as was required in previous versions of MicroStation.

NOTE: *This control is available only if environment maps have been defined.*

Fresnel Effects

If on, Fresnel effects are rendered. These account for the increased reflectivity and decreased transparency of elements when viewed at sharp angles. For example, a window appears more reflective than transparent when viewed at a sharp angle.

If off, Fresnel effects are not rendered.

>	RAYTRACE FRESNEL
>	RAYTRACE SET FRESNEL ON
>	RAYTRACE SET FRESNEL OFF

Quick Display

If on, you can preview the Ray Traced view more quickly. This is done by ray tracing the view in multiple passes. The first pass provides a rough view in one-eighth of the time it takes to ray trace the final image. The image is then refined on successive passes until finished.

>	RAYTRACE QUICKDISPLAY
>	RAYTRACE SET QUICKDISPLAY ON
>	RAYTRACE SET QUICKDISPLAY OFF

NOTE: *Quick Display is especially useful when performing test renderings to check lighting or texture mapping. You can usually tell on the first pass whether or not more adjustments need to be made, rather than render the entire image. On a multitasking workstation, the actual time may vary from the estimate depending on system load. You can abort the render process at any time by Resetting.*

NOTE: *When Quick Display is on, at the end of each pass, the amount of time that remains to complete the image is displayed in the Message Center. This can be opened by clicking near the middle of the status bar.*

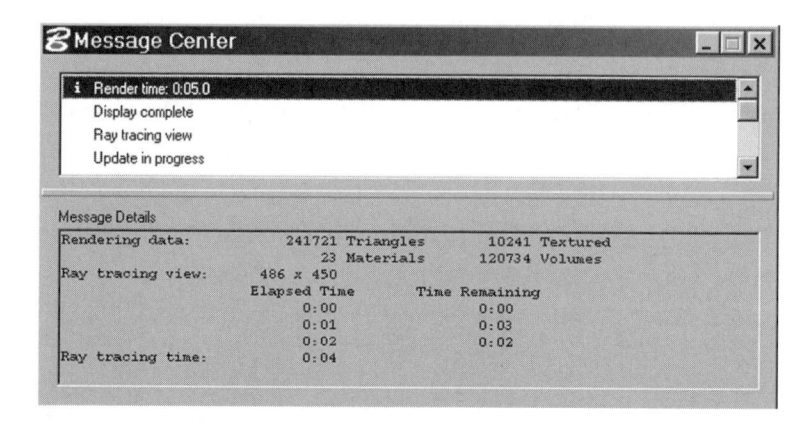

Render All Objects

If on, all elements are considered when rendering instead of only those that are visible in a view or inside a fence.

If on, reflections of, or shadows cast by, elements outside the view or fence contents are rendered.

If off, only those elements are rendered that appear within the view or are in the fence contents.

>   RAYTRACE EXTENTS
>   RAYTRACE SET EXTENTS ON
>   RAYTRACE SET EXTENTS OFF

Real World Lighting

When this setting is enabled, ray traced images are rendered using the same lighting attenuation and lumen values as those used with radiosity and particle tracing. This lets you set lighting levels using Ray Trace, without having to create multiple radiosity or particle-tracing solutions. Just like radiosity and particle tracing, Real World Lighting uses the Lumens values of light sources, forces attenuation on for all lights, and uses the same type of physically accurate attenuation (with the intensity of the light falling off with the square of the distance). With Real World Lighting enabled for ray tracing, you can use the interactive brightness and contrast sliders to adjust the rendered views.

With Real World Lighting off, ray tracing ignores the Lumens values of light sources, uses the attenuation distance specified for each light, if enabled, and the intensity of the light falls off linearly with distance (as opposed to the square of the distance). This mode is offered to provide lighting that is more compatible with phong rendering.

Adapt to Brightness

This sets the intensity (in lumens per square master unit) of the middle of the display range. That is, when the image is rendered, the brightness range of the image is adjusted so that the specified intensity is near the middle of the display range.

Display Contrast

This sets the display contrast for subsequent rendered images. Allowable values range from 1.0 (maximum contrast) to 5.0 (softer image).

Antialiasing Settings

The controls in this section set how antialiasing is performed for ray traced images.

In most cases, the default antialiasing settings for Ray Tracing are adequate. You should become familiar with the following material before adjusting these settings.

Antialiasing improves image quality by reducing jagged edges. For example, you might find a red region in part of a pixel and a green region in another part. Antialiasing examines different parts of a pixel and combines the values to achieve a smooth image.

MicroStation uses an adaptive antialiasing technique.

- A small number of initial samples is taken in a pixel (determined by the Samples Min setting in the More Ray Tracer Settings dialog box).
- The variation between samples is determined.
- If the variance exceeds the Contrast Threshold, another sample is taken and the variance is reevaluated.
- This procedure is repeated until the variance between the samples is acceptable, or until the maximum number of samples is reached (determined by the Samples Max setting).
- When done, all the samples are combined into a final pixel value.

You can improve antialiasing image quality by doing the following:

- Take a larger number of initial samples.
- Allow a larger number of total samples.
- Lower the threshold at which sampling stops.

Quality

This sets the number of samples taken during antialiasing calculations. Choosing any of the following options—Very Low, Low, Medium, High, or Very High—automatically sets the values for Samples, Min and Max. Choosing Custom lets you manually edit the values for Min and Max Samples.

(Samples) Min

This sets the minimum number of samples taken per pixel during antialiasing. This setting is automatic when a Quality setting other than Custom is chosen. Values can be an integer from 2 through 64. The values for the various Quality settings are Very Low 4, Low 5, Medium 6, High 9, Very High 13, and Custom, where you can enter a number from 2 to 64. The default of Very Low, or 4 Samples, is adequate in most cases.

> **NOTE:** *As a rule of thumb, to determine the minimum time to render an antialiased image, take the amount of time taken to Ray Trace the view without antialiasing and multiply by Min.*

RAYTRACE SET MINSAMPLES <value>

(Samples) Max

This sets the maximum number of samples taken per pixel during antialiasing. This setting is automatic when a Quality setting other than Custom is chosen. Values can be an integer from 2 to 64. The values for the various Quality settings are Very Low 9, Low 9, Medium 16, High 25, Very High 36, and Custom, where you can enter a number from 2 to 64. The default of 9 is adequate in most cases.

No more than this number of samples are taken for any pixel during Ray Tracing. In general, it is rare that this many samples are taken.

RAYTRACE SET MAXSAMPLES <value>

Contrast Threshold

This sets the degree of antialiasing for a given pixel. When the contrast between all the samples of a pixel exceeds this value, more samples are taken. When the contrast drops below this value, or when the maximum number of samples is reached, antialiasing is stopped for the pixel.

The default value of 0.1 is adequate in most cases. This can be a floating point number between 0.001 and 1.0. A lower value achieves a higher degree of antialiasing and results in longer rendering times. A higher value will often result in fewer samples being taken per pixel, leading to shorter rendering times with some loss in image quality.

> **NOTE:** *In mathematical terms, contrast is defined as the ratio of variance of the samples within the pixel to the average value of the pixel. This means that the more samples differ from the average value of the pixel, the higher the contrast within the pixel. For example, a*

contrast of 0.1 means that there is a 10% variance between the samples of the pixel. A contrast threshold of 0.1 implies that more samples need to be taken if the current samples vary by more than 10% from the average of the pixel.

RAYTRACE SET CONTRAST <Value>

Jitter Samples

If on, antialiasing samples are taken in a non-uniform manner.

This can be used to create a softer image, and is especially useful for still images. It helps reduce moiré patterns introduced by fixed-grid sampling of high-frequency (noisy) images. A good example is a checkerboard disappearing into the distance.

If off, each antialiasing sample is taken on a fixed grid.

RAYTRACE JITTER
RAYTRACE SET JITTER ON
RAYTRACE SET JITTER OFF

NOTE: *Since using jitter is similar to adding noise to an image, horizontal and vertical edges in an image may become slightly ragged. Turning jitter samples off reduces this effect.*

NOTE: *Jitter samples usually should be turned off when creating animations. This prevents temporal aliasing, where elements pop in and out from frame to frame.*

Depth of Field

Enable this setting to vary the focus according to distance, with the target of the camera always in focus. This produces images more like those from conventional cameras.

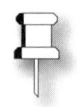

NOTE: *This feature works in conjunction with antialiasing only.*

f-Stop

This is used in conjunction with depth of field to adjust the lens aperture. As with a conventional camera, larger numbers result in sharper images.

In the following images, the one on the left was rendered without Depth of Field enabled, and that on the right was rendered

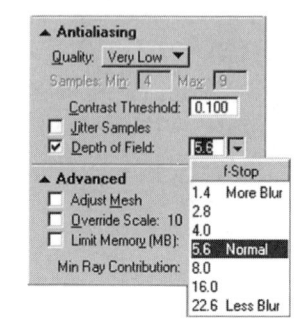

| Ray Tracing Dialog Box | **129**

with it enabled. In the image on the left, everything is sharp and in focus. The image on the right side has the fire hydrant in the foreground (the camera target point) in focus, while the background becomes progressively blurry after that point. Adding Depth of Field can provide you with more realistic, softer images and can be especially useful where the background is not the focus of the image.

Images without *(left)* and with *(right)* Depth of Field set.

NOTE: *If you are using a background image with Depth of Field enabled, the background will not be blurred. You may want to consider blurring the image you are using for the background using an image editor. In the image above, the background is applied as a sky cylinder, and therefore it is correctly blurred by depth of field during rendering since the geometry is quite a distance from the camera focal point.*

Advanced Rendering Settings

You can use these controls to adjust the precision of Ray Traced renderings.

Adjust Mesh

If on, curved surfaces are adjusted by a distance proportional to their radius of curvature to correct for irregular shadows.

In rare cases, curved surfaces or spheres that are partially illuminated and partially in darkness may produce irregular shadows along the line separating light and dark. This is known as the *terminator*. This can be corrected by turning Adjust Mesh on.

If off, surfaces are not adjusted for irregular shadows along the terminator.

```
RAYTRACE ADJUST
RAYTRACE SET ADJUST ON
RAYTRACE SET ADJUST OFF
```

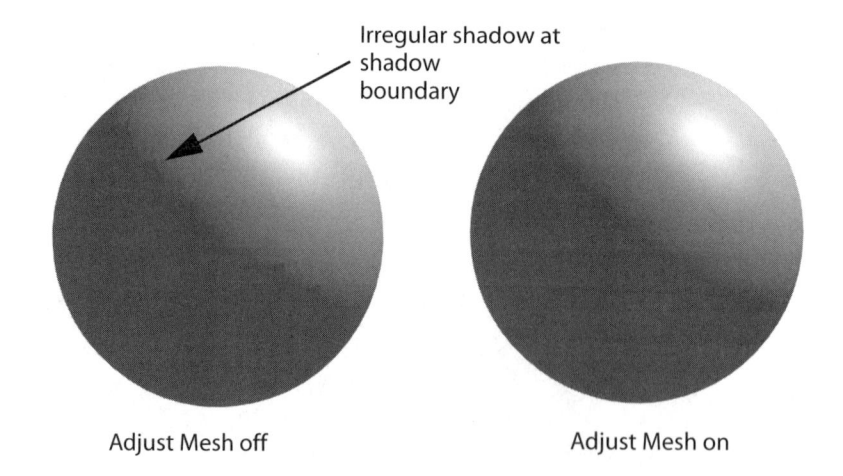

Adjust Mesh off — Irregular shadow at shadow boundary

Adjust Mesh on

Override Scale: 10

If on, (the default) sets the scale at which the model is rendered using a floating point number from 0.0 through 15.0. The number represents the exponent of the scale factor used to scale the model. For example, a value of 5.0 scales the model down by a factor of 10^5, or 100,000. The model is not changed.

The default value is $1/_{1000}$ of the size of the model, which generally produces the optimal rendering. This number can be changed if precision problems cause unexplained missing surfaces, or surface speckling, to appear in the rendered image.

RAYTRACE SET SCALEFACTOR <value>

Limit Memory (Mb)

If on, this lets you limit the amount of memory (RAM) used in preprocessing for ray tracing. This can improve performance, particularly on larger models, by avoiding the necessity for the system to page out to disk during ray tracing.

Min Ray Contribution

If on, this sets a limit (from 0 to 100) on the number of rays that will be traced through a given pixel. It does this by specifying the minimum contribution that a reflected or transmitted ray needs to have before that ray will be computed. This can be very useful in rendering animations that comprise thousands of frames. If you have many reflective and/or

| Ray Tracing Dialog Box | 131

transparent materials, a small adjustment between 5 and 10% could potentially save you hours of computing time with no discernible loss in image quality.

Adjusting Ray Trace settings

In the next few exercises, you will be making adjustments to the Ray Tracer settings and visually comparing the results to see the effects.

✔ Exercise 3-20: Adjust basic settings for ray tracing

1   Open *ray settings.dgn*.

    To see where the camera is positioned in relation to the model, you can turn on the camera view cone display.

2   Select the Define Camera tool.

3   Enter a data point in View 2.

    The camera cone is displayed in View 2. Notice how the camera is positioned so that you are looking through several windows.

4   Select the Render tool with the following tool setting:

    Render Mode: Ray Trace

    Open the Ray Tracing dialog box by clicking the magnifying glass icon in the Render tool dialog box.

    The Ray Tracing settings dialog box opens.

5   In the Ray Tracing dialog box, turn on:

    Quick Display
    Render All Objects
    Real World Lighting

    Since you just opened this design file, there is no solution in memory. The default mode is Create New Solution. Also note that Render current solution (in any view) is grayed out.

6   Enter a data point in View 2.

| Chapter 3: Rendering Options and Settings |

NOTE: *In the Ray Tracer settings dialog box, the following can be adjusted without the need to recompute a new rendering solution — Shadows, Reflections, Transparency, Fresnel, Quick Display, and the Max number of reflections and transparency. These settings are view related and can be adjusted while using the solution currently loaded in memory.*

Changes to the state of Render All Objects or Real World Lighting would require a new solution in order to actually see the effects of toggling these options on or off.

✔ Exercise 3-21: Enable shadows, transparency, and reflection

1. Continuing in *ray settings.dgn*, in the Ray Tracing dialog box, turn on:

   Shadows
   Reflections with Max set to 2
   Transparency with Max set to 1

   The next step will show the results of ray tracing using the above settings for the Ray Trace render mode.

2. In the Render tool dialog box, click the Render current solution (in any view) icon.

3. Enter a data point in View 3 to ray trace the view with Shadows, Reflections, and Transparency enabled.

   While this is an improvement, the settings need refining: the number of transparency planes set is too low (at 1). In the rendering of View 3, you can see through the first window only.

View 2 *(left)*, with no shadows, reflections, or transparency, compared to View 3 *(right)*.

| Environment Mapping | 133

✔ **Exercise 3-22: Increase the Transparency setting**

1 Continuing in *ray settings.dgn*, in the Ray Tracing dialog box, change the Transparency value from 1 to 999.

2 Ray trace View 5 with the current solution.

Now you can see through all the window panes.

View 3 *(left)* with transparency Max set to 1 and View 5 *(right)* with Max set to 999.

NOTE: *The Transparency setting Max (integer) defines the number of consecutive transparent objects you can look through. If you work with solids, each window you look through would require a transparency setting of 2, as there would be both an inner and an outer surface. In the exercise example file, the windows are just shapes, having no thickness, so each window requires only one transparency. In this example, the camera angle and position is such that it is looking through all seven window panes; thus, you would need to set the transparency Max to at least 7.*

ENVIRONMENT MAPPING

Remember, from the earlier ring models exercises, that the environment map consists of six images forming an imaginary cube around the model. These images appear in both transmitted and reflected rays and, when Visible Environment also is enabled, they appear in place of the background color of the view. You will now look at environment maps in more detail.

| Chapter 3: Rendering Options and Settings |

✔ Exercise 3-23: Set up environment maps for model

1   Open *Environment Mapping.dgn*.

    This model consist of six reference files — four buildings, street lights, and a light ring of distant lights to provide realistic global illumination from any camera angle.

2   Select the Apply Material tool in the Render tools tool box.

    The Apply Material dialog box opens.

3   In the Render tool dialog box, click the Environment Maps tool.

    The Environment Maps dialog opens to let you select the individual environment maps for the Front, Back, Left, Right, Top, and Bottom faces of the environment cube. Initially, only the Front face can be selected and only its browse icon is enabled. When you select the initial Front face, all other faces then will default to this first image, until you specify a different image for each of them.

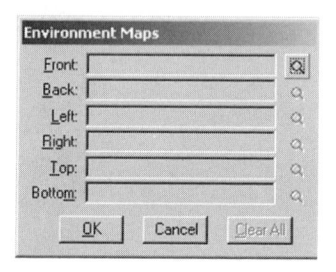

4   Click the browse icon for Front.

    The Select Environment Map [All] dialog box opens.

5   Browse for and choose *skybox front.jpg* from the course *Image Library\Skybox* folder.

6   Click OK.

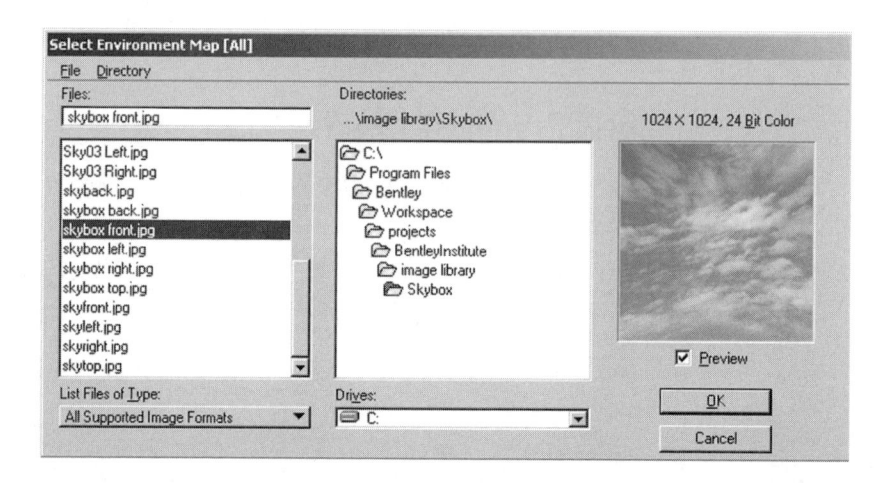

Select Environment Map [All] with *skybox front.jpg* selected.

| Environment Mapping | **135**

7 Repeat this process for the remaining faces, selecting *skybox back.jpg* to be the back image, *skybox left.jpg* as the left image, *skybox right.jpg* as the right image, and *skybox top.jpg* as the top image.

NOTE: *When you select the browse icon for a face, the Select Environment dialog box includes the face name in its title, such as Select Environment Map [Right].*

NOTE: *The bottom image in this exercise can be left as the originally chosen image since it is located below the ground plane and won't be seen.*

8 Click OK in the Environment Maps dialog box to finish.

9 Select the Render tool.

10 Open the Ray Trace settings dialog and verify that Environment Maps is enabled and Visible Environment is disabled.

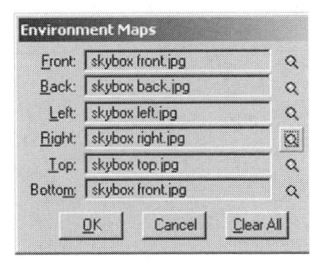

Select Environment Maps

11 Enter a data point in View 2.

The view is rendered and the environment map images are visible as either reflections or as transmitted rays through the glass in the building model.

12 Ray trace the current solution in View 3.

Notice that the environment maps are visible through the windows in View 3.

View 2 *(left)* and View 3 *(right)*, with reflected and transmitted environment map images visible.

| Chapter 3: Rendering Options and Settings |

While the environment maps are visible in reflections, or through transparent materials, they are not evident elsewhere. To make the maps visible generally, you can turn on Visible Environment.

✔ Exercise 3-24: Turn on Visible Environment

1. Continuing in *Environment Mapping.dgn*, in the Ray Tracing dialog box, enable Visible Environment.

2. Ray trace the current solution in Views 2 and 3.

   The environment maps are evident wherever the background would normally be seen, or reflected.

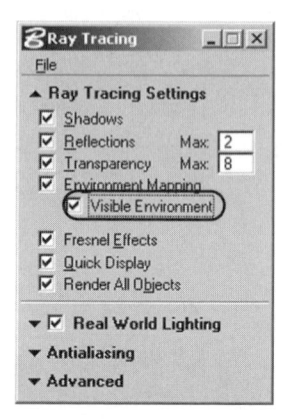

View 2 *(left)* and View 3 *(right)* with Visible Environment enabled.

NOTE: *The Visible Environment can be very useful for animations, since the sky would change correctly as the camera is moved through a scene. Using a background image for animation would be a mistake as the background would appear the same, or unmoving. Another option for a realistic sky background would be to use a sky cylinder that has a sky image defined as a material and then applied to a cylindrical surface around the model. Sky cylinders will be covered in more detail in a later chapter.*

FRESNEL EFFECTS

When enabled in the Ray Tracing settings, the Fresnel effect calculates the increased reflectivity of a surface when viewed at a sharp angle. You can see this effect for yourself. Look at your watch, holding your wrist up to view the time. Now rotate your wrist slowly away from you so the watch crystal is on edge. As you do so, you will see the increased reflectivity and, when rotated to a severe enough angle, the crystal will act like a mirror and reflect nearly all light rays.

✔ Exercise 3-25: Fresnel effects

1. Open *bridge render day.dgn*.
2. Select the Render tool with the following tool setting:

   Render Mode: Ray Trace
3. Click the magnifying glass icon to open the Ray Tracing dialog box.
4. Verify that Fresnel Effects is disabled.
5. Enter a data point in View 2 to ray trace the view and create a new solution.
6. In the Ray Tracing dialog box, turn on Fresnel Effects.
7. Select Ray Trace Current Solution (in any view).
8. Enter a data point in View 4 to ray trace it with Fresnel Effects on.

Images with Fresnel Effects off *(left)* and enabled *(right)*.

As you can see, with Fresnel Effects enabled, the water appears much more reflective when ray traced from the camera view angle. The sharper the angle, the more reflective the water would appear. In contrast, rendering the top view would not produce any difference whether Fresnel Effects were enabled or not.

RENDER ALL OBJECTS

When you ray trace a view with Render All Objects turned off, you only render what the camera sees in the view and any elements that the camera view cone crosses. If Render All Objects is not enabled, it is very likely that some objects behind the camera may not show up either as reflections or shadows. To prevent objects located behind the camera from being improperly left out of a scene, it is a good idea to enable Render All Objects.

In the next exercise, you will be ray tracing a camera view of a mirror. The position of the camera or eye point is in the middle of the room looking at the mirror on a wall. The 3D scene consisting of a room with furniture, table lamp, wall pictures, and the like will be rendered first with Render All Object disabled and then again with it enabled to compare the results.

✔ Exercise 3-26: Render All Objects

1 Open *render all objects.dgn*.

2 Select the Render tool, with Render Mode set to Ray Trace.

3 Open the Ray Tracing settings dialog box and verify that Render All Objects is disabled.

4 With Create New Solution selected, enter a data point in View 2.

   The view is ray traced and a new solution is created. This includes only those objects in the model that are within the view cone, or whose elements are crossed by the camera view cone frustum.

   NOTE: Frustum *denotes a geometric shape used to describe the viewing volume in computer graphics, where the viewing plane sits at the top of a truncated pyramid that extends into the 3D environment. More rendering terms like this can be found in the glossary section at the end of this book.*

5 In the Ray Tracing settings, enable Render All Objects.

| Rendering Setup dialog box | **139**

6 With Create New Solution selected, in the Render tool dialog box, enter a data point in View 4.

The view is rendered and the objects that were behind the camera now appear as reflections in the mirror.

Ray traced image with Render All Objects disabled *(left)* and enabled *(right)*.

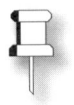

NOTE: *The reflections in the mirror, prior to enabling Render All Objects, are from the environment maps. With Render All Objects enabled, the environment maps still can be seen through the reflected window in the mirror image.*

Reviewing the effects of the ray tracing operations from the last exercise, the image on the left does not include any of the objects that were behind the camera. These were not visible in the rendering until you enabled the Render All Objects setting. If you ray trace your model with Render All Objects enabled, you can then ray trace the resulting solution in any view you choose since every element is rendered, not just those in the current camera view.

By setting the option to Ray Trace current solution in any view, you can move the camera to another vantage point and immediately render without the need to preprocess or read in the textures again. This saves considerable time in large models and is useful when animating a camera through a scene.

RENDERING SETUP DIALOG BOX

This dialog box is a combination of all the rendering-related dialog boxes. Using this dialog box, not only can you create rendering setup files that can be recalled later, you can use it as a reminder of all the settings available.

| Chapter 3: Rendering Options and Settings |

A variety of rendering settings can have a major impact on rendering times. For initial working images, coarse settings can be used to produce images quickly. For final images, however, you must remember to adjust the settings to improve the quality. The Rendering Setups dialog box streamlines these procedures. This dialog box lets you create rendering setups and save them with the model. You can create multiple setups that cover different rendering scenarios, for example:

- ▶ Working setup — With coarse settings, useful for initial rendering to check the placement of lights and materials.

- ▶ Check setup — With finer settings, to give a near-final-quality image for last minute checking.

- ▶ Final setup — With all settings chosen, to produce the final high-quality, photorealistic rendered image.

To load the settings relative to the current requirements you select the appropriate named setup from the Setup Name option menu.

Setup files also can be exported to an external file. The exported file then can be imported into a new model and, subsequently, saved with that model. Using this procedure, you need to go through the initial setup process once only.

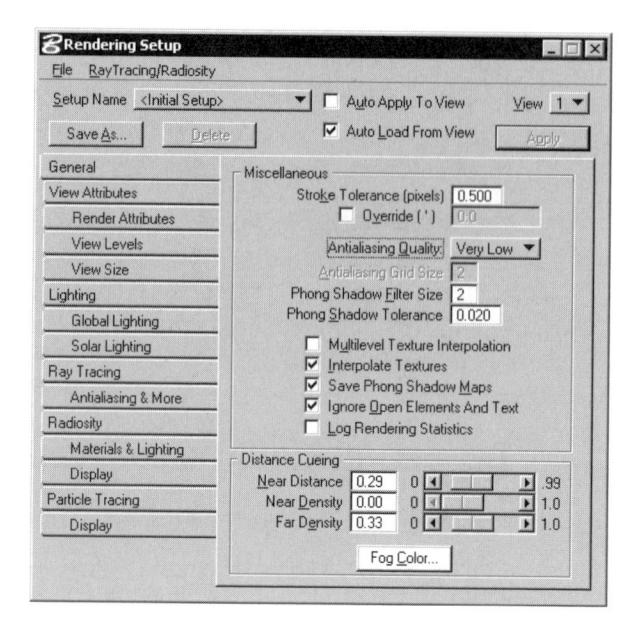

| Rendering Setup dialog box |

Setup Name

This option menu displays the name of the rendering setup file currently loaded. Where no file has been saved or loaded, the default name <Initial Setup> appears.

Auto Apply To View

When on, the settings of a selected setup file automatically are applied to the current view (as displayed in the View option menu).

View

This displays the currently selected view.

Save As

This opens the Save Setup As dialog box, which is used to save a setup file (with the active model).

Delete

This deletes the current setup file. It is not available (dimmed) if no setup file has been saved or loaded—that is, when <Initial Setup> is the current file.

Auto Load From View

This loads the settings from the currently selected view.

Apply

This applies the current settings to the selected view.

File menu

Items in this menu let you import a previously saved setup file, or export the currently loaded settings to an external file. These files have the extension *.rsf* (Rendering Setup File).

✔ **Exercise 3-27: Create a Rendering Settings Setup**

1. Open *hole8-17-model.dgn*.
2. Open the Rendering Setup dialog box (Settings > Rendering > Setup).

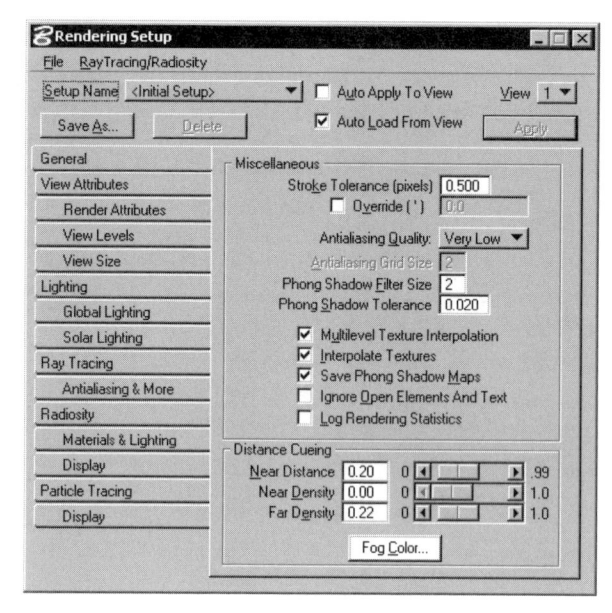

3 Select the Solar Lighting tab.

4 Set the following:

Time: 2:00 PM
Click Cities and choose your city or one near you.
Date: Today's date.

5 Click Save As.

6 In the Name field of the Save Setup As dialog box, enter *my_setup*.

7 Click OK.

The dialog box closes and the new settings file name appears in the Setup Name option menu. You can recall this rendering setup with the saved Solar settings later. Using this method, you can create several rendering setups.

Once you have created a rendering setup, you can export it to an external file. You then can import this saved setup into other models. These straightforward processes are performed as follows.

To export a rendering settings setup file:

1 From the Setup Name option menu, choose the setup to export.

2 In the Rendering Setup dialog box, select File > Export Setup File.

The Export Setup File dialog box opens.

3 In the Export Setup File dialog box Files field, enter a name for the settings file.

4 Click OK.

The file is saved to disk and the dialog box closes. Where a setup file is required for other models, you first must export it to an external file in this way.

To import a rendering settings setup file:

1 In the Rendering Setup dialog box, select File > Import Setup File.

The Import Setup File dialog box opens.

| Review Questions | **143**

2 If necessary, select the directory where the required file is stored.

3 Select the required file from the list.

4 Click OK.

The Import Setup File dialog box closes and the Import Setup As dialog box opens. This lets you name the rendering setup for the current design file.

5 Optionally, enter a new name for the imported rendering setup.

6 Click OK.

The dialog box closes and the imported settings are loaded with the chosen setup name displayed in the Setup Name option menu.

REVIEW QUESTIONS

1 Which rendering mode—Phong, Smooth, or Constant—produces the most realistic result?

2 Which shading mode calculates colors at the vertices of the polygons and then blends these across each polygon's surface?

3 Both ray tracing and phong renderings produce shadows. Which one can produce colored shadows?

4 What Ray Tracing settings can be turned on to increase reflectivity of elements viewed at sharp angles?

5 Which shadows are more accurate: those produced by phong shading or those produced by ray tracing?

6 You can phong shade a single element in a view (as an option). Can you do this with ray tracing?

7 What is the default Max value for reflections in the Ray Tracer Settings dialog box?

8 What shading type requires the use of 3D glasses for viewing?

9 Which setting affects all rendering and hidden line routines and affects both rendering time and image quality, where curved surfaces are involved?

10 What can be done to reduce the jagged edges that are particularly noticeable on low resolution displays?

11 Which view control tool is used to set the clipping planes for a view and adjusts how fog or depth cueing appears?

Chapter Summary

In this chapter, you have learned how to use all of MicroStation's display modes, from wiremesh to hidden line, and the rendering routines Constant, Smooth, Phong, and Ray Trace. You have learned how they differ and which settings have an effect on the routine you decide to use. You were taught the importance of stroke tolerance and how this one setting can affect all rendering modes. You have learned the importance of anti-aliasing, environment mapping, Fresnel effects, and Render All Objects. You also learned how to turn on Depth of Field to achieve photographic-quality renderings. In addition to all of these, you have become skilled at how to apply Distance Cueing, such as Fog and Depth Cueing effects.

4 Global and Source Lighting

Of all of the tools and techniques for achieving truly photorealistic results, when rendering with MicroStation, lighting has the most impact. Without correct illumination, a 3D scene will look very flat and two-dimensional. This chapter presents the lighting tools in MicroStation and how to properly use them to improve your rendering results.

MicroStation provides two types of lighting: source and global. Source lighting is created via special cells that you place in a model and is covered later in this chapter. Global lighting is available for a DGN file (all models) via settings in the Global Lighting dialog box.

GLOBAL LIGHTING

When you first began to render with MicroStation, you picked a rendering method and hoped for the best. If you were lucky, the model already had decent global lighting configured, and the rendering results were acceptable, if not a bit mediocre. This was a result of the Solar, Ambient, and Flashbulb Light settings, inherited from the original 3D seed file.

In the following exercises, you will begin by ray tracing a view in a model, using the current global lighting settings. Following this, you will adjust settings for the global lighting to improve the image.

✔ Exercise 4-1: Review the effect of global lighting

1. Open *Global Lighting.dgn*.

   You will ray trace View 2 with the current global lighting settings. Since you do not have a ray trace solution yet, the only option will be to Create a new solution.

2. Select Render with the following tool setting:

   Render Mode: Ray Trace

3. Enter a data point in View 2 to ray trace the view.

   The view renders but is very dark. To remedy this, you will need to adjust the Global Lighting settings.

Global Lighting Types

Three main sources of global lighting are found in every DGN file: ambient, flashbulb, and solar. Additional to these light sources is the option to add sky lighting (to solar and distant lights). In the following, you will inspect the effects of each of the global light source types.

The following table describes the Global Lighting settings.

Tool setting	Effect
Ambient	If on, enables controls for setting the intensity and color of ambient lighting.
	Intensity — Can vary from no light (0) to full light (1).
	Color — Opens the Modify Color dialog box, to set the Ambient lighting color.
Flashbulb	If on, enables controls for setting the intensity and color of the view flashbulb.
	Intensity — Can vary from no light (0) to full light (1).
	Color — Opens the Modify Color dialog box, to set the Flashbulb lighting color.
Solar	If on, enables controls for setting the intensity and color of the solar lighting. Clicking the Show Solar Settings button, at the left, expands the dialog box to display all Solar lighting settings.
Add Sky Light to all Solar and Distant Lights	If on, enables the color button for the lighting. Clicking the Show Sky Settings button, at the left, expands the dialog box to display all relevant settings.

| Global Lighting |

Ambient

Ambient light is all-pervasive. That is, it illuminates all surfaces equally. It is controlled in the Global Lighting dialog box. The intensity of ambient light can vary from None (0) to Full (1.0), and its color can be adjusted. Whether or not a material is affected by ambient light depends on a material's ambient property. If its ambient value is set to 0, then the material will not be illuminated by the global ambient light regardless of how high you make it.

Because ambient light illuminates all surfaces equally, increasing its intensity reduces the depth, or contrast, of the shaded view.

Ambient light is useful, however, in simulating background office lighting or illuminating surfaces that would not otherwise receive light. No shadows are cast by ambient light.

> **NOTE:** *For radiosity solving and particle tracing rendering operations, it is normal to turn off Ambient lighting. If you forget to do this, an alert box gives you the option to do so prior to commencing the rendering process.*

✔ Exercise 4-2: Adjust ambient light settings

1. Continuing in **Global Lighting.dgn**, open the Global Lighting dialog box by selecting the Global Lighting tool or else Settings > Rendering > Global Lighting.

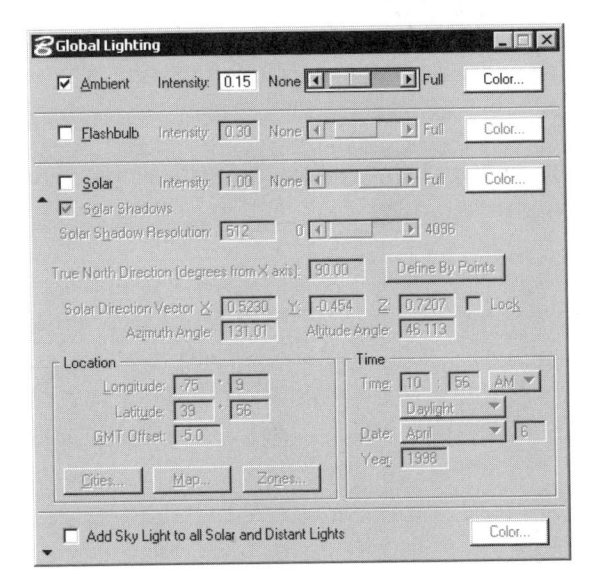

   From here, you make all adjustments to global lighting. Because changes to the global settings are immediate, there is no OK or Cancel button.

   In the current Global Lighting settings, the only light on at the moment is Ambient, with a low value of 0.15 or 15%.

2. In the Global Lighting dialog box, change the Ambient value from 0.15 to 0.50.

   Unlike other light sources, Ambient immediately affects the view display. It is not a true light source because it has no origin. You can make changes to Ambient and ray trace the current solution without needing to create a new solution, as you would with all other light types.

3 In the Render tool dialog box, click the Ray Trace current solution (in any view) icon.

4 Enter a data point in View 3.

The view is ray traced and now is much brighter but only in the sky and the water. This is due to the fact that only the sky material has an ambient value above 0. The water appears brighter only because it is reflective and is reflecting the changes in the sky material's brightness.

5 Change Ambient from 0.50 to 1.0.

6 With the Render tool still active, enter a data point in View 5.

As you increase the global ambient, notice that the sky gets progressively brighter along with the reflections in the water.

The effect of using only ambient light. *(Left to right):* Settings of 0.15, 0.50, and 1.0.

From this, you can see that ambient lighting affects only those materials that have an ambient value above 0.

Material Ambient

In this following exercise, you will find it easier to understand how the global lighting ambient and the material's ambient properties affect one another. While you will be learning about material definitions later in this course, you will be working briefly with the Define Material tool for part of this exercise. You will open the main design file containing the

| Global Lighting |

city model that is referenced by *Global Lighting.dgn* and use the Define Material tool to switch to a different material palette. In this new material palette, all of the material definitions, with exception of the sky cylinder material (the background sky image), have ambient set to 60% rather than 0.

✔ **Exercise 4-3: Change material definitions by switching palettes**

1. Open *Longbeach.dgn*.
2. In the Rendering Tools tool box, select the Define Materials tool.
3. In the Material Editor dialog box, select Palette > Unload.

   An Alert dialog box appears, warning you that the palette has materials in use by the material table and unloading the palette will send these to the missing materials list.

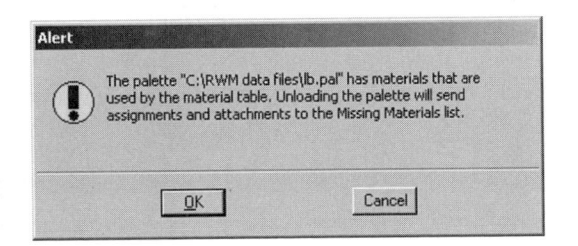

4. Click the OK button to unload the palette.
5. In the Material Editor dialog box, select Palette > Open.

   The Open Palette dialog box opens.

6. Choose *LB ambient.pal* from the list in the course *dgn* folder.
7. Click OK to load the palette.
8. Reopen the file *Global Lighting.dgn*.

   An Alert box appears, asking you if you want to save changes to the *Longbeach.mat* file.

9. Click Yes.

   The material file is saved before *Global Lighting.dgn* is opened.

Having changed the material definitions, the following exercise will show more clearly how ambient lighting can affect your rendered images.

Exercise 4-4: View the effect of ambient lighting on materials

1. Continuing in *Global Lighting.dgn*, in the Rendering Tools tool box, select the Global Lighting tool.

    The Global Lighting dialog box opens.

2. Verify that Ambient is turned on and its value is set to 0.15.

3. Select the Render tool with the following setting:

    Render Mode: Ray Trace

4. Enter a data point in View 2.

    The view renders and, although it is dark, unlike in the previous exercise all the materials appear to be illuminated at least a little by the ambient light.

5. In the Global Lighting dialog box, change the Ambient value from 0.15 to 0.50.

6. Ray trace the current solution in View 3.

    Now the image is much brighter.

7. Change the Global Lighting Ambient value from 0.50 to 1.00 (you can do this by moving the Ambient slider all the way to the right).

8. Ray trace the current solution in View 5 or 6.

    Now the view is too bright and lacks contrast.

The effect of using only ambient light. *(Left to right)*: Settings of 0.15, 0.50, and 1.0.

On its own, ambient lighting is not meant to be the main source of lighting. It can be used in conjunction with other lighting to add "background" light to materials that have an ambient setting above 0.

| Global Lighting |

Flashbulb

Flashbulb provides a point light source coincident with the eye point of the view. Like Ambient, it is controlled in the Global Lighting settings box. The intensity of Flashbulb light can vary from None (0) to Full (1.0), and its color can be adjusted. Also like Ambient, Flashbulb lighting does not cast shadows.

NOTE: *For radiosity solving and particle tracing, it is normal to turn off Flashbulb. If you forget to do this, an alert gives you the option to do so prior to commencing rendering. There are drawbacks to using Flashbulb just as there are to using a flashbulb on a real camera. You do not have to worry about "red eyes," but you will experience hot spots on highly specular and reflective surfaces. This occurs especially where the camera is directly opposing these surfaces. For this reason, when creating a walkthrough animation, it is good to use very little flashbulb intensity or disable this feature altogether.*

NOTE: *If the camera is moving through a scene while rendering animation frames, using Flashbulb requires a new ray trace solution to be calculated for each frame. The proper use of Flashbulb in these cases could also add considerable processing time for each frame in the animation. When animating a camera through a scene, it is recommended that Flashbulb be turned off, unless other objects, materials, or lights are animated. In these cases, as with using Flashbulb, a new rendering solution must be computed for each frame.*

✔ **Exercise 4-5: Adjust the Flashbulb settings**

1. Open **Global Lighting2.dgn**.

   This model references Longbeach.dgn and has six views displayed.

2. In the Rendering Tools tool box, select the Global Lighting tool and check the following settings:

   Ambient: Disabled
   Flashbulb: Enabled and set to 1.0.

3. Ray trace View 2, creating a new solution.

   With Flashbulb intensity at 1.0, the face of the building is brightly illuminated because all of the light energy hits this face straight on.

4 Ray trace View 3, creating a new solution.

If you compare the two renderings, you can see that, in View 3, the light from the flashbulb is directed at both sides of the building and is more evenly distributed. The rendering also looks better, since the camera is not directly opposing the building faces as it is in View 2.

Flashbulb lighting straight on or directly opposing the building *(left)* and at an angle to the building *(right)*.

Because you created a new solution for View 3, the flashbulb lighting was recalculated from the different camera (eye point) location. If you had ray traced View 3, using the current solution from the first rendering, you would have seen a different result, as the following exercise shows.

✔ **Exercise 4-6: Ray trace the current solution with Flashbulb lighting**

1 Continuing in *Global Lighting2.dgn*, ray trace View 5, creating a new solution.

In the next step, you will be redisplaying a solution that has flashbulb energy from a different camera angle.

2 In the Render tool dialog box, click the Ray Trace current solution icon.

3 Enter a data point in View 6.

View 6 is rendered, using the existing solution from the previous rendering where the flashbulb was directly in front of the building.

You can see clearly that the right side of the building is darker than the front. You can also compare View 3 and View 6 to see that, in View 3, the right side of the building is illuminated by the flashbulb. Since you creat-

| Global Lighting |

ed a new solution, the flashbulb energy actually hit the right side of the building. In View 6, the flashbulb energy and direction was from a different camera angle (directly in front), and none of the energy hit the right side of the building.

Images with flash from current camera position *(left)* and with flash from previous camera angle *(right)*.

Solar lighting

Ambient light and the flashbulb produce images that lack depth and have a flat, or two-dimensional appearance. What is missing from the previous images are shadows, such as those cast by overhangs and other features in the model. Since neither Ambient nor Flashbulb produces shadows, you need to engage the third type of global lighting—solar light—and its ability to cast shadows.

When Solar global lighting is enabled, its Intensity and Color settings become active. Selecting the Show Solar Settings button, located to the left of the Solar toggle, expands the Solar section of the dialog box to reveal more solar lighting settings. The following table describes the effect of each setting.

Solar setting	Effect
Intensity	Sets the intensity of the Solar light — Can vary from no light (0) to full light (1).
Color	Opens the Modify Color dialog box, to set the Solar lighting color.
Solar Shadows	If on, solar shadows are created in phong rendering, ray traced and particle traced images, as well as radiosity solutions.
	This requires also that Shadows be on in the Rendering View Attributes dialog box and, for ray tracing, in the Ray Tracing dialog box.

Solar setting	Effect
Solar Shadow Resolution	Sets the resolution of the shadow map generated for the solar light with phong rendering. The lower the value, the less resolute the solar shadows will be, and processing time will be reduced. Has no effect on ray traced images.
True North Direction (degrees from X axis)	Specifies the direction of North as degrees from the X axis.
Define By Points	Lets you define the direction of North, graphically, with two points.
Solar Direction Vector X, Y, Z	Specifies the direction vector from the solar light. Dimmed if Lock is off.
Azimuth Angle	Sets the azimuth direction of the solar light (from 0 to 360°). Dimmed if Lock is off.
Altitude Angle	Sets the angle of the "sun" above the horizon (from 0 to 90°). Dimmed if Lock is off.
Lock	Sets how the position of the solar light is determined: • On — The position of the solar light is determined by Vector values. • Off — The position is determined by Location and Time settings.
Location	Contains controls to set the model's location for calculating solar light. These controls are dimmed if Lock is on. • Longitude — Sets the longitude at the model's location. • Latitude — Sets the latitude at the model's location. • GMT Offset — Sets the time difference from Greenwich Mean Time (GMT) at the model's location. • Cities — Opens the Location By City dialog box, which is used to set the location by selecting a city from the list. • Map — Opens the Location By Map dialog box, which is used to set the location by pointing at the location on a map of the world. • Zones — Opens the GMT Offset By Time Zone dialog box, which is used to set the GMT Offset by selecting a time zone.
Time	Sets the time of day and the year for the rendering. • Time — Sets the hours and minutes, with option menus for AM or PM and Standard or Daylight time. • Date — Sets the date for the rendering. • Year — Sets the year for the rendering.

| Global Lighting |

You can make adjustments to the solar direction using azimuth angle and altitude. You can also make adjustments by entering the month, year, and time of day, provided you know where the model is on the planet. You can easily pick a large city near you to determine your longitude and latitude which would also give you the time zone offset from Greenwich Mean Time (GMT).

NOTE: *Using azimuth and altitude angles to adjust the solar direction vector is an easy way to get the light to shine exactly where you want it. Keep in mind that this method lets you have the sun shine in any direction. For example, you could have it shine directly on the north face of a building in North America. While this may look nice, it does not happen in the real world.*

✔ Exercise 4-7: Enable and configure solar lighting

1 Open *Global Lighting3.dgn*.

2 In the Rendering Tools tool box, select the Global Lighting tool, and check the following settings:

Ambient: Enabled and set to 0.10
Flashbulb: Disabled
Solar lighting: Enabled and set to 1.0

3 If necessary, click the Show Solar Settings arrow, to the left of the Solar check box, to display further settings for solar lighting.

4 Turn off Solar Shadows.

5 If necessary, enable the Lock check box for Solar Direction Vector.

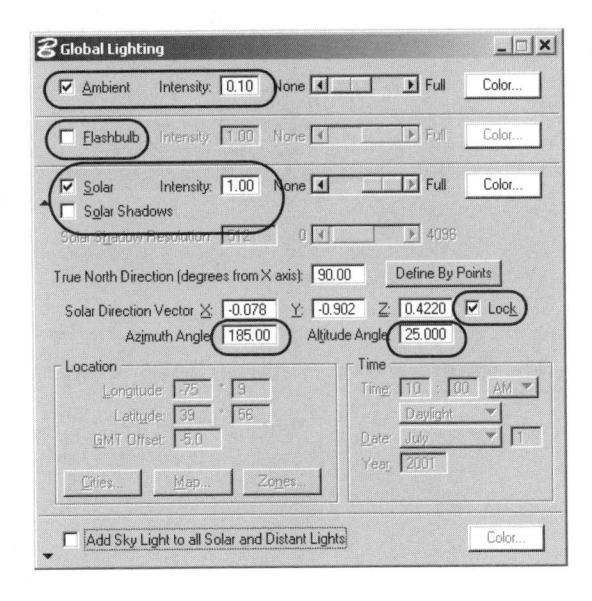

| Chapter 4: Global and Source Lighting |

6 In the Azimuth Angle field, enter 185.

The azimuth angle is measured in a clockwise fashion from North, with North or 0 being straight up in the Top view (the y-axis).

7 In the Altitude Angle field, enter 25.

The altitude angle defines the angle of the sun off the horizon (positive values indicate the angle above the horizon).

8 Select the Render tool with the following setting:

Render Mode: Ray Trace

9 Enter a data point in View 2.

10 If necessary, adjust the brightness of the image with the Brightness slider until you are happy with the result.

11 Ray trace View 3 using the current solution.

The views are rendered without shadows and, while lacking depth, they look somewhat better than the same views rendered in the previous exercise using just Flashbulb and Ambient lighting.

Ray traced solar lighting without shadows.

To add depth to the images, you will now turn on Solar Shadows.

Exercise 4-8: Turn on Solar Shadows

1 Continuing in *Global Lighting3.dgn*, in the Global Lighting dialog box, turn on Solar Shadows.

2 Ray trace View 5, creating a new solution.

The image is rendered complete with shadows.

| Global Lighting | **157**

3   Ray trace View 6 using the current solution.

Ray traced using solar lighting with shadows.

Comparing Views 5 and 6 with Views 2 and 3, you can clearly see that adding shadows provides much more depth and contrast to the rendered image.

Add Sky Light to All Solar and Distant Lights

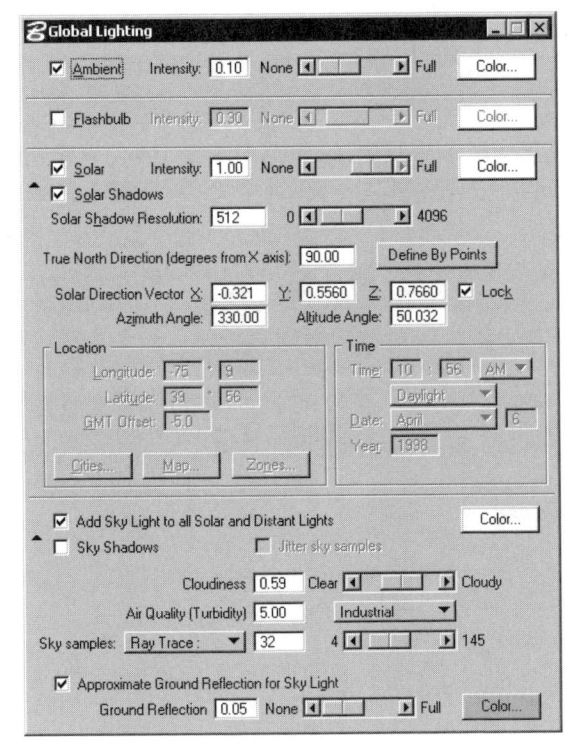

Global Lighting with sky light.

With this setting enabled, an additional atmospheric lighting effect is created, to increase the realism of solar lighting and other distant lighting sources. With solar lighting, for instance, the intensity of the light is modified by the angle of the sun, providing a more realistic solar study. As in the real world, when cloudiness increases, the direct sunlight decreases but the amount of light from the sky increases. Similarly, the light from any distant light sources is modified.

As with other global lighting sources, you can adjust the color of the sky light by clicking the Color button and selecting a new color.

Once Sky Light is enabled, you can set the degree of Cloudiness and the Air Quality (Turbidity) to create the desired conditions. On a clear day, for example, the sky is not uniformly lit. More sky light comes from the direction of the sun, thus producing darker, sharper shadows. Alternatively, on a cloudy day, the sky is uniformly lit with softer, less pronounced shadows.

With Air Quality (Turbidity) set to Perfectly Clean, there is a small amount of coloring from the sky lighting. When Air Quality (Turbidity) is set to Industrial, the coloring effect of the sky lighting is more pronounced.

Sky light is a directional light, coming from an imaginary sky hemisphere and pointing in toward the center. The precision of the hemisphere is determined by the Sky samples setting: the slider control range is from 4 to 145, with larger numbers increasing precision. You can enter a number higher than 145 by entering a value directly into the field.

When using solar lighting or distant lights to illuminate an interior scene through openings such as windows, it is much more efficient to create sky openings at these locations. As you will see later, the sky openings, once defined, focus both solar and skylight through only these openings. Using sky openings reduces the computations and improves both rendering performance and the resulting image. Sky openings, which are placed using the Define Light tool, are discussed later in this chapter.

Ray traced image without added sky light *(left)* and with added sky light *(right)*.

With Sky Light enabled, shadows are less dark and more detail is apparent in objects located in the shadows of other objects.

| Global Lighting |

Approximate Ground Reflection for Sky Light

This setting is used to create an approximation of all sun and sky light reflected by the ground. A Color button lets you define the color for the ground reflection. Typically, this setting would be used where a model has been created without any ground geometry.

NOTE: *If you have ground geometry in the design, and are using particle tracing or radiosity, the ground geometry and material colors or textures would cast shadows and reflect light instead.*

✔ Exercise 4-9: Render with solar lighting and shadows

1. Open *Global Lighting4.dgn*.
2. Open the Global Lighting dialog box.

   This DGN file has been saved with Ambient enabled and set to 0.10, Flashbulb disabled, and both Solar lighting and Solar Shadows enabled.

3. Verify that Add Skylight to all Solar and Distant lights is disabled.
4. Use the Render tool to ray trace View 2.

   The view is rendered without sky lighting and looks quite good where the faces are lit directly by the solar light.

5. Select Ray Trace Current Solution (in any view) and enter a data point in View 3.

   Again the rendering looks good.

6. Enter a data point in View 5 to ray trace with the current solution.

   From this camera angle, the building appears very dark since the sides are not illuminated directly by the solar light and are in the shadow.

7. Enter a data point in View 6 to ray trace with the current solution.

   Again, from this camera angle, the building appears extremely dark since these sides are not illuminated directly by the solar light.

This is an example where you need to have sky light added to reduce the starkness of the shadows and to reveal some degree of detail in the shadowed areas.

Rendered images showing views from the sunny side *(top)* and from the dark side *(bottom)*.

• •

✔ **Exercise 4-10: Add sky light to reduce starkness of Solar shadows**

1. Continuing in *Global Lighting4.dgn*, in the Global Lighting dialog box, if necessary open the Add Sky Light to all Solar and Distant Light settings by clicking the arrow to the left of the toggle.

   The dialog box expands to display settings for Sky Light.

2. Turn on Add Skylight to all Solar and Distant lights.

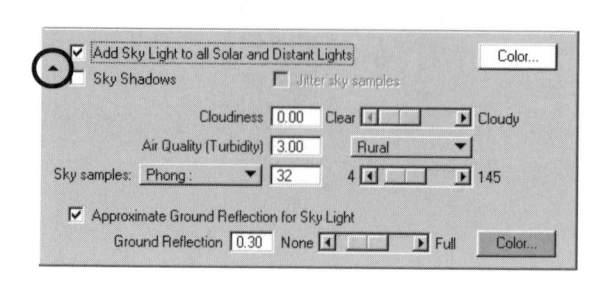

3. Turn on Sky Shadows.

4. Ray trace View 2, creating new solution.

   Since you have made a change by adding sky light, a new solution is required to see the effects.

| Light Ring and Solar Cluster | **161**

The resulting image rendered in View 2 is somewhat lighter in the shadow areas now. When using the particle trace or radiosity render modes, the effects of adding sky light will be much more pronounced.

5   Disable Sky Shadows and ray trace View 3, again creating a new solution.

Notice that the view renders much faster without Sky Shadows enabled and without much difference in the resulting rendered image. You may want to consider disabling this setting for best performance.

6   Ray trace Views 5 and 6 using the current solution.

Now the areas that were too dark before have some illumination and look more realistic.

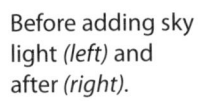

Before adding sky light *(left)* and after *(right)*.

LIGHT RING AND SOLAR CLUSTER

In the last exercise, you saw that by adding sky lighting you could brighten up the dark areas in an exterior scene. In the next exercise, you will look at using a ring of distant lights to create uniform illumination and, in addition, soften the hard ray traced shadows for a more realistic look. The light ring can be in a reference file, letting you easily rotate the file to change the azimuth angle.

NOTE: *Distant lights are one of the source lighting types that are discussed in the next section. In going through this exercise, you will get a brief look at the Define Light tool, which is used to create source lighting and is covered in the section following this.*

| Chapter 4: Global and Source Lighting |

✔ **Exercise 4-11: Use Light Ring**

1. Open the DGN file *villa.dgn*.
2. Ray trace View 2.

   The view is rendered but appears too dark in the shadow areas.

3. In the Rendering Tools tool box, select the Global Lighting tool.

4. In the Global Lighting dialog box, turn off Solar Light.

   Scene ray traced with solar light.

5. In the Rendering Tools tool box, select the Define Light tool and set the following:

   Mode: Modify
   Method: Edit Light

6. If necessary, open the light list by clicking the Show Light List arrow to the right of the Mode option menu.

7. In the light list box, select the reference file *Ref 6 (lightring10 30deg.dgn)*.

8. Enable the On setting to turn on all the lights in the reference file.

9. Ray trace View 4, creating a new solution.

10. Adjust the brightness to match that of View 2.

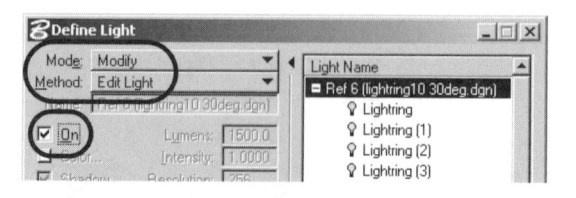

    Scene ray traced with ring of distant lights.

The image is a great improvement over the previous rendering where only solar light was used.

NOTE: *The reference file containing the light ring consists of 28 distant lights. Eighteen of the lights are non-shadow-casting and are 20° apart with an intensity of 0.0278. These 18 lights make up half of the total solar illumination and completely encircle the model. The remaining 10 are shadow-casting and make up the solar cluster to mimic the sun. Each light in the solar cluster has an intensity of 0.05. Their intensities totaled account for the remaining half of the solar light energy. To achieve softer shadows, the 10 shadow-casting lights are placed 0.5° apart, forming a solar cluster that is spread over 5° of arc.*

Using a "light ring" in this way simulates solar lighting conditions but gives you softer shadows. It's now time to look at source lighting in detail.

SOURCE LIGHTING

Although every design file contains the global lighting capabilities just described, there is another optional source of lighting that you can use to add even more realism: source lighting. These light sources are created by placing special cells containing the lighting information. This lighting information is then used during the rendering process.

MicroStation supports four source lighting types: point, spot, distant, and area lights. All are contained in the cell library *lighting.cel*, which is delivered with MicroStation. It can be found in the *Bentley\Workspace\System\Cell* folder. In addition to these standard light source cells, you can select from a number of sample predefined light sources in the delivered file *lightlist.dgn*. Additionally, you can create your own predefined light sources in any DGN file.

Light source cells have a number of settings that adjust the lighting output and characteristics of each lighting cell you place. In addition, the rendering options ray tracing (with Real World Lighting enabled), radiosity, and particle tracing can take advantage of IES (Illuminating Engineering Society) photometric lighting definition files to define the lighting output even more accurately. IES photometric lighting files can be applied to point, spot, and area light source cells.

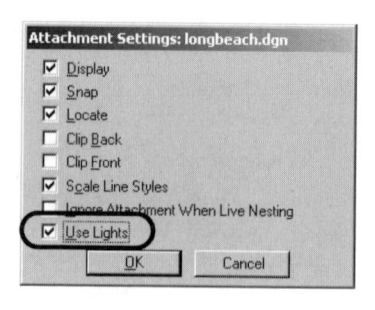

During the rendering process, all active source lighting cells placed in the design affect the outcome. Source lighting cells located in references, however, are ignored unless the Use Lights setting has been enabled for each reference, and the lights are enabled using the Define Light tool. You can activate the Use Lights setting in the Attachment Settings dialog box at the time you attach the reference. This is one of the additional options found when you click Options in the Reference Attachment Settings dialog box.

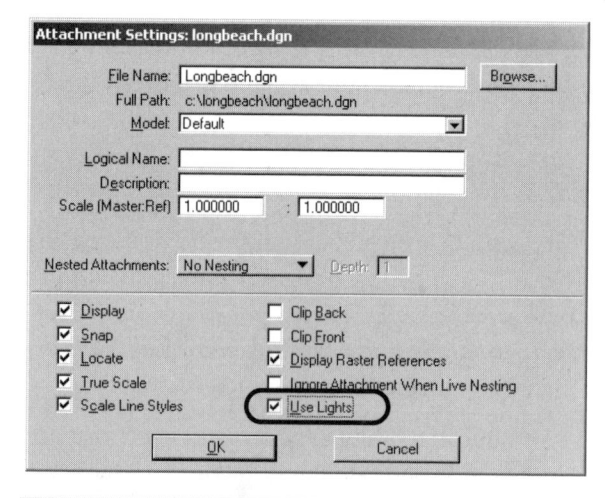

Where the Use Lights setting was not enabled during reference attachment, you can enable it in the Attachments Settings dialog box. This is opened from the References dialog box by selecting Settings > Attachment.

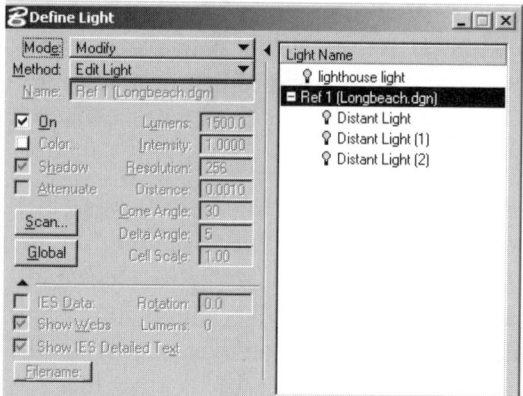

NOTE: *Light sources present in references will appear in the Lights list of the Define Light tool and may be turned on or off using the Define Light tool. Regardless of whether you enabled the lights at the time of attachment, the Define Light tool can be used to control the on/off behavior of lights in reference files. Displayed in the list box are the light source names, the reference number, and the reference name. While you can also view the settings of light source cells in references, you cannot edit them from the active file.*

Define Light tool settings with the Light Name list displaying lights in both the active file and a reference.

Using light sources in references, you can experiment with different lighting setups. For example, you can create multiple lighting files with various source lighting setups. You then reference these files and turn on/off the reference file lights as required.

One of the settings for each light source, Lumens, is used for ray tracing (when Real World Lighting is enabled), radiosity solving, and particle tracing only. It is ignored by the other rendering modes. It lets you work with real-world lighting values when using ray tracing, radiosity, and particle tracing solutions.

While not a light source in itself, there is a fifth source lighting option: Sky Opening. This can be used in conjunction with solar and sky light global lighting, and distant light source lighting, when using ray tracing, radiosity, or particle tracing rendering modes. They restrict the calculations of the effects of solar lighting, sky lighting, and distant lights, to only that area represented by the sky opening. That is, only the illumination from solar lighting or distant lights that shine through the sky openings is considered in the calculations. Similarly, when particle tracing, all particles from these same light sources are focused to pass through the sky opening(s).

DEFINE LIGHT TOOL

Let's explore this tool in more detail. Located in the Rendering Tools tool box, or opened by selecting Settings > Rendering > Source Lighting, it is used to access MicroStation's full lighting capabilities. The Define Light tool's settings contain controls that are used to create as well as modify light sources in a model. When modifying light source values, you can select several lights at once and modify their parameters or toggle them simultaneously.

A description of the settings and their purpose follows.

Tool Setting	Effect
Mode	Sets the general type of operation to be performed using the tool: • Modify — Modify a light source. • Create — Create a light source. • Clear Shadow Map(s) — (Phong rendering only) Lets you clear existing shadow maps if the design has been phong rendered previously with Save Shadow Maps enabled in the Rendering Settings dialog box (select Settings > Rendering > General). Otherwise, clears the shadow maps from memory so that they will be recomputed.

Tool Setting	Effect
Method	(Mode set to Modify only) Sets the specific type of operation to be performed with the tool: • Edit Light — Change a selected light source's settings. • Apply Values — Apply the currently displayed settings to a selected light source. • Delete Light — Delete a light source. • Move Light — Move a light source. With directional light sources, both the location and target points are redefined separately. • Target Light — Reposition a directional light source's target point, without changing the light source's location. • Position Light — Reposition a directional light source, without changing its target point. • Dolly Light — Move a directional light source, without changing its relative direction.
Type	(Mode set to Create only) Sets the type of light source to create: Distant Light, Point Light, Spot Light, Area Light, or Sky Opening.
Name	This text field lets you define a name for the light source that you are creating. Giving light sources unique names helps you identify them if you want to modify them in some way, or delete them. Where no name is input, MicroStation gives the light a default name that identifies the type of light source. Where there are other light sources of the same type, with the same name, then the name is incremented—for example, *Spot Light, Spot Light (1), Spot Light (2)*, and so on—for spot light sources. If predefined lights are available, then this field becomes a combo box with a drop-down list that lets you select from the predefined lights. You then can give the selected light a unique name and, if required, modify the settings.
On	Sets whether the light source is on or off.
Color	Opens the Modify Color dialog box, which is used to specify a color for the light source.
Shadow	If on, the light source can cast shadows in a phong, or ray traced, rendered image, as well as with a radiosity solution, or a particle traced image. • In phong rendered images, only distant, area, and spot lights can cast shadows. • In ray traced, particle traced, or radiosity rendered images, all light source types can cast shadows.
Attenuate	If on, the light source is attenuated; its intensity decreases over distance.

Tool Setting	Effect
Lumens	Sets the light source brightness, for use with radiosity solving, particle tracing, and ray tracing with Real World Lighting enabled. Acts as a multiplier of the light source's Color and Intensity values to simulate real-world lighting values. This value, when multiplied by the intensity of the light, specifies the overall brightness, in lumens.
Intensity	Sets the intensity of the light source (default is 1.0).
Resolution	(Phong rendering only) Sets the resolution of the shadow map generated for the light source. The lower the value, the less resolute the shadows from the light source will be, and processing time will be reduced.
Distance	(Attenuate setting on only) Sets the distance from the light source, in working units, at which its attenuated intensity is one-half of its original intensity. For radiosity, particle tracing solutions and ray tracing with Real World Lighting enabled, the Distance value is ignored. In these cases, the attenuation of lighting is relative to the square of the distance from the source light.
Cone Angle	(Type set to Spot Light only) Sets the angle of the beam cone of a spot light source. Used to "focus" the beam.
Delta Angle	(Type set to Spot Light only) Sets the angle, at the edge of the beam cone, through which a Spot Light beam falls from full intensity to zero.
Cell Scale	Controls the size of the construction class light source element.
Samples	(Type set to Area Light only) Sets the number of samples to be taken when computing ray traced shadows only.
Min Samples	(Type set to Sky Opening only) Sets the minimum number of samples taken. When computing shadows from sky openings, the distance from the opening determines the number of shadows samples taken. When a point is very far from the opening, it can only see a small portion of the sky, and only the number of samples defined in "Min Samples" are taken.
Max Samples	(Type set to Sky Opening only) Sets the maximum number of samples taken. When computing shadows from Sky Openings, the distance from the opening determines the number of shadow samples taken. As points closer to the opening are illuminated, those points can see more of the sky and the number of shadow samples will increase, up to "Max Samples."
Global (button)	Opens the Global Lighting dialog box, which is used to control settings for Ambient, Flashbulb, Solar, and Sky Light.
Scan (button)	(Mode set to Modify only) Starts the light scanning process.

Tool Setting	Effect
Show Light List (icon)	Located at the top right of the Define Light dialog box, clicking this icon opens the Light List list box, which displays a list of all the source lights present in the design and any references. You can use this list box to identify a light source for modification to light sources in the active file, or to enable/disable lights in the references.
Show IES Data (icon)	Located at the bottom left of the Define Light dialog box, clicking this icon opens a group box that contains IES data details for the selected light source. • IES data — If on, the IES data is used in the calculation of the light from the light source. • Show Webs — If on, the photometric characteristics for the IES light source are displayed graphically. • Show IES Detailed Text — If on, a text window opens to display the Photometric Data File Information for the IES light source. • Rotation — Lets you enter a value to rotate the photometric characteristics for the IES light source. • Lumens — Displays the brightness value, in lumens, for the IES light source. This setting is used in ray tracing (with Real World Lighting enabled), radiosity solving, and particle tracing only. • Filename (button) — (IES Data on only) Clicking this button opens the Select IES lighting file dialog box, which lets you select a new IES lighting file for the light source.

Light Source Types

Each of the four light source types, plus sky openings, have their own characteristics. By default, the delivered light sources all have their Intensity set to 1 and their Lumens value set to 1500.

A light source's settings are stored in its representative cell. When a light source is selected, its values appear in the Define Light tool settings window.

NOTE: *IES lighting files can change the way that the point, spot, and area lights direct their light.*

Distant Light

This is a directional light source, behaving the same as solar light, producing parallel light rays, throughout the model. That is, the light source's orientation defines the direction of uniform light that illumi-

| Define Light Tool |

nates all surfaces facing in its direction. By default, distant light sources have the same brightness as solar lighting.

Only the direction of distant light sources is important, since they provide identical lighting to sunlight. No matter where in the model you create a distant light source, all surfaces facing that direction are equally illuminated. That is, they will be illuminated whether the geometry is in front of or behind the light source in the model. In creating a distant light source, you define first the location of the light source, and then its direction.

Distant lights, if pointing upward and enabled, behave differently in the various rendering modes, as follows:

- Constant, smooth, and phong — Distant light sources always will shine.
- Particle tracing — A distant light source is presumed to be a realistic representation of a sun and is considered off if pointing upward (similar to the sun being below the horizon).
- Radiosity — As with particle tracing, a distant light is presumed to be a realistic representation of a sun, and is considered off when pointing upward.
- Ray tracing — When Real World Lighting is enabled, a distant light is presumed to be a realistic representation of a sun, and is considered off when pointing upward. Otherwise, upward-pointing distant lighting will shine.

By default, the Intensity of a distant light source is defined as 1.0 and is equivalent to the intensity of the sun at the brightest point on Earth, on the brightest day when the sun is directly overhead (120,000 lumens per square meter). In contrast, for a scene requiring an overcast day, you might, for example, have a distant light with an intensity of 0.001.

To simulate the yellowish color of sunlight at high angles, you can set the light source Color to the following RGB values: 255, 247, 235 (or, on a scale of 0 to 1, to 1.00, 0.97, 0.92). To simulate the more reddish color of sunlight at low angles, such as at sunset, decrease the green and blue values from those specified.

Point Light

Acting like an electric light bulb, light from a point light is radiated in all directions from the origin of the light source.

Spot Light

This is a directional light source having a conical beam, similar to a flashlight. Spot light sources having the same Lumens and Intensity settings as a point light source may appear brighter in rendered images because the energy is restricted to the cone angle.

Area Light

Area lights are useful for many diffuse lighting situations, such as simulating fluorescent lighting, where the light source is neither a point light nor a spot light. Area light sources are created from existing polygonal shapes in the design.

Unlike the preceding light sources, area lights that are created from Primary class elements will be visible in the rendered images (as the shape of the polygon used to create them). To create an area light source that is not visible in rendered images, simply use a Construction class element to create it, and then turn off the display of constructions in the rendered view prior to rendering.

Sky Opening

Though not a light source, sky openings used in conjunction with ray tracing, radiosity solving, and particle tracing generate more efficient solutions for indoor scenes lit with solar lighting, sky light, or distant light sources. Typically, this would be through an opening in a wall or ceiling. Rather than consider the entire "sky" for calculating the lighting effect, only the lighting that is visible through the opening or openings are considered. You can define as many sky openings as you like, although one large opening can be created for a row of windows rather than a separate opening for each window.

Once you define a sky opening or multiple openings, only the light that passes through the opening is considered. If you wanted to look out the window and see, for instance, a courtyard, you would need to create a large enough sky opening and place it far enough back for light to enter the courtyard. In the case mentioned above, if you were to create the opening right outside this same window, the courtyard would be completely dark. You might think of the sky opening as a one-way light valve in which you can only see light on one side. If this seems a little confusing now, don't worry, it will make a little more sense once you visually see how it works in rendering.

PREDEFINED LIGHT SOURCES

You can create predefined light sources, which are selectable from the Define Light tool. When you have predefined light sources available and you set the Mode to Create, the Name field is replaced with an option list which contains all of the predefined lights of that type. If you select a predefined light from the list, the settings for that light replace the values in the dialog box. You then can further adjust these settings as required prior to placing the light source.

MicroStation is delivered with a selection of predefined light sources in the file *lightlist.dgn*. This file is in the *Bentley\Workspace\system\cell* directory. The location of this file, and any other DGN files containing predefined lights, is defined by the configuration variable MS_LIGHTLIST, which is defined as:

$(_USTN_SYSTEMROOT)*cell/lightlist.dgn*

$(_USTN_SITE) *cell/lightlist.dgn*

$(_USTN_PROJECTDATA) *cell/lightlist.dgn*

This lets you create your own predefined lights in a *.dgn* file named *lightlist.dgn*, which you then can place in either:

$(_USTN_SITE)cell/ (typically ...\ *Workspace\standards\cell*), or

$(_USTN_PROJECTDATA)cell/ (typically...\ *Workspace\projects\ YourProject\cell*).

Lights defined in these additional files then would be added to the initial list of predefined lights. Alternatively, you can use any DGN file in any location, and simply add the file to the MS_LIGHTLIST configuration variable.

Creating Predefined Light Sources

Creating predefined light sources is as simple as placing a cell in a DGN file. For maximum efficiency, it is highly recommended that no elements be placed in these files other than the light sources.

To create a list of predefined light sources:

1 Create a new DGN file.

2 Use the standard Define Light tool to place any number of lights, with the desired settings, anywhere in the DGN file.

PLACING LIGHTS

In the following exercises, you will be creating, placing, and adjusting each of the four types of source lights as well as creating a skylight opening. This will help you to understand source lighting and the effects their parameters can have on the rendering process. You will be rendering with Real World Lighting enabled in the Ray Tracing Settings dialog box. This will force accurate attenuation of all lights based on the lumens and intensity of the light used.

✔ Exercise 4-12: Place a Distant Source light

1. Open the DGN file *simple interior.dgn*.

2. In the Rendering Tools tool box, select the Global Lighting tool and verify the following settings:

   Ambient: Enabled and set to 0.25
   Flashbulb: Enabled and set to 0.50
   Solar and *Add Sky Light to all Solar and Distant Lights:* Disabled

3. Ray trace View 2.

   The resulting rendered view appears dark and lacks contrast.

4. In the Rendering Tools tool box, select Define Light.

   The Define Light dialog box opens.

5. In the Define Light dialog box set the following:

   Mode: Create
   Type: Distant

   In the lower left corner of the MicroStation window, the prompt reads: "Place light source > Define light position."

6. In View 1 - Top, snap to the center of the green circle at location 1 and accept with a data point.

   You will see a light cell on the end of your cursor, the graphic is in the shape of an arrow. The prompt reads "Place light source > Define light target point."

7. Still in View 1 - Top, snap to the center of the red circle at location 2 and accept with a data point to define the direction of the Distant light and to complete its placement.

| Placing Lights | **173**

When placing a distant light, you will see an arrow and dotted line in dynamics, indicating direction.

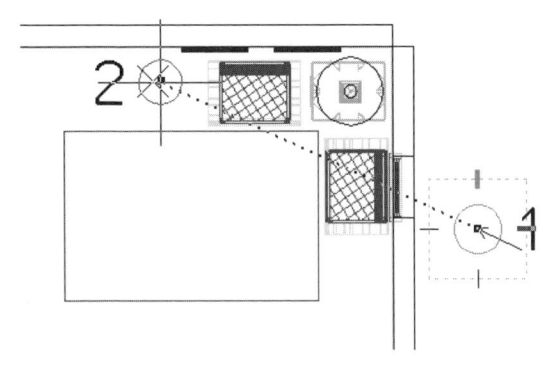

NOTE: *When placing a distant light, it is important to note that it behaves identical to solar lighting, having parallel light rays. Also, like solar light, it is not attenuated. When you place this light type, you merely define a direction vector to indicate where the sun is shining.*

8 In the Global Lighting dialog box, turn off Flashbulb.

9 Ray trace View 2, creating a new solution.

Distant light only, with an Ambient setting of 0.25.

The resulting rendered image of the room appears very dark, except where the light directly strikes a surface. Notice how the lamp shade appears brighter than the surrounding objects. This is due to the fact that the material assigned to the shade has an ambient of 1.0 while all other materials have no ambient value. The other materials, therefore, are not affected by the global ambient lighting.

| Chapter 4: Global and Source Lighting |

✔ Exercise 4-13: Add sky light to the distant light source

1. Continuing in *simple interior.dgn*, in the Global Lighting dialog, turn on Add Sky Light to all Solar and Distant Lights.

2. Ray trace View 2, creating a new solution.

    The rendering takes much longer and you really can't see much of a difference other than the light appears to come from different directions through the window. To focus the sky light energy more efficiently through the window, you will need to create a Sky Opening.

    Scene ray traced with sky light.

Creating a Sky Opening

When used in conjunction with distant lights or solar light, sky openings are a very efficient way of focusing solar energy through openings such as windows and skylights.

In the next exercise, you will create a sky opening using the same 3D model as in the previous exercise. By re-rendering the view, you will be able to better appreciate what the sky opening can do to improve your interior renderings.

✔ Exercise 4-14: Create a Sky Opening

1. Continuing in *simple interior.dgn*, select the Place Block tool, Tools > Main > Polygons.

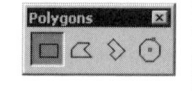

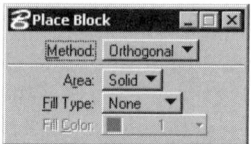

2. In View 5, with AccuDraw enabled and set to Side Rotation, place a block on the outside of the window opening by snapping to the geometry at the window corners.

| Placing Lights |

You will use this block to create the sky opening.

3 Select the Define Light tool and set the following:

Mode: Create
Type: Sky Opening
Min Samples: 16
Max Samples: 32

4 Select the block you just placed.

An arrow appears. This points in the direction the sun will shine through your sky opening.

5 Move your pointer until the arrow points toward the room interior; then accept with a data point to create the sky opening.

6 Ray trace View 2, creating a new solution.

The view is considerably brighter than that created prior to adding the sky opening.

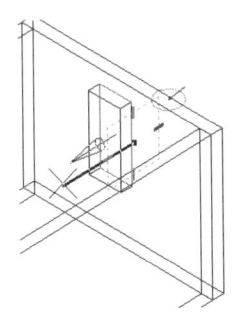

Creating a sky opening with dynamic arrow indicating the direction the light will shine.

Distant light through a sky opening.

Even though the rendering is much improved after adding the sky opening, it still is missing something. You can see some very distinctive banding in the shadows produced by sky light hitting the window mullions and the chair. To further improve this image, you can increase the sky samples and turn on Jitter sky samples.

7 Select the Define Light tool and set the following:

Mode: Edit

| Chapter 4: Global and Source Lighting |

8. Select Sky Opening in the Light Name list and change samples to the following:

   Min Samples: 64
   Max Samples: 512

9. Enable Jitter sky samples in the Global Lighting dialog box.

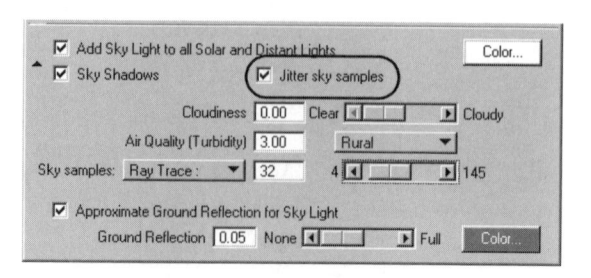

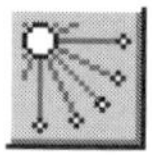

10. Ray trace View 2, creating a new solution.

    As you can see, increasing the sky opening's samples and turning on Jitter sky samples helps to reduce the shadow banding and also produces softer shadows but at the expense of increased rendering time.

Distant light with sky opening samples min 64 max 512 and Jitter sky samples.

The ray tracing routine does not compute any of the light that normally would be reflected by the walls and surfaces in the scene. As you could clearly see in the last two renderings, the side of the room not being hit directly by light remains dark. To include the reflected light, you would need

Example of the scene when particle traced.

| Placing Lights |

to create a radiosity or particle tracing lighting solution. These more advanced lighting solutions will be discussed in detail in a later chapter.

NOTE: *When ray tracing without a lighting solution from particle tracing or radiosity, only those surfaces in the direct path of the light sources are illuminated. With ray tracing alone, none of the reflected light is considered.*

NOTE: *To illuminate the ceiling in an interior scene without using particle tracing or radiosity, a workaround is to place a non-shadow-casting area light below the floor and point it at the ceiling.*

Placing Point Lights

Point lights emit light radially in all directions, like the filament of an ordinary incandescent bulb. By emitting light in all directions, point lights work well to illuminate interior scenes when ray tracing. Since point lights are non-directional, they tend to illuminate more surfaces than would a directional light such as a spot light. Since point lights are considered to be non-directional, these lights will not produce shadows when using the phong rendering routine.

In the next exercise, you will place two point lights in the scene you have been working on.

NOTE: *Depending on your computer, you may want to edit the sky opening and set the Min Samples to 16 and the Max Samples to 32 to improve the rendering performance.*

✔ Exercise 4-15: Place Point Lights

1. Continuing in ***simple interior.dgn***, select the Define Light tool and set the following:

    Mode: Create
    Type: Point Light

2. Click on the down arrow to the right of the Name field and, from the list that displays, choose Incandescent 40W.

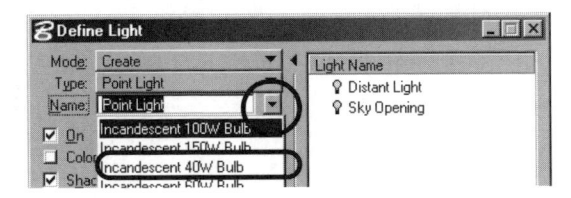

| Chapter 4: Global and Source Lighting |

3   Using 3D data points, or AccuDraw, along with the Top and Front views, place the point light in the center of the lamp shade.

Using the Top and Front views to place the light source at the center of the lamp shade.

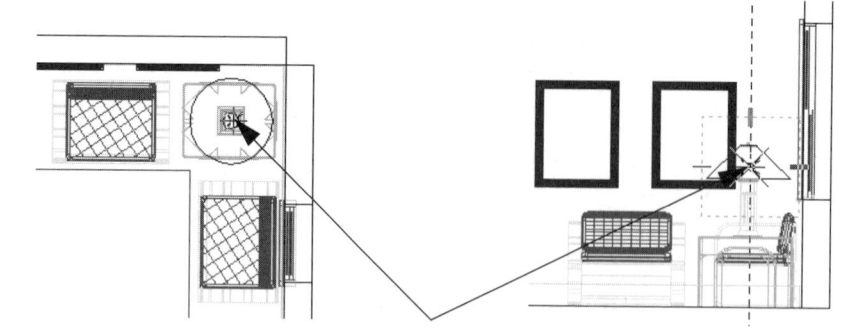

4   Ray trace View 2, creating a new solution.

The view is a little brighter with the added point light but the shadow on the wall, from the lamp shade, is too strong.

5   Select the Define Light tool and, from the list of predefined lights, choose halogen 150W Bulb.

6   Again, using the Top and Front views, place the light in the center of the room, midway between the ceiling and the floor.

Using the Top and Front views to place the light source at the center of the room.

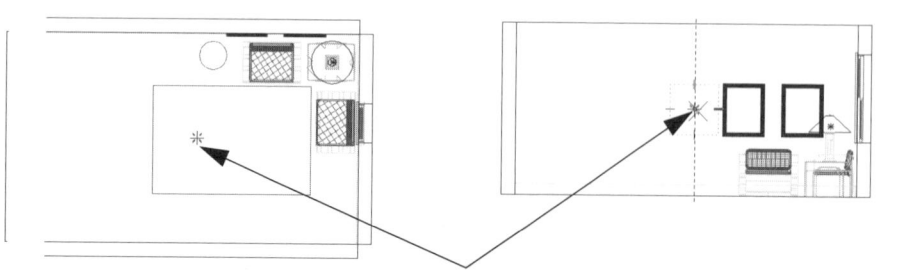

7   Again, ray trace View 2, creating a new solution.

You may want to dynamically adjust the brightness and contrast to achieve the best results.

Still, the right side of the room appears a little too

| Placing Lights | **179**

dark, since the two point lights are not very bright when compared to the distant (solar) light. They are overpowered by the distant light, and it needs to be dimmed to let the point lights contribute more to the scene.

✔ Exercise 4-16: Reduce the intensity of the Distant light

1. Continuing in *simple interior.dgn*, select the Define Light tool with the following settings:

   Mode: Modify
   Method: Edit Light

2. In the Light Name list, select the Distant Light.

3. In the light settings, change Intensity from 1.0 to 0.1

   Since the distant light is so much brighter than the interior lights, this reduction in its intensity will make the two point lights provide a greater portion of the overall light output. They will appear brighter and more effective.

4. Ray trace View 2, creating a new solution.

5. Use the Brightness and Contrast sliders to make final adjustments to the rendered image.

   Now the image looks much more convincing, and is much more evenly lit.

By lowering the intensity of the distant light, the two point lights appear brighter.

Placing Spot Lights

Spot lights are directional lights having a point of origin and a target point. These lights will produce shadows with both phong and ray trace rendering. The spot light produces a beam of light with a range or spread of light, based on a cone angle from 1° to 90°, which you define. You can define a delta angle also, which is the soft falloff of light along the edge of the cone of light produced by the spot light.

The cone angle is measured from the center, so in 3D space the cone actually is twice this angle when measured across the entire cone. The delta angle is measured from the inside edge of the defined cone angle toward the center, producing a smaller cone. A 0 delta angle produces a sharp edge where the light strikes an object. This is the effect you might expect to see on stage in a theatrical production. By using a delta angle, the edges of the cone can be softened to produce a more realistic effect. Placing a spot light requires you to define the origin or position of the light source, and a target for the spot light's beam.

Graphic showing spot light with cone angle and delta angle.

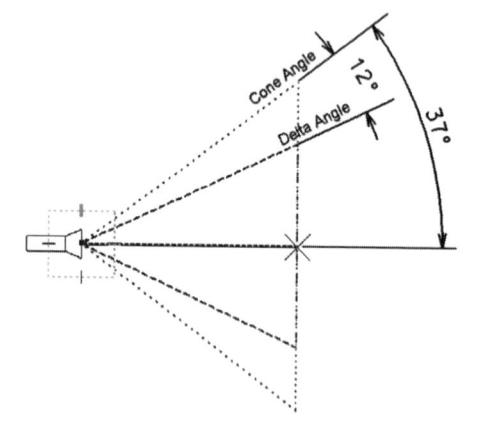

Exercise 4-17: Place spot lights

1   Open DGN file *Spot lights.dgn*.

    This model consist of an interior scene with the camera facing a wall having three pictures. You will be placing spot lights to illuminate each of these pictures. You will be giving each spot light a different cone angle and delta angle so you can see how these settings affect the rendered view.

| Placing Lights | **181**

Weighted lines are visible in the Top, Front, and Right views. You will use these as guides when placing the spot lights.

2 Enable AccuSnap if not already enabled.

3 Select the Define Light tool and set the following:

Mode: Create
Type: Spot Light
Lumens: 825
Intensity: 1.0
Cone Angle: 30
Delta Angle: 5

4 Ensure that the Light is on and enable Shadows and Attenuation.

The graphic of the spot light appears on the end of your pointer, and you are prompted to Place light source > Define Light position.

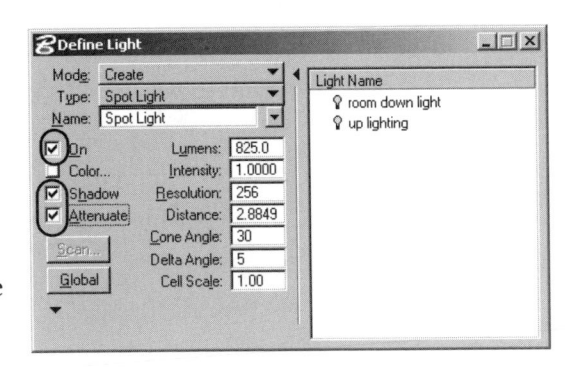

NOTE: *When you are using Real World Lighting (RWL) mode, MicroStation's ray tracing engine will correctly attenuate the lights regardless of whether the Attenuate box is checked. If, however, you render without RWL mode, your scene could be overly bright without enabling attenuation. Attenuation is covered in detail later in this chapter.*

5 In View 3, the Front view, snap to the top of the rightmost weighted line and accept with a data point.

At this point you will see dynamic cone angle and delta angle graphics as you move your pointer in a view.

The next step is to define the target for light.

6 Snap to the bottom of the same weighted line, in View 3, and accept with a data point to define the target and place the spot light.

| Chapter 4: Global and Source Lighting |

Spot light being placed in View 3.

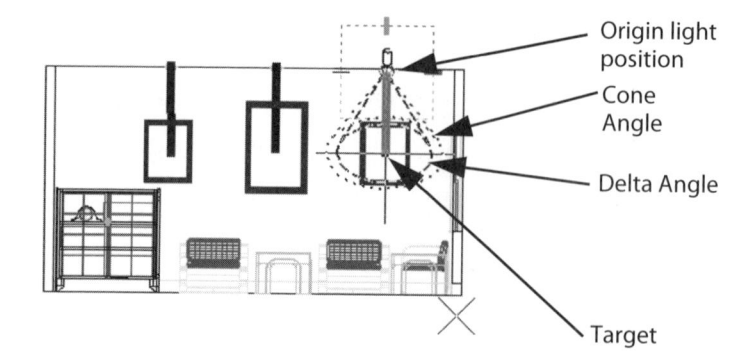

Origin light position
Cone Angle
Delta Angle
Target

7 In the Define Light dialog box, make the following changes:

   Cone Angle: 37
   Delta Angle: 12.

8 Place a second spot light using the weighted line for the middle picture. Snap to the top of the line for the light position and the bottom of it for the target.

   Notice how the cone angle and delta angle dynamic graphics are both larger than when placing the previous light.

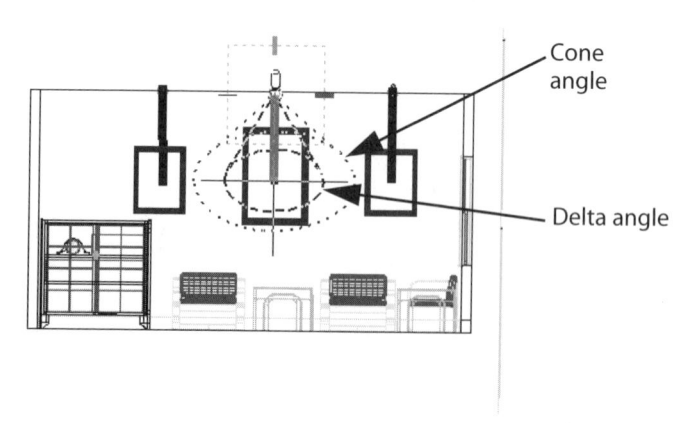

Cone angle
Delta angle

9 In the Define Light dialog box, make the following changes:

   Cone Angle: 20
   Delta Angle: 0.

10 Place a third spot light using the weighted line for the left picture. Snap to the top of the line for the light position and the bottom of it for the target.

| Placing Lights | **183**

When placing the third light with a 0 delta angle, you can clearly see from the dynamics while placing that only the cone angle is visible.

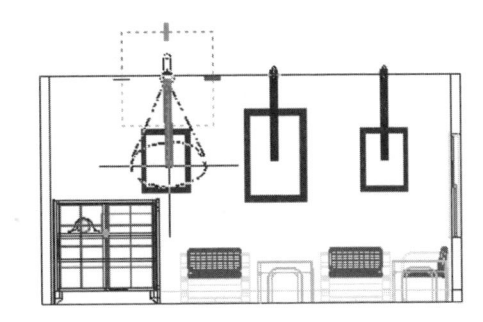

NOTE: *If you want to make your cone angle very small, the delta angle would need to be either zero or an integer smaller than the cone angle.*

11 Ray trace View 2, creating a new solution.

You can clearly make out the differences in each spot light in the ray traced image. The light on the right with a cone angle of 30 and delta angle of 5 produces a smaller spot on the wall and the edge is not a soft as the middle light. The middle light with a cone angle of 37 and delta angle of 12 produced a large cone with a much softer edge than the first light you placed. Looking at the left light with a cone angle of 20 and a delta angle of 0, it is pretty apparent that this cone is smaller than the first two and has a razor sharp edge since the delta angle is 0.

Looking at the image, you may decide that the center spotlight is more to your taste, so a quick edit of the already placed spot lights can be made to make the outer lights match the middle one.

| Chapter 4: Global and Source Lighting |

✔ Exercise 4-18: Edit already placed lights

1. Continuing in *Spot lights.dgn*, in the Rendering Tools tool box, select the Define Light tool.

2. If necessary, click the Show Light List icon to open the Light Name list box.

3. In the Define Light dialog box, set the following:

   Mode: Modify
   Method: Edit Light

4. In the Define Light dialog box light list box, click and drag to select all three spot lights in the list.

5. While all the spot lights are selected, set the following:

   Cone Angle: 37
   Delta Angle: 12.

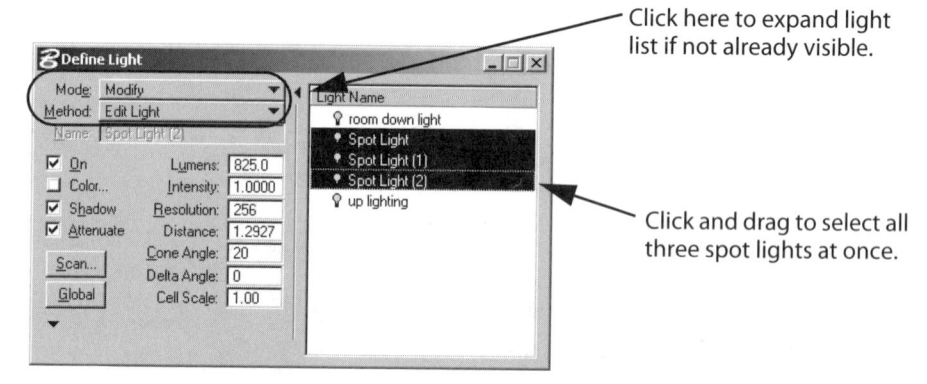

   — Click here to expand light list if not already visible.

   Click and drag to select all three spot lights at once.

6. Ray trace View 2, creating a new solution.

Ray traced image with all spot lights having the same values.

| Placing Lights | **185**

As you just experienced, selecting several lights and making changes is very easy. You can use this method to make any value changes available in the Define Light dialog box. For instance, you could have changed the color, disabled shadows, or turned off the lights, just as easily. You cannot, however, change a light type from one to another by editing. In other words, you cannot, for example, turn a distant light into a point light, or any other type, by editing the light.

Creating Area Lights

Area light sources are useful for simulating lighting such as that from fluorescent lighting. You can create an area light source from any existing convex polygon. That is, you first define a (polygonal) shape for the geometry. You then select the Define Light tool, with Mode set to Create and Type set to Area Light, select the geometry, and then define the direction that the area light "shines."

Polygons used to create area light sources may have any number of vertices, but they must be convex polygons.

During processing, area light sources are first converted into triangular-shaped light sources. A rectangular area light source, for example, is converted into two triangular light sources, while a pentagon is converted into five triangular light sources, one for each edge.

If a radiosity solution is being computed, each (converted) triangular light source is processed separately. In a design containing only one rectangular light source, therefore, there will be shots for two light sources (one for each triangle).

Area light sources have an additional setting, Samples, that is applicable only to ray tracing. This includes the ray traced display of radiosity and particle tracing solutions where Ray Trace Direct Illumination is enabled. The Samples setting affects how the light source is treated during ray tracing processing. The effects of the settings are most noticeable in the appearance of shadows cast by the area light source. Higher Samples values produce smoother shadows but take longer to process.

The size of the area light source also affects the appearance of shadows. Smaller area light sources may require fewer samples than larger ones to produce reasonable ray tracing results.

| Chapter 4: Global and Source Lighting |

✔ Exercise 4-19: Create area lights

1. Open the DGN file *office scene.dgn*.
2. Ray trace View 2.

    This model contains only one light source, a point light in the desk lamp. The rendering is fairly dark with just this one light.

    The ceiling of the model has two rectangular holes into which two blocks have been drawn. These are clearly seen in View 4. You will now use these blocks to create area lights.

3. Select the Define Light tool.
4. In the Define Light tool settings, set the following:

    Mode: Create
    Type: Area Light
    Lumens: 2800
    Samples: 4

5. Select the left block with a data point (reset if you select the ceiling, so that the block highlights).
6. Move your pointer downward until the dynamic arrow points down, indicating the direction the area light will shine, and accept with a second data point to create the area light.
7. Repeat this procedure for the remaining block, to create a second area light.
8. Ray trace View 2, creating a new solution.

(Left) With desk lamp point light; and *(right)* after adding two area lights.

| Placing Lights | **187**

NOTE: *To improve the shadows cast by the area lights, make the Samples field higher. This can be changed after placing the light by editing the light with the Define Light tool.*

NOTE: *It is a good idea to use Construction class elements for your area lights if you intend to use texture maps for the light fixtures. You then can turn off the display of Construction elements to ensure that only the light from the area light is present in the rendering, and not the original element used to construct it.*

Attenuation

Attenuation is the falloff of a light's intensity over distance. In the real world, the intensity of all manmade lights falls off, or diminishes, with the square of the distance. Real World Lighting forces attenuation on all lights except solar and distant lights.

With Real World Lighting off, ray tracing behaves as in earlier releases, ignoring the lumens values of light sources. It uses the attenuation distance specified for each light, where the intensity of the light falls off linearly with distance (as opposed to the square of the distance). This mode is provided for compatibility with earlier ray tracing, as well as to provide lighting that is more compatible with phong renderings.

If you are not using Real World Lighting, it is very import to enable the Attenuation setting for your source lights, and specifying the distance over which the light will halve in intensity. If left disabled, or with no attenuation, the source light will be overly bright since the light's intensity would remain the same over an infinite distance. Forgetting to use attenuation is a common mistake made by newer users.

✔ **Exercise 4-20: Attenuation of source lights**

1   Open the DGN file *demo attenuation.dgn*.

2   Select the Render tool with Render Mode set to Ray Trace.

3   Click the Open Ray Tracing settings dialog icon.

    The Ray Tracing dialog box opens.

| Chapter 4: Global and Source Lighting |

4. Verify that Real World Lighting is enabled.

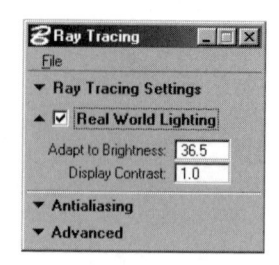

5. Ray trace View 1.

   The view is ray traced with Real World Lighting, forcing attenuation on all the source lights used in this scene.

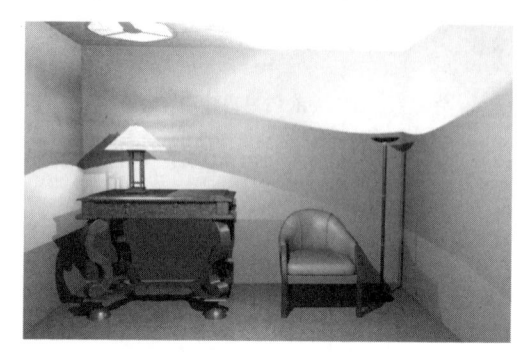

   Rendering with Real World Lighting on.

6. In the Ray Tracing dialog box, turn off Real World Lighting.

   With Real World Lighting (RWL) turned off, the lights will not attenuate unless checked and a distance entered. The design file currently has attenuation turned off on all lights. Leaving it off, you can render a view and then enable attenuation and render again to compare results.

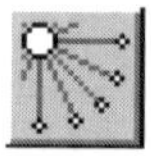

7. Ray trace View 2.

   The image is quite bright and has a noticeable hot spot on the wall between the table lamp and the floor lamp. Since none of the light's intensity is falling off over distance, the hot spot is coming from the point light located in the center of the room.

   Ray trace without RWL, and no attenuation.

   You can turn on Attenuation for light sources, individually, when Real World Lighting is not enabled.

| Placing Lights | **189**

✔ **Exercise 4-21: Turn on attenuation for each light source**

1   Select the Define Light tool and set the following:

    Mode: Modify
    Method: Edit

2   Click and drag on the lights in the list to select all three lights.

3   Turn on Attenuate.

4   Ray trace View 3.

    With all three lights attenuated, the hot spots are no longer present in the rendered image.

Attenuation Distance

The attenuation distance refers to the distance from the light source where the light intensity is reduced to 1/2 of its original value. This reduction is linear in nature when using the ray trace rendering mode. When placing spot lights, the distance field will be based on the distance to the target and automatically filled in.

RWL off and all lights attenuated.

For area lights and point lights, you will need to enter the distance in this field. The distance should be the distance from the light to the surface you intend to illuminate. You may want to use the measure tool to accurately determine this distance. When using ray tracing with Real World Lighting, radiosity or particle tracing, attenuation is calculated based on the brightness of the light in lumens and the value of this field is ignored.

Review Questions

1. What are the three main sources of Global Lighting found in every DGN file?
2. What global light source is all-pervasive, equally illuminating all surfaces?
3. Does the flashbulb cast a shadow?
4. By default, what direction is north as it relates to solar light?
5. What lights types are never attenuated?
6. Name the four different types of source lights.
7. What is the special source lighting type that is not actually a light?
8. Which one of the four source light types behaves identical to the sun?
9. Which one of the four source light types radiates light in all directions from the light's origin?
10. What can you do to improve the shadows cast by an area light?

Chapter Summary

In this chapter, you learned about global and source lighting and how lighting is one of the most important, if not the most important, aspect of producing renderings from 3D computer models. You were taught the importance of ambient light and how the materials that you create can be made to utilize this light, from completely ignoring it to amplifying its effect on your renderings. You learned how Flashbulb works and how it can be used to illuminate your scenes. In this chapter, you also were taught how each of the source light types used by MicroStation differs and how they can best be used to effectively render your scenes. You learned how a special sky light opening can be used to more effectively bring light through windows and openings in structures. Lights play such an important role in the rendering process that you will be given a more in-depth look at all of these lights in later chapters.

5 Introduction to Materials

MicroStation's rendering capabilities let you create photorealistic images of your designs. To create these images, elements in your models need to have materials applied to them such that, when rendered, they take on the appearance of the real-life object rather than just the color of the design element.

Material definitions and assignments in MicroStation rely on two types of files:

- Palette *(.pal)* file — where material definitions are stored.

- Material *(.mat)* file — material allocation table that references the palette files and records the assignments by level/color.

Both palette and material files are ASCII text files. Typically, each DGN file will have one material *(.mat)* file, which will reference one or more palette *(.pal)* files. This lets you store similar materials in separate palette files. For example, all your glass definitions can be stored in a single palette file, all your floor definitions in another, and so on.

In previous chapters, you worked with DGN files and models that already were set up to render. They were set up with both palette and material files, containing the material assignment information. In addition, each model already had custom materials assigned or attached to the geometry.

MicroStation's Color Table

When you render a 3D scene in MicroStation without a material file, the surfaces are rendered using the element color. The currently attached color table is used when a material file is not present. You can customize the color table, which consists of 255 colors each of which can be customized from a palette of 16,777,216 possible colors. Changes made to the color table automatically are applied to any rendered image where an assignment from a palette file has not been made via a material file.

✔ **Exercise 5-1: Render with MicroStation's color table**

1. Open *materials.dgn*.

   The simple 3D model in this file consists of a matrix of spheres on a square surface, with no material assignments.

2. Select the Render tool with the following tool setting:

   Render Mode: Ray Trace

3. Enter a data point in View 2.

   The spheres are rendered with their respective element color based on the color values associated with the current color table. Note, in particular, the blue sphere second from the left in the topmost row in the view.

4. Open the default color table (Settings > Color Table).

5. Double-click on the first blue square in the color table, color 1.

   Alternatively, select color 1 and then click the Change button.

6. In the Modify Color dialog box, change the Color Component RGB values to the following:

   Red: 175
   Green: 240
   Blue: 255

| MicroStation's Color Table |

7 Click OK.

The Modify Color dialog box closes, and the color square for color 1 changes to the newly defined color.

8 Click Attach.

The modified color table is attached, and the color of the second sphere, in the topmost row, updates to reflect the modification you just made.

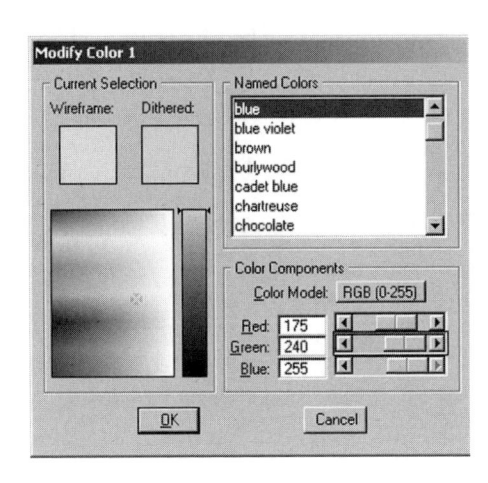

9 Ray trace View 2, using Create New Solution.

The second sphere renders in the modified color.

You have seen the difference made by editing a single color in the color table. Next you will attach a previously created color table with custom colors.

✔ **Exercise 5-2: Attach a different color table**

1 Continuing in *materials.dgn*, open the Color Table dialog box (Settings > Color Table).

2 In the Color Table dialog box, select File > Open.

3 Locate *materials.tbl* in the course \dgn folder and click OK.

The color definitions stored in *materials.tbl* are displayed in the Color Table dialog box. Next, you need to attach the new color definitions to the active design file.

4 Click Attach.

All of the wireframe spheres are updated to the new color definitions.

5 Ray trace View 2.

Notice that the elements are rendered in the new colors as specified by the color table.

Now, you will return the model to its original state by attaching the default MicroStation color table.

6 Open the Color Table Settings dialog box.

7 From the Color Table dialog box, select File > Default.

8 Click Attach.

The model returns to its original appearance.

You have seen that the model renders with the elements using their defined colors when there is no material table attached, and no materials assigned to the elements. It's time now to look at how you can assign materials to elements in your model.

ASSIGNING MATERIALS

Typically, the most common method of assigning a material is simply by level and color. That is, the material is assigned to all elements of a particular color on a particular level (multiple colors and levels also may be defined).

Remember, a palette file stores the material definitions, while a material table stores the assignment information (which material is assigned to which level and color combination). In the following exercises, you will use an existing palette file and assign a material from it, to elements in the model.

✔ **Exercise 5-3: Assign materials based on level and color**

1 Open the file *simple stuff.dgn*.

This model, consists of two 3D columns. It has been saved with the four standard views open — Top, Front, Right, and Isometric. Although, when rendered, the outside shape of both columns is identical, the left column is constructed from four separate solids, while the right column is a single united SmartSolid. Both columns are on the same level, and are the same color.

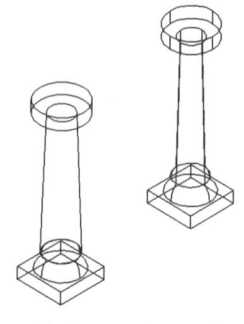

Columns shown in wireframe.

| Assigning Materials |

2 In the Rendering Tools tool box, select the Apply Material tool.

The name on the Apply Material tool dialog box varies, depending on the current operation that is selected via its icons. For example, if you select the Remove Assignment icon, the dialog box title will change to Remove Material Assignment.

Currently, the dialog box has most options disabled, since no palette file is associated with the material file.

Before you can make any assignments, you need to open a palette file.

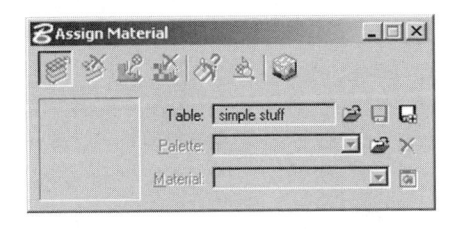

Assign Material dialog with no palette.

3 Click the Open Palette icon to browse for a palette file.

The Open Palette dialog box opens.

4 In the Open Palette dialog box, navigate to the course \dgn folder and select *simple stuff.pal*.

5 If necessary, select the Assign by Color/Level icon in the Apply Material dialog box.

Assign Material dialog after choosing the *simple stuff* palette file.

Column dark is selected as the material to be assigned since it is the first material in the material list.

6 Move the pointer over any of the model's geometry and enter a data point to select it.

7 Accept the assignment with a second data point.

8 Select Render from the Rendering Tools tool box, with the following tool setting:

Render Mode: Ray Trace

Since this is the first time you have ray traced this model, the only option available is Create New Solution.

9 Enter a data point in View 2.

| Chapter 5: Introduction to Materials |

In the resulting image the columns both have the same material applied, as they are both on the same level and the geometry for both is the same color.

Next, you will change the color of the right column to see how this affects the rendering.

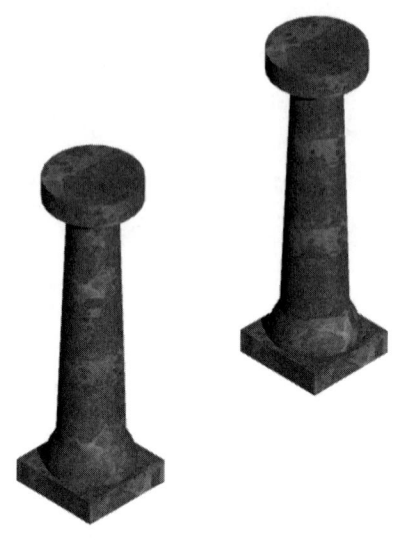

✔ Exercise 5-4: Effect on material of changing element color

1. Continuing in *simple stuff.dgn*, select the Change Element Attributes tool with the following settings:

    Method: Change
    Color: On and set to red (color 3)

2. Identify the right column and accept with a data point to effect the change.

    The right column is a single element, a SmartSolid, and now is red.

3. Ray trace View 2.

Notice that the right-hand column now is rendered in the new element color (red) rather than the material definition assigned earlier. Since the method used for the material assignment was Level/Color, changing the level or the color of the geometry causes the material assignment to be lost.

Similarly, if you change an element to a level/color combination that has a different material assignment, the geometry will render with that material.

| Attaching Materials |

In the foregoing, you used the most common method for applying materials to a model, based on level and color. This method is especially effective when you need to assign a material to a large number of objects in a design. But, as you saw, changing the color or level of an element results in elements losing their material assignment. In the following section, you will learn another method for assigning material definitions.

ATTACHING MATERIALS

MicroStation provides an alternative to the level/color method for applying materials, where you attach material definitions directly to the elements. This works much like other display attributes such as color, weight, or line style. Once a material is attached to an element, that element will render with the attached material regardless of the element's color or level. The only caveat is that MicroStation must have access to the attached material's definition, which resides in a palette file *(.pal)*, via a reference in a material file *(.mat)*. If not, the element will render in its native color, or in a material assigned by level and color if there is one. Thus, you must ensure that you have a material file for the DGN file that, in turn, references the correct palette files for the attached materials.

NOTE: *Any material that is attached to an element has priority over materials assigned by level and color.*

Exercise 5-5: Attach material to one of the columns

1. Continuing in *simple stuff.dgn*, select the Apply Material tool.
2. In the Material menu, select *Column light* to make it the active material.
3. In the Assign Materials dialog box, click the Attach icon.
4. Identify the right column.
5. Accept with a second data point, away from the geometry, in any view.

   The material *Column light* now is attached to the right column.

6. Ray trace View 2.

The right-hand column renders with the material *Column light*.

Now that the material for the right column is attached, not assigned by level/color, you can change the column to any level or color and it still will render with the attached material.

✔ **Exercise 5-6: Change the level/color of the right column**

1. Select the Change Element Attributes tool with the following tool settings:

   Method: Change
   Level: On and set to level Another Level
   Color: On and set to color 7

2. Identify the right column and accept with a data point to effect the changes.

   The column now appears in a cyan color.

3. Ray trace View 2.

   The right column still renders with the *Column light* material even though you changed both its level and color.

Attaching materials has many advantages over assigning materials by level/color. For instance, you can create a cell library with photorealistic materials attached to the geometry for each cell. This results in render-ready cells that can be placed in any design without concern about level and color assignments. As long as MicroStation can find the definition of the material attached to the cell geometry, the cell will render with the correct material definition.

If the attached definitions cannot be found in any open palettes, the definitions will appear as missing in the Material Editor dialog box. When this occurs, the required definitions can be imported into the current palette. Alternatively, you can open a palette containing the definitions that are attached.

MODIFYING MATERIALS USING QUERY

Occasionally you will need to change a material that someone else has created and assigned, or you may forget which material is assigned to an

| Removing Assigned or Attached Materials | **199**

element. The easiest way to determine current material assignments or attachments is using the Query Material tool.

✔ **Exercise 5-7: Use Query Material to check materials and assignments**

1. Continuing in *simple stuff.dgn*, select the Apply Material tool.

   From the earlier exercise, where you attached a material, the dialog box title reads Attach Material. Note the current preview material is *Column light*, again from the earlier exercise.

2. In the Attach Material dialog box, click the Query Material icon.

   The dialog box name changes to Query Material.

3. Enter a data point over the left column.

   The preview image changes to *Column dark*, the material assigned to the left column.

4. Double-click on the material preview window in the Query Material dialog box.

   The Material Editor dialog box opens with the material, identified by the Query Material tool, ready for modification.

5. Select Query Material.

6. Enter a data point over the right column.

   The preview changes and the Material Editor dialog box updates with the material *Column light* ready for editing.

7. Close the Material Editor dialog box.

   NOTE: *Using the Query Material tool in conjunction with AccuSnap provides instant information regarding material assignments or attachments. Simply by moving your cursor over elements of your model, information will display regarding any material assignment or attachment.*

REMOVING ASSIGNED OR ATTACHED MATERIALS

There may come a time when you want to remove the association of a material to one or more elements in your model. In the case of a material assignment by color/level, this could be very important. With these

| Chapter 5: Introduction to Materials |

assignments, changing geometry color or level could leave you with a level/color assignment that is no longer relevant (sometimes referred to as a *zombie* assignment).

✔ Exercise 5-8: Remove material

1   Continuing in *simple stuff.dgn*, in the Rendering Tools tool box, select the Define Material tool.

The Material Editor dialog box opens. This is the same dialog box that you opened in the previous exercise by double-clicking the material preview in the Query Material dialog box.

The Material Editor dialog box displays materials currently available. Clicking the + sign for a material displays the Level and Color for assignments (such as *Column dark*) and the element type and model name for material attachments (such as *Column light*).

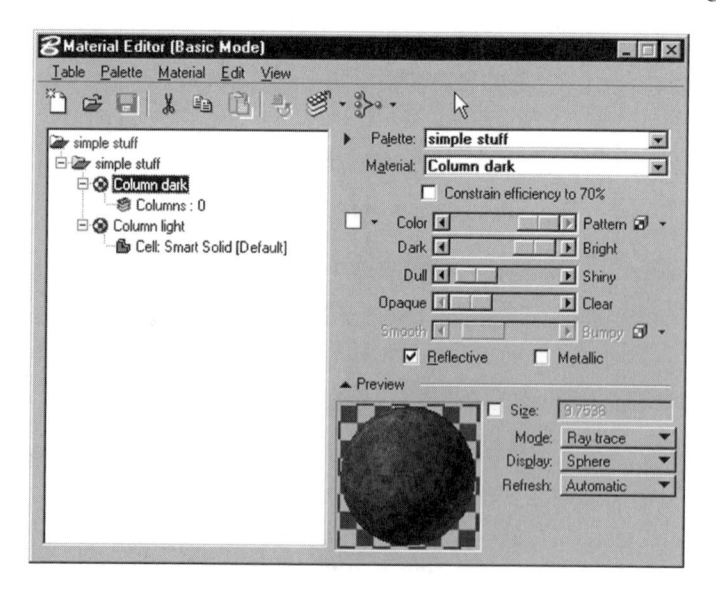

Material Editor with assignments and attachments shown.

2   Use the Element Selection tool to select all the geometry that makes up the left-hand column.

3   Select the Change Element Attributes tool with the following settings:

Method: Change
Level: Foundation
Color: 6

| Removing Assigned or Attached Materials |

4 Enter a data point in any view to accept the change.

5 Release the selection set by entering a data point away from the geometry while the Selector tool is active.

NOTE: *Since the material assignment still exists but there is no geometry that meets the criteria as previously assigned, the material assignment becomes a zombie. If you look in the Material Editor, you will see that Column dark is still assigned to the level Columns and color 0. If you then place some new geometry on the Columns level that is color 0, you might end up with an unwanted assignment.*

6 Undo the element attribute change.

This returns the column's element attributes to level Columns and color 0.

7 Select the Apply Material tool and, in its dialog box, click the Remove Assignment icon.

The name for the dialog box now becomes Remove Material Assignment.

8 Identify any element in the left column.

The element highlights.

9 Accept the removal with a data point.

The assignment is removed. Confirm this by looking in the Material Editor and notice that the assignment is no longer listed.

10 In the Remove Material Assignment dialog box, click the Remove Attachment icon.

11 Identify the right column.

12 Accept the removal with a data point.

The attachment is removed, as can be confirmed in the Material Editor dialog box.

NOTE: *As an alternative method, you can right-click on the material assignment or attachment in the Material Editor list box and select Delete from the menu to remove unwanted assignments or attachments.*

| Chapter 5: Introduction to Materials |

WORKING WITH SOLIDS

When working with SmartSolids or Feature Solids in a design, you have the option to attach materials either to the entire solid or to the individual faces of the solid.

In the sample model you are working with, the left column consists of individual solids, while the right column is a single united SmartSolid. If you wanted to change the materials for the columns so that the dark material was at the top and base sections, with the light material in the center section, it can be done with both columns as the following exercises will show.

✔ Exercise 5-9: Attach materials to solids

1 Continuing in *simple stuff.dgn*, select the Apply Material tool and, in its dialog box, click the Attach icon.

   The name of the tool dialog box changes to Attach Material.

2 In the Attach Material dialog box, set the material to be *Column dark*.

3 Identify the top (cylinder) of the left column and accept with a data point away from the geometry.

4 Identify the base (slab) of the left column and accept with a data point away from the geometry.

5 Identify the top of the right column and accept with a data point away from the geometry.

6 Set the material to be *Column light*.

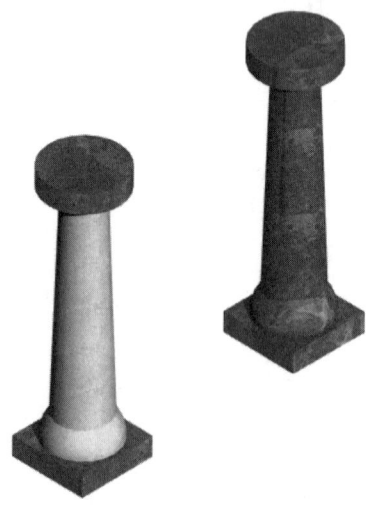

Rendered result after attaching materials to solids.

| Working with Solids | 203

7 In turn, identify and accept the two center sections of the left column.

8 Ray trace View 2.

Notice that the right column has the *Column dark* material applied to all of it, not just the top section that you identified. This is because it is a single element, a SmartSolid. The left column, on the other hand, consists of four separate solids, thus letting you apply different materials to each section. To get the same result on the right column, you can attach the light material just to the required faces of the SmartSolid, as follows.

✔ Exercise 5-10: Attach materials to faces of a SmartSolid

1 Continuing in *simple stuff.dgn*, select the Apply Material tool and click the Attach icon.

2 Identify the right column.

The entire column highlights.

3 Move the pointer over the solid and note how the separate surfaces highlight.

4 Move the pointer so that the rounded section, just above the square base, is highlighted and enter a data point.

5 Holding down the <Ctrl> key, move the pointer so that the surface just above it is highlighted and accept with data point (still with the <Ctrl> key depressed).

6 Releasing the <Ctrl> key, move the pointer away from the geometry and accept with a data point.

7 Ray trace View 2.

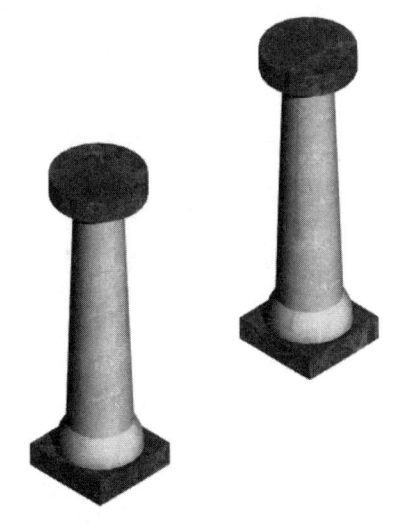

Rendered results after attaching material to the faces of the right column.

Notice that the SmartSolid (right column) now has a different material applied to its center surfaces.

In the Material Editor, you can see the attachment of the two materials to the SmartSolid elements.

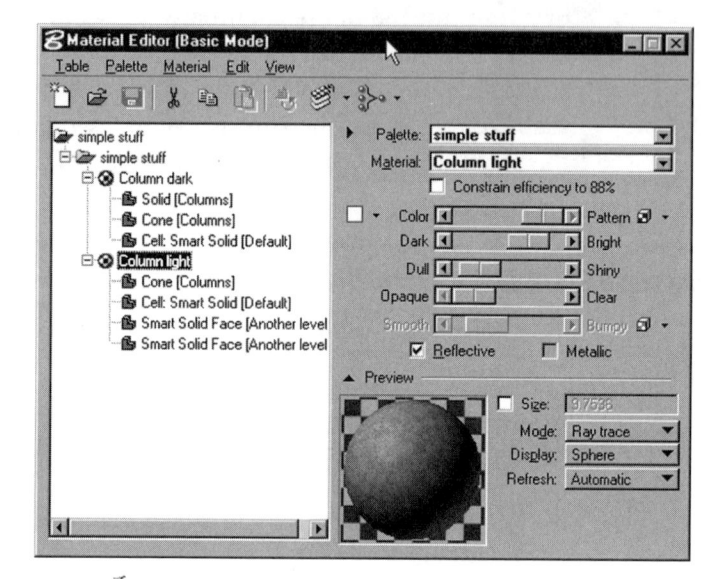

Material Editor with SmartSolid Attachments shown in list box.

RENDER READY CELLS

Now that you have learned how to attach materials to your geometry, you may already be thinking of useful ways to utilize this feature. I have been using this method for years to create what I refer to as *render ready cells*. The cell library used in next exercise contains numerous cells, all of which have photorealistic material attached rather than assigned. Since the materials are attached, you can place the cells in any design file without worrying about a conflict with your current assignments. Regardless of their color or level, the render ready cells will render with the attached materials, provided a path to the material definition can be found in any open palette.

In the next exercise, you will be placing a few render ready cells to quickly add content to a small room.

| Render Ready Cells | 205

✔ Exercise 5-11: Use render ready cells

1. Open the design file **RR Cells.dgn**.

   You can see several weighted points.

2. Ray trace View 2.

   The view renders and, as you can see, the lighting looks good and materials have been applied.

3. Attach the *RR Cells.cel library* file, Element > Cells.

   The Cell Library dialog box opens.

4. Select Chair Emile Lounge from the list of cells and click the Placement button or double-click on the cell in the list to make this cell the active cell.

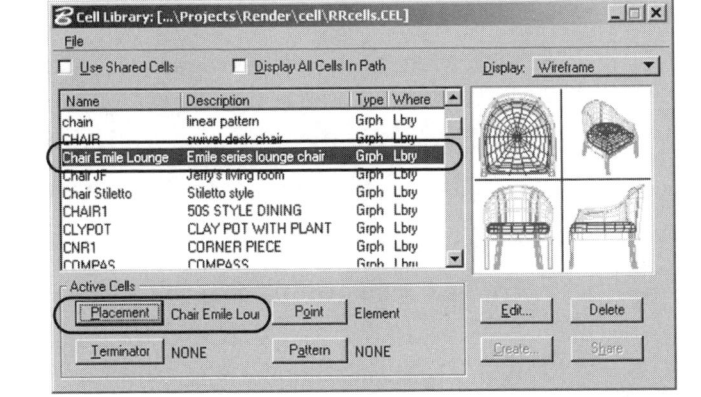

RRcells cell library with Chair Emile Lounge selected.

5. Open the Cell tool bar Tools > Main > Cells.

6. Click on the Place Active Cell tool.

   The cell will be visible as you move your cursor in a view.

7. In the Place Active Cell dialog box, set the Active Angle to 300.

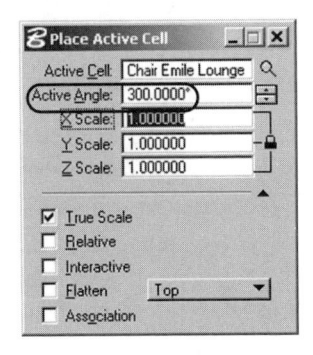

The Place Active Cell dialog.

| Chapter 5: Introduction to Materials |

8 With the AccuDraw compass rotated to Top, snap to the magenta-colored weighted point in view 1 and enter a data point to place the active cell.

9 Select the Mirror tool, Tools > Main > Manipulate.

10 Apply Mirror copy about Horizontal to the cell you just placed. When prompted to identify an element, pick the chair and then snap to the blue weighted point in the view as the mirror line. Enter a data point to accept the mirrored copy.

11 Select Element > Cells to reopen the Cell Library dialog box.

12 From the list of cell names, scroll down and select *Small round table*. Click on the Placement button to make this the active cell.

13 Click on the Place Active Cell tool.

The table cell will be visible as you move your cursor into a view.

14 With AccuDraw compass rotated to Top, snap to the blue weighted point in View 1 and enter a data point to place the cell.

15 From the list of cell names, scroll up and select *floor lamp*. Click on the Placement button to make this the active cell.

16 Click on the Place Active Cell tool.

The floor lamp cell will be visible as you move your cursor into a view.

17 With AccuDraw compass rotated to Top, snap to the green weighted point in View 1 and enter a data point to place the cell.

18 Ray trace View 2, creating a new solution.

Notice that the cells are rendering in their element colors, and they do not appear to have materials attached.

NOTE: *The next step will be one of the most import things to know about when using render ready cells. As mentioned in the beginning, in order to render with the attached materials, MicroStation must be able to find the definitions of the attached materials in an open palette. Since the material (.MAT) file was already saved with a palette statement pointing to a palette containing the RR Cells material definitions, you would think the cells would have rendered with these materials. In fact, MicroStation has no way of knowing that these*

| Render Ready Cells | **207**

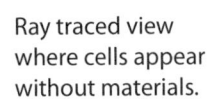

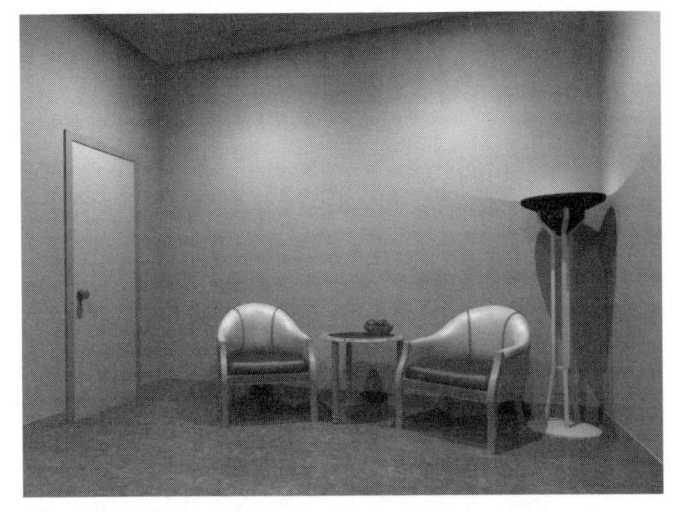

Ray traced view where cells appear without materials.

materials were introduced, since they were added using the Place Cell tool. In order for MicroStation to reparse the file and look for these materials, you will need to enter a key-in.

19 Open a Key-in window if not already open: Utilities > Key-in.

20 In the Key-in window, enter **define materials**.

> **NOTE:** *You only need to key in* **de m**; *you don't have to type every character.*

21 Ray trace View 2, creating a new solution.

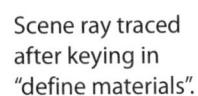

Notice that the cells now render with realistic materials attached.

Scene ray traced after keying in "define materials".

| Chapter 5: Introduction to Materials |

22 From the Cell Library dialog box, make *PICT3* the active cell.

23 In the Place Active Cell dialog box, set the Active Angle to 0.

24 Snap to the red weighted point on the wall in View 4, and enter a data point to place the picture.

25 Ray trace View 2, creating a new solution.

26 Notice that the cell you added does not have materials and renders with just the element colors.

27 Key in **define materials**.

28 Ray trace View 2, creating a new solution.

Now the cell of the picture renders with the attached materials.

Final render with picture added.

As you can see from the previous exercise, render ready cells provide a very quick and efficient method of adding photorealistic entourage to your 3D scenes.

NOTE: *When creating your own render ready cells, you should consider carefully naming the materials that you will be attaching to the individual pieces of geometry. You should use a name that describes where it is being used. For instance, the cell Chair Emile Lounge uses two materials,* Emile chair cushions *and* Emile chair legs. *By editing these definitions using the Material Editor, you can* *completely change the look of the cell without attaching another material.*

NOTE: *When using RR cells, consider creating a* RR Cells.pal *palette with your original definitions. You can easily copy these definitions into your current working palette, and then any edits you make will only be for the current scene, leaving your original definitions unaltered.*

REVIEW QUESTIONS

1. Material definitions and assignments rely on what two types of files?
2. Without a material file, elements in MicroStation are rendered based on element color. What determines the element color?
3. Which has precedence: a material assignment or an attachment?
4. If a material is already attached or assigned, what tool can be used to easily determine what material is used?
5. What file stores the material definitions?
6. What method is used to apply materials to render ready cells?

CHAPTER SUMMARY

In this chapter, you were introduced to MicroStation's material assignment and editing tools. You learned how to apply materials to geometry in a model and how to remove material assignments where necessary. You learned how to attach materials to individual faces of solids. To see the power of attached materials in action, you also learned to use render ready cells.

6 Defining and Applying Materials

When you create a 3D model from scratch, you will need to create and/or assign materials for photorealism. The model otherwise will be rendered only in its element's colors. In the previous chapter, you were introduced briefly to the tools for assigning materials to elements in a model. This chapter teaches you, in more detail, how to create and assign materials to your models.

THE MATERIAL EDITOR

One of the most important rendering tools for achieving photorealistic results is the Material Editor. Whether you are a visualization novice or an expert, you will spend a great deal of time with this tool, and mastery of it is all-important in visualization projects both small and large. The Material Editor provides you with the means to create custom materials with such interesting properties as transparency, translucency, reflection, refraction, texture maps, and more.

| Chapter 6: Defining and Applying Materials |

✔ Exercise 6-1: Tour the MicroStation Material Editor

1. Open the file *materials.dgn*.

2. In the Rendering Tools tool box, select the Define Materials tool.

   The Material Editor dialog box opens. Since no palettes are open, nor materials defined, most items are grayed out. To start off, you must create a palette or open an existing material palette.

3. In the Material Editor, select Palette > Open.

4. In the Open Palette dialog box, locate and select the file *starter.pal* in the course \dgn directory.

5. Click OK.

   The material definitions in the selected palette file are read into MicroStation, and a list of materials now appears in the palette tree on the left side of the Material Editor dialog box.

   NOTE: *Using this starter palette is an excellent way to create new materials. You can select the finish you want, copy those material properties to a newly named material, and then make edits such as changing the color or adding a texture.*

6. In the Preview section, set Mode to Ray Trace.

   NOTE: *It is a good idea to change the Preview Mode to Ray Trace so that you can see the reflections, transparency, and refraction properties for the selected material.*

7. Click each material listed and observe the preview image.

   Note the difference between the two glass materials, *glass start no refraction* and *glass start refract*.

8. Click the starter folder icon in the Material Editor.

   All the materials are displayed in the preview window as phong rendered spheres. As you move your pointer over a material in the preview, you will see the material's name display—that is, provided the focus is on the Material Editor dialog box.

| The Material Editor |

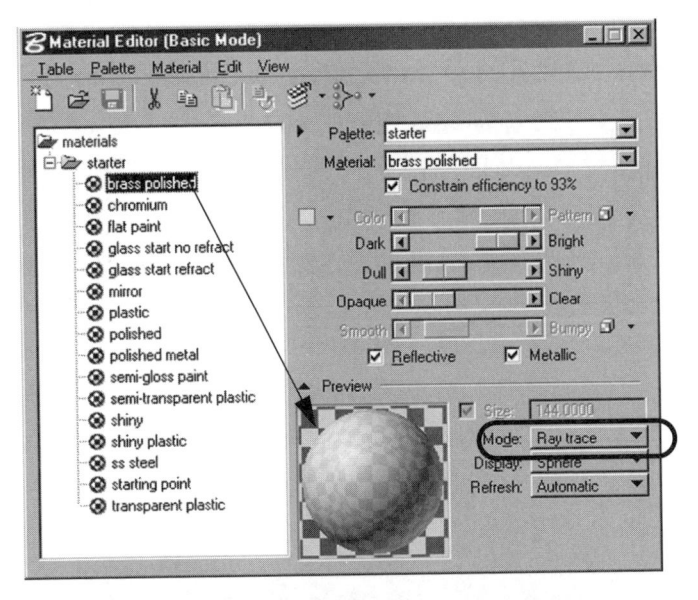

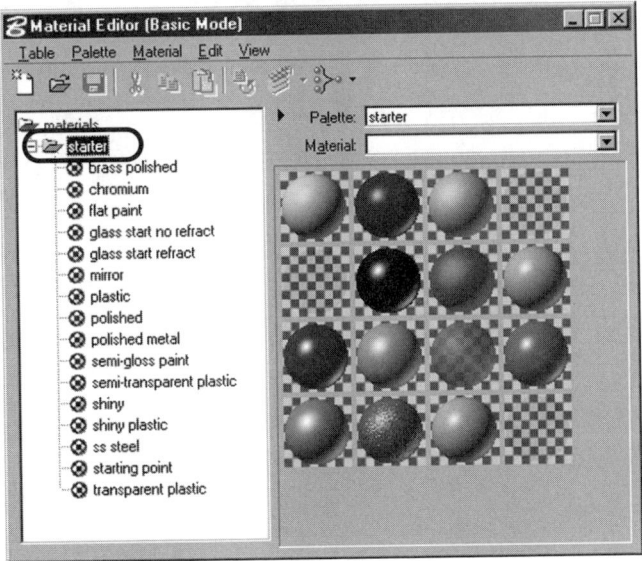

Assigning Materials by Level and Color

Assigning materials in MicroStation typically is by level and color. This means that once assigned, everything that is on the same level and has the same color will be rendered with the assigned material. In the next exercise, you will be assigning material definitions to several 3D spheres, each of which resides on the same level but has a different color.

| Chapter 6: Defining and Applying Materials |

✓ Exercise 6-2: Assign materials by level and color

1 Continuing in *materials.dgn*, in the Material Editor, right-click on the material *brass polished*.

2 From the menu, select Assign.

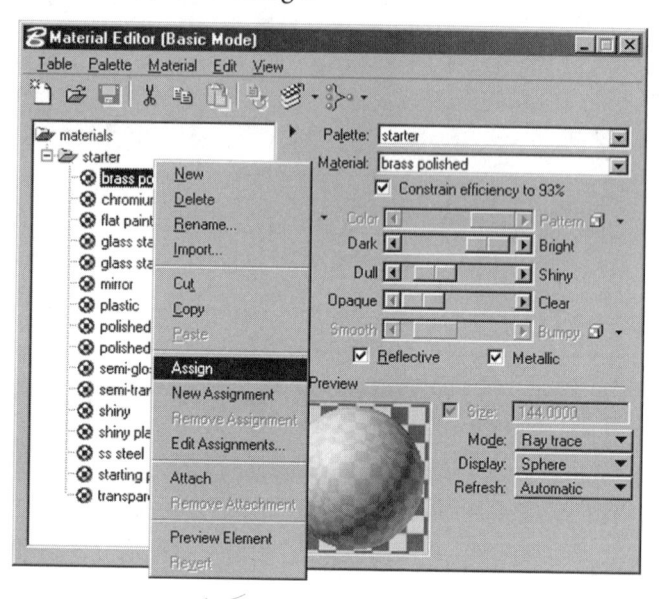

The Assign Material dialog box opens. This is the Apply Material tool dialog box with the Assign by Level/Color icon preselected.

NOTE: *Alternatively, you can select the Apply Materials tool in the Rendering Tools tool box, and then click the Assign by Level/Color icon.*

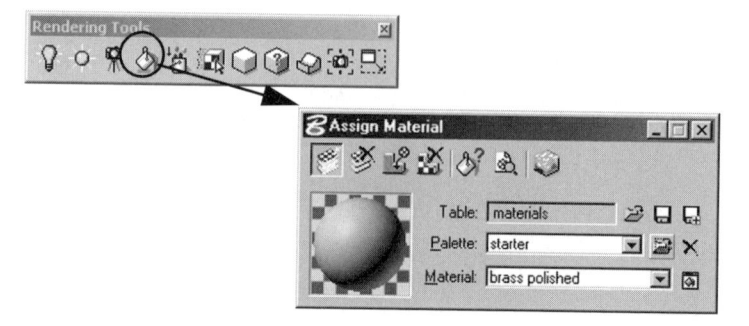

3 With a data point, identify the first white sphere in the upper left corner of the Top view.

| The Material Editor | 215

The sphere highlights.

4 Enter a second data point to accept the assignment.

In the Material Editor, a plus sign (+) appears next to the brass material in the list. This indicates the material has been assigned, and in this case it is to a level/color combination.

5 Ray trace View 2 to render with the material assignment you just made.

The sphere you selected renders with a brass appearance, the result of assigning the *brass polished* material definition to the element's level and color.

6 In the Material Editor, click on the plus sign next to *brass polished*.

The level name and color number you assigned are displayed below the material name.

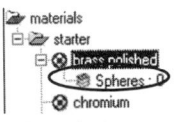

7 In the Rendering tools tool box, select the Apply Material tool.

8 From the Material list (drop-down menu), select *chromium*.

9 In the Top view, with a data point, identify the blue sphere to the right of the first one and accept with a second data point.

10 Similarly, assign additional materials to some of the remaining spheres.

11 Ray trace View 2 to see the effect.

When working with the Apply Material tool, the names of materials that already have been assigned appear in bold type in the Material list of the dialog box.

Removing Material Assignments

You can remove material assignments made previously. This can be performed individually, or you can use a selection set to remove multiple materials.

✔ Exercise 6-3: Remove a single material assignment

1. Continuing in *materials.dgn*, make sure that AccuSnap is enabled (Settings > Snaps > AccuSnap) with Pop-up Info also enabled and set to Automatic.

   AccuSnap is a drawing aid that automatically locates the elements and provides feedback as to what materials, if any, are assigned or attached.

2. Select the Apply Material tool and click the Remove Material icon.

   The title of the dialog box changes to Remove Material Assignment.

3. In one of the views, move the pointer over a sphere not assigned any material.

   Observe the universal No symbol. The tool tip informs you that no material is assigned, and notes the level and the color assigned to the element.

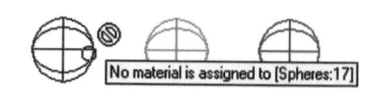

4. Move the pointer over the blue sphere to which you assigned the material *chromium*.

   The pointer changes to indicate selection is possible. The tool tip indicates that *chromium* is currently assigned to the level Spheres and color 1.

5. Enter a data point to highlight the element.

   Notice that the material *chromium* now is selected in the tool settings.

6. Enter a second data point to accept the removal of the *chromium* material assignment.

7. Ray trace View 2 to see that, once again, the sphere is rendered in blue.

| The Material Editor |

If you select multiple elements, you can remove materials assigned to them in one step.

✔ **Exercise 6-4: Remove multiple material assignments**

1. Continuing in *materials.dgn*, select the Element Selection tool.
2. Select all of the spheres to which you assigned materials.

   It does not matter if you select some that do not have assignments.
3. Select the Apply Material tool with Remove Material Assignment active.
4. Enter a data point to remove all material assignment to the select elements.
5. Ray trace View 2 to see that all materials have been removed and the spheres render in their respective colors.

   NOTE: *You can also make assignments to multiple elements by selecting the elements first and then clicking Assign by Level/Color.*

Materials Attached as Attributes

In the previous section, you applied materials by level and color. With this method, all elements of a particular level/color are assigned the chosen material. If you move the element to another level, or change its color, then the initial material definition is lost. A second option for applying materials lets you attach the material as an attribute. When you do this, you can move the element to another level, or change its color, or both, and the material definition remains. A material that is attached to an element takes precedence over a material that is assigned by level/color.

Recovering missing material attachments

One advantage of the material attachment method is that, even without a material table file, MicroStation will be able to display the names of the missing materials once a view has been rendered. You then can recover missing attached materials either by recreating them or by opening a palette file that contains the missing definitions.

✔ Exercise 6-5: Check for missing materials

1. Open DGN file *cool home.dgn*.

   This model is set up with the required source lighting. You can check the lighting setup in the Define Light tool dialog box.

2. In the Render tools tool box, select the Define Light tool to see the lights used.

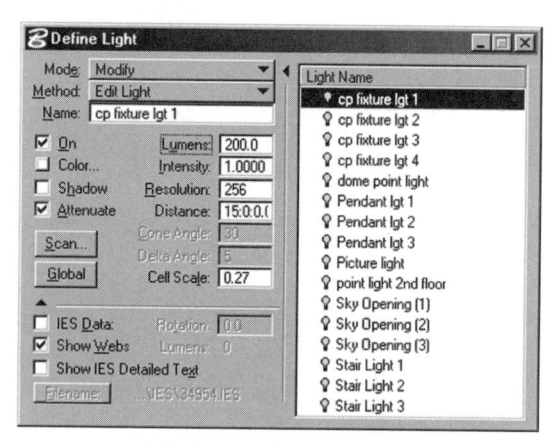

3. Ray trace View 2.

   The lighting for the this model is set up, but no photorealistic materials are applied. Some things may appear overly bright since the default setting of a material with no assignment or attachment of custom material will have a diffuse of 60, meaning 60% of the light is reflected by the material.

4. Select the Define Material tool.

   The Material Editor dialog box opens and displays a list of missing materials in a default Missing Materials palette. Even though these materials are attached to elements rather than assigned by level and color, MicroStation needs the material definitions in order to render these materials. These definitions are stored in a palette file.

Before proceeding with material definitions, rendering the design will let you see how the lighting and materials currently are set.

Ray traced scene with no materials assigned or attached.

| The Material Editor |

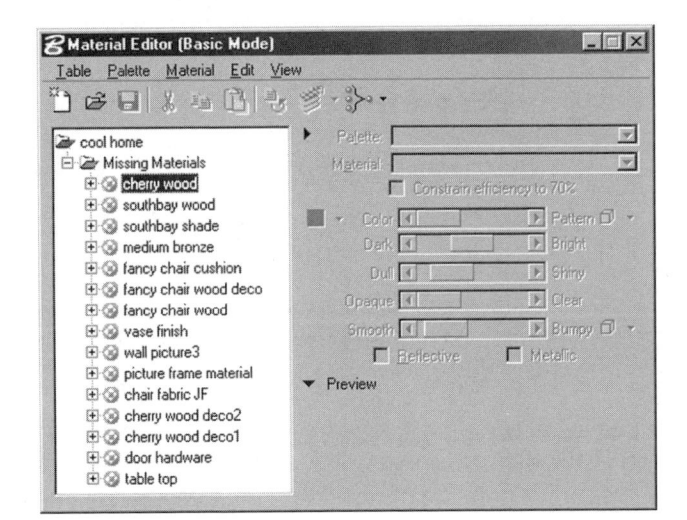

Material Editor with missing materials.

You have several options when materials are missing. They are:

- Open the palette containing the missing definitions so that MicroStation will find the materials.

- Where the original definitions are lost, you can recreate the material using the same name as the original.

- Remove the attached material by clicking the plus sign and expanding the list to display the missing attachments. You then can select the elements in the expanded list and choose Material > Remove Attachment.

In the next exercise, you will create a new palette file and then open an existing palette file that contains the required material definitions. You will then copy the missing definitions into your newly created palette.

✔ Exercise 6-6: Create a new palette and add/load an existing palette

1. Continue in *cool home.dgn*, with *cool home* selected in the Material Editor dialog box.

2. Click the New Material icon on the Material Editor dialog box.

   New Palette [1] and New Material [1] items appear in the list.

3. In the Material Editor dialog box, select Palette > Save As.

| Chapter 6: Defining and Applying Materials |

4   In the Save Palette As dialog box, change the name from *New Palette [1].pal* to *cool home* (*.pal* will be added automatically).

5   Click OK.

6   In the Material Editor dialog box, select Palette > Open.

7   Select the palette *stairs.pal,* which is located in the course *dgn* directory, and click OK.

The *stairs* palette is loaded. The palette Missing Materials no longer is present in the Material Editor because all of the missing definitions are contained in the palette just loaded.

The next step is to copy all the required materials into the new palette file that you created. You can do this by first filtering the display so that only the materials used in the model are available for copying.

✔ **Exercise 6-7:   Copy the required materials to the new palette**

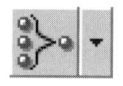

1   Continuing in *cool home.dgn*, in the Material Editor, click the Filter button, set to Filter Used, to turn on the filter.

This ensures that only the used materials from the palette display in the list box.

You will now copy the used definitions from the *stairs* palette to your *cool home* palette.

2   Select all the filtered (Used) materials from *stairs.pal* by clicking on the first material in the list and shift-click on the last material in the filtered list.

3   Press and hold the <Ctrl> key, and then drag the selected materials into *cool home*.

NOTE: *Holding the <Ctrl> key makes a copy of the definitions. If you do not hold the <Ctrl> key, the operation will move the definitions.*

With the materials now added to your *cool home* palette, you can unload the *stairs* palette file.

| The Material Editor |

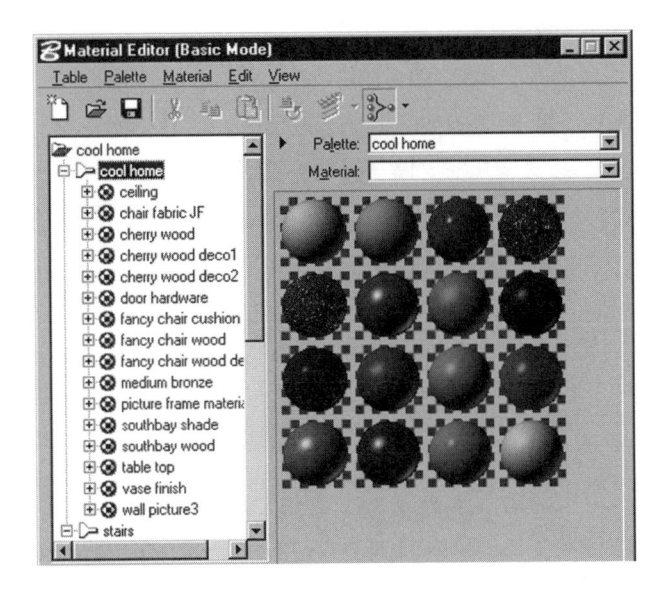

✔ **Exercise 6-8: Unload the original material palette**

1 Continuing in *cool home.dgn*, in the Material Editor dialog box, right-click on *stairs* (the stairs palette file), and select Unload from the menu.

The palette *stairs* is unloaded from memory. It is removed from the Material Editor dialog box.

2 Click the Filter button to turn off filtering.

The entry New Material [1] again appears in the material list. This is the default material that was created when you created the new palette file. In the following exercise, you will rename this material and adjust its settings to create a new material.

Creating New Materials

To achieve photorealistic results with your rendered images, you need photorealistic materials to assign or attach to your design geometry. In the following exercises, you will be given a more in-depth look at the Material Editor, creating a variety of materials and then assigning or attaching them to the geometry in the scene.

First, you will rename the default new material that you created previously. You will then use it to create a floor material.

✔ Exercise 6-9: Rename the default material

1. Continuing in *cool home.dgn*, in the Material Editor dialog box right-click on New Material [1] and select Rename from the menu.

2. Change the name to *floor*.

3. Press <Enter>, or click in the list box, to accept the name change.

You just created a material definition containing default properties. In this next exercise, you will adjust the base properties of the material to appear shiny. Later, you will add a pattern map so that the finished material is a shiny wooden floor.

✔ Exercise 6-10: Adjust the new material's properties

1. Continuing in *cool home.dgn*, in the Material Editor dialog box, check in the dialog box title that it is in Basic Mode.

2. If the Material Editor is in Advanced Mode, select View and turn off Advanced Mode.

3. Verify that the Preview render mode is Ray Trace.

   You want the floor to have the reflective appearance of well-waxed wood. To see how reflective your material is, you must ray trace the preview.

4. In the material list, select the new material floor (if it is not already highlighted).

5. Verify the following settings:

   Reflective: Enabled
   Metallic: Disabled

6. Use the controls in the Dull/Shiny setting to move the slider until the Constrain Efficiency value is 57%.

   NOTE: *Efficiency is defined as the percentage of the total light that is reflected or transmitted by a material. The efficiency value for a realistic material should never exceed 100%.*

   As you move the slider toward Shiny or Dull, notice that more or less of the checkered background is reflected. This gives you a visual representation of how the setting affects the finished material.

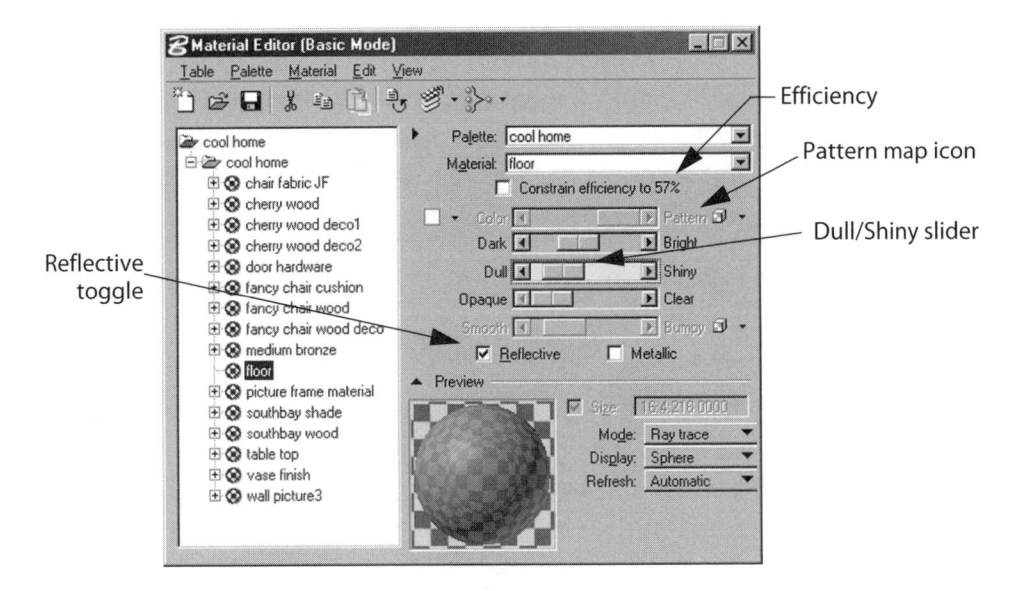

| The Material Editor | 223

Labels on Material Editor figure: Efficiency, Pattern map icon, Dull/Shiny slider, Reflective toggle

With the finish now defined for the new floor material, you will add a pattern map, or texture, to give it a real-world appearance.

NOTE: *The Metallic toggle in the Material Editor dialog box sets the color of the shiny specular highlights. If checked, the shiny highlights will be the same color as the base color. If unchecked, they will be the color of the reflected light, typically white. Also, when Metallic is disabled, you can customize the highlight color using the Material Editor's Advanced Mode.*

✔ **Exercise 6-11: Add a pattern map to the material definition**

1. Continuing in *cool home.dgn*, in the Material Editor, click the Pattern Map icon, which is located to the right of the Color/Pattern slider.

   The Open Image File dialog box opens.

2. Select *Wdfloor13.jpg* from the course *Image Library\Patterns* directory.

3. Click OK.

   The Pattern for floor dialog box opens.

4. Note the Image Size: 893 x 1000 (lower right of the dialog box).

| Chapter 6: Defining and Applying Materials |

> **NOTE:** *It is a good idea to check the image size when using a texture. Since many textures are tiled or repeated, you should select the size of the texture carefully with an eye toward maintaining the same aspect ratio of the original pattern image. This ensures that the image isn't stretched or otherwise distorted during the rendering process.*

5 Set the Mapping mode to Parametric.

6 Set Units to Master.

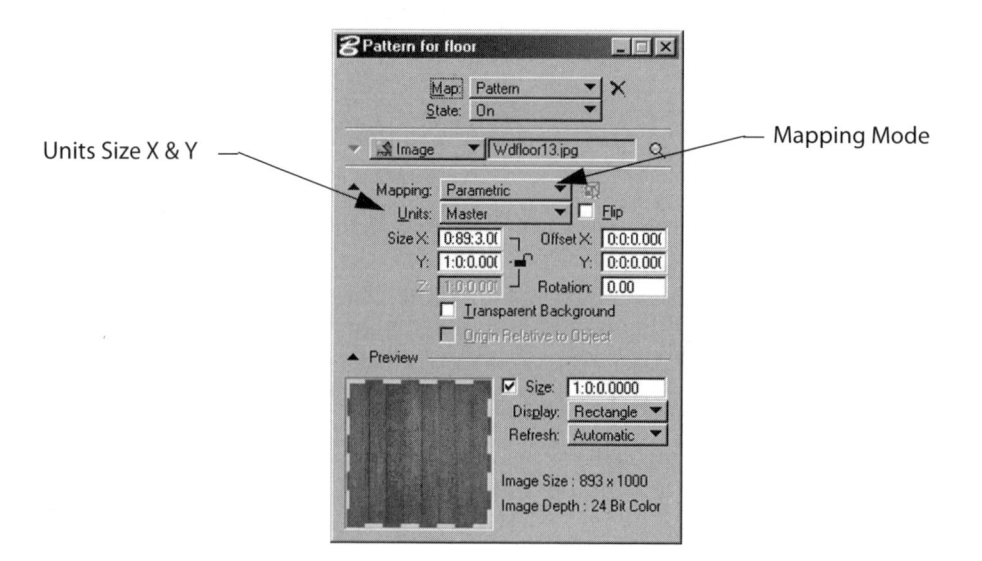

Units Size X & Y ← → Mapping Mode

7 Set the Size X to 0:89:3 (0.893 meter), leaving Y at 1:0:0 (1.0 meter).

This will preserve the aspect ratio of the texture to be tiled (893 x 1000). Note the Working Units currently are set for a Master Unit in meters and a Sub Unit measure in centimeters.

8 In the Material Editor dialog box, move the Dull/Shiny slider to the right until the efficiency is 55%.

The wood pattern map image pixels are darker than the original white default color, so the amount of light reflected off the texture is considerably lower. When you chose *Wdfloor13.jpg* as the pattern map, the efficiency dropped from 57% to 42%.

> **NOTE:** *So far, all your changes to the palette have been stored in memory only. In the Material Editor, they are displayed in blue and the Save Palette icon is active. Now would be a good time to save the palette to disk.*

| The Material Editor | **225**

9 Click the Save Palette icon in the Material Editor.

The changes to the palette file are saved to disk. The entries in the Material Editor now appear in black, and the Save Palette icon is dimmed.

This completes the definition of the floor material for the scene. Before continuing, we will discuss pattern mapping modes.

Pattern Mapping Modes

When using a texture map, you have three possible mapping modes: Parametric, Planar, and Elevation Drape. These modes affect the way a texture is mapped to elements in a model. Following is a description of how these different modes work.

Parametric is the default mapping mode, where the image is mapped to the element relative to the origin of the element. For this mapping mode, if you rotate an element that has the material assigned to it, the pattern map and/or bump map rotates with it

Planar mapping mode aligns the horizontal axis of the pattern map with the horizontal plane (X-Y) of the DGN file. The image then is tilted to match the slope of the selected surface. This mode is useful for materials attached to SmartSolids. Planar mapping mode should be used for solids in general, and when working with TriForma models. This mode keeps the texture oriented the same way on the walls or sides of building models.

Elevation Drape lays the texture on elements in the view, similar to what would happen if you took a blanket, shook it out, and let it drape across the model. This is the mode you would use to pattern map a digital terrain model (DTM) consisting of many triangles. When using this option, the elements are seen as one large object to which the pattern map is applied, rather than individual triangles, each with the pattern map applied to them.

Preview Material

Now that you have the material defined, you can preview it on the intended element. This will give you a better idea of how the texture will be mapped and allows you to tweak the settings, if needed, prior to actually assigning it.

| Chapter 6: Defining and Applying Materials |

✔ Exercise 6-12: Preview the floor material

1. Continuing in *cool home.dgn*, in the Material Editor list box, right-click on the material *floor* and, in the menu, select Preview Element.

   Alternatively, select the material in the list and then select Material > Preview Element.

2. In View 1, with a data point, select the large orange polygon surrounding the geometry.

3. Enter a second data point in View 2 to accept the polygon and preview the material in View 2.

   The floor is smooth rendered in View 2 with the selected material. This shows you how this texture will map to the floor geometry, allowing you to easily see how it is scaling and if the rotation is what you expect.

   NOTE: *When previewing a material, you can make the selection of the geometry in any view. The second data point accepts the element and determines the view to render.*

It's time now to assign your new material to the floor element in the model.

✔ Exercise 6-13: Assign the floor material

1. Continue in *cool home.dgn*, with the material *floor* highlighted in the Material Editor dialog box.

2. Select Material > Assign. Alternatively, you can right-click on the material *floor* and select Assign from the menu.

   The Apply Material tool dialog box opens, with the Assign by Level/Color icon already selected and the material floor as the chosen material.

3   Select the geometry for the floor in any view and enter a data point to accept the material assignment.

4   Ray Trace View 2 to see the floor rendered with the wood finish material.

Notice that the furniture, which is located in a reference file, now renders with realistic materials. These materials are attached to the geometry, rather than assigned. They were the missing materials that you copied earlier from the stairs palette into your cool home palette.

Notice also how the ceiling in part of the room (at the left in the view) also now renders with the wood material. This is because the element used to construct it, a solid, is the same color and on the same level as the polygon used for the floor. The solid forms the floor of the upper level and the ceiling of the lower level.

You can change either the level or color of the geometry to fix this. Alternatively, you can use the attach mode to apply a different material to the face that is forming the ceiling geometry. Later, you will use this method to attach a different material to the ceiling face of the solid element.

MATERIAL EDITOR ADVANCED MODE

To this point, you have been working with the Material Editor in its basic mode. The advanced mode provides you with many additional material adjustments that can be very useful in creating photorealistic material definitions.

✔ Exercise 6-14: Explore the Material Editor's Advanced Mode

1   Continuing in *cool home.dgn*, in the Material Editor, select View > Advanced Mode.

The Material Editor switches modes, and now you can see several additional options.

2   Observe that as you move the pointer over each setting and pause, a tool tip is displayed for a short time, explaining the function.

3   Move the pointer over the Efficiency setting and pause.

This is an excellent way to become familiar with each setting.

The Advanced Options

In the Material Editor dialog box, when it is set to Advanced Mode, there are many options for tweaking your material definitions. A summary is provided in the following table.

Option	Effect
Palette	Displays the currently open palette.
Material	Displays the current material. You can select a material from this field.
Efficiency	The total amount of incoming light that is not absorbed. It is the sum of the diffuse, specular, transparency, and translucency components. Controlled by slider or key-in, valid values should be from 0 to 100. Higher values, however, are possible but not recommended for physically accurate materials.
	Additional Efficiency option: Efficiency lock. When locked, modifying the material's diffuse, specular, transparency, or translucency components will automatically adjust the other components so that efficiency does not change.
Color	Determines the material color. A slider from 0 to 100 determines percentage of color to mix with the pattern map if one is used. If a pattern is present, a higher value mean a greater percentage of pattern map will be displayed. For instance, setting this to 25 would mean 25% color and 75% pattern map. To use a custom color, click on the icon to the left of the color slider.
Diffuse	The amount of all incoming light that is reflected in all directions equally. It affects the overall brightness of the material. Controlled by slider or key-in, values can be from 0 to 100.
Translucency	The amount of incoming light that is transmitted through the material and scattered in all directions as it exits the material. Controlled by slider or key-in, values can be from 0 to 100.
Specular	The amount of incoming light that is reflected in the opposite direction to the incoming light. Controlled by slider or key-in, values can be from 0 to 100.
	Additional Specular options (Plastic, Metal, and Use Element) determine the specular highlight color. If set to Plastic, the color will be white; if to Metal, the color will be the same as the base color. To use a custom color, click on the icon to the left of Specular in the Material Editor. If set to Use Element, the highlight color will be determined by the element to which the material is assigned.

Reflect	The amount of incoming light that is reflected from other objects in the scene. Additional Reflect options are Custom and Link to specular. Custom allows the reflect value to be less than or equal to the specular value. Link to specular locks the Reflect and Specular components so that they remain equal and locked when adjusting.
Finish	Determines the roughness or smoothness of a material. Small values result in rough surfaces that have large specular highlights. Larger values result in smooth surfaces with narrow specular highlights. Finish options are Custom, Off, or Link to specular. Custom values can be 0 to 100. Off means that Finish is not used. Link to specular locks Specular and Finish to be equal; therefore, adjusting one will change the other.
Transparency	The amount of incoming light that is transmitted directly through the material.
Refract	The index of refraction controls how much the direction of light passing through a transparent object is modified. A value of 1.0 will not change the light direction, values farther from 1.0 will bend the light more. Refract is only adjustable for materials with some degree of transparency. Additional Refract option, Thickness, is measured in Master Units. It is useful for describing refractive thicknesses for surfaces that are modeled with no thickness.
Bump	Modifies the surface normal to give the appearance of a bumpy surface when rendered. Controlled by slider or key-in, typical value can be from 0 to 100. Higher values (over 100) may be keyed in.

CREATING PHOTOREALISTIC MATERIALS

In the following exercises, you will create definitions for the other materials required for the example model. After you have defined and assigned the materials, you will ray trace the scene to see the results of your work.

> **NOTE:** *When creating photorealistic materials, particularly for the global lighting rendering solutions — radiosity, particle tracing, and ray tracing (with Real World Lighting) — the value for the Efficiency setting is important. It is the sum of the diffuse, specular, transparency, and translucency components and should never exceed 100 for physically accurate materials.*

Working from Existing Materials

When creating materials, often there are one or more settings that are valid for a number of different materials. For example, several materials may have the same Color and Specular settings but different pattern maps. To speed up the creation of such materials, it is a good idea to have a "starter" palette that contains basic materials. These are materials that you can import and then modify with adjustments to the settings for the finished material. This method of importing and modifying existing materials is a great way to quickly generate several different material definitions. Similarly, you can make a copy of an existing material in the current palette and modify its settings to create a new material.

To create materials from those existing in other palettes, you can use either of two methods. You can:

- ▶ Import definitions from a starter palette.
- ▶ Open the starter palette and copy the definitions by dragging and dropping, and then unloading the starter palette from memory.

In both methods, once the definitions have been imported/copied into your current palette, you should rename them and make the required adjustments.

You will use the import material technique in the following exercises. The supplied starter palette contains several different finishes, from shiny to flat, as well as some metals and glass materials, to start you off.

✔ Exercise 6-15: Create the ceiling material

1. Continuing in *cool home.dgn*, in the Material Editor, select Material > Import.

   The Select Palette File dialog box opens.

2. Select *starter.pal* in the course *\dgn* directory.

3. Click OK.

   The Import Materials dialog box opens.

4. In the Import Materials dialog box, select *flat paint*.

| Creating Photorealistic Materials | **231**

5 In the Import As field, change the name to *ceiling*.

6 Click Import to import this material into the *cool home* palette.

7 In the Material Editor, with the material *ceiling* selected, decrease the Diffuse component value to 55.

NOTE: *Diffuse is a measure of the incoming light that is reflected; higher values result in brighter materials. If you happen to have hot spots from your source lights when ray tracing with Real World Lighting enabled, you can lower the diffuse component on the offending material, reduce the lumens value of the source light, or do both. This process often is referred to as* tweaking.

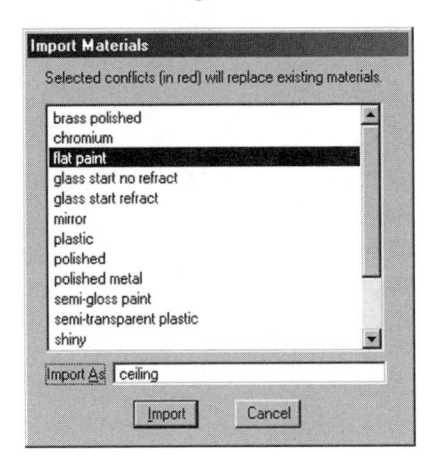

8 Click Save Palette to save the modified definition to disk.

NOTE: *You could wait until you have all your definitions complete before saving to disk. But remember that all your work is in memory until saved to disk. As a visual clue to whether or not a material is saved to disk, the text for saved definitions appears in black while text for definitions in memory appears in blue.*

NOTE: *Do you see now why you should change the name of the material when you import it? You have just changed the new definition slightly, while preserving the original starter palette definition. Even though MicroStation would have read the definition correctly, it is good practice to avoid having, on your system, different material definitions with identical names. If two definitions exist, and both palettes are loaded, MicroStation will use the definition from the first palette loaded and ignore the definition in any palette loaded subsequently.*

Where a required material is similar to one already present in the loaded palette, you can make a copy of the original and work with the copy.

Pay close attention to the preview when changing any material parameter. If you are working to achieve a satin or matte finish, adjusting the

Specular and Finish component can help you create the finish you are looking for. Setting the preview to use a sphere, cone or cylinder works best for discerning adjustments made to Specular and Finish.

✔ Exercise 6-16: Create a second ceiling material

1. Continuing in *cool home.dgn*, in the Material Editor dialog box, right-click on the material *ceiling*.
2. In the menu, select Copy.
3. Right-click again (anywhere in the list box) and choose Paste.

   The ceiling material is pasted but the name is *ceilingl[1]*.
4. Right-click on *ceiling[1]* and, from the menu, choose Rename.
5. Change the name from *ceiling[1]* to *dome ceiling*.
6. Change the diffuse component value to 33.

   Several lights are used in the dome area. Reducing the diffuse value will prevent the material from appearing overly washed out when ray traced.
7. Change Specular to 12.
8. Change Finish to 5.

   You may find that some materials have Finish and Specular linked so that Finish takes the same value as Specular. In these cases, you can unlock Finish from Specular by selecting the Custom option to the left of the Finish slider.
9. Click Save Palette to save the modified definition to disk.

✔ Exercise 6-17: Create main wall material

1. Continuing in *cool home.dgn*, in the Material Editor, select Material > Import.
2. From the Select Palette File dialog box File menu, select *starter.pal* (this should be the default selection from the previous operation).
3. Click OK.

| Creating Photorealistic Materials | 233

4. Select *semi-gloss paint* from the list of materials, and change the Import As name to *main wall*.

5. Click Import.

   To turn this material into that required for the main wall, you need to adjust some of its properties.

6. Click the Color icon (to the left of the Color field) in the Material Editor.

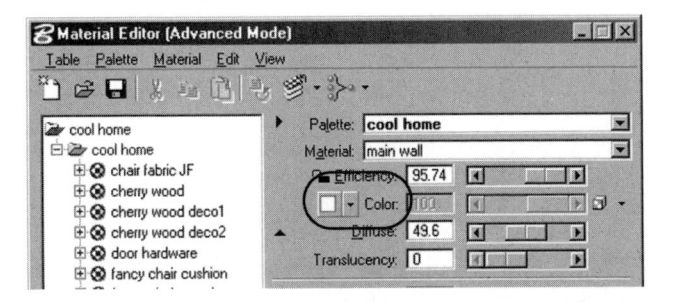

   The Base Color dialog box opens.

7. In the Base Color dialog box, with Color Model set to RGB (0-255), set the following values:

   Red: 250
   Green: 255
   Blue: 219

8. Click OK.

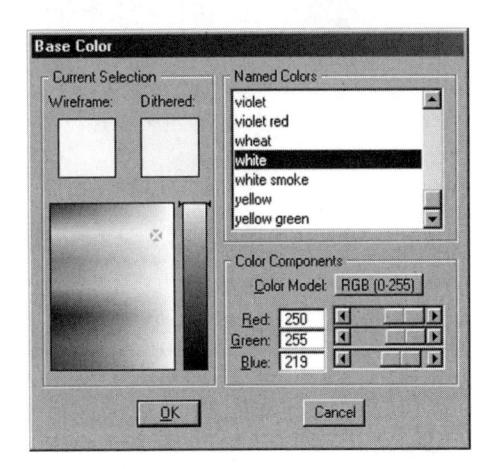

9. Click the Save Palette icon.

Using Transparent Background

To create the next material, the stair railing, you will import a predefined finish from the starter palette, and then add a texture (image file). The texture image will be mapped to the stair railing surface and will look very realistic when rendered, without the need to model the intricate geometry. By enabling the Transparent Background setting in the Pattern dialog box, you will see only the railing, as the material between the railing will be rendered transparent. This will save you time in regard to both modeling and rendering time.

✔ Exercise 6-18: Create stair railing material

1. Continuing in *cool home.dgn*, in the Material Editor dialog box, select Material > Import and, from the Select Palette File dialog box File menu, select *starter.pal*.

2. Click OK.

3. Select *semi-gloss paint* from the list of materials and change the Import As name to *stair railing*.

4. Click Import.

   Now that you have a predefined finish, all you need to complete the definition is a texture image for the stair railing.

5. In the Material Editor, click Pattern Map.

   The Open Image File dialog box opens.

6. Navigate to the course *Image Library\Objects* directory.

7. Select *spiral rail.tif*.

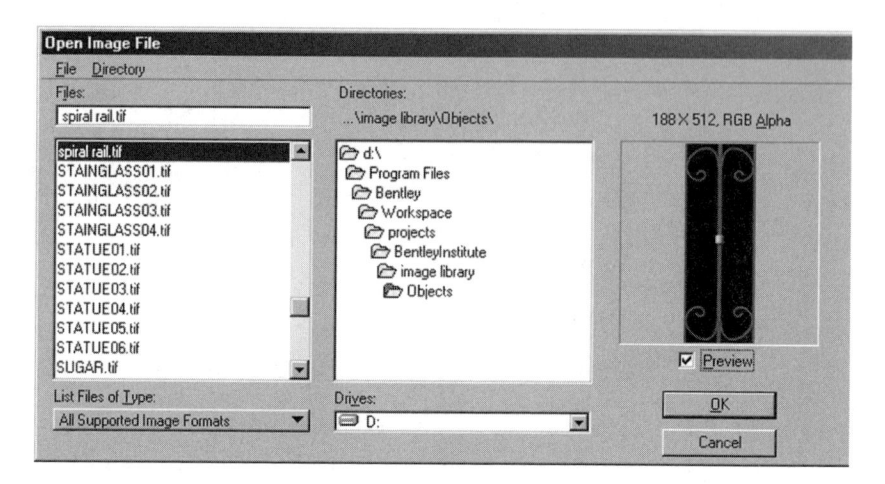

8. Click OK.

9. In the Pattern for railing dialog, set the following:

| Creating Photorealistic Materials | **235**

Mapping: Parametric
Units: Master
Size X: 0:30:5.00
Size Y: 0:76:20.00

Turn on Transparent Background.

10 In the Material Editor dialog box, click the Save Palette icon.

NOTE: *All the images in the* Image Library\Objects *folder are intended to be used with Background Transparency enabled. These images are TIFF format and are saved with either a single background color, or they may be saved as 32-bit RGB Alpha images. If background color is used, the upper left-hand corner pixel determines the color that is considered transparent. If RGB Alpha is used, only those pixels inside the mask that is saved with the image are seen.*

NOTE: *The Size Y setting in this case is set to the measured vertical distance for the railing geometry. The image will be tiled in X every 30.5 centimeters but will not appear tiled in Y since the distance is set to the same height as the measured geometry for the railing.*

Creating More Materials

In the following exercises, you will continue creating materials for the sample model.

Exercise 6-19: Create pendant lamp finish material

1 Continuing in *cool home.dgn*, in the Material Editor, select Material > Import and select *starter.pal* in the Select Palette File dialog box.

2 Click OK.

3 Select *polished* from the list of materials to import and change the Import As name to *pendant lamp finish*.

4 Click Import.

5   In the Material Editor dialog box, click the Color icon.

The Base Color dialog box opens.

6   In the Base Color dialog box, with Color Model set to RGB (0-255), set the following:

Red: 125
Green: 75
Blue: 40.

7   Click OK.

8   In the Material Editor dialog box, click the Save Palette icon.

Next, you will copy and paste the already created floor material to create a similar material for the stairs. The stair material will have a different pattern rotation, but all other parameters will remain the same.

✔ Exercise 6-20: Create the stair material

1   Continuing in *cool home.dgn*, in the Material Editor, right-click on the material *floor* and, from the menu, choose Copy.

2   Right-click again and choose Paste.

The floor material is pasted but the name is *floor[1]*.

3   Right-click on the copied material and, from the menu, choose Rename.

4   Change the name from *floor[1]* to *stairs*.

5   Click the Pattern icon.

The Pattern for stairs dialog box opens.

6   Set the value for Rotation to 270.

7   In the Material Editor dialog box, click the Save Palette icon.

In the next exercise, you will create a Tiffany lamp material for the pendant lamp hanging from the ceiling. You will create this material from scratch, rather than from an imported starting material.

| Creating Photorealistic Materials | **237**

✔ Exercise 6-21: Create the pendant lamp bowl material

1. Continuing in *cool home.dgn*, in the Material Editor, select Material > New.

2. Change the name from New Material[1] to *pendant lamp bowl*.

   Remember to accept the name change by clicking in the list box, or pressing <Enter>.

3. With the new material selected, set the following fields:

   Diffuse: 38
   Translucency: 20
   Specular: 22
   Reflect: 8
   Finish: 80

   NOTE: *You may need to unlink Finish from Specular by clicking the chain link icon, to the left of the setting, and choosing Custom from the menu.*

   Transparency: 22
   Ambient: 100

4. In the Material Editor, click Pattern Map.

5. From the list of patterns in the course *Image Library\Patterns* directory, select *tiffany01.jpg* and click OK.

6. In the Pattern for pendant lamp bowl dialog box, set Mapping Mode to Elevation drape.

   Elevation-draping the material will lay the image onto a revolved surface with much less distortion than the other mapping modes.

7. Lock the Size X: and Y: settings by clicking their lock icons.

8. Set Size X: to 0:80.

   You will need to modify the X and Y offsets to center the image in the lamp bowl, which you can do

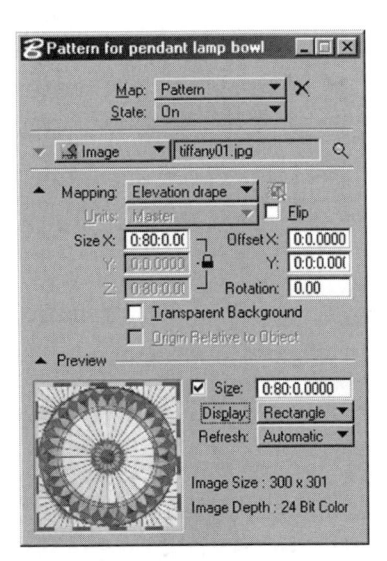

Exercise 6-22: Create rug material

1. Continuing in *cool home.dgn*, in the Material Editor, select Material > Import and select *starter.pal* in the Select Palette File dialog box.
2. Click OK.
3. Select *flat paint* from the list of materials and change the Import As name to *rug*.
4. Click Import.
5. Change the Specular setting to 6.
6. In the Material Editor, click the Pattern Map icon.

   The Open Image File dialog box opens.
7. Navigate to the *Image library\Objects* directory and select *RUG01.tif*.
8. Click OK.
9. In the Pattern for rug dialog box, turn on Transparent Background.
10. In the Material Editor dialog box, click the Save Palette icon.

Exercise 6-23: Create window sill material

1. Continuing in *cool home.dgn*, in the Material Editor, select Material > Import and select *starter.pal* in the Select Palette File dialog box.
2. Click OK.
3. Select *shiny* from the list of materials and change the Import As name to *window sill*.
4. Click Import.
5. In the Material Editor, click Pattern Map.
6. From the list, in the *Image Library\Patterns* directory, select *Marble09.jpg*.

| Creating Photorealistic Materials |

7   Click OK.

8   In the Material Editor, set the following:

   Diffuse: 70
   Specular: 30
   Reflect: 5
   Finish: 80

9   Click the Save Palette icon.

✔ **Exercise 6-24: Create window pane material**

1   Continuing in **cool home.dgn**, in the Material Editor, select Material > Import and select *starter.pal* in the Select Palette File dialog box.

2   Click OK.

3   Select *glass start no refract* from the list of materials and change the Import As name to *window pane*.

4   Click Import.

5   Click the Save Palette icon.

✔ **Exercise 6-25: Create window frame material**

1   Continuing in **cool home.dgn**, in the Material Editor, select Material > Import and select *starter.pal* in the Select Palette File dialog box.

2   Click OK.

3   Select *semi-gloss paint* from the list of materials and change the Import As name to *window frame*.

4   Click Import.

5   In the Material Editor, click the Color icon.

   The Base Color dialog opens.

6   In the Base Color dialog box, with Color Model set to RGB (0-255), set Red, Green, and Blue to a value of 20.

7   Click OK.

8   Click the Save Palette icon.

Exercise 6-26: Create trim material

1. Continuing in *cool home.dgn*, in the Material Editor, select Material > Import and select *starter.pal* in the Select Palette File dialog box.

2. Click OK.

3. Select *semi-gloss paint* from the list of materials and change the Import As name to *trim*.

4. Click Import.

5. In the Material Editor, set the following:

   Diffuse: 70
   Specular: 20
   Finish: 20

6. Click the Save Palette icon.

Blending Texture with Base Color

When you include an image file in a material definition, you can control the balance between the image file and an underlying color that appears in the rendered image. The underlying color may be the element color in the model, or you can specify another custom color. The following material uses this technique of balancing between the image and a specified color.

Exercise 6-27: Create the base for the stair top rail material

1. Continuing in *cool home.dgn*, in the Material Editor, select Material > Import and select *starter.pal* in the Select Palette File dialog box.

2. Click OK.

3. Select *polished* from the list of materials and change the Import As name to *stair top rail*.

4. Click Import.

5. In the Material Editor, click the Color tile and, in the Base Color dialog box, set the following:

| Creating Photorealistic Materials | **241**

>   *Red:* 184
>   *Green:* 15
>   *Blue:* 9

6   Click OK.

7   In the Material Editor, click Pattern Map.

8   From the list in the *Image Library\Patterns* directory, select the image file *Wood43.jpg*, and then double-click or click OK.

9   In the Pattern for stair top rail dialog box, set the following:

>   *Mapping*: Parametric
>   *Units*: Master
>   *Size X*: 1:12:90.00
>   *Size Y*: 0:38:90.00

10 In the Material Editor, set the Color value to 59.

>   Reducing this value lets the underlying red color, which you just made, bleed through the pattern map image to change the color of the material.

11 In the Material Editor, set the following:

>   *Diffuse*: 50
>   *Specular*: 20
>   *Reflect*: 5
>   *Finish*: 80

12 Click the Save Palette icon.

In the previous exercises, you imported materials from the starter palette, changing the names of the materials and any settings that were required for the new material. By creating your own materials with new unique names, you know that the material definition comes from your own project material definitions. This ensures that they do not come from a globally defined material that may be subject to change whenever you update software.

Using Bump Mapping

Bump mapping uses the brightness of an image to, in effect, displace the geometry when rendered. This displacement is based on light and dark areas, where the light areas of bump maps tend to create raised areas, or ridges, while the dark areas create depressions in the appearance of the

| Chapter 6: Defining and Applying Materials |

material. For bump maps, you can use either grayscale or color images to produce materials with a 3D effect when rendered.

In the next exercise you will add a bump map to the previously created material *main wall*, which will give the wall a 3D stucco finish.

✔ Exercise 6-28: Edit material main wall to include a bump map

1. Continuing in ***cool home.dgn***, in the Material Editor, select *main wall* from the list of materials.

2. In the Material Editor, click Bump Map (the icon to the right of the Bump setting).

3. From the list of bump image files, in the course *Image Library\Bumps* directory, select *STUCCO01.JPG*.

4. Click OK.

    The Bump for main wall settings dialog box opens.

5. Change the Units to Master.

6. Set the Size X and Y to 0:50.

    The bump map will be tiled in master units and will give the wall a textured appearance when rendered.

    This completes the material definition for main wall.

7. Click the Save Palette icon.

Just to have a little contrast and make the room more interesting, you can create another wall material with the same properties as the main wall but with a different color. You can do this easily by copying and pasting the main wall material and then editing the color settings.

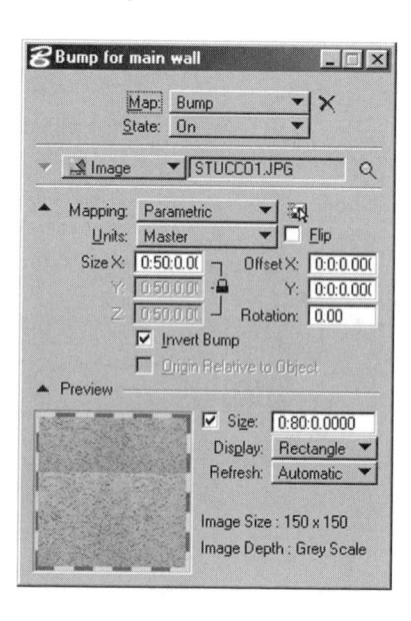

| Creating Photorealistic Materials |

✔ Exercise 6-29: Create second material for walls

1. Continuing in *cool home.dgn*, in the Material Editor, right-click on the material *main wall* and, from the menu, choose Copy.

2. Right-click again and choose Paste.

    The material *main wall* is copied, but the name is *main wall[1]*.

3. Right-click on the copied material and, from the menu, choose Rename.

4. Change the name from *main wall[1]* to *wall*.

5. Click on the color tile.

    The Base Color dialog opens.

6. With Color Model set to RGB (0-255) set:

    Red: 255
    Green: 211
    Blue: 145.

7. Click OK.

8. Click the Save Palette icon.

    NOTE: *It is a good idea to name your material files with broadly descriptive terms. A "floor covering" could be tile, wood, carpet, or some other material. Naming the material* blue carpet, *for example, would not be such a good idea, since it describes a property of the material that could change. For instance, if you later wanted to use wood flooring instead, you would need to create another material and assign it. The name* floor covering *lets you edit the material definition only, to completely change the look, without having to assign a new material.*

To complete the material definitions, you will use an existing material to create a material that includes a bump map, for the Tiffany lamp.

✔ Exercise 6-30: Decorative bump for Tiffany lamp

1. Continuing in *cool home.dgn*, in the Material Editor, right-click on the material *pendant lamp finish* and, from the menu, choose copy.
2. Right-click again and, from the menu, choose paste.

   The material *pendant lamp finish* is pasted, but the name is *pendant lamp finish[1]*.
3. Right-click the copied material and, from the menu, choose Rename.
4. Change the name from *pendant lamp finish[1]* to *pendant lamp deco*.
5. In the Material Editor, click Bump Map.
6. From the list of bump image files, in the course *Image Library\Bumps* directory, select *cornice01.jpg*.
7. Click OK.
8. In the Bump for pendant lamp deco dialog box set:

   Size X: 0.1
   Size Y: 1.868.
   Offset Y: -0.18.
9. In the Material Editor dialog box, set the Bump value to 50.
10. Click the Save Palette icon.

That completes the creation of materials for this model. Next you will make the assignments and attachments of these materials to the geometry.

APPLYING MATERIALS

In the following exercises, you will learn how to apply the materials you just finished creating. You will make assignments based on the color and level of the elements, as well as by attachment, where the material is attached as an element attribute.

Making assignments by color and level is very easy. You need only select one element in order to apply a material to all elements having the same color and level. On the other hand, attaching materials as attributes has

| Applying Materials |

its own advantages. A material attachment has precedence over a material assigned by level and color. When a material is attached, it does not matter what color or level it is on—the material attachment is honored. This method works well for cell libraries. In these cases, you can attach materials to the elements in the cell and the cell is ready to render. That is, you do not have to worry about a conflicting assignment with other materials assigned by level and color.

In the example model, you may remember that the furniture elements already have materials applied to them. These elements are located in a reference file. For the following exercises, where you will be applying materials to elements in the active file, it will be less confusing if the reference file elements are not displayed. Turn off the display of the reference now.

✔ Exercise 6-31: Turn off display of the referenced elements

1. Continuing in *cool home.dgn*, open the References dialog box.

2. In the References dialog box, turn off the display for the reference file.

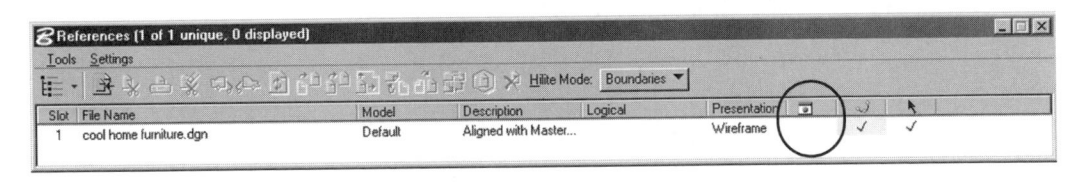

References dialog box showing the reference display turned off.

Earlier you rendered View 2 and saw that the floor material was assigned also to the ceiling in part of the room under the landing. This is because the elements for both the floor and the ceiling are the same color and are located on the same level. You could change the color of the ceiling element, but then this might later cause a conflict with another material. The ceiling element is a solid. Its bottom face is the ceiling of the lower room, and its upper face is the floor for the upstairs area. As you can attach materials to faces of solids such as this, you can have different materials on the top and bottom faces. Here, you will attach a ceiling material to the solid's lower face.

✔ Exercise 6-32: Attach ceiling material to the face of a solid

1 Continuing in *cool home.dgn*, make *floors* the active level and, in View 2, turn off all other levels.

This will make it easier to select the correct geometry to make the assignments.

2 In the Material Editor dialog box, right-click on the material *ceiling* and select Attach from the menu.

The Attach Material dialog box opens.

In View 2, enter a data point on the orange solid used for the upper floor.

The slab highlights.

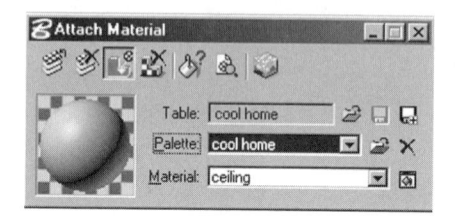

3 Move the pointer to a position within the area of the lower face and enter a data point (MicroStation finds the surface nearer to the viewer).

The lower face highlights.

4 Enter a further data point to accept the attachment.

5 In the Material Editor, click the plus sign, next to the material *ceiling*, to expand the entry and show the attachment.

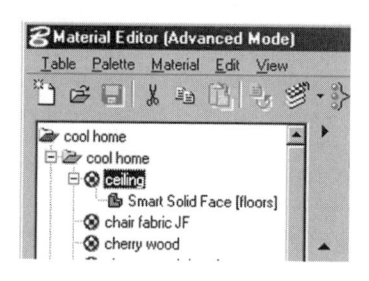

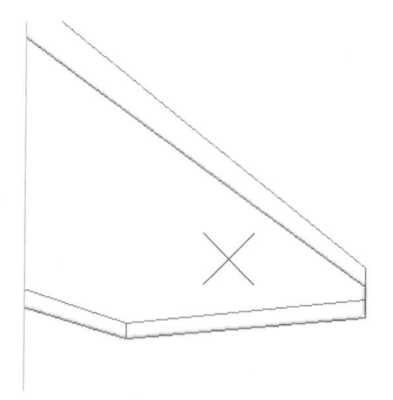

The ceiling material is expanded to show the attachment to a SmartSolid face.

For other elements, you can assign materials by level and color.

| Applying Materials |

✔ Exercise 6-33: Assign materials stair top rail and stair railing

1. Continuing in **cool home.dgn**, in View 2, turn on level *Railing*.

2. In the Rendering tools tool box, select the Apply Material tool.

   The Attach Material dialog box opens. The tool retains the Attach Material option that was used previously.

3. In the Attach Material dialog box, click the Assign Material icon.

   The dialog box name changes to reflect that the mode now is Assign rather than Attach.

4. In the Material list, select the material **stair top rail**.

5. Enter a data point on the yellow element that makes up the stair railing.

   The geometry highlights.

6. Enter a second data point to accept the assignment.

7. Using the same method, select *stair railing* from the material list, in the Assign Material dialog box, and assign it to the green-colored surface immediately below the stair top rail.

✔ Exercise 6-34: Assign the trim material

1. In View 2, turn on levels *trim, columns,* and *balcony*.

   The *trim* material will be assigned to geometry on levels *balcony* and *trim*.

2. In the Apply Material tool dialog box, click the Assign Material icon and select *trim* as the Material.

3. Select any of the geometry making up the balcony.

4. Accept with a second data point.

5. Select the red-colored geometry either around the arch door or along the stairway.

6. Accept with a second data point.

| Chapter 6: Defining and Applying Materials |

    7 Using the same method, assign the trim material to the cyan-colored column.

    8 Ray trace View 2 creating a new solution to verify you have correctly made the assignments so far.

✔ Exercise 6-35: Assign the wall materials

    1 Make *walls* the active level and, in View 2, turn off all other levels.

    2 Turn on level *dome ceiling*.

    3 Select the Assign Material tool and set *main wall* as the material.

    4 In View 2, select any of the geometry making up the main walls.

    5 Accept with a second data point.

    6 Similarly, set *wall* as the material and, in View 2, assign it to the light green-colored polygon.

    7 Now, set *dome ceiling* as the material and assign it to the dome geometry above the main walls.

✔ Exercise 6-36: Assign further materials

    1 Continuing in **cool home.dgn**, make *rug* the active level.

    2 In View 2:

        Turn off level *walls*.

        Turn on levels *sills*, *stairway,* and *window framing*.

    3 Click on the Assign Material tool.

    4 Using the same method as before, assign the following materials:

        rug to the green polygon on the floor.
        stairs to the green stairway geometry.
        windowsill to the green window sill geometry.
        window frame to the orange window frame geometry.

    5 Ray trace View 2, creating a new solution to verify you have correctly made the assignments so far.

| Applying Materials |

You may have noticed that, when you selected the window frame geometry, the entire window frame highlighted. In fact, the window frame geometry is a cell that contains elements for both the frame and the window glass. In order to assign a material to an individual element of a cell, you may need to determine the level and/or color of the element and then assign by color and level rather than by just identifying the element. You can determine this by using the element info tool.

NOTE: *To assign a material to an individual element in a cell, you can also drop the cell, make the assignment, and then undo the dropping of the cell.*

✔ Exercise 6-37: Assign a material to an element in a cell

1. Continuing in *cool home.dgn*, select the Element Information tool in the Primary Tools tool bar.

2. Select the window frame.

   The Element Information dialog box opens.

3. From the list of elements, select Complex Shape [14] and notice that the window pane element highlights.

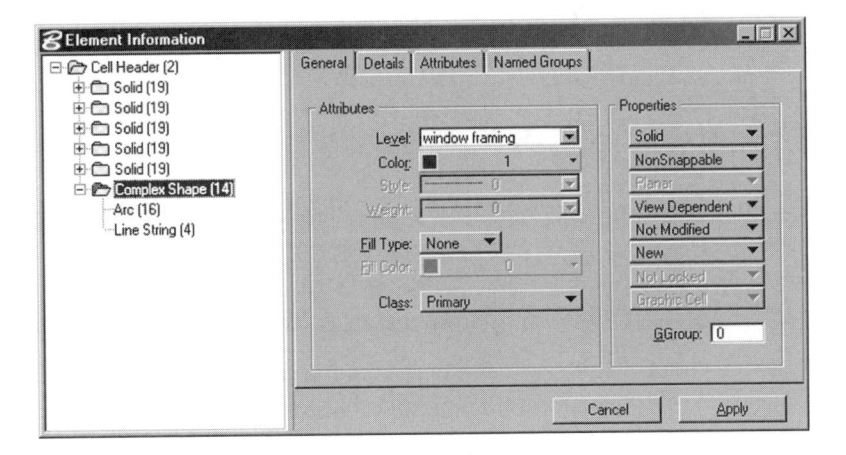

4. Note that the element color is 1.

5. Select the Apply Material tool, with the Assign Material option active.

| Chapter 6: Defining and Applying Materials |

6 Make *window pane* the active material and click the Material Assignments icon located to the right of the material field.

7 In the Material Assignments dialog box, select level *window framing* and color blue (color 1).

8 Click Apply to see the assignment in the list box.

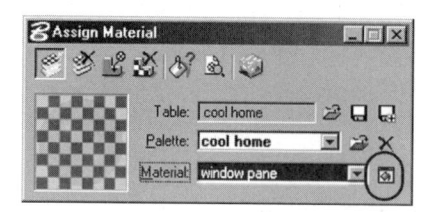

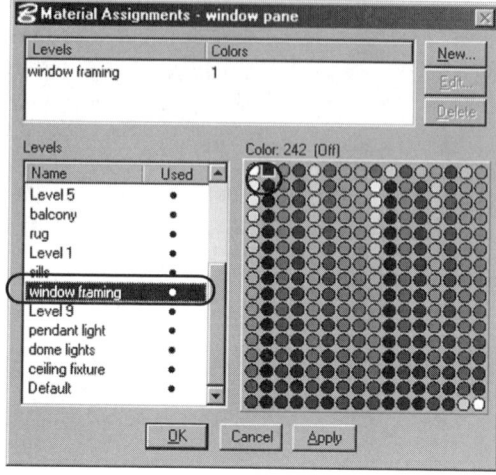

9 Click OK to complete the assignment.

10 In the Assign Material tool dialog box, click the Save Material Table icon to save the material assignments file.

11 Ray trace View 2, creating a new solution to verify you have correctly made the assignments so far.

Finally, you will apply materials to the pendant light.

✔ Exercise 6-38: Assign materials to the pendant light

1 Continuing in ***cool home.dgn***, make *pendant light* the active level and turn off all other levels in Views 1 and 2.

2 Fit View 1.

3 Select the Apply Material tool.

From the previous exercise, this tool still is in Assign Material mode.

4 Select material *pendant lamp finish* in the Material list.

| Applying Materials |

5 In View 2, select any part of the geometry for the supporting chain and accept with a second data point.

6 Select material *pendant lamp bowl* in the Material list.

7 In View 1, select the red geometry for the lamp bowl and accept with a second data point.

8 Select material *pendant lamp deco* in the Material list.

9 In the Assign Material dialog box, click on the Material Assignments icon to the right of the Material field.

The Material Assignments dialog box opens for the selected material.

10 In the Material Assignments dialog box, select level *pendant light*, and the color cyan (color 7) in the color picker.

11 Click Apply button to see the assignment.

12 Click OK to complete the assignment of the material.

13 Use the Render tool to Smooth render View 1.

The Tiffany lamp texture is not centered on the bowl. For these situations, you can dynamically adjust the positioning, scaling, and rotation of a texture once it has been assigned, as you will see in the following section.

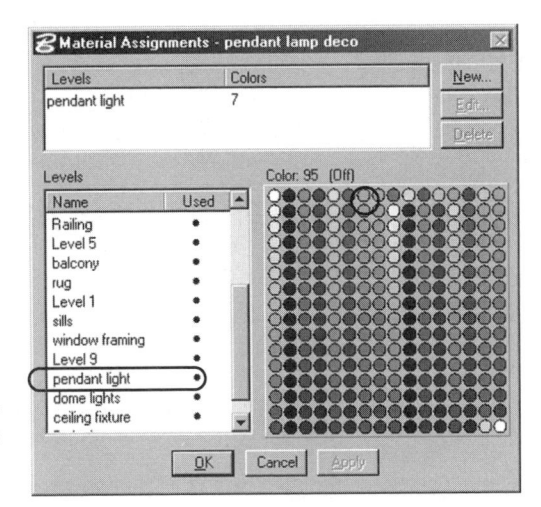

Dynamic Map Adjust

One of the most exciting visualization enhancements in the past couple of years is the ability to dynamically adjust a pattern map or bump map. Once a material with a texture has been assigned, you can dynamically adjust the texture by moving, scaling, or rotating.

| Chapter 6: Defining and Applying Materials |

Prior to this enhancement, you had to manually make changes to X,Y offsets, Size X,Y, or Rotation Angle and render each time to see the results. This trial and error method could be very time consuming, and frustrating as well.

In the next exercise, you will see for yourself how easy it is to move a texture such as the pattern for the Tiffany lamp.

✔ Exercise 6-39: Dynamically adjust texture map

1. Continuing in *cool home.dgn*, in the Rendering Tools tool box, select the Dynamically Adjust Map tool.

   NOTE: *Disabling AccuSnap will make it easier to manipulate the image.*

2. Check that the Move Map icon is selected, with Map set to Pattern.

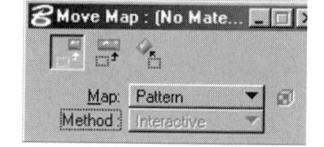

3. In View 1, identify the red geometry that makes up the lamp bowl.

   The bowl is rendered with the Tiffany pattern map. Note the prompt in the lower left corner of the MicroStation window, "Material Map Dynamic > Identify point on element to move image from."

4. Click near center of the circular pattern of the pattern image.

   The pattern image now moves with the pointer.

5. Center the image on the lamp bowl and enter a data point to accept the change.

Before *(left)* and after *(right)* adjusting the pattern image.

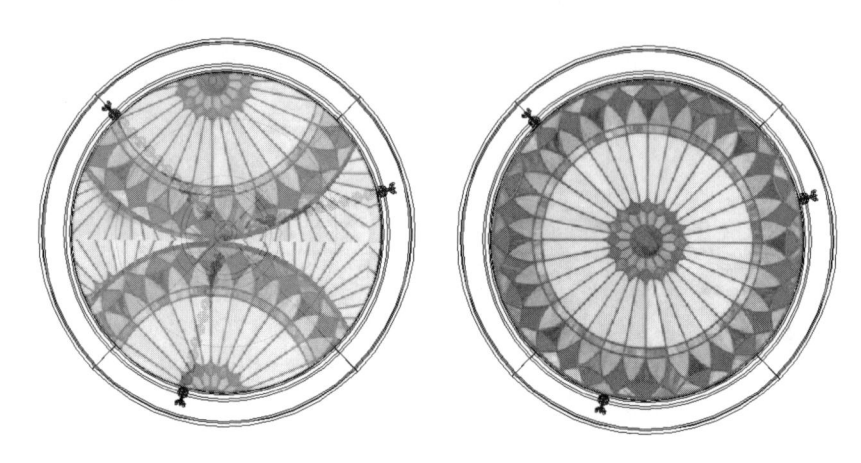

| Applying Materials |

Rendering the Scene

After applying the photorealistic materials, the next step is to render the scene. You can use ray tracing or particle tracing to achieve a realistic look.

✔ **Exercise 6-40: Render the scene**

1. Continuing in *cool home.dgn*, turn on the display for reference file *cool home furniture*.
2. Turn on all levels in View 2.
3. Ray trace View 2.

Image before *(left)* and after *(right)* adding materials.

As you can see, the rendered view looks much more realistic after creating and applying realistic materials.

Review Questions

1. Which tool provides you with the means to create custom materials with such interesting properties as transparency, translucency, reflection, refraction, texture maps, and more?
2. Which preview mode in the Material Editor lets you see reflections and refraction?
3. What drawing aid automatically locates the elements and provides feedback as to what materials, if any, are assigned or attached?
4. What advanced material setting is defined as the percentage of the total light that is reflected or transmitted by a material?
5. What does the Metallic toggle do if checked?
6. What are the three possible mapping modes when using a texture map?
7. Which material property determines the amount of all incoming light that is reflected in all directions equally?
8. Which material property determines the roughness or smoothness of a material with small values resulting in rough surfaces that have large specular highlights?
9. When using background transparency, which pixel determines the background color used for transparency in a 24-bit color image?
10. To use mask information rather than background color for transparency, what image format should you use?

Chapter Summary

In this chapter, you have learned how to define new materials and how to apply those materials to elements in a model. You have been provided with a more in-depth look at the Material Editor and all the settings for adjusting and fine-tuning materials. You learned to assign materials by their color and level attributes and also how to attach materials to the geometry. You have also learned:

- how to use both patterns and bump maps to create truly photo-realistic materials.
- how to dynamically adjust pattern maps of previously assigned materials.
- how to use background transparency in a material definition.

7   Advanced Materials

You have worked with materials that incorporate pattern maps and bump maps, which are created from digital images. In this chapter, you will continue working with other definable materials, namely procedural textures and gradient maps. Finally, you will look at ArchVision's Rich Photorealistic Content (RPC).

PROCEDURAL TEXTURES

In addition to being able to define materials using pattern maps from digital images, MicroStation's rendering engine also supports several procedural textures. These procedural textures have pros and cons. Here, you will learn both the advantages and the disadvantages of using these materials.

Several of the procedural textures that ship with MicroStation are 3D in that they have Size Z information in addition to Size X and Size Y. For these materials, the procedure calculates pixel information in the z-axis. For example, wood, marble, and stone work very well as procedural textures, particularly when applied to a solid. If you make a cut into a solid with any of these 3D procedural materials applied, the procedural material will look correct in the cut. The grain, veins, or joints will align correctly with the 3D procedural texture, whereas a 2D texture may fall short and require extra steps to make the joins align and look natural.

| Chapter 7: Advanced Materials |

This could include requiring multiple definitions for the different faces of the solid to work around this shortcoming.

Procedural textures are wholly created by MicroStation Development Language (MDL) applications and are calculated by your computer. They tend to look less realistic than a texture made from an actual photograph. Also, they can take a little longer to render, as each pixel must be computed rather than being loaded from memory.

Being programs, the procedural textures are not something you can create yourself. Each procedural texture, however, has several adjustable parameters that let you customize or tailor the texture to meet your rendering needs. You will know when a texture is 3D by looking at the Size Z value in the Pattern dialog box. If this area is grayed out, then the texture is 2D. If not grayed out, so that you can adjust the Z value, then it is 3D.

Working with Procedural Textures

In the next exercise, you will look at a model where 2D pattern maps are applied to some solid materials in a real-world scene. You will create replacement materials, using procedural textures, and then compare the results.

✔ Exercise 7-1: Select a procedural texture

1 Open the file *livroom procedural1.dgn*.

2 Ray trace View 2.

As you can see, the fireplace is rendered with a stone pattern map, and the material also uses a bump map for added realism. The shortcomings of this particular material are obvious. The edges of the stones do not align with each other along the meeting of the front edge with the sides of the fireplace.

3 Select the Define Material tool to open the Material Editor.

4 From the list of materials, select *stone texture1*.

5 In the Material Editor, click Pattern Map.

| Procedural Textures | 257

The stone does not line up along edge boundaries.

The Pattern for stone texture1 dialog box opens. Notice that Mapping is set to Planar, and the Size X and Y fields are set to 5. Notice also that the Size Z area is grayed out.

6 Click the New Material icon on the Material Editor dialog box.

New Material [1] appears in the list.

7 Change the name of the new material to *stone procedural*.

8 In the Pattern for stone procedural dialog box, from the Image button option menu, select Procedure.

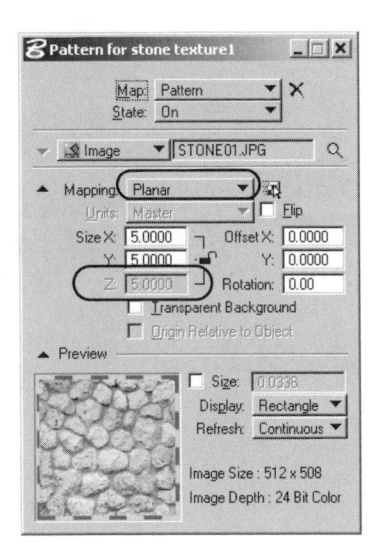

Pattern for stone texture1.

| Chapter 7: Advanced Materials |

Options for this menu are Image, Gradient, and Procedure. Gradients will be discussed immediately following procedural textures.

9 When you select Procedure, a second button appears, to the right of the Procedure button. It has the name of the currently selected procedural texture, such as Boards.

10 Click the material button to see the entire list of available procedural textures, and from it select Stone.

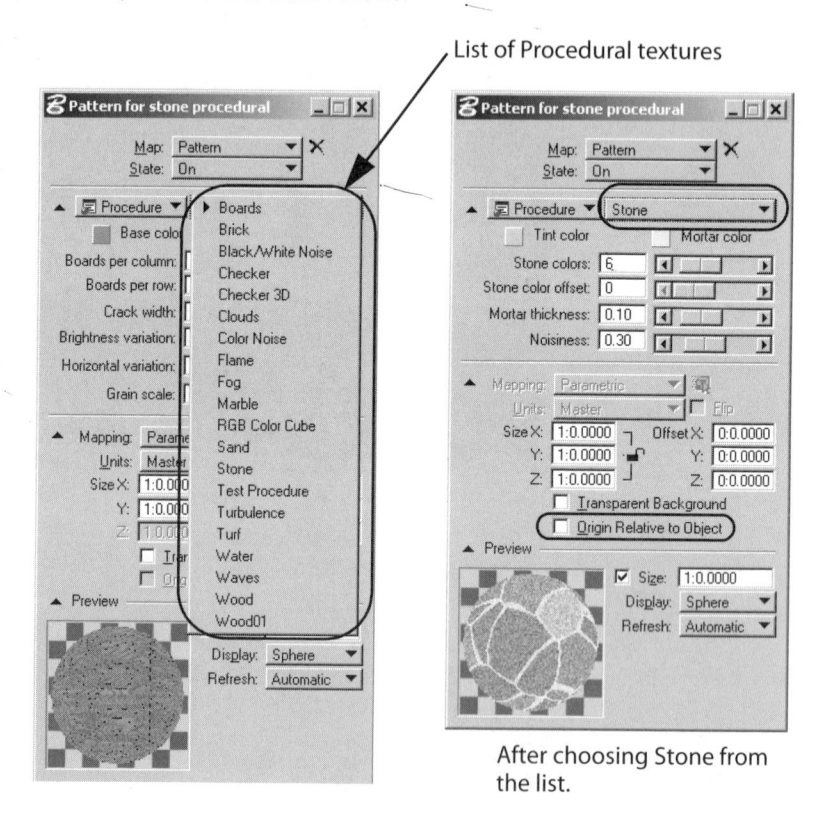

List of Procedural textures

After choosing Stone from the list.

NOTE: *Remember that you can see information about any field or setting in the dialog boxes simply by hovering the pointer momentarily over it.*

Next, you will modify the parameters for the stone procedural texture.

| Procedural Textures |

✔ Exercise 7-2: Set the parameters for the Stone procedural texture

1. Continuing in *livroom procedural1.dgn*, in the Pattern for stone procedural dialog box, set the following:

   Stone colors: 1
   Stone color offset: 4
   Mortar thickness: .14
   Noisiness: .15
   Size X: 1.5 (Lock the Size by clicking on the lock icon; this will make Y and Z sizes equal to X.)
   Origin Relative to Object: Disabled

2. Click on the Mortar color button.

   The Base Color dialog box opens.

3. In the Base Color dialog box, set Red, Green, and Blue to 84, and click OK.

4. In the Material Editor dialog box, set the following:

   Diffuse: 48
   Specular: 5

5. In the Rendering Tools tool box, select the Apply Material tool.

6. Set the mode to Assign Material by clicking the Assign by Level/Color icon.

7. Set Material to *stone procedural*.

8. Select the fireplace geometry, in View 5, and accept with a data point to make the assignment.

9. Ray trace View 5, creating a new solution.

Comparing the two images on the following page (from Views 2 and 5), notice that the procedural stone texture in the right image (from View 5) has no discontinuity of the stone at the edges. This is not so with the left image, which uses a stone texture pattern map from a photograph. While the stone procedural material looks quite good, it may not appear as realistic as the image mapped material.

> **NOTE:** *You could fix the discontinuity in the left image by dynamically adjusting the pattern map and using more than one*

Texture mapping *(left)* vs. Procedural stone *(right)*.

material definition to apply to the faces of the fireplace. This task, however, can be rather tedious and time consuming.

In the next exercise, you will create a wood procedural texture to apply to the fireplace mantel. In the previous exercise, you may have noticed that when you rendered View 5, the mantel geometry rendered in the element color (red). The data set has two fireplace models and two mantels. This was done so you could easily compare between the two different methods. Views 2 and 6 display the levels for the pattern mapped textures, while Views 5 and 7 display the levels for procedural textures.

In creating the wood procedural texture, because it is a 3D texture like the stone texture, you will be able to adjust the size in the X, Y, and Z directions.

| Procedural Textures |

✔ Exercise 7-3: Create a wood procedural texture

1. Continuing with **livroom procedural1.dgn**, in the Material Editor dialog, right-click on material *mantel* and select Copy from the menu.

2. Right-click again and select Paste from the menu.

   The copy of the material is pasted as *mantel[1]*.

3. Right click on *mantel[1]* and choose Rename from the menu.

4. Change the name to *mantel procedural*.

   By doing this, you are copying all the finish characteristics of the current mantel material. The only property you will need to change will be the texture, which you will change from a pattern map to a procedural texture.

5. In the Material Editor, click the Pattern Map icon.

6. In the Pattern for mantel procedural dialog box, change the Type from Image to Procedure.

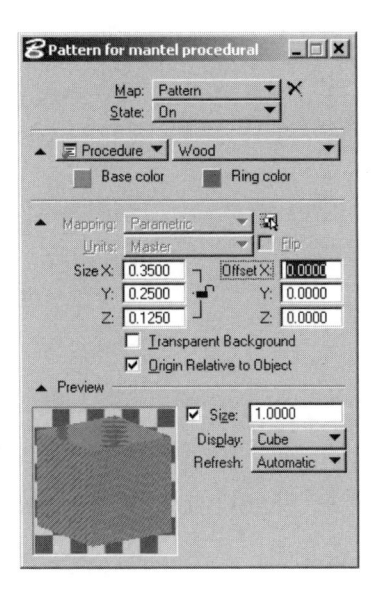

7. From the list of procedural materials, select Wood.

8. In the settings, set the following sizes:

   X: 0.35
   Y: 0.25
   Z: 0.125

   NOTE: *Doubling the value in the Size X field, relative to those for Y and Z, stretches the pattern of the wood grain along the x-axis. Doubling the value in the Size Y field, relative to those for X and Z, stretches the pattern of the wood grain along the y-axis.*

9. Select the Apply Material tool, and use it to apply the new material, *mantel procedural*, to the red mantel geometry in View 7.

10. Ray trace View 6, creating a new solution.

11 Ray trace View 7, creating a new solution.

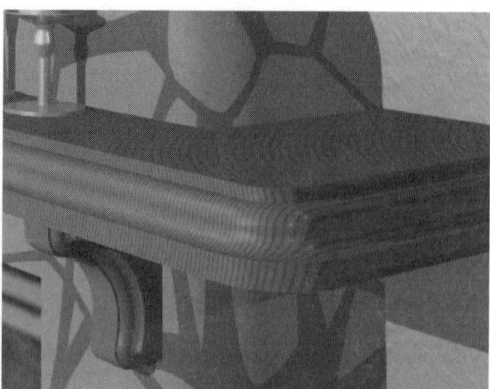

Texture using pattern map *(left)* and procedural texture *(right)*.

Comparing the two renderings, notice in the right image that the procedural texture's grain looks like what you might expect to see in a piece of wood that has been cut with a router. The grain in the left image is not very accurate in the cut area since it is a two-dimensional pattern map with no easy control over the mapping in the cut area.

There are several procedural textures to choose from in the materials delivered with MicroStation. Not all are 3D but each is worth trying, particularly Stone, Clouds, and Flame. MicroStation's online help files provide additional information on working with procedural textures.

In this next exercise, you will look at the procedure Clouds, which is used to provide a sky background.

✔ Exercise 7-4: Procedural texture clouds

1 Open the design file *clouds.dgn*.

This model consists of a revolved arc that creates a 360° hemispherical dome surface. The other geometry is from reference files and consists of a bridge model and terrain. The lighting is from a reference with an array of distant lights.

2 Ray trace View 2.

| Procedural Textures |

Looking at the resulting ray traced camera view, notice the clouds and sky look quite realistic. This is the procedural texture Clouds that has already been created and applied to the dome surface.

NOTE: *The material properties for the dome will be similar to that for a sky cylinder covered in Chapter 9. The material has been set up with Diffuse and Specular both 0, Shadow casting disabled, and Ambient set to 1000. By making Diffuse 0, the material is unaffected by any of the source lights, other than Ambient, making the material the same brightness no matter where you point the camera. By disabling Shadow casting, the distant lights or solar light can shine through the dome to illuminate the model. Making Specular 0 eliminates any shiny spots appearing on the sky dome.*

Procedural Clouds.

Let's look now at the settings available for the procedural texture Clouds.

✔ **Exercise 7-5: Work with settings for procedural texture Clouds**

1. Continuing in *clouds.dgn*, select the Define Material tool to open the Material Editor.

2. From the list of materials, select Clouds.

3. In the Material Editor, click the Pattern Map icon.

| Chapter 7: Advanced Materials |

The Pattern for clouds dialog box opens. Notice that the texture is a procedure.

The Clouds procedure contains several user-adjustable settings. The following is a description for each.

Cloud color: Lets you define the color of the clouds. The default color is white.

Sky color: Lets you define the color of the sky. The default color is a sky blue.

By adjusting these colors, you can create sunset skies or stormy skies.

Thickness: Controls the relative scaling factor for the thickness of the clouds (default 1.5). The minimum is 0.0 and the maximum is 5.0. Values less than 1.0 produce more wispy clouds, and values above 1.0 produce more patchy clouds.

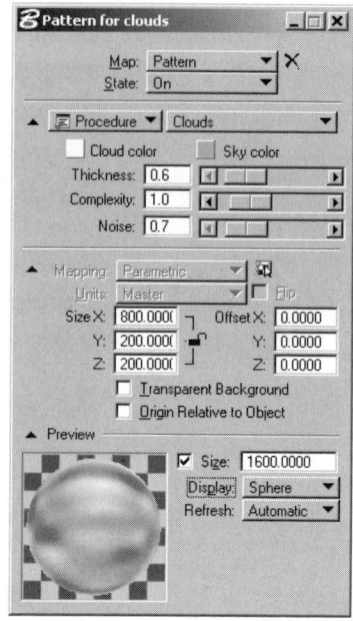

Procedural texture settings for Clouds.

Complexity: The number of levels of detail in the cloud pattern, with a range of 0.0 to 24.0 (default 4.0). The calculation time increases one-for-one with changes in this value, with lower numbers taking less time to render.

Noise: Controls the appearance of the clouds, with allowable values from 0.0 to 5.0. Low values produce smoother clouds, while higher values produce grainier results.

Origin Relative to Object: Determines how the texture will be mapped to an object. If enabled, the texture's origin will remain the same no matter where it resides in 3D space. If disabled, the origin of the texture would be based on the global origin of the model. If the geometry it is applied to is a cell, then the cell origin would be used.

Like Wood and Stone procedural textures, Clouds is three-dimensional, letting you scale the texture in X, Y, and Z. Unlike a standard texture, the Clouds procedure will correctly map to a sphere or, as in this case, a dome. A pattern mapped image would wind up tight at the poles or be stretched at the equator, making a dome surface unsuitable for an image mapped pattern. The Clouds procedural texture, on the other hand, will look natural even if you point the camera straight up, thus providing a completely immersive environment. In a later chapter you will learn to create VR Panoramas, so make a note now that by using the procedural Clouds and a sky dome, you can create a completely immersive environment perfect for exterior scenes rendered to cubic panoramas.

Try experimenting with the settings, ray tracing the view to check the effects. You can also see that the clouds palette already has several definitions. Try assigning these to the sky dome and ray trace View 2 to see the results.

Gradient Maps

Along with pattern/bump maps and procedural textures, the Material Editor in MicroStation lets you create gradient maps. Two types of gradient maps are available, linear and radial, which are applied as follows:

Linear gradient — Color is constant in the Y direction of the map. Its colors are interpolated or blended from one color to another along the X direction of the map.

Radial gradient — Colors are interpolated based on the distance from the origin of the map.

When you work with gradient maps:

- Linear gradients may be rotated, while the angle setting has no effect on radial gradients.

- When creating a gradient as a map, you can specify up to 50 different color keys. Colors can be edited, and the color keys can be repositioned as required.

- When you want to use a gradient as a repeating map, with a smooth transition, you should set the first and last colors to be identical.

In the next exercise, you will be using gradients and transparency to create the effect of deepening water levels in a swimming pool and also a circular jacuzzi. The materials have been created to show you a real-world example of how gradients can be used. You will be examining the settings rather than creating and assigning these materials.

Chapter 7: Advanced Materials

✔ Exercise 7-6: Work with linear gradient maps

1. Open the DGN file *gradients1.dgn*.

   In this model, Views 2 and 4 are camera views, from the shallow end of the pool, looking toward the deep end.

2. Ray trace View 2, creating a new solution.

   You can see the water appears to all be of the same depth.

Pool ray traced with no gradient map.

3. Ray trace View 4, creating a new solution.

   Notice how the water now appears to get deeper away from the camera. This view has a copy of the complex shape used for the water just a little below the original and, with a gradient map applied, it is also on a separate level which is not on in View 2.

Pool ray traced using a gradient map.

| Gradient Maps |

Looking at the settings helps to explain the settings used, including how the gradient map was created.

✔ Exercise 7-7: Inspect the gradient material settings

1. Continuing in *gradients1.dgn*, select the Define Material tool to open the Material Editor.

2. From the list of materials select *pool gradient*.

3. Set the Preview Display to:

   Mode: Ray Trace
   Display: Rectangle

4. With Material Editor in Advanced Mode, look at the current settings:

   Diffuse is fairly low at 18.
   Transparency is 100.
   Ambient is 100.

5. In the Material Editor, click the Pattern Map icon.

   In the Pattern for pool gradient dialog box, notice that the option menu on the left is set to Gradient. Notice also that the option menu on the right is set to Linear.

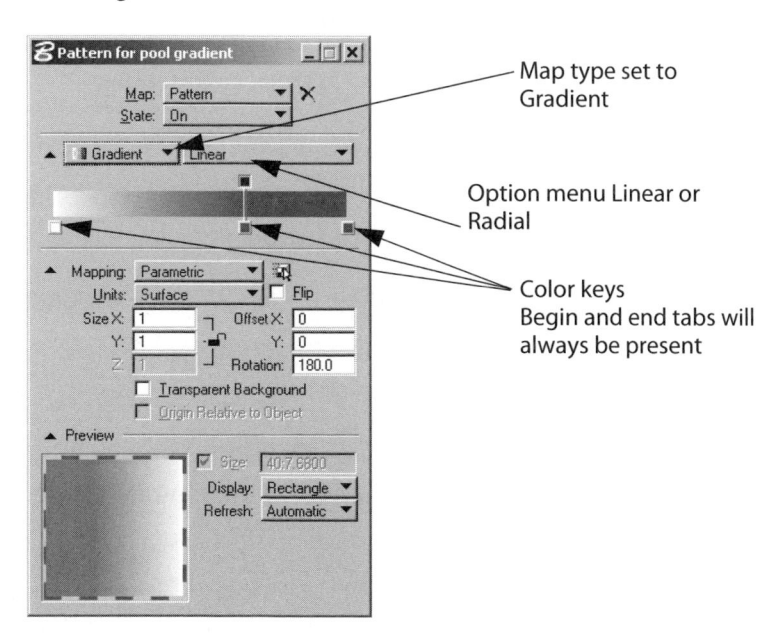

   - Map type set to Gradient
   - Option menu Linear or Radial
   - Color keys Begin and end tabs will always be present

Using gradient maps to create the effect of deepening water is just one application for using gradients. You can use gradients also to create a twilight sky background. Used for this purpose, like the Clouds procedure, a gradient will map to a dome surface.

There are several options available to you when creating gradient maps.

To add color keys when creating your own gradients:

1   If necessary, in the Map Editor dialog box, expand the section displaying the image type (Gradient) and gradient type, to reveal the gradient color bar.

2   Enter a data point on the color bar at the desired position for the key.

    The key is added. Initially, the color is set to the interpolated value of the gradient at that point.

3   Repeat the above step for further color keys, as required.

To reposition a color key on a gradient:

1   Click on the vertical bar for the desired color key, and drag it to its new location.

You cannot drag a key past another key, but they can be abutted to cause a sharp edge between adjacent colors. The first and last keys of the gradient cannot be moved, but if you try to drag them, a copy is made of the key. If you drag another key all the way to either end of the gradient color bar, then that key will replace the end key.

To change the color of a color key:

1   Click on the color (lower) button for the color key.

    The Gradient Color Chooser dialog box opens.

2   Use the controls in the dialog box to define the required color.

3   Click OK.

    The dialog box closes and the gradient displays with the new color included.

To delete a color key(s) of a gradient:

1   Click on the vertical bar, or the top button, for the required key.

| Gradient Maps | **269**

The button at the top of the color key highlights.

2 (Optional) Use <Ctrl> data points to select additional keys to delete.

3 Press the <Delete> key.

or

While the top button is highlighted, right-click to open a menu and select Delete.

NOTE: *The first and last keys cannot be deleted. If, however, you drag another key all the way to either end of the gradient color bar, then that key will replace the end key.*

In an example similar to the previous, this time using radial gradients, you can make the round jacuzzi in the pool scene appear deeper in the middle. For this effect to work, a polygon was placed a little below the circle used for the water. The polygon then was mirrored to create quarter flips of the gradient map, thus forming a circular image.

Single polygon *(left)* and four polygons mirrored and quarter flipped *(right)*.

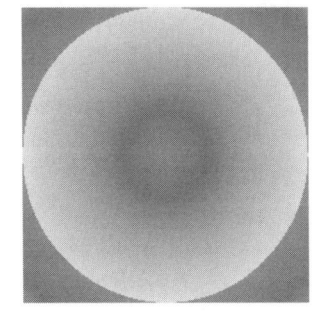

✔ Exercise 7-8: Use radial gradients

1 Continuing with ***gradients1.dgn***, ray trace View 5, creating a new solution.

Notice that the water in the jacuzzi all appears to be of the same depth.

2 Ray trace View 6, creating a new solution.

As in the previous exercise, the radial gradient provides the effect of a deepening pool, only this time it is circular.

| Chapter 7: Advanced Materials |

Without gradient map.   With radial gradient map.

In the following exercise, the steps explain the settings used, including how the gradient map was created.

✔ **Exercise 7-9: Inspect the radial gradient settings**

1. Continuing in *gradients1.dgn*, select the Define Material tool to open the Material Editor.

2. From the list of materials, select *jacuzzi gradient*.

3. If necessary, set the Preview Display to Rectangle.

4. With Material Editor in Advanced Mode, look at the current settings:

   Diffuse: Quite low at 15
   Transparency: 100
   Ambient: 100

5. If necessary, in the Material Editor, click the Pattern Map icon to open the Pattern Map Editor.

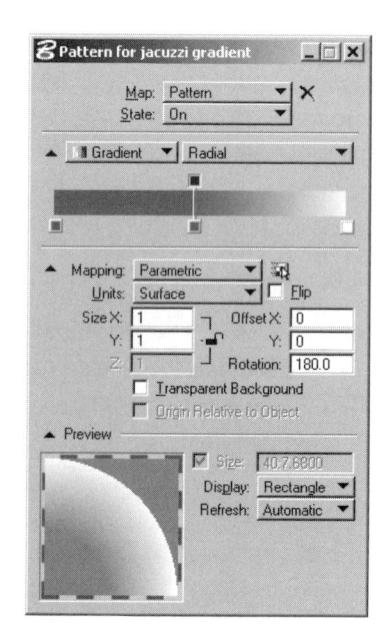

Radial Gradient used for Jacuzzi

Notice in the Map Editor dialog box that the option menu on the left is set to Gradient and the Type is Radial. The color of the keys is slightly different from that used for the swimming pool, leaning a little more toward green than blue.

Gradients can make nice backdrops for models and work well when adding colors to glass bottles or wine goblets. You can see from the previous examples that they definitely work well for creating the illusion of depth in a pool of water. They are another tool in your rendering tool box — just let your imagination be your guide.

USING ARCHVISION RPC FILES

MicroStation supports ArchVision's Rich Photorealistic Content, or RPC, 3D textures such as realPeople and realTrees, and RPC 3.0 content such as RPC Automobiles and Objects. RPCs are replaced dynamically, at render time, with images from the RPC files that are appropriate for the current viewing direction. That is, during rendering, RPCs are replaced by geometry and texture maps extracted from the RPC files. The maps selected are determined by the orientation of the camera with respect to the RPC and the current animation frame number for an animated RPC.

ArchVision Content Manager

For newer RPC content, ArchVision Content Manager is required, along with an ArchVision licence. From MicroStation, you can access the ArchVision Content Manager via the Configure Content button in the RPC Thumbnail Viewer. Refer to ArchVision *(www.archvision.com)* for information on RPC and their licensing.

Where required, MicroStation's thumbnail browser may be disabled via a configuration variable. To disable the RPC thumbnail browser, set the configuration variable **MS_DISABLE_RPCBROWSER** to a value of 1. To re-enable the browser, set the configuration variable to 0 (zero), or leave blank.

The RPC Tool Box

Tools for placing and editing RPCs are located in the RPC tools tool box, which is opened by selecting Tools > Visualization > RPC.

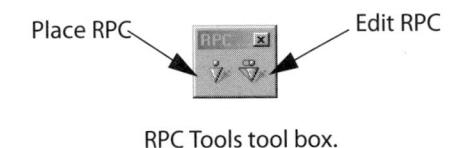

Place RPC   Edit RPC

RPC Tools tool box.

You use the Place RPC tool to place RPC in a model. Settings for this tool let you select, via combo boxes, a Directory, Category, and Name for the RPC. Additional controls let you browse for a directory, refresh the combo boxes, or view the RPC content via a thumbnail browser.

If you're placing an RPC for the first time, you will automatically be presented with the file browser. Other tool settings let you set the height, scale, and size variation for the RPC. A Random rotation setting lets you place RPCs with random rotation, without having to define the target direction for the RPC.

When you first use this tool, all the directories in the search path will be scanned for RPC files. The search path is the list of directories defined by the environment variables MS_PATTERN, MS_BUMP, MS_IMAGE, and MS_DEF. Any time the contents of a directory is changed, it will be rescanned. If for any reason the combo boxes do not accurately list the RPC files present, you can click the Refresh button (immediately to the right of the Browse button. A Reset will abort the scanning for RPC files.

You use the Edit RPC tool to edit the settings for an existing RPC in a model. This includes the option to change the RPC as well as to modify its various settings.

Placing RPCs

When you place an RPC, you can choose to place the RPC with random rotation or you can manually specify the direction of the RPC. This manual rotation option is especially useful when placing people in a scene.

After you select the Place RPC tool, you will first be prompted for the RPC position, which locates the center of the bottom edge of the RPC. Once you have set the RPC position, you will be prompted for the RPC target point, which is the point to which the RPC will face. In other words, it defines the rotation of the RPC about the global z-axis. RPC placement is always such that the vertical axis is parallel to the model's vertical axis. If Random rotation is enabled, each RPC will be placed with a randomly selected orientation, and no additional data point is needed to select the target point.

| Using ArchVision RPC files | 273

✓ Exercise 7-10: Place an RPC

1. Continuing in *cool home.dgn*, enable AccuDraw if not already enabled.
2. Turn on all levels in View 1, and Fit View 1.
3. Make RPCs the active level and make the active color 0.

   RPCs are placed using the active level and color.
4. Select Tools > Visualization > RPC to open the RPC tools tool box.
5. Select the Place RPC tool.
6. Click on the Browse for file icon in the Place RPC dialog box.

   The Select RPC Directory dialog box opens.
7. Navigate to the *Workspace\projects\render\RPC* folder and click OK.
8. In the Place RPC dialog box, from the Category menu, select People [Casual].
9. From the Name menu, select Vicki & Sierra.

   At this point the RPC will appear at the pointer location and move with it. Notice that there are two profiles of the subject in wireframe display at 90° to each other. Notice also that the base of the wireframe representation comes to a point on one side. This indicates the front in the RPC.
10. Check the following RPC settings:

    Random rotation: Off

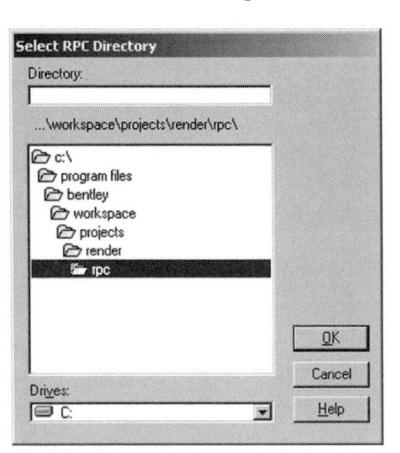

| Chapter 7: Advanced Materials |

Scale: 100%
Size Variation: 0%.

NOTE: *The Random rotation and Size variation features are useful for quickly placing a number of trees or plants in a file.*

11 With Snap mode set to Center Snap, snap to the edge of the green polygon for the rug in View 2.

The pointer snaps to the center of the polygon (rug).

12 Accept with a data point to place the RPC.

13 Set the AccuDraw compass to Top rotation to make it easier to orient the RPC. The RPC will rotate as you move your cursor to set orientation.

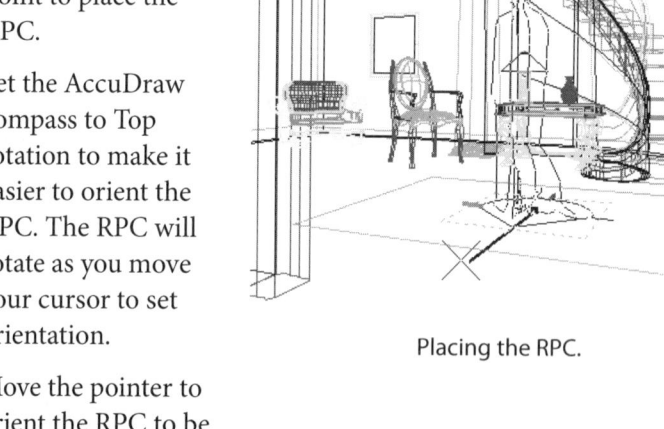

Placing the RPC.

14 Move the pointer to orient the RPC to be facing the archway and enter a data point to finish.

• •

✔ **Exercise 7-11: Place a second RPC**

1 Continuing in *cool home.dgn*, with the Place RPC tool still active, select Tina[2] from the Name list.

2 Disable AccuSnap if on.

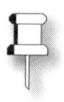

NOTE: *With the focus on AccuDraw, entering a j toggles AccuSnap on and off.*

| Using ArchVision RPC files | 275

3 In View 2, move your pointer to place the RPC near the bottom of the stairs.

You can check in the Top view to make sure you are in the right location and not too far back where the stair geometry could interfere.

4 Enter a data point to place the RPC.

5 Enter a second data point to orient the RPC to face toward the previously placed RPC.

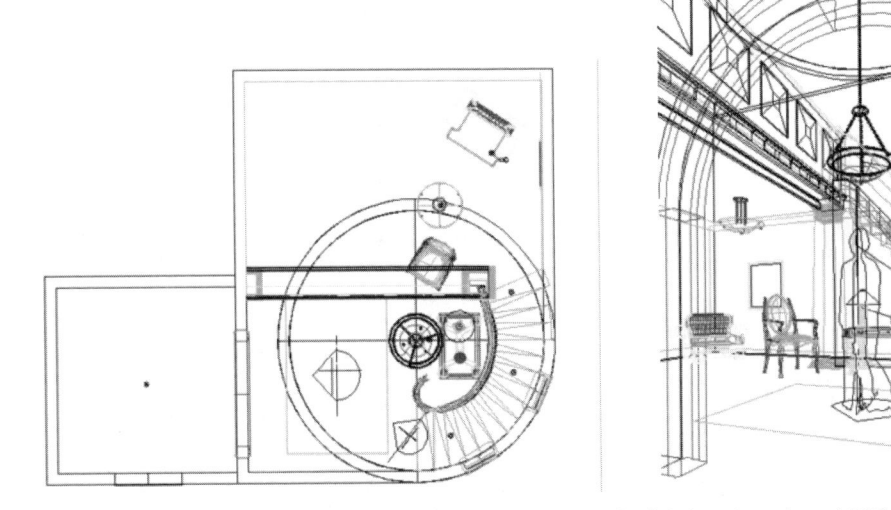

Wireframe Top view *(left)* and camera view *(right)* showing placed RPCs.

Some RPCs may appear to be floating slighting above the surface when rendered. To correct this, you can move them vertically downward a small amount. A few test renderings may be required to make sure they appear to be on the ground or floor.

6 Ray trace View 2, creating a new solution.

Notice that the rendered RPCs appear to be floating just above the floor.

7 Using the Selector tool, select both RPCs.

8 Using AccuDraw, move both RPCs downward 0.0254 units in Z.

9 Release the RPCs from the selection.

| Chapter 7: Advanced Materials |

10 Ray trace View 2, creating a new solution.

Both RPCs you just placed and rendered are image objects, meaning that they have multiple images and will display a different image if the camera angle is changed. For instance, Tina[2] has the following properties: Images 362, Frames 1. This information is available in the Place RPC tool dialog box. You can display these properties by clicking the arrowhead icon at the lower left corner of the dialog box (the same icon is used to close the Properties section).

Exercise 7-12: Render another view

1 Continuing in *cool home.dgn*, attach the saved view *rpc view 2* to View 6.

2 Ray trace View 6 using the current solution.

Ray traced views with RPC added.

As you can clearly see in the above rendered views, the images within the RPC changed with the different camera angle. RPCs like these will appear three-dimensional when animating a camera

| Using ArchVision RPC files |

through a scene. They can be very useful also for quickly adding render ready content to your scene.

Editing RPCs

You can use the Edit RPC tool to edit the values applied to an RPC, as well as to change it to another RPC in the library.

In the next exercise, you will use the Edit RPC tool to change one of the RPCs that you placed in the previous exercise.

✔ Exercise 7-13: Edit RPC

1. Continuing in *cool home.dgn*, in the RPC tools tool box, select the Edit RPC tool.

2. Move your cursor over the first RPC you placed and enter a data point.

   The Edit RPC dialog box opens.

3. From the Name menu, select Lisa.

4. If necessary, click the Show RPC properties icon at the lower left corner of the dialog box to display the RPC properties.

   NOTE: *Notice that the wireframe display changes and you see only a single profile rather than two as before. The RPC you selected on this occasion is two-dimensional. Notice, in the Properties section, the Images value is 1 and the Frames value is 600. These values, along with the word Motion and the figure 600, in the preview, indicate that this is a special type of RPC that will animate automatically when you create an animation in MicroStation. For these RPCs, you do not need to add anything special to your animation script; they will animate automatically. Additionally, all 2D RPCs will billboard, or face the camera, at all times, so you do not have to worry about seeing them at severe camera angles, or edge on.*

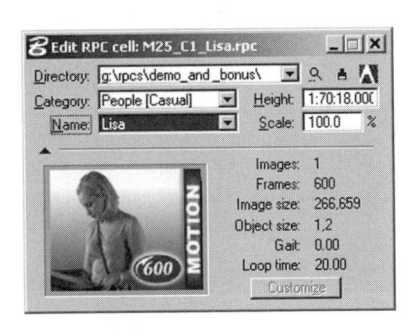

| Chapter 7: Advanced Materials |

5 Enter a data point in any view to accept the change.

6 Ray trace View 2, creating a new solution.

The new RPC, Lisa, appears in place of Vicki & Sierra.

7 Ray trace View 6 using the current solution.

Comparing the two renderings, you can see that, while there is a variation in the pose for Tina [2] in the two views, Lisa looks the same in both.

NOTE: *Additional information on using RPC files can be found in MicroStation's help files.*

Review Questions

1 How can you tell whether a procedural texture is 3D or not?

2 Name one advantage to a procedural texture.

3 When using the Clouds procedural texture mapped to a dome around your model, what should the diffuse and specular properties be?

4 Making the clouds appear bright requires you set a high value to which material property?

5 What are the two types of gradient maps?

6 How many different color keys can you specify when creating a gradient as a map?

7 What does RPC stand for?

8 Name three different types of RPC.

Chapter Summary

In this chapter, you learned about MicroStation's advanced materials, and ArchVision's "Rich Photo-realistic Content" RPCs. You saw how to define and edit procedural textures, and how to apply gradient maps to material definitions. You saw the difference between ArchVision's 2D and 3D RPCs, and how the 3D RPCs simulate 3D objects in rendered views.

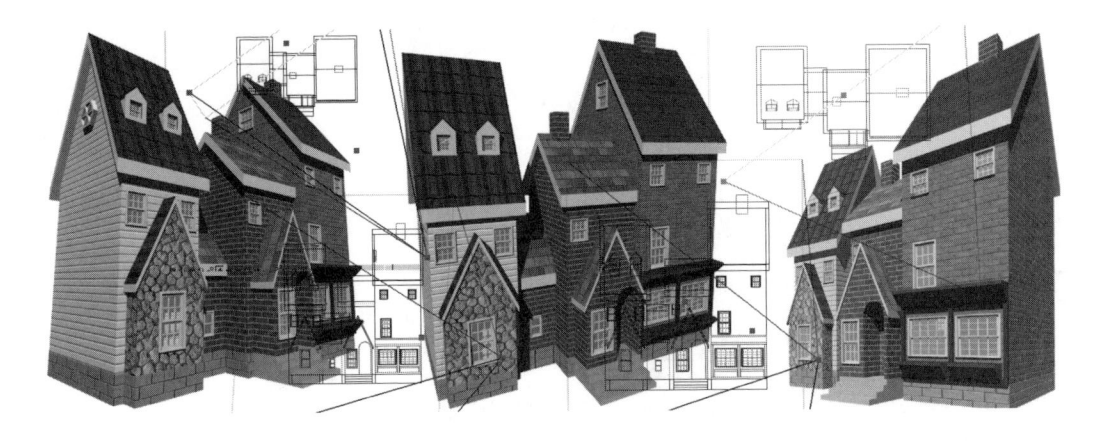

8 Facet Smoothing and Elevation Draping

MicroStation's Facet Smoothing tool is used to improve the rendered quality of discrete polygons. It is used to apply smoothing to any polygonal model. In this chapter, you will learn to use the Facet Smoothing tool to smooth models constructed from individual polygons.

This chapter continues the subject of applying materials to elements in a model, but with the focus on digital terrain models (DTM). It covers items that are essential for working with DTMs: Facet Smoothing and Elevation Draping.

SURFACE NORMALS

Prior to a discussion on facet smoothing, one needs to know a little bit about "surface normals" since they play an important role in the use of the Facet Smoothing tool. A *surface normal* is a vector perpendicular to a surface pointing outward. A solid or 3D primitive such as a cone, slab, or sphere will have surface normals as well. With a solid, the surface normals will always face away from the solid. Every time you place a polygon in MicroStation, it will have a surface normal. For performance reasons, most virtual reality software packages will only render the sides of those polygons that have the normal pointing toward the

| Chapter 8: Facet Smoothing and Elevation Draping |

viewer. MicroStation always renders both sides of surfaces; however, you can toggle this feature off when using radiosity or particle tracing.

When a surface is mirrored in MicroStation, the surface normals are flipped, as seen in the following image.

Dome with surface normals pointing out *(left)*, and the same dome after being mirrored pointing inward *(right)*.

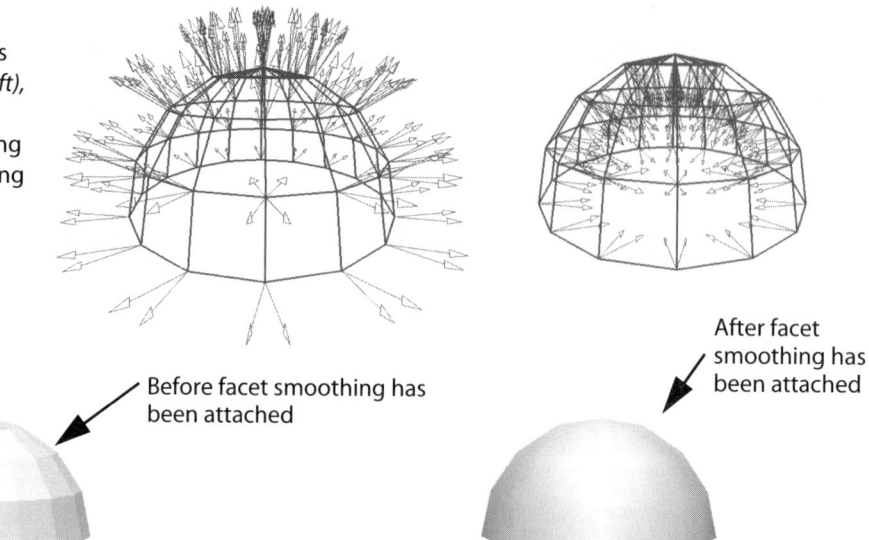

Before facet smoothing has been attached

After facet smoothing has been attached

Since all the normals for the dome are reversed, the facet smoothing will still work fine. What if you were to create half of the symmetrical geometry and mirror that?

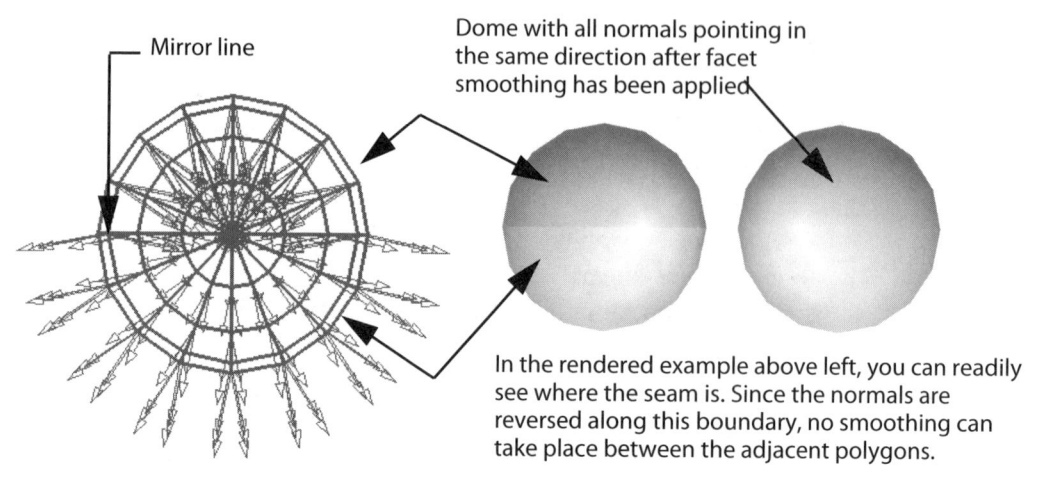

Mirror line

Dome with all normals pointing in the same direction after facet smoothing has been applied

In the rendered example above left, you can readily see where the seam is. Since the normals are reversed along this boundary, no smoothing can take place between the adjacent polygons.

Top view of dome showing flipped surface normals.

| Facet Smoothing |

From the Modify Surfaces tools, you can use the Change Normal Direction tool to flip a normal or a selection set of normals.

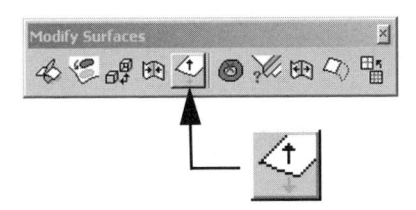

The Change Normal Direction tool is used, in 3D only, to change the surface normal direction for a surface (cone, extruded surface, surface of revolution, or B-spline surface).

It is also used in conjunction with other tools to control the way that elements are treated.

To change a surface's normal direction:

1   Select the Change Normal Direction tool.

2   Identify the surface.

    The surface normals display.

3   Accept to change the direction of the surface normals.

Alternative method to change a surface's normal direction:

1   Use the Element Selection tool to select the surface(s).

2   Select the Change Normal Direction tool.

    The normal direction is changed for the selected surface(s).

FACET SMOOTHING

Facet Smoothing rounds the edges of intersections of discrete polygons. To do this, the normals for the polygons are calculated by averaging the normals of adjacent polygons, thereby softening their otherwise harsh, or faceted, appearance. Applications where this is desirable include digital terrain modeling and cases where approximated surfaces have been created, usually as a result of translating a file. Where facet smoothing is used, the new normals are written to the selected polygons as attribute linkage data. The polygons themselves are not modified.

| Chapter 8: Facet Smoothing and Elevation Draping |

✔ Exercise 8-1: Attach facet smoothing to a DTM

1. Open the DGN file *example dtm.dgn*.

   The file opens with four views displayed, View 2 being a camera view.

2. Ray trace View 2.

   If necessary, adjust the Brightness/Contrast to display the detail in the image.

   Notice how the faceting of the triangles is clearly visible in the rendering.

3. From the MicroStation main menu, choose Utilities > Named Groups.

   The Named Groups dialog box opens.

4. In the Named Groups dialog box, select the named group *portion* in the list box.

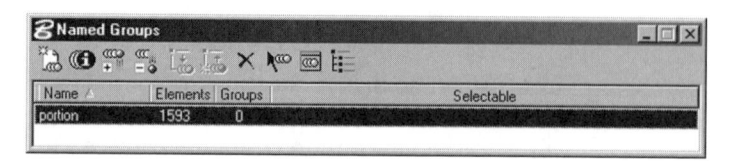

   The named group *portion* is a predefined selection of polygons in part of the DTM.

5. In the Named Groups dialog box, click the Select Elements icon.

   A portion of the polygons in the DTM are selected.

6. In the Rendering Tools tool box, select the Facet Smoothing tool.

   The Facet Smoothing dialog box opens.

7. In the Facet Smoothing tool settings, set the following:

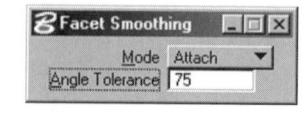

   Mode: Attach.
   Angle Tolerance: 75

8. Enter a data point in any view to attach the smoothing attribute to the selected polygons.

9. Ray trace View 2, creating a new solution.

| Facet Smoothing | **285**

Notice how the polygons from the selection set now appear smooth when rendered.

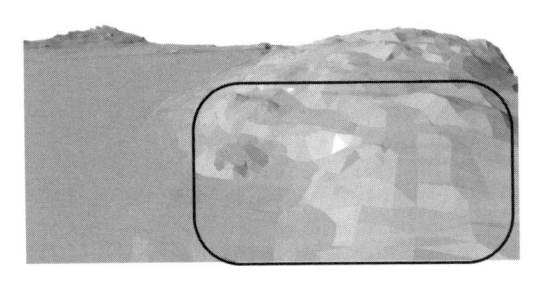

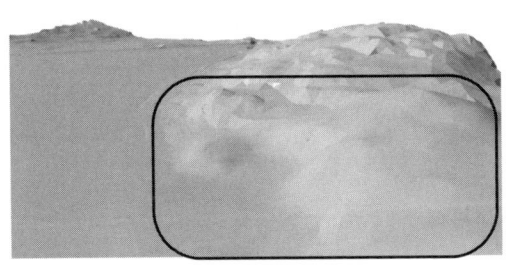

Highlighted area shows the rendered polygons before *(left)* and after *(right)* applying facet smoothing.

NOTE: *When facet smoothing large files, it may be considerably faster if you apply smoothing to several selections separately, rather than trying to smooth all the polygons at once. It is acceptable to apply smoothing to polygons that already have the smoothing attribute attached, so you can overlap your selections.*

✔ **Exercise 8-2: Attach all the polygons for smoothing**

1 Continuing in *example dtm.dgn*, in View 1, use the Selector tool to select all the polygons in the DTM.

   This design file only contains triangles, so you could optionally select all elements by choosing Edit > Select All from the main tool bar.

2 In the Rendering Tools tool box, select the Facet Smoothing tool.

3 Using the same settings as for the previous exercise, enter a data point in any view to attach the smoothing attribute to all the polygons.

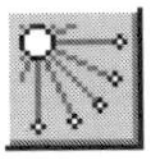

4 Ray trace View 2, creating a new solution.

Rendered DTM after facet smoothing all polygons.

ELEVATION DRAPING

In Chapter 6, you used elevation draping as the pattern mapping mode for the Tiffany lamp texture. Elevation Draping lays the texture onto elements like a blanket being shaken out and allowed to fall. In that regard, it falls only in the Z-direction, so you can think of it as being affected by gravity and always falling toward the ground plane.

The main purpose of the elevation draping mode is for draping aerial photos, or other materials, over a large number of individual polygons such as you may get in a digital terrain model (DTM). Typically, a DTM file is represented by a network of thousands of individual planar triangles that are created from survey data.

In the following exercises, you will drape an aerial photograph of the terrain over the geometry in the model. To do this, you need to know some details of the geometry—namely, its location and dimensions. This will let you properly set up the image for the material with the correct size and location.

The aerial photo that you will be using in the following exercise needs to precisely match the extents of terrain model. You will need to determine the extents of the geometry in the design X-Y plane, limiting the measurement to a single X-Y plane. While using the Measure between Points tool, you can lock the z-axis with AccuDraw after snapping to the first corner.

✔ Exercise 8-3: Get information for material map

1. Continuing with *example dtm.dgn*.

2. From the Main tool, click on the Measure Distance tool with the Distance option set to Between Points.

3. Enable AccuDraw and AccuSnap if not already enabled.

4. Snap to the lower left corner of the geometry in View 1 and enter a data point to start the measurement. Move your cursor toward the right and hit the <z> key, followed by the <Enter> key. This will turn on AccuDraw's Lock Z function.

5. Snap to the lower right corner of the geometry and enter a data point.

| Elevation Draping | 287

You should see Last Distance 800.00m in the Measure Distance dialog box.

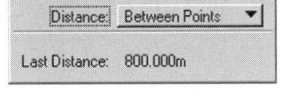

6   Enter a Reset to start a new measurement.

7   Snap to the lower right corner of the geometry in View 1 and enter a data point to start the measurement. Turn on Z-Lock by hitting the <z> key followed by the <Enter> key.

8   Snap to the upper right corner and enter a data point to measure the distance between points.

    Note the measurement is 600.00m.

    NOTE: *For this model, the four corners have the same Z value but it is more likely that you would not have this condition. By locking the z-axis during measurement of your terrain model, you can make sure your measurements are planar.*

9   Determine the X,Y coordinates of the lower left corner of geometry with a tentative snap.

    The readout is located just to the right of the message center, where you should see 40800.000, 104200.000, 0.000. Make note of the X and Y values, as you will need them for the X,Y Offset when creating the material.

    NOTE: *If you don't see the coordinate values for your tentative snap point, it may be that you need to set your tentative point mode to locate. From the main tool window select Utilities > Key-in to open the Key-in dialog box if not already open. Use the following key-in:* **SET TPMODE LOCATE.** *After this, when you snap to a point, its coordinates will appear in the status bar.*

You now are ready to define the material to drape over the DTM.

✔ **Exercise 8-4:   Create the elevation drape material**

1   In the Rendering Tools tool box, select the Define Materials tool.

    The Material Editor dialog box opens.

2   In the Material Editor, click the New Material icon.

    A new palette and a new material are created.

3   Right-click on New Material[1] and choose Rename in the menu.

| Chapter 8: Facet Smoothing and Elevation Draping |

4 Change the name to *aerial photo*.

5 With the Material Editor in Advanced mode, set Specular to 0 by moving the slider all the way to the left.

You do not want the ground to appear shiny. Setting Specular to 0 makes the material appear dull or flat.

NOTE: *When using a bump map, you will need to have the Specular value above 0.*

6 Click the Pattern Map icon located to the right of the color slider.

The Open Image File dialog box opens.

7 Navigate to the course *Textures* directory, select *aerial_photo.jpg*, and then click OK.

The Pattern for aerial photo dialog box opens.

8 In the Pattern for aerial photo dialog box, set the following:

Mapping: Elevation Drape
Size X: 800
Size Y: 600
Offset X: 40800
Offset Y: 104200.

The Offset X and Y settings define where the lower left corner of the image corresponds to the geometry.

9 In the Material Editor select Palette > Save As.

10 Change the name to *aerial.pal* and click OK.

With the elevation drape material defined, you now can apply it to the geometry in the model.

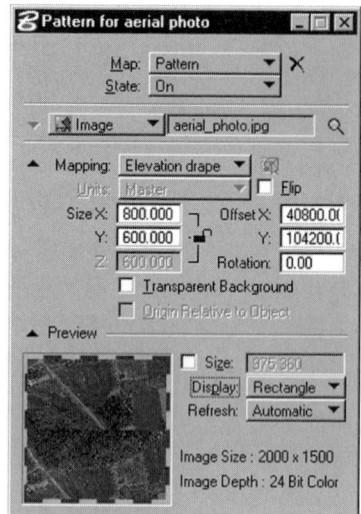

Exercise 8-5: Assign the elevation drape material

1 In the Rendering Tools tool box, select the Apply Material tool.

You will be assigning the material by color/level, so that all the polygons are included in the elevation drape.

| Review Questions | **289**

2 Click the Assign by Color/Level icon.

3 Identify any of the polygons in the DTM and accept with a second data point.

4 Ray trace View 1.

5 With the current solution, ray trace View 2.

Notice that the aerial photo covers all the polygons as one large image. The origin of the image is the lower left corner of geometry as determined by the Offset X, Y settings. The image covers exactly the 800x600 meters area as determined by the Size X,Y settings.

Rendered image of View 2.

REVIEW QUESTIONS

1 In which direction do surface normals point on a solid?

2 What happens to surface normals when a surface is mirrored in MicroStation?

3 What is the name of the technique that can be used to improve the rendered quality of discrete polygons?

4 What pattern mapping mode is used to apply aerial photos, or other materials, over a large number of individual polygons such as you may get in a digital terrain model (DTM)?

CHAPTER SUMMARY

In this chapter, you have learned how to attach facet smoothing to a digital terrain model to smooth out, for rendering, an otherwise faceted model. In addition, you learned how to create a material using an aerial photo as a texture map, and then how to apply this material by elevation draping it onto the model.

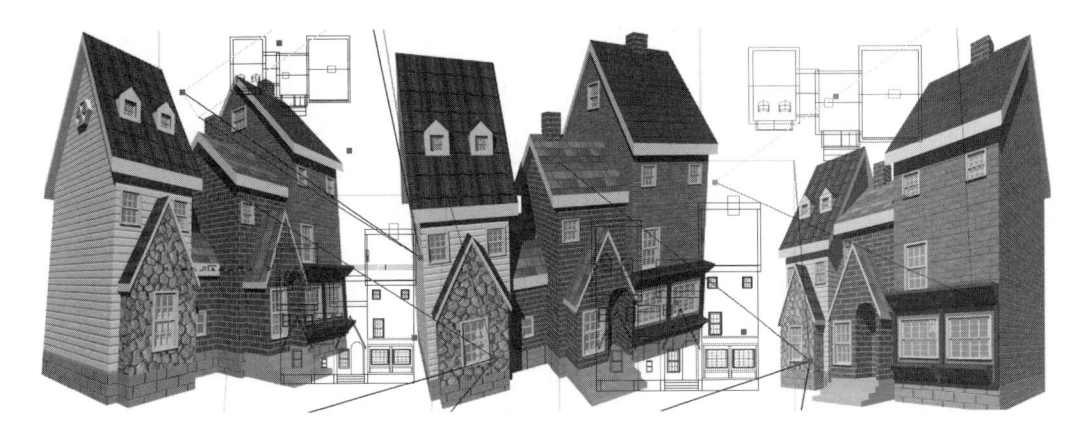

9 Exterior Rendering

Renderings of exterior models are affected by several factors, including the choice of materials and the lighting settings, both Global Lighting and Source Lighting. Even an outstanding model can look dull if it is poorly illuminated. This chapter shows you how to set up lighting for both day and nighttime renderings.

In addition to lighting, you will use fog and depth cueing as both of these rendering view attributes can add a great deal of realism to your exterior renderings.

For exterior renderings to look photorealistic, you will want to include images of the sky. You can do this by adding a background image, using a sky cylinder, or using environment maps in conjunction with a sky box. These techniques are presented in this chapter.

DAYTIME LIGHTING SETUP

Using solar lighting alone can provide good lighting for those surfaces that are directly illuminated by solar light, but it also can leave the shadowed areas much too dark. To solve this problem, you could use the particle tracing or radiosity routines to obtain a more complete lighting solution for your model. These rendering modes take into account the light reflected by the surfaces in the model and thereby illuminate the shadow areas with indirect lighting.

| Chapter 9: Exterior Rendering |

While either of these routines can provide the most realistic results, they require much more computational time to complete a rendering. Instead of using these more complex rendering modes, you will first learn how to effectively illuminate exterior scenes, generating excellent results, using the ray trace rendering method.

✔ Exercise 9-1: Check the global lighting

1. Open model *Site_Exterior*, in DGN file *site.dgn*.
2. Select Global Lighting.

   Note the current settings.

   NOTE: *The azimuth angle associated with the solar direction is measured in degrees clockwise with North (0°) along the y-axis, in the Top view. For example, an azimuth angle of 0.0 would shine directly on the North face, 90.0 would shine directly on the East face, 180.0 on the South face, and 270.0 on the West face. The altitude angle is a measurement of the sun angle in degrees off the horizon. The current settings mean the sun is to the SW and at about 37° above the horizon.*

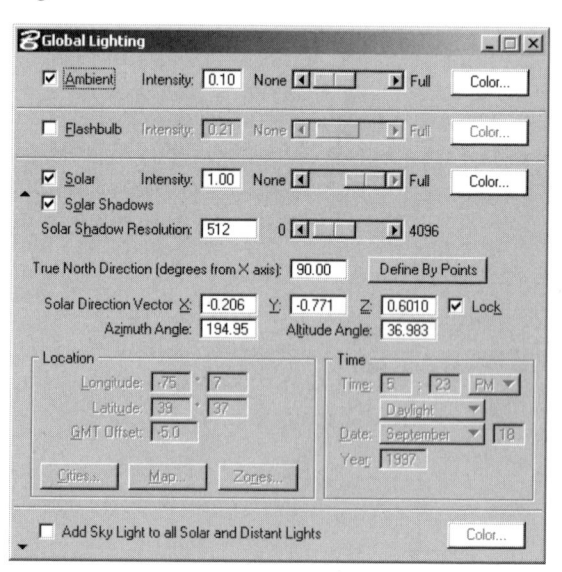

3. Apply the saved view *south side* to View 2 (Utilities > Saved Views).
4. Ray trace View 2, creating a new solution, and adjust the Brightness slider until the grass texture looks good.

   NOTE: *After you interactively adjust the brightness, you will need to redisplay the current solution to correctly render the sky cylinder since the main illumination for the sky cylinder is ambient.*

| Daytime Lighting Setup | 293

Rendering of saved view *south side*.

The lighting looks fairly good, but these faces are directly illuminated by solar lighting.

5 Apply the saved view *from right* to View 4.

6 Ray trace the current solution in View 4.

The view from the right is rendered, and now you can see that this side of the building is in the solar shadow and appears much too dark.

Building viewed from the right side.

Using Sky Light

One option for providing more uniform light is to turn on the setting Add Sky Light to all Solar and Distant Lights, which is located in the Global Lighting dialog box. With this setting enabled, you can add atmospheric lighting from the sky. A Color button lets you define the color of the sky light.

While this feature was discussed in an earlier chapter, it is important for exterior renderings. Hence, we will again look at its use here.

When this setting is turned on with solar lighting, the intensity of the light is modified by the angle of the sun (providing a more realistic solar study). As cloudiness increases, the direct sunlight decreases and the lighting becomes more diffused. On a clear day, for example, the sky is not uniformly lit—more sky light comes from the direction of the sun, thus producing darker, sharper shadows. Alternatively, on a cloudy day, the sky is uniformly lit—producing softer, less pronounced shadows. These same rules are applied to the light from any distant light sources in the model.

Additionally, the amount of coloring from the sky lighting varies. With Air Quality (Turbidity) set to Perfectly Clean, there is a small amount of coloring from the sky lighting. When Air Quality (Turbidity) is set to Industrial, the coloring effect of the sky lighting is more pronounced.

Using the controls in the Global Lighting dialog box, you can set the amount of Cloudiness and the Air Quality (Turbidity) to create the desired conditions for your image.

Sky light is a directional light, coming from an imaginary sky hemisphere and pointing in toward the center. The precision of the hemisphere is determined by the Sky samples setting: the slider control range is from 4 to 145, with larger numbers increasing precision. You can enter a number higher than 145 by entering a value directly into the field.

✔ **Exercise 9-2: Adding Sky Light**

1 Continuing in model **Site_Exterior**, open the Global Lighting dialog box if not already open from the previous exercise.

| Daytime Lighting Setup | **295**

2 In the Global Lighting dialog, click the small down arrow located left of the Add Sky Light to all Solar and Distant Lights setting.

The dialog box expands to display the Sky Light settings.

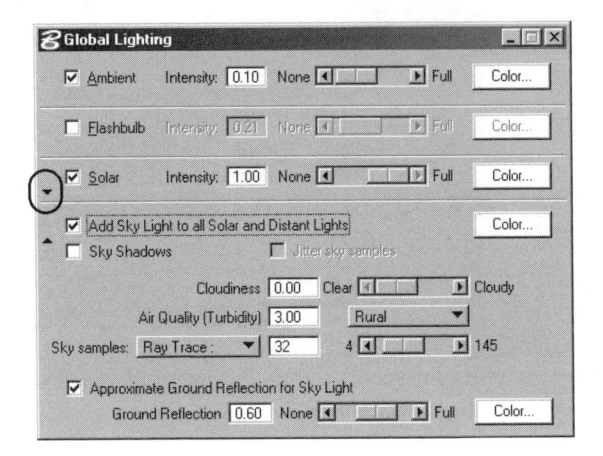

Sky Light settings.

3 Turn on Add Sky Light to all Solar and Distant Lights.

4 If necessary, turn off Sky Shadows.

NOTE: *Turning off Sky Shadows will dramatically improve rendering speed. Sky Shadows work best with particle tracing, and you will not be able to see much of a difference in the final rendering when just ray tracing. It is therefore recommended that you disable this feature for ray trace rendering.*

5 Verify that Sky samples for Ray Trace is 32 (which is the default setting).

6 Turn on Approximate Ground Reflection for Sky Light with the following settings:

Ground Reflection: 0.60.
Color: White (RGB set to 255, 255, 255)

7 Attach the Saved View *from right* to View 5.

8 Ray trace View 5, creating a new solution.

Model rendered with added sky light.

As you can see, the image is much brighter in the shady areas and the entire building model is more uniformly lit.

Using Light Ring and Solar Cluster

In this section, you will be reintroduced to an alternate method for achieving uniform global illumination using a ring of distant light sources. In addition, this method will provide softer shadows than would be provided by solar light alone.

Distant light sources produce directional light, like the sun, with parallel light rays that travel throughout the design. That is, the orientation of the light source defines the direction of uniform light that illuminates all surfaces facing in its direction. This applies whether the surfaces are in front of, or behind, the distant light source in the design. By default, distant light sources have the same brightness as solar lighting.

Distant lights do not shine if pointed upward, when used with ray tracing (with Real World Lighting enabled), particle tracing, or radiosity. This is because they behave identically to the sun and would be below the horizon if they were pointing upward. They will, however, shine upward while ray tracing if Sky Lighting and Real World Lighting are disabled. They also will shine, if pointing upward, for constant, smooth, and phong rendering modes.

In the next exercise, you will add distant light sources to fill in the shadows with additional light. These light sources already have been placed in a DGN file that is referenced to the main model file.

| Daytime Lighting Setup | 297

✔ **Exercise 9-3: Add distant lights to fill in shadows**

1. Continuing in model *Site_Exterior*, in the Global Lighting dialog box, set the following:

   Solar: Off
   Add Sky Light to all Solar and Distant Lights: On
   Sky Shadows: Off

2. Open the References dialog box (File > Reference).

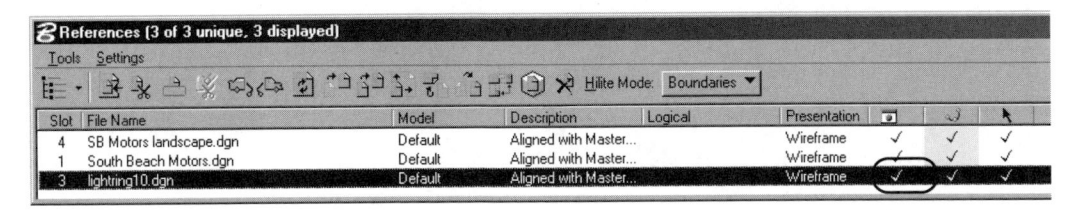

3. Enable display of *lightring10.dgn*.

   Now the reference file lights will be used. These consist of 18 non-shadow-casting distant lights and 10 shadow-casting distant lights.

4. Ray trace View 4, creating a new solution.

5. Adjust the brightness slider so that the grass matches that of the previously rendered View 5 where solar and sky light were used.

6. Ray trace current solution in View 4.

   The dynamic adjustment may not accurately represent the rendered view. Ray tracing the current solution will provide an accurate representation of the image.

View 5, with solar light and sky light.   View 4, with light ring and sky light.

| Chapter 9: Exterior Rendering |

By comparing the results, you can readily see that the light ring method in conjunction with sky light provides even more uniform illumination than that produced using solar light and sky light.

Now you can move the camera to any exterior vantage point and get good results, even in the solar shadows.

7 Try applying the other saved views such as *across pond*, and use the Ray Trace current solution tool to view other aspects of the model using the light ring solution.

(Left): Image with solar light and sky light. *(Right):* Image with light ring and sky light.

In two ray traced images from the saved view *across pond* above, it's clear that shadows appear to be much softer with the light ring method than when using solar lighting.

ADDING BACKGROUND IMAGES

Now that you have learned about lighting setups, the next step is to learn about adding sky backgrounds for a photorealistic touch. One method is to add a background image to the view(s) that you use for rendering.

✔ **Exercise 9-4: Add background images**

1 Open the DGN file ***Bridge Daytime.dgn***.

2 Apply the saved view *River* to View 2 and View 4.

3 Ray trace View 2.

The view renders with just a background color.

| Adding Background Images |

4 Select Setting > Design File to open the DGN File Settings dialog box.

5 Select the Views category, and set the following:

View: 4
Background: On

6 Click the magnifying glass icon to browse.

7 In the Select Background Image dialog box, set the following:

List Files of Type: All Supported Image Formats
Preview option: On

8 Navigate to the course *image library\Backgrounds* folder and select *sky37.jpg*.

Click OK.

9 In the DGN File Settings dialog box, click OK.

Sky37.jpg becomes the background image for View 4.

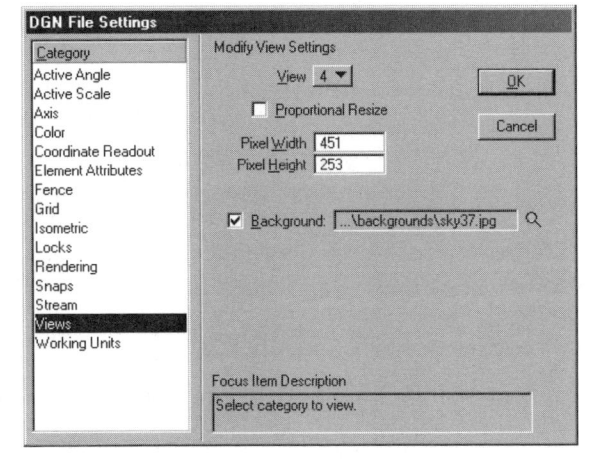

NOTE: *Once you have applied a background to a view, you can open the Select Background Image dialog using the key-in:* **active background.** *The display of a background image is a view attribute. You can open the View Attributes dialog by holding down the <Ctrl> key and entering* **b** *from the keyboard.*

10 Ray Trace View 4 using the current solution.

Since only the background was changed, you can use the ray tracing solution from the previous rendering.

Notice how much more realistic the rendered image appears with the added background image.

Rendered view without *(left)* and with *(right)* background image.

APPLYING FOG TO ADD REALISM

Now that you have added a background, you can make the rendering look even more realistic by adding a touch of fog. One problem with computer images is that they tend to look a little too perfect. Adding a touch of atmospheric fog improves the final appearance of the rendered image.

✔ Exercise 9-5: Apply fog

1. Continuing in model ***Bridge***, turn on the background image for View 2 (Settings > Design File and turn on Background in the Views category).

2. Open the Rendering View Attributes dialog box (Settings > Rendering > View Attributes) and set the following:

   View Number: 2
   Distance Cueing: Fog

3. Click Apply to apply the view attribute settings to View 2.

4. Ray trace View 2 using the current solution.

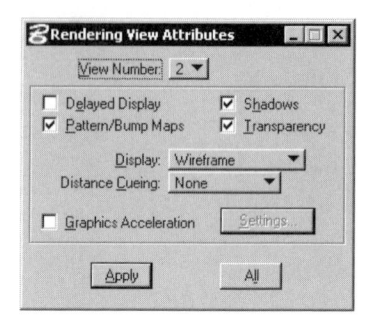

| Applying Fog to Add Realism |

The view is rendered with fog. Since fog only affects how the image is viewed and does not change the solution, you can make adjustments to the fog without having to recompute the ray trace solution.

Bridge after applying fog.

You can see that adding a little fog adds additional realism to the rendered model. Items farther back in the view, including the background image, now look slightly hazy compared to the items that are in the foreground.

Remember that display depth affects the depth cueing of a view. Changing the back clipping plane adjusts where the fog is at a maximum, or far density. You also can change the values for the fog, as you will do now.

✔ **Exercise 9-6: Adjust the values for fog**

1. Open the Rendering Settings dialog box (Settings > Rendering General).

   The Rendering Settings dialog box is where you make changes to distance cueing and change the density and appearance of fog and depth cueing.

2. Change Near Distance to 0.20.

   Near Distance is a percentage of the distance measured from eye point to far clipping plane. This distance when set is seen as clear air before the fog begins.

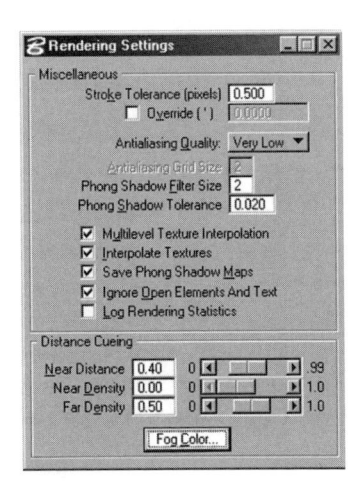

3. Change the Far Density setting from 0.30 to 0.50.

4. In the Rendering View Attributes dialog box, turn on Fog for View 4.

5 Ray trace the current solution in View 4.

The view is rendered with the new Far Density setting, and you can see the fog is much heavier than before. The far density occurs at the back clipping plane for the view. The back clipping plane can be set using the Set Display Depth tool. Also you can see there is some clear air in the foreground before the fog begins.

Bridge with fog Far Density of 0.5 and Near Distance of 0.2.

DEFINING AND USING SKY CYLINDERS

In the previous exercise, you used a background image which works well for still images. However, they do not work so well if you intend to create an animation or save a panorama. If, for example, you are animating a camera through a scene, the scene will move and change while the background image remains constant. This gives a very unnatural look to the animation. In addition, background images are not saved in panorama views. If you want a sky background to be saved as part of a panorama, you need to use either a sky cylinder or an environment map.

NOTE: *The procedure used to save a panorama image is covered in Chapter 12.*

Using a sky cylinder is an easy way to add a seamless sky background around a model. Several sky cylinder images are included in the image library data set delivered with this course.

Exercise 9-7: Create a new material for the sky cylinder

1 Open *sky cylinder.dgn*.

The design file consists of a large cylinder with the *bridge* render model and other models, attached as references, within the cylinder.

2 Select the Define Material tool.

| Defining and Using Sky Cylinders | 303

Currently, the Material Editor is empty, since no materials are yet associated with this DGN file.

3 If not already in Advance mode, set the Material Editor to Advanced Mode by selecting View > Advanced Mode.

4 Select Palette > New.

A new palette file is created with the name New Palette [1].

5 Select Material > New.

A new material definition is created with the default name New Material [1].

6 Right-click New Material [1] and select Rename from the menu.

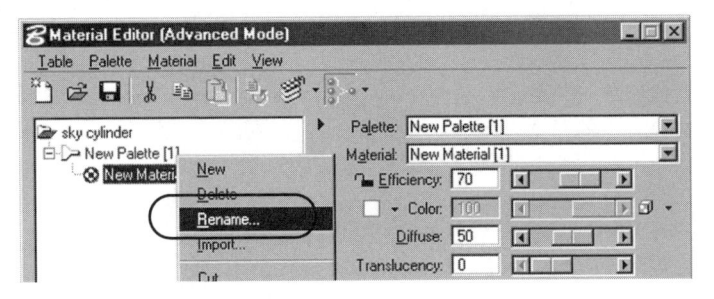

7 Rename the material Sky Cylinder.

With the material created, you now can add a pattern map and define the settings.

✔ Exercise 9-8: Define the new material

1 Continuing in *sky cylinder.dgn*, in the Material Editor dialog box, click Pattern Map.

2 In the Open Image File dialog box, navigate to *image library\backgrounds* and select file *skycyl13.jpg*.

3 Click OK.

4 In the Pattern for Sky Cylinder dialog box, set the following:

Units: Surface
Preview Display: Cylinder (to review how the pattern will look on the cylinder)
Size X: 0.5 and *Y:* 1.0

This causes the image map to repeat horizontally around the cylinder two times, which prevents the image map from appearing too stretched.

5. In the Material Editor dialog box, move the Diffuse slider all the way to the left, making Diffuse 0.

Since you are using real world lighting, you do not want the sky material to be light reflective or sensitive to hot spots from the solar lighting or any other source lights. Making the Diffuse component of the material 0 prevents this from happening.

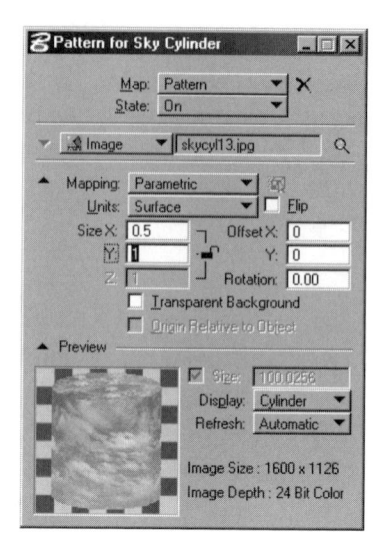

Pattern - Sky Cylinder dialog with preview display set to cylinder

6. Similarly, move the Specular slider all the way to the left, making Specular 0. You do not want the sky to have any specular highlights or to appear shiny.

In order for the sky cylinder to look realistic, you need to increase the ambient light level of the material so the sky will appear self-illuminated and bright, no matter what direction you view it from.

7. In the Ambient field, enter 1000.

   NOTE: *You can manually key in values above 100 in the Ambient field, but the slider goes from 0 to 100 only.*

   NOTE: *When using a sky cylinder, you can make the sky material self-illuminated using a high value for its Ambient. For a material to be self-illuminated in this way, by ambient light, the Ambient light setting in the Global Lighting dialog box must be turned on and have some value.*

8. Turn off Cast Shadows.

   This prevents the sky cylinder geometry from casting a shadow on the model after you make the assignment or attachment of this material.

| Defining and Using Sky Cylinders | 305

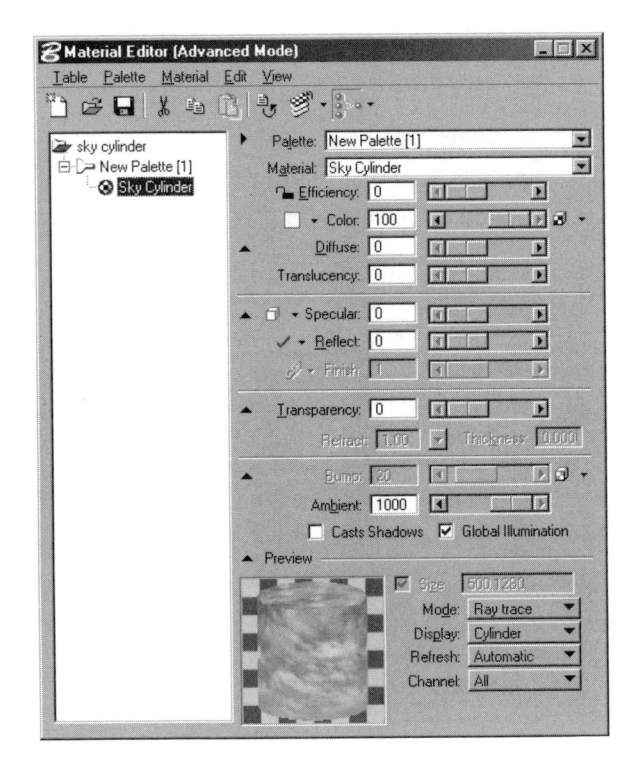

Sky Cylinder material settings.

9 In the Material Editor, select Palette > Save As.

10 Save the palette as *skycyl.pal*.

With the material completed, you now can apply it to the cylinder element.

✔ Exercise 9-9: Apply the material to the cylinder

1 Continuing in ***sky cylinder.dgn***, select the Apply Material tool in the Visualization tools tool box.

By default, the palette you just saved is loaded.

2 In the Apply Material dialog box, click the Assign by Color/Level icon.

3 In View 3 (the Isometric view), identify the blue cylinder surrounding the design geometry.

4 Accept with a data point.

5 Ray trace View 2, creating a new solution.

6 Ray trace View 4 using the existing solution, and compare the two images.

The sky appears quite different in each of the rendered views since you are looking at a different part of the sky cylinder in each view. If you were using a background image, the background would appear the same in both views.

Images from View 2 *(left)* and View 4 *(right)* showing the scene from different camera angles.

ADDING SKY BACKGROUND WITH ENVIRONMENT MAPPING

Using a sky cylinder to assign a material to a cylinder placed around the design geometry is one method for adding a background that changes with camera movement. Another option is to use a sky box and make the environment maps visible. Seamless sky cylinders are easier to create than seamless environment boxes, although environment boxes have the advantage of completely enclosing the model. Since environment boxes provide a more immersive environment, they work better for rendering cubic panoramas. You also have to be more careful when animating a camera through a scene that uses a sky cylinder: it is possible to see a big hole in your sky if the camera looks up to the top edge of the cylinder.

An environment map is simply a set of images that can be used to enclose a model in an imaginary cube. The environment maps are assigned using the Environment Maps option of the Apply Material tool. Like sky cylinders, environment maps can work well for saving panoramas and for creating exterior animations.

Visible Environment Maps

In order to see the environment maps directly, you needed to place a slab (or other object) around the entire scene with a transparent material assigned to it (commonly referred to as *visible environment* geometry). Thus, when a ray from the eye would see no other objects, it still would see through the visible environment geometry to the environment maps.

When Visible Environment is enabled, with Environment Mapping, all rays will now see environment maps directly, without the need for visible environment geometry. If some visible environment geometry is present, it will continue to work as before. A Visible Environment toggle has been added to the Ray Tracing settings dialog to optionally disable this feature—for example, when rendering with a photomatched raster reference.

When environment maps have been defined and a view is ray traced with

- Environment Mapping alone enabled, environment maps are visible only in reflected and transmitted rays.

- Visible Environment also is enabled, environment maps display in a view as a background, as well as in reflected and transmitted rays.

✔ Exercise 9-10: Select Environment Maps

1. Open *environment map1.dgn*.

2. Select the Apply Material tool, and click the Environment Maps icon.

   The Environment Maps dialog box opens. It contains six fields, one for each face of the environment cube. Initially, only the magnifying glass browse icon is enabled for the Front face. Once you have selected the Front environment map, which will be inserted into the field for each face, the browse icons for all faces are enabled. You then can use browse for alternative image files for each respective face.

| Chapter 9: Exterior Rendering |

3 Click the magnifying glass for the Front field.

4 In the Select Environment Map [All] dialog box, navigate to the course *Image Library\Skybox* folder and select file *skybox front.jpg*.

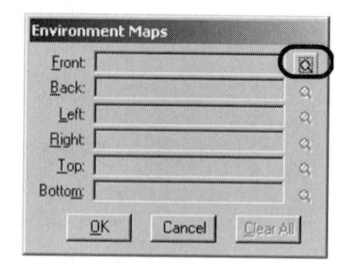

5 Click OK.

Environment Maps for all faces are set to use the same image.

6 Using the browse icons for each face, select their respective image files. For example, the Back face will use *skybox back.jpg*, the Left face will use *skybox left.jpg*, and so on.

You do not need to select a bottom image. Leave it set to *skybox front.jpg*.

7 Select the Render tool with Render Mode set to Ray Trace.

8 In the Render dialog box, click the magnifying glass icon to open the Ray Tracing settings dialog box.

By default, the Environment Mapping option automatically is enabled, along with Visible Environment, after defining the environment maps in the previous step.

9 Ray Trace View 2, creating a new solution.

10 In the Render tool dialog box, select Render current Solution in any view and ray trace View 4.

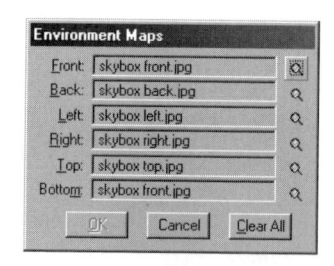

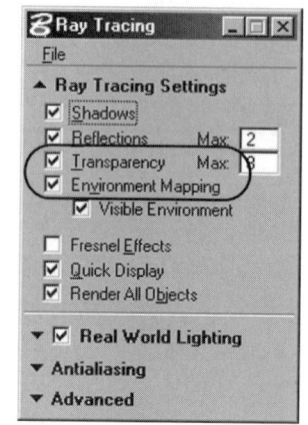

Notice how the sky changes with the change in the camera view, unlike using a background image. In this example, the sky image actually is stretched quite a bit when compared to the images that were used to define the environment. In these images, however, it still is acceptable since sky images usually can be stretched quite a bit, but you could turn your puffy white clouds into cirrus clouds.

| Adding Sky background with Environment Mapping | 309

Two different camera views with environment maps visible.

Optimizing for visible environment

When you define environment maps and toggle on Visible Environment in the Ray Tracing settings, the sky will be seen through a block that is based on the range of elements for the model and any reference files. This may have a rectangular rather than square shape, whereas environment maps should be seen through a cube. To overcome this possible problem, you can place a cube around your model geometry. As you will see shortly, this cube does not have to be displayed when rendering the view; it just has to be present in the model. Effectively, this will make the range of elements in the model cubic and prevent any distortion of the environment maps.

In the next exercise, you will see how the environment maps look completely different when seen through a cube rather than the rectangular range block of the sample model geometry.

✔ Exercise 9-11: Environment maps seen through a cube

1   Open the design file *environment map2.dgn* file.

    This model is identical to the last one with one exception: there is a large cube around the model. This geometry is made of construction elements placed on level Skybox. In addition, the same skybox images as used in the previous exercise already are defined.

2   Ray trace View 2.

Notice that clouds look more like the actual images and are not stretched as they were in the previous exercise.

3 Ray trace View 4 using the current solution.

As in the previous exercise, you can see the environment looks different when seen from different camera angles.

The same environment images seen through an oblong range block *(left)* and through a forced cubic range block *(right)*.

With this method, the large cube placed around the design geometry can consist of Construction class or Primary class elements, and may be placed on any level. When the range block is calculated for the visible environment, the cube will determine the extents of the range block.

You have various options for creating the cube geometry. You can:

- Use Construction class elements and turn off display of constructions in the rendering view.

- Use Primary class elements and turn off display of the level containing the cube geometry in the rendering view.

- Create the cube with linear elements and enable Ignore Open Elements And Text checked in the Rendering Settings. The cube geometry then will not render even if its level is displayed in the rendering view.

NOTE: *You can even use a line placed in the model to change the range block. You do not have to place a block to change the extents of the model. In other words, a diagonal line from one upper corner of a box to the opposite lower corner would accomplish the same thing, so you could delete the box and use the line instead.*

NIGHTTIME OR DUSK-TO-DAWN RENDERING

Occasionally, you may need to create a lighting setup to render night, sunset, or early morning scenes of a building model. Doing this can lead to spectacular rendered images, provided you add all the right ingredients, such as solar lighting, source lighting, and an appropriate sky background.

Sunset Rendering Setup

In the next exercise, you will work with a sunset setup that creates a photorealistic image for that time of day.

✔ **Exercise 9-12: Sunset rendering setup**

1. Open **BC1 sunset.dgn**.
2. Select Global Lighting from the Rendering Tools tool box.
3. Verify, or set the Global Lighting Settings to match the following:

   Ambient: On and set to 0.15
   (Ambient) Color: Red 255, Green 253, Blue 191
   Flashbulb: Off
   Solar: On and set to 1.00
   (Solar) Color: Red 255, Green 232, Blue 204
   Solar Shadows: On with Azimuth 145.03, Altitude Angle 12.954
   Add Sky Light to all Solar and Distant Lights: On
   (Sky Light) Color: Red 255, Green 218, Blue 196
   Approximate Ground Reflection for Sky Light: On with Ground Reflection set to 1.0.
   (Ground Reflection) Color: Red 255, Green 231, Blue 207

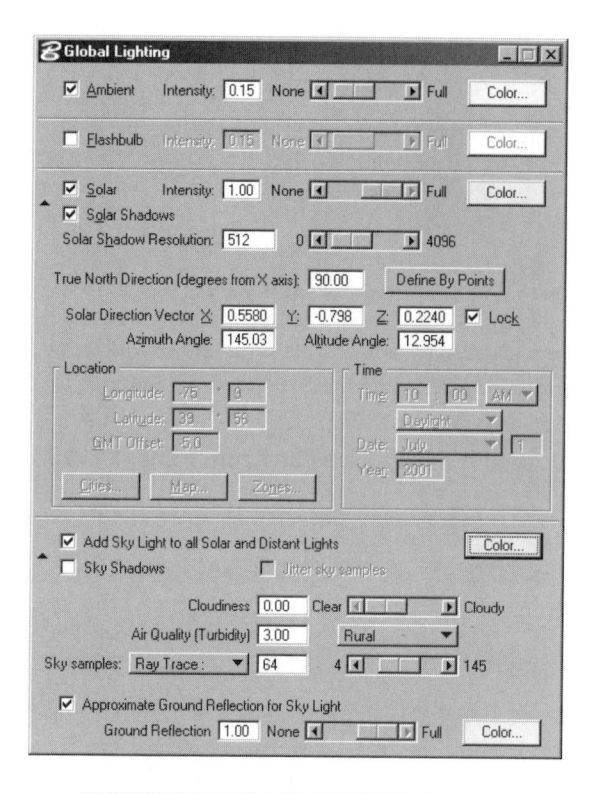

The Altitude Angle for Solar is about 13° above the horizon, producing long shadows. Because you want it to appear to be sunset, Ambient Color, Solar Color, Sky Light Color, and Ground Reflection Color are set to colors you might expect to see at sunset.

4. Ray trace View 2, creating a new solution.

   Observe the long shadows, as you would expect to see them at sunset.

The sunset background is a sunset environment map. The environment map images are seen in the view because Environment Mapping and Visible Environment are both enabled in the Ray Tracings settings dialog box. The range block is modified by a line in space that represents the diagonal of the required range block. This has the same effect on the range block as the cube did in the previous exercise. The light posts seen in the rendered image are cells with source lights built into them. For this rendering, those light sources have been turned off.

Dusk or Twilight Rendering

For this following exercise, the rendering setup is configured for the time of day shortly after sunset. A similar setup also would work for an early morning scene, just before dawn.

Sunset rendering.

| Nighttime or Dusk-to-Dawn Rendering |

As with the previous exercise, the goal is for you to understand the settings required to achieve the final result, not necessarily to perform every step. In this case, the file is ready to render with source lights and other material settings set up in advance.

For the twilight rendering, the building model is set up with two sets of windows residing on different levels. The reason for this is that the material applied to the windows on one level is for day renderings, while the other is for night rendering. You can select which type of window you want by turning on or off the appropriate levels. In this model, the night version has a few windows set up with a material that has much higher ambient value applied, making the glass appear to be self-illuminated. The high ambient material is randomly applied so the building appears to have lights on in several offices but not all, adding even more to the realism. This method is fairly easy to use for faking lighting, with none of the overhead required when using real light sources.

✔ Exercise 9-13: Twilight setup

1. Open *BC1 Twilight.dgn*.

    This file contains source lights to illuminate the building interior. In addition, the lamppost lights that were turned off in the sunset version are enabled for this setup.

2. Apply the saved view *twilight* to View 2.

3. Select Global Lighting.

4. Review the Global Lighting settings (on following page).

    NOTE: *Even though the sun is supposed to be below the horizon, setting the Altitude Angle to 5° will provide some illumination on the building. The Solar Intensity now is only 0.02, down from 1.0 as used in the sunset setup. Since you are using Real World Lighting, setting the solar intensity very low prevents the solar light from overwhelming the source lights. The color of all global lights used are much cooler now, leaning toward blue or pink rather than the warm orange, yellow, or reds you might use in a sunset setup.*

    The design file has a twilight background image displayed in View 2, rather than using an environment box. The source lights are enabled in the reference files for this rendering, including spot lights, point

| Chapter 9: Exterior Rendering |

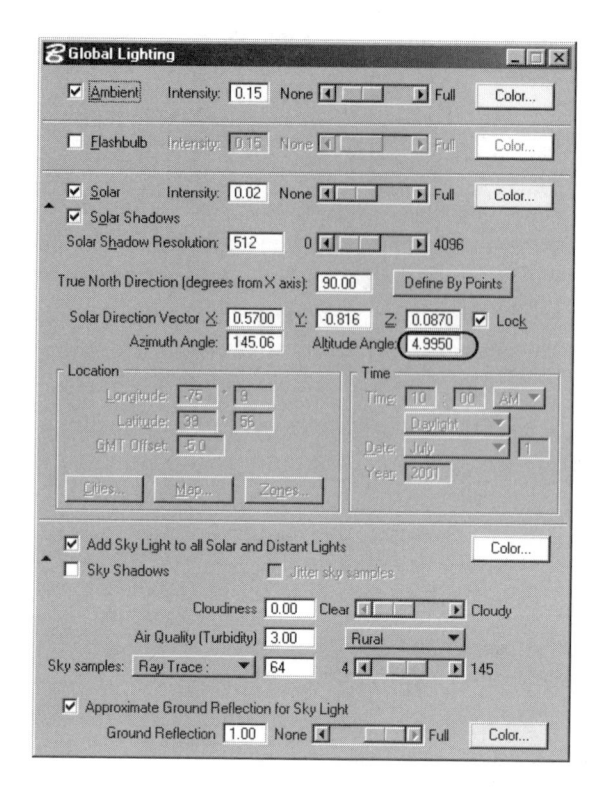

lights and area lights, to achieve the desired effect. The addition of several shadow-casting lights slows down the rendering noticeably.

5   Ray trace View 2, creating a new solution.

Twilight rendering.

Inspect the rendered image in View 2 and notice how, in the background image, the sun has set but the sky is still illuminated.

| Nighttime or Dusk-to-Dawn Rendering | **315**

This fits the time of day you are trying to match. The lights in the building now are on, as are the street lights and shop signs.

6 Select the Define Light tool.

The Define Light dialog box opens, displaying the light list for this model. There are no light sources in the main model. The light sources used are those in the references. The reference *BC1 street lights.dgn* uses IES point lights for each of the six street lights. The reference *BC1 Night.dgn* has numerous point lights and area lights to illuminate the signs and to provide light within the building

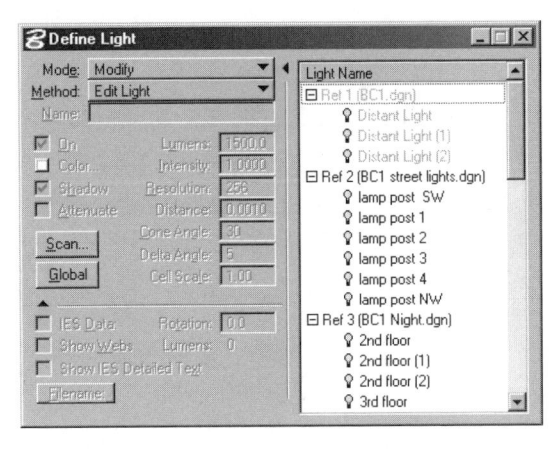

The Define Light dialog with the Light list shown.

NOTE: *When Real World Lighting is enabled, ray traced images are rendered using the same lighting attenuation and lumen values as those used with radiosity and particle tracing. This lets you set lighting levels using Ray Trace, without having to compute multiple radiosity or particle tracing solutions. Just like radiosity and particle tracing, Real World Lighting uses the lumens values of light sources. As well, it forces attenuation on for all lights and uses the same type of physically accurate attenuation (with the intensity of the light falling off with the square of the distance). Another benefit, with Real World Lighting, is that you can use the interactive Brightness and Contrast sliders to adjust the ray traced views.*

Nighttime Rendering Setup

Following on from the previous section, here you will review the settings needed for a nighttime rendering. The setup will be very similar to the previous example for twilight rendering, with a few adjustments to global lighting, background image, and depth cueing.

| Chapter 9: Exterior Rendering |

✔ Exercise 9-14: Nighttime setup

1 Open *BC1 Night.dgn*.

The file opens with a nighttime background image displayed in View 2.

2 Select the Global Lighting tool.

The Global Lighting dialog box opens.

In the night rendering setup, you can see that Solar light is disabled. As no distant lights are used, Add Sky Light to all Solar and Distant Light also can be disabled. It would have no effect, even if enabled.

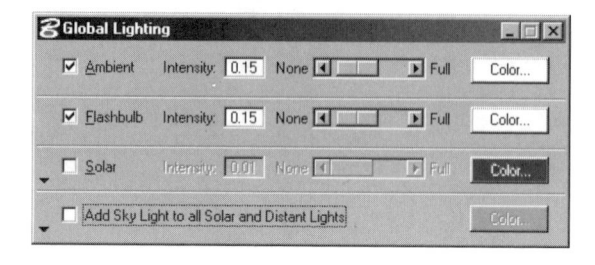

3 Ray trace View 2, creating a new solution.

The view is ray traced using only source lights, along with 0.15 Ambient and a 0.15 Flashbulb. Notice how the night sky background adds additional photorealism to the rendering.

4 In the Render tool dialog box, select Ray Trace current solution in any view.

5 Select View 4.

| Nighttime or Dusk-to-Dawn Rendering | 317

Notice that this time the rendered image fades into black and the background image disappears completely. This is due to Depth Cueing being enabled in the Rendering View Attributes for this view. Remember, from earlier exercises, that depth cueing is similar to black fog. It is controlled by the display depth and also settings in the Rendering Settings dialog box.

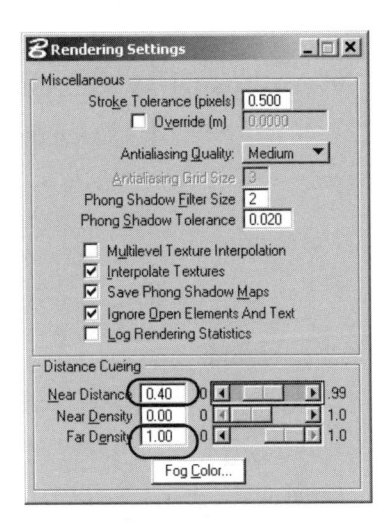

6 Open the Rendering Settings dialog box and review the settings used for this nighttime scene.

NOTE: *Rendering Settings let you adjust both the Fog and Distance Cueing settings. For these settings to affect your rendering, you must also enable Fog or Distance Cueing for the individual view. This is set in the View Attributes dialog box (Settings > Rendering > View Attributes).*

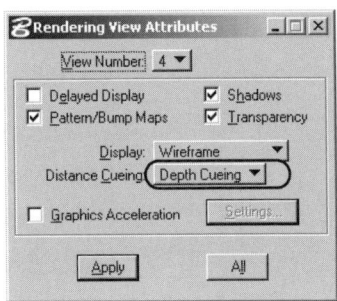

Rendering View Attributes with Depth Cueing enabled in View 4.

7 Open the Rendering View Attributes dialog box and note the Depth Cueing setting.

Nighttime Particle Traced Rendering

In this next exercise, you will be rendering a bridge model using a previously calculated particle traced lighting solution. Particle tracing will be discussed in detail in a later chapter, but for now you will get a glimpse of what can be accomplished using particle tracing. Particle tracing calculates the paths of light particles as they are emitted from light sources and are reflected and transmitted through the scene. When ray traced, these lighting solutions provide photorealistic images, including reflections, refraction, and other caustic lighting effects such as light reflected by mirrors or focused through lenses.

Exercise 9-15: Particle trace exterior night scene

1. Open the design file *LightDesign.dgn*.

   This model consists of a bridge with typical highway lighting fixtures using IES photometric files to accurately represent the lumen output and spread of lighting.

2. Select the Render tool in the Visualization tool box.

3. In the Render dialog box, set Render Mode to Particle Trace.

4. Click the Open Particle Tracing settings dialog icon (the magnifying glass) in the Render dialog box.

   The Particle Tracing dialog box opens.

5. Choose File > Load from the Particle Tracing dialog box.

   The Load Rendering Database dialog opens.

6. Navigate to the course *\dgn* folder and select *LightDesign1.ptd*.

7. Click OK, to load the previously computed particle traced lighting solution.

   The title for the Render dialog box now displays the number of shots used in the loaded file. Also, the Display current solution in any view button is enabled.

8. In the Render tool dialog box, click the Display current solution in any view icon.

9. Enter a data point in View 2.

   View 2 is rendered using the loaded particle traced solution.

   Where required, you can configure Particle Tracing to produce a display showing where the light hits surfaces in the view, referred to as the *illuminance* of the scene. The display is color coded from blue through to red, indicating least to most light, respectively.

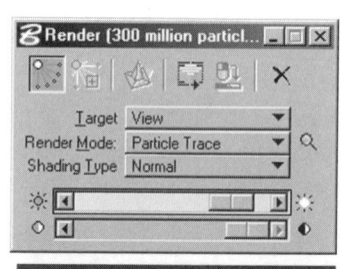

| Nighttime or Dusk-to-Dawn Rendering | **319**

✔ Exercise 9-16: Display Illuminance of view

1 Continuing in *LightDesign.dgn*, in the Particle Tracing dialog box, switch to the advanced mode by choosing Interface > Advance.

2 In the Particle Tracing dialog box, set:

Display Mode: Illuminance.

Illuminance is a false color display of the light hitting the surface.

3 With Display current solution in any view selected in the Render tool dialog box, enter a data point in view 2.

The view is rendered with a false color display showing illuminance or light hitting the surfaces of the model.

4 Move the interactive Brightness slider and see how the hot spots of light dynamically change, showing exactly how the light is spread out along the bridge.

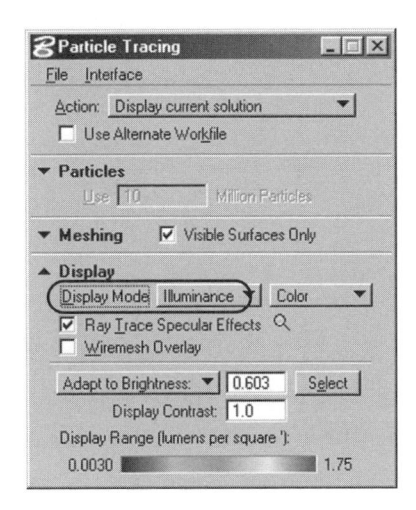

Bridge rendered with particle traced solution and display set to Illuminance.

REVIEW QUESTIONS

1. How do you add atmospheric lighting from the sky in the Global Lighting dialog?

2. Do distant lights shine upward when ray tracing with Real World Light enabled?

3. Does sky light work with distant lights?

4. How can you turn on and off the display of a background image applied to a view?

5. Which view control tool can be used to adjust where the far density occurs when using fog?

6. Assuming you will be using Real World Lighting, when using sky cylinders, the material applied should have a zero _____ and a high_____.

7. When would you turn off a material's ability to cast shadows?

8. When particle tracing, what is the false color display of light hitting the surface of a model?

9. When particle tracing, what is the false color display of light reflected by the surface of a model?

CHAPTER SUMMARY

In this chapter, you learned how to set up global lighting. You saw how you can add distant lights for fill-in lighting and how to use sky lighting to provide a more uniform global illumination of a ray traced exterior scene. You learned how to define and apply a sky cylinder material to a large cylinder surrounding your model, to provide a realistic backdrop for your rendered images. You have gained knowledge of how to apply background images and to apply and adjust fog effects. You were taught how to use visible environment maps and how to set up global and source lighting to achieve sunset, twilight, and nighttime rendering of exterior scenes. The chapter ended with particle tracing of a bridge model, and you learned how to ascertain lighting design information, such as luminance, from the rendered view.

10 Interior Spaces and Global Illumination

When you create an image using ray tracing alone, additional source lights often are required to effectively illuminate the various surfaces in the 3D scene. This is to account for the fact that the Ray Tracer does not calculate the light reflected or absorbed by the materials used in a model. Ray tracing requires you to add lights that would not be required in real life.

When you use either of the global illumination methods, radiosity or particle tracing, you create a lighting solution for the model. That is, the reflection and absorption of light is calculated. These two methods, though similar in their results, differ greatly in their approach to solving the lighting for a 3D scene. In this chapter, you will learn how the two differ and what steps you must take to set them up to render a realistic and accurate lighting solution.

RADIOSITY

Radiosity, as defined in the literature of physics, is the total power leaving a point on a surface, per unit area on the surface. In the context of rendering, power is light energy.

Radiosity solving is a sophisticated technique that calculates the light that is reflected between diffuse surfaces. It can be used to demonstrate effects such as color bleeding (where one colored surface lends a tint to another nearby surface) and light dispersion (the reflection of indirect light onto other surfaces in a scene). Radiosity does not distribute specular light, and thus it does not produce caustics. To display specular highlights in a radiosity solution, you must set Final Display to Ray Trace (this setting is found on the Display portion of the Radiosity dialog box).

Radiosity solving, unlike ray tracing, is not a rendering technique on its own. It merely generates a lighting solution that, in turn, can be rendered. In fact, radiosity solving and ray tracing capabilities can be used together to produce realistic images with the best qualities of both methods. Radiosity solving operates as a rendering preprocess that computes the global, view-independent (diffuse) lighting solution. Ray tracing uses this radiosity solution to render a view-dependent image, adding specular highlights and reflections.

Since the radiosity solution is view-independent, it can be reused to render additional images of the design from different views. Each image can be rendered using either ray tracing or smooth shading. Smooth shading can be faster than ray tracing, but does not include any of the specular effects such as reflections, refractions, and specular highlights.

The radiosity solving process produces useful intermediate solutions in a short amount of time. It then automatically and continuously refines them into the final solution. This makes it possible to display intermediate results so that you can decide when the solution is satisfactory and stop the calculations.

Also, you can specify the stopping criteria, either as a fixed number of shots or as a fraction of the total global illumination to be distributed.

When viewing a radiosity solution, whether it is an intermediate solution or a completed calculation, you can adjust the brightness of the image interactively, using the slider control in the Render tools dialog box.

Radiosity and Lighting

MicroStation's radiosity solving calculates the dispersion of light energy in a scene. Radiosity calculations require different lighting settings than those used for standard phong or ray traced images where Real World

| Radiosity | 323

Lighting is disabled. When Ray Tracing is used with Real World Lighting enabled, it too works with the same settings as Radiosity.

For global illumination options, such as Radiosity, Particle Tracing, and Ray Tracing with Real World Lighting enabled, the Define Light tool has a Lumens setting. This setting is the number of lumens in the light source which determines how bright the light is. The Intensity value acts as a multiplier of a light source's lumens or brightness, like a dimmer switch. With an Intensity setting of 1.0, the specified value of lumens will appear at full (100%) brightness. With an Intensity setting of 0.5, by contrast, the specified brightness of the Lumens will be dimmed by half.

How Radiosity Solutions are Generated

Understanding the basics of the radiosity solving process can help you determine the necessary trade-offs between solution time and solution quality that are critical to successful use. The main control over solution quality is determined by the subdivision settings, which specify how finely each surface in the design is meshed.

> **NOTE:** *Radiosity solving is a processing-intensive operation. As such, the practical minimum hardware requirements for radiosity solving may exceed the general minimum requirements for using MicroStation.*

Patches and elements

During processing, surfaces are first subdivided into a set of triangles controlled by the MicroStation Stroke Tolerance setting. These triangles are further subdivided into patches. From here, each patch is subdivided into one or more triangular elements, thus forming an element mesh. A further adaptive subdivision may occur along shadow boundaries. Settings in the Radiosity dialog box determine the sizes of the patches and elements, as well as the degree of adaptive subdivision.

The settings in the Radiosity Settings section control the size of the patches and elements. Another setting in the Radiosity Settings section controls the way the elements are further subdivided along shadow boundaries. Take, for example, a simple 10 × 10 unit square surface.

With the Radiosity settings:

Maximum Patch Area: 50
Maximum Element Area: 12.5

the surface is first subdivided into patches having a maximum area of 50 square units.

From here, the patches are further divided into elements having a maximum area of 12.5 square units.

Light energy is received by the elements. Illumination is calculated at each vertex, and the mean value is calculated for the element. Also calculated is the amount of energy that is absorbed and reflected. This is dependent on the material definition for the surface. Finally, the amount of light energy to be shot (reflected) is calculated for each patch by gathering the values for all elements contained within it (the patch).

Each shot during radiosity solving shoots the light energy from a single patch to each of the elements of the other surfaces. By selecting and shooting the brightest unshot patch each time, the intermediate solution progresses as quickly as possible toward the final solution.

Adaptive subdivision

If a spotlight is placed above the lower right corner of the surface, and the radiosity solution is calculated and then ray traced, the resulting image is less than satisfactory. This is due to the element mesh being too coarse to accurately depict the circular light beam.

This can be corrected by decreasing the size of the element mesh. However, only the lower right corner of the image needs the extra resolution, not the entire surface.

Setting Maximum Element Subdivisions to a value greater than 0 meshes surfaces more

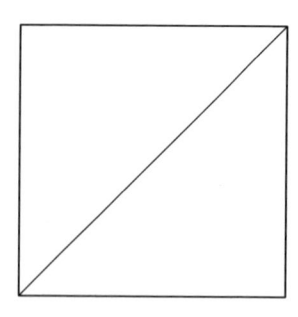

A 10 x 10 square divided into two patch areas of 50 square units.

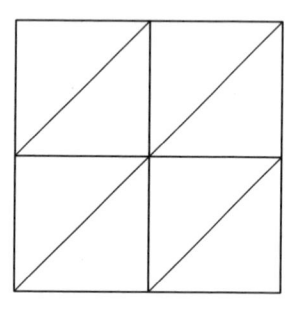

A surface divided into element areas of maximum 12.5 square units.

The Maximum Element Subdivision set to 1.

| Radiosity |

finely at shadow boundaries. For example, a setting of 1 allows each element to be further subdivided into four triangles, and a setting of 2 allows each of these to be further subdivided into four, and so on. Thus, the higher this value, the more accurate the boundary becomes, but at a greater cost in processing time.

Setting Maximum Element Subdivisions to 7 produces the results in the next image. As you can see in the wiremesh image, the element areas are further divided along the shadow boundary into very small triangles. Since this only occurs where the contrast differs more than 10% as set by the Subdivision Contrast Threshold, it is referred to as *adaptive subdivision*.

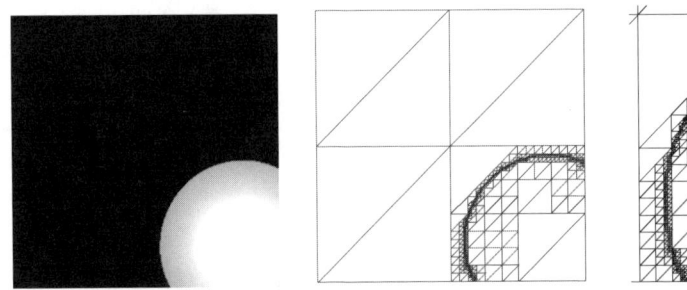

(Left to right): Rendered, wiremesh overlay, and close-up view of subdivision.

Controlling calculation time and accuracy

Geometric accuracy of the shooting operations is determined by the sizes of the patches, with smaller patches giving a more accurate result at a greater cost in time. In general, each patch can shoot to the elements of every other patch, so the time needed to compute an exact solution can increase with the square of the number of patches. For example, a solution with twice as many patches takes about four times as long to compute; one with 10 times as many patches takes about 100 times as long to compute, assuming the ratio of the patch areas to the element areas remains the same.

When the element area remains constant, the time to compute a solution may vary linearly with the number of patches. For example, if the maximum patch size is 10.0 and the maximum element size is 1.0, reducing the patch size to 5.0 would require twice as many shots to be taken (with the time per shot remaining constant), taking twice as long to reach a similar solution of higher quality.

Sky Openings and Radiosity

When using distant light sources or solar lighting, the light rays are present throughout the model, not just in the vicinity of the design geometry. For efficiency, you can create one or more sky openings that restrict the calculations to the light that passes through the sky opening only.

You should use sky openings in particular where you have an interior space illuminated from outside by distant light sources and/or solar lighting. For exterior scenes, you can use sky openings to focus the processing on the region of the model where the design geometry is located.

✔ Exercise 10-1: Create a sky opening

1. Open *simple interior rad.dgn*.

    This model of a room with furniture is set up with internal lighting provided by a source lighting cell in the table lamp. Solar lighting provides further illumination through the window. To ensure that calculations for the Solar light apply only to the area through the window, you will first place a sky opening just outside the window.

2. Open View 5.

    View 5 opens with only the walls and a polygon for creating a sky opening displayed.

3. Select the Define Light tool with the following tool settings:

    Mode: Create
    Type: Sky Opening
    Min Samples: 5
    Max Samples: 20

    Because the solar lighting is entering through a single window, increasing the minimum samples to 20 will produce a better spread of this light.

4. In View 5, click on the polygon just outside the window in the wall.

| Radiosity |

A dynamic arrow appears in the view, indicating the direction in which the light will shine.

NOTE: *This tool will identify only the polygon, ignoring the solid forming the wall with the window opening. Solids are not valid elements for a sky opening.*

5   With the arrow pointing into the room, enter a data point to create the sky opening.

NOTE: *A light that could be used for ray tracing alone can be seen grayed out in the Define Light dialog box. This indicates that it is turned off.*

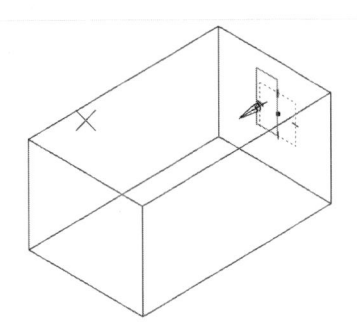

Create a skylight opening with a dynamic arrow.

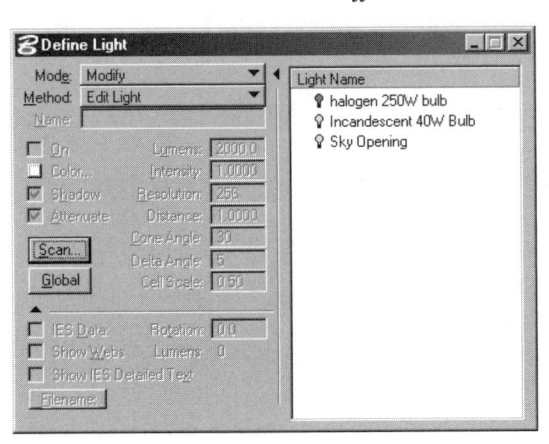

6   Close View 5.

With the sky opening in place, you now will check the Global Lighting settings and proceed to create the radiosity solution.

Exercise 10-2: Create a radiosity solution

1   Continuing in *simple interior rad.dgn*, apply the saved view *simple* to View 2.

2   Select Global Lighting in the Rendering Tools tool box.

3   Check that the Global Lighting values match those shown (see next page).

| Chapter 10: Interior Spaces and Global Illumination |

4 Close the Global Lighting dialog box.

5 Select the Render tool with the following tool setting:

   Render Mode: Radiosity

6 In the Render tool dialog box, click the Open Radiosity settings dialog icon (the magnifying glass).

The Radiosity dialog box opens.

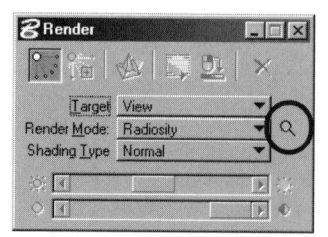

7 Check that the Radiosity settings are as shown at right.

8 Enter a data point in View 2 to obtain a radiosity solution with 10 shots.

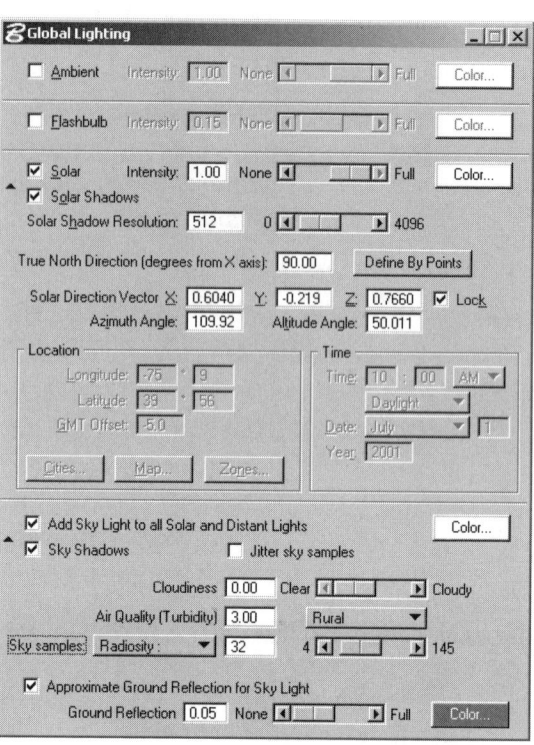

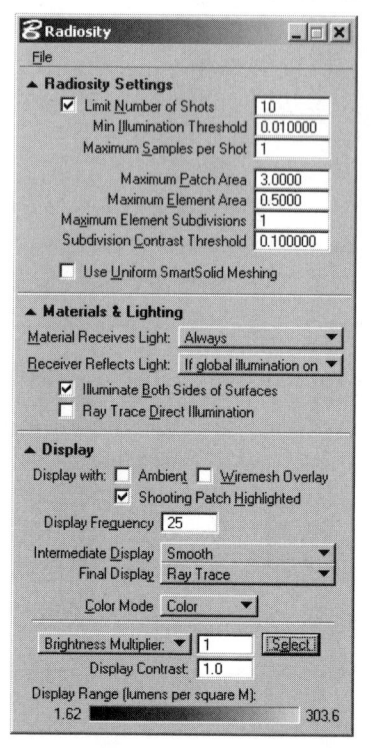

| Radiosity | **329**

The resulting rendered image is rather coarse, with some of the meshing triangles clearly visible in the shadows. You need to refine the settings to improve the image quality.

In the following exercise, you will increase the Maximum Element Subdivisions so the adaptive meshing can be used to improve the image, especially at the shadow boundaries. The meshing along the shadow boundaries then can be subdivided as required where the contrast threshold is greater than 0.10 or 10%.

✔ Exercise 10-3: Adjust the radiosity settings for a better result

1 Continuing in *simple interior rad.dgn*, in the Radiosity dialog box, change Maximum Element Subdivisions to 5.

2 Enter a data point in View 2.

An Alert dialog box prompts you about clearing the current solution.

3 Click OK to start a new solution.

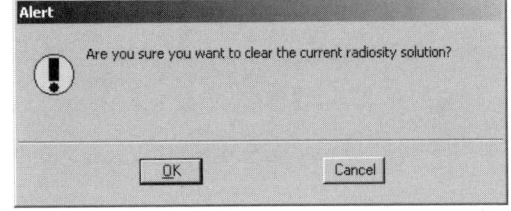

The Radiosity Shot progress displays in the status area.

Image with one element subdivision *(left)* and with five *(right)*.

After changing the Maximum Element Subdivisions to 5, the shadow boundary looks better defined but still has a decidedly stepped appearance. To refine this further, you can:

- make the Maximum Element Area smaller,
- increase the Maximum Element Subdivisions, or
- adjust both of the above.

Refining Radiosity Settings

By making a few simple adjustments, you can greatly affect the final rendered output. You will do just that now. You will make adjustments to obtain a radiosity solution that will be used to create the final rendering.

✔ Exercise 10-4: Refining settings for final radiosity solution

1. Continuing in *simple interior rad.dgn*, in the Radiosity dialog box, set Maximum Element Subdivisions to 6.

   This causes the adaptive subdivisions along the shadow boundaries to be divided into extremely small triangles.

2. Change the Maximum Patch Area from 3.0 to 1.0.

   Setting this to a smaller value increases the accuracy at the expense of longer rendering time.

3. Change the Maximum Element Area from 0.5 to 0.1.

   Setting this to a smaller value results in an adaptive subdivision with an initial area five times smaller than before, that is, subdivided as needed into smaller areas.

4. Change the Maximum Samples per Shot from 1 to 5.

   This will further improve the accuracy of the solution and resulting rendered image.

   NOTE: *If you are using a relatively small patch size, generally you can use a smaller number of samples. If you are using a larger patch size, generally you will need to use a larger number of samples. Similarly, if you wish to decrease the number of samples, you may need to decrease the patch size as well. If you increase the number of samples, however, you still may be unable to increase the patch size significantly without adversely affecting the accuracy of the lighting calculations.*

5. With the Render Mode set to Radiosity, render View 2, creating a new solution.

| Radiosity | 331

With Limit Number of Shots set to 10, the solution stops after 10 shots. View 2 is ray traced with the 10 shot solution.

Image before *(left)* and after *(right)* refining the radiosity settings.

Ray Trace Direct Illumination

Where a scene primarily is lit by direct light from light sources, the Ray Trace Direct Illumination setting can reduce rendering times. With this setting enabled, the Ray Tracer is used to compute shadows from light sources, but not from reflected light. In these cases, very high-quality images can be obtained using much larger element sizes and therefore much less memory.

✔ Exercise 10-5: Use Ray Trace Direct Illumination

1 Continuing in *simple interior rad.dgn*, in the Materials and Lighting section of the Radiosity dialog box, turn on Ray Trace Direct Illumination.

2 Render View 2, creating a new solution.

To this point, you have restricted the number of shots to 10. To obtain a more complete radiosity solution, you can remove the limit of 10 shots. This will let the solution progress until another of the limiting factors is reached, or the entire light energy is used.

The resulting ray traced solution after 10 shots.

You can interrupt radiosity solving between shots by Resetting. After the current shot is completed, the final display is rendered. The final display can be interrupted with a Reset.

If an intermediate solution is being displayed, a single Reset interrupts the display, and the solution continues with the next shot. A second Reset then interrupts the radiosity solution, and a third Reset interrupts the final display.

You can restart the radiosity solution from the next shot by selecting Add more shots to solution (to current limits). Radiosity settings, such as Limit Number of Shots, can be changed before the solution is restarted, and in most cases changes will take effect immediately. Other settings, such as the initial subdivision settings, will not take effect until the rendering database is cleared and a new solution commences.

Exercise 10-6: Create a more complete solution

1. Continuing in *simple interior rad.dgn*, in the Radiosity Settings section of the Radiosity dialog box, turn off Limit Number of Shots.

2. In the Render tool dialog box, click Add More Shots to solution (to current limits) and enter a data point in View 2.

    The process continues from the stopping point, starting with shot 11. After 25 shots the view will be smooth rendered, as the Intermediate Display currently is set to Smooth. The process will continue until the minimum illumination threshold is met or until you enter a Reset, at which point the final display will be ray traced.

3. Let the process continue for about 55 shots and then Reset.

    The radiosity process stops and the view is ray traced, using the radiosity solution. You also can use the Display current solution (in any view) option to render the view. Turning the Limit Number of Shots back on will prevent further shots from being computed, provided the number is less than what has already been computed.

    The completed image.

4. If necessary, use the sliders in the Render tool dialog box to adjust the image to suit.

| Radiosity |

Adjusting image brightness/contrast

Whether radiosity calculations are interrupted or are completed, you can use the Brightness and Contrast sliders in the Render tool settings to interactively fine-tune an image. Move the Brightness slider to the right to brighten or to the left to darken. Similarly, move the Contrast slider to the right to increase contrast or to the left to reduce it.

Using the Brightness slider is similar to using the Brightness Multiplier/Adapt to Brightness setting in the Display section of the Radiosity dialog box. Using the Contrast slider is similar to using the Display Contrast setting in the same section of the Radiosity dialog box.

As mentioned in the beginning of Chapter 3, a gamma correction may be necessary to achieve the same results as those depicted here in this book. You can adjust this by choosing Workspace > Preferences > View Options from the MicroStation main window. A gamma correction of 1.7 would be a good starting point if you are not using an LCD monitor.

Saving the radiosity solution

Once you have a solution, you can save it to a disk file. Later, you can reload it to render further views, or save images to disk, or animate a camera though a model.

When saving a radiosity solution, the default name given is comprised of the name of the design file plus the active model. For instance, if your design file is named *office.dgn* and the active model you were working with was *First Floor*, the default file name would be *office_first floor.rad*. If you switched to another model, perhaps the second floor model, then the default particle solution file would be *office_second floor.rad*.

NOTE: *There is one exception to this naming rule. When you are in the default model, the file name is the design file name with the .rad extension.*

✔ Exercise 10-7: Save the radiosity solution

1. Continuing in ***simple interior rad.dgn***, in the Radiosity dialog box, select File > Save Solution.

   NOTE: *You also can right-click in the Render tool dialog box icon tool bar and select Save Solution from the pop-up menu.*

2. In the Save Rendering Database dialog box, set List Files of Type to Radiosity Solution Files [*.rad].

3. Click OK.

   Because you are working in the default model, this will save the solution to a file with the same name as the DGN file, but with a *.rad* extension.

Loading a previously calculated solution

You can save a radiosity solution with any name, meaning you can have multiple solutions with different names and different lighting setups.

In the following exercise, you will clear the current rendering solution from memory and then reload your saved radiosity file.

✔ Exercise 10-8: Loading a radiosity solution from a file

1. Continuing in *simple interior rad.dgn*, in the Render tool dialog box, click Clear current rendering solution.

   An Alert box asks if you are sure that you want to clear the current radiosity solution.

2. Click OK.

   Notice, in the Rendering tool dialog box, that Display current solution (in any view) now is disabled.

3. In the Radiosity dialog box, select File > Load Solution.

   Alternatively, right-click in the Render tool icon bar and select Load Solution.

4. In the Load Rendering Database dialog box, select the database that you created in the previous exercise *(simple interior rad.rad)*.

5. Click OK.

   The file is loaded and progress is displayed in the status area. Notice that the Display current solution (in any view) button again is enabled.

6. Ray trace View 2 using the current solution.

| Particle Tracing | **335**

From here, you can add use the Add More Shots to solution (to current limits) option to add extra shots and produce a more refined image.

The image at right, which has been allowed to process through to a complete solution, is now very photorealistic.

Image with complete radiosity solution.

PARTICLE TRACING

Particle tracing is not a rendering process in itself, but a special global lighting solution that can be used during the rendering process. Particle tracing is an alternative to traditional radiosity, with significantly lower memory requirements. It is especially well suited to visualizing very large designs. Because particle tracing solutions are computed directly to disk rather than in memory, solutions can be generated for designs of virtually any size.

Particle tracing solutions are view-independent. Once computed, the solution can be displayed from any vantage point. This feature is particularly useful for creating animations and interactive walkthroughs.

Particle tracing calculates the paths of light particles as they are emitted from light sources and are reflected and transmitted through the scene. When ray traced, these lighting solutions provide photorealistic images, including reflections, refraction, and other caustic lighting effects such as light reflected by mirrors or focused through lenses. To view specular highlights, reflections, and refraction in a particle traced image, you must enable Ray Trace Final Display in the Display Settings section of the Particle Tracing dialog box.

Particle Tracing Compared

To clearly show how particle tracing can improve your images, you will compare the rendered result of ray tracing a scene first without and then with a particle traced lighting solution.

| Chapter 10: Interior Spaces and Global Illumination |

✔ Exercise 10-9: First look at particle tracing

1. Open *simple interior PT.dgn*.

   This model is identical to the one used for radiosity. It also includes the sky opening defined as part of the radiosity exercise.

   NOTE: *When one or more sky openings are present in a model, all particles from distant or solar light are forced to pass through the sky openings. This speeds up the rendering process by letting you use fewer particles than would be required were there no sky openings present.*

2. Apply saved view *simple* to Views 2 and 4.

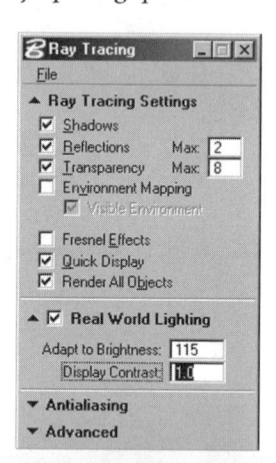

3. Select Render, with the following tool setting:

   Render Mode: Ray Trace

4. Click the magnifying glass icon to open the Ray Tracing settings dialog box and set the following:

   Real World Lighting: On
   Adapt to Brightness (in the expanded Real World Lighting section): 115

5. Close the Ray Tracing settings box.

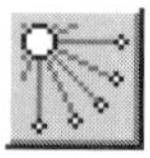

6. Ray trace View 2, creating a new solution.

   The rendered view is very dark on the right side where no direct light strikes any surface. The image is typical for ray tracing without adding additional lights to simulate reflected light.

   Scene ray traced with Real World Lighting.

7. Set the Render Mode to Particle Trace.

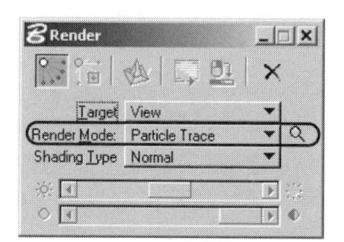

| Particle Tracing |

8 Click the magnifying glass icon to open the Particle Tracing settings dialog box and set the following:

Action: Create New Solution
Particles: Use 1 Million Particles
Ray Trace Specular Effects: On

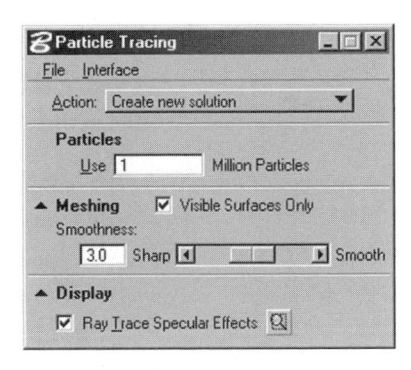

Particle Tracing basic user interface.

9 Enter a data point in View 4.

The particle tracing process begins by shooting one million particles, with progress displayed in the status area. It begins with the shooting phase, followed by the meshing and ray tracing phase, which continues to completion.

The right side of the image now is illuminated. Light particles bouncing off other surfaces provide this illumination.

Scene particle traced with 1 million particles.

Typically, when working with particle tracing, increasing the number of particles will improve the image. One of the options you have is to add to the existing particles. That is, you do not have to start shooting particles from zero. In this example, the shadows from the chairs are very indistinct, and the window frame and mullions have a few splotches. Adding particles will improve the definition of the shadows, and more hits on the window will smooth out the splotches. You will now add nine million particles to the solution to bring it up to 10 million.

✔ Exercise 10-10: Add particles to the solution

1 Continuing in *simple interior PT.dgn*, in the Particle Tracing dialog box, set Action to Add more particles and redo mesh.

2 Set Particles to Use 9 Million Particles.

These will be added to the initial 1 million particles.

| Chapter 10: Interior Spaces and Global Illumination |

3 Enter a data point in View 2.

An alert box appears, warning you that the current solution files will be overwritten.

4 Click OK in the Alert box.

The additional particles have helped to sharpen the shadows from the window on the carpet and added a little more detail to the shadows around the chairs. Still, this could be better.

Because much of the light that is creating shadows for this scene is from direct lighting, you can try another option, in the advanced settings for Particle Tracing. You can turn on Ray Trace Direct Illumination. This requires a new calculation of the particle traced image.

Scene particle traced with 10 million particles.

✔ Exercise 10-11: Turn on Ray Trace Direct Illumination

1 Continuing in *simple interior PT.dgn*, in the Particle Tracing dialog box, select Interface > Show Advanced Settings.

2 Set the following:

Action: Create New Solution

Particles
Ray Trace Direct Illumination: On
Use 10 Million Particles

Meshing: Enable Visible Surfaces Only
Smoothness: 3.0
Mesh Detail: 1.5

NOTE: *The default for Meshing is for Visible Surfaces Only to be enabled. This will produce the quickest results since only the meshing required for the view to render is completed. Where you want a complete solution that meshes all elements, you can disable this setting.*

| Particle Tracing | **339**

Particle Tracing dialog Advanced Interface.

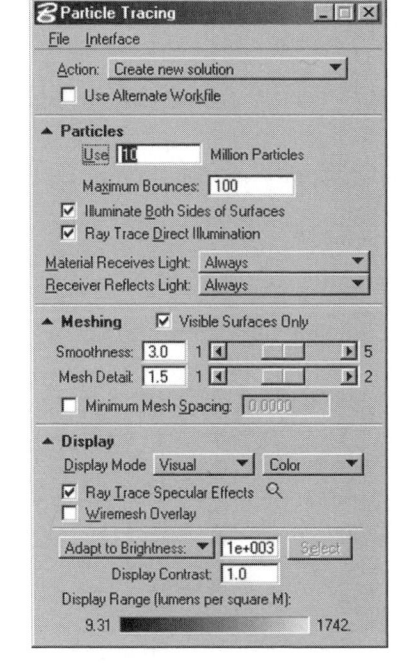

Action section options are Create New Solution, Add more particles redo mesh, Redo mesh only, Display current solution, and Continue after reset.

Particles section defines number of particles and how they react with design.

Meshing section controls the level of detail and smoothness of the rendering mesh.

Display section defines the display of the particle traced solution.

3 Enter a data point in View 4.

An Alert box warns that current solution files will be overwritten.

4 Click OK in the Alert box.

Upon completion of the meshing phase, the final image is ray traced with direct illumination. Notice that the shadows are much sharper than in the previous solution.

NOTE: *You can see some distinct banding in the shadows produced by the chair's arm, on the side wall at the left. This is due to a low number of samples on the sky opening. You can improve the appearance of these shadows by increasing the sky samples, but at the expense of longer rendering time.*

Scene with 10 million shots particle traced with Ray Trace Direct Illumination enabled.

In the next exercise, you will make a few more adjustments to fine-tune the image.

| Chapter 10: Interior Spaces and Global Illumination |

✔ Exercise 10-12: Fine-tune the lighting

1. Continuing in *simple interior PT.dgn*, click on the Define Light tool.
2. Change the Mode to Modify and Method to Edit Light.
3. Click on the Sky Opening in the Light Name list box.
4. Change the Max Samples to 512 and Min Samples to 32.
5. Open the Global Lighting dialog box and enable Jitter sky samples.

Global Lighting with Jitter sky samples enabled.

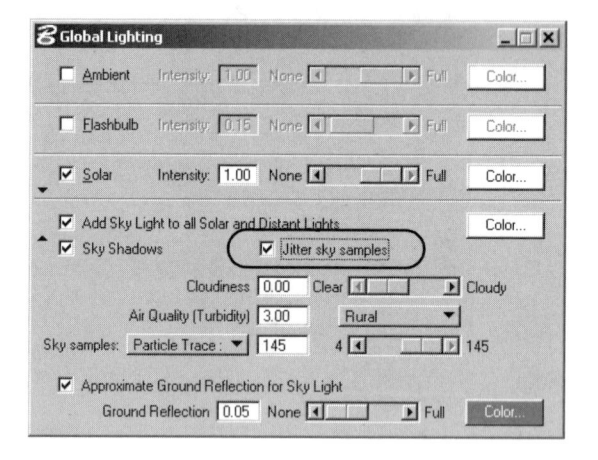

6. With Render Mode set to Particle Trace, create a new solution using 10 million particles in View 2.

Scene rendered with Jitter sky samples on.

As you can see, a little fine-tuning of lighting and the particle traced image rendered in this simple scene produced very realistic and convincing results.

How Particle Tracing works

Particle tracing works by calculating the paths of light particles as they are emitted from light sources and are reflected and transmitted throughout the scene. This process occurs in two separate phases.

The Particle Shooting Phase

During this phase particles are emitted, or shot, into the scene from each light source. You can specify the total number of particles to be shot. From this total figure, the relative value of the Lumens setting for each light source then determines the number of particles shot by each source. The particles are distributed based on the brightness in lumens for the lights in the scene, brighter lights shooting more particles overall than those that are less bright.

Particle paths are traced through the scene, interacting with the surfaces of any objects encountered along the way. These interactions can include caustics, which are the lighting effects caused by light reflected off surfaces or refracted through transparent objects. Examples of the caustic effect are sunlight reflecting off the face of a watch and flashing in someone's face, or the light focused through a lens. A caustic reflection differs from a ray traced reflection in that the caustic reflection bounces light from the surface receiving the light to the surface receiving the reflected light or caustic. A ray traced reflection just shows what the viewer would see.

When a particle strikes a surface, it is either absorbed or bounced. A bounce can be a diffuse reflection, a specular (mirror) reflection, or a specular transmission with refraction. Each time that a particle is diffusely reflected or absorbed, a hit point is recorded for that surface. All hits are recorded to disk in a hit point file which has the extension .shp.

Each surface's material properties determine the relative probabilities of these interactions. Take, for example, a diffuse white surface having a Diffuse setting of 0.7 and a Specular setting of 0.0. This surface will diffusely reflect 70% of the particles that hit it and absorb the remaining 30%. If the material also has a specular value greater than 0, then a percentage of the particles will be specularly reflected. Similarly, if the material is partially transparent, then some particles will be transmitted as well.

Display Phase

Once the shooting phase has finished, the display phase begins, meshing surfaces as needed. During this phase, the hit points on each surface are processed to determine the illumination of the surfaces. As each illumination mesh is computed, it is stored to disk in a mesh file, which has the extension *.um*.

When Visible Surfaces Only is enabled, the progress bar estimates the amount of time required to complete the view, not the complete solution.

When Visible Surfaces Only is disabled, the view is rendered, meshing surfaces as needed first. When the view is complete, all remaining surfaces are meshed. For these situations, the progress bar estimates the amount of time required to complete the entire solution. Note that the view is likely to be fully rendered long before the progress bar reaches 100%. After meshing is completed, the particle traced solution can be displayed quickly and easily from any view point. Because the solution automatically is saved to disk, it is not lost even if you close the design or exit MicroStation.

In some cases, the smooth shaded display created during the meshing phase is sufficient, since shadows and caustics are part of the particle traced solution. When additional specular effects are desired, such as views with reflective or refractive objects, the final display can be ray traced by enabling Ray Trace Specular Effects in the Display Settings section of the Particle Tracing dialog box.

> **NOTE:** *Particle tracing stores most of its data in temporary files. These files are located in the directory specified by the variable* MS_PTDIR. *If this variable is not defined, then the files are stored in the directory defined by* MS_TMP.

Disk Space Requirements for Particle Tracing

Because particle tracing computations are written to disk, you need to ensure that you have enough free space for the image being rendered. Specifically, 8 bytes are required for each hit point initially, in the un-

| How Particle Tracing works | 343

sorted hit point file (.*uhp*). Later, this reduces to 4 bytes / hit point when that file is converted into a sorted hit point file (.*shp*).

The ratio of hit points to particles can vary greatly, of course, depending on the geometry and materials used in your design. This ratio, however, remains relatively constant as you add more particles. Thus, you can get an estimate of the disk space required as follows:

- First run a small (1 million particle) solution, and check the size of your hit point file (.*shp*).

- You can use this figure then to estimate how much free space you'll need.

For example, if a 1 million particle solution produces a 4 MB hit point file (.*shp*), then for a 400 million particle solution, the final hit point file would be 1600 MB (400 x 4 MB). The disk space required, however would be double that, 3200 MB, to allow for the initial .*uhp* file.

Where you don't have enough free space, there is a trick that you can use to overcome the shortage. What if, in the above example, you had only 3000 MB free? You could still get a 400 million particle solution, as follows:

- Shoot 200 million particles, which requires 1600 MB for the initial .*uhp* file and then reduces to 800 MB for the final .*shp* file.

- Add 200 million particles, which requires only 2400 MB (800 MB for the first .*shp* file, plus 1600 MB for the second .*uhp* file).

In this example, the final .*shp* file still will be 1600 MB, exactly the same as if you did it all in one step.

NOTE: *In order to create files greater than 4 GB, you must be using an NTFS file system. FAT file systems are limited to 4 GB for a single file.*

Meshing Settings

Smoothness

Particle tracing calculates the paths of light particles as they "bounce" around a model and then calculates the effect of the light particle "hit points" on each surface. The more particles you use, the more hit points the particle tracer has to work with, resulting in a better image. The Smoothness setting controls the size of the local area over which hit points are spread out. The Smoothness setting involves a trade-off between "noisiness" and "blurriness." In brief, setting the Smoothness setting

- ▶ Too low — will make your details (such as shadows and caustics) sharp, but you will also see noise (more commonly known as "splotches") in your image
- ▶ Too high — will make everything normally appear smooth, but you will lose detail in your shadows and caustics.

NOTE: *A smoothness setting of 3.0 is a good starting point and also the default. If you still have noise using a setting of 3.0, add more particles and redo the mesh to reduce the noise.*

Scene with Mesh Smoothness set to 3.0 *(left)* and 1.0 *(right)*.

Mesh Detail

(Visible only when Show Advanced Settings is on.)

This setting lets you control the resolution of the rendering mesh. Values (from 1 through 5) may be entered in the text field. Recommended values from 1 to 2 also may be input via the Mesh Detail slider. In general, this value should be set at the default value of 2.0. Increasing this value will generate more mesh points, which will take longer but may produce more detail. Decreasing the value will generate fewer mesh points, which will reduce processing time but may show less detail.

Minimum Mesh Spacing

(Visible only when Show Advanced Settings is on.)

If on, this setting sets the minimum size of a rendering mesh. The size of the rendering mesh defines the amount of feature detail, such as shadows and highlights, that will be visible in a particle traced solution. Setting this to an appropriate value can reduce the processing time and disk space required.

This value, which is specified in master units, should be set to the width of the smallest feature that should be visible in a solution. The appropriate value to use is, of course, dependent on your design and how you intend to render it. Where close-up detail is required, a smaller value is needed to produce a finer mesh. For more distant images, a larger value may be used with little or no noticeable degradation in the image quality, but a noticeable reduction in processing time.

Saving Particle Traced Solutions

You can save a particle traced solution to disk. It can be retrieved and, providing the geometry and the lighting have not changed, you can add more particles or render additional images with the particle traced solution already calculated.

When saving a particle traced solution, the default name given is comprised of the name of the design file plus the active model. For instance, if your design file is named *office.dgn* and the active model you were working with was *First Floor*, the default file name would be *office_first floor.ptd*. If you switched to another model, perhaps the second floor model, then the default particle solution file would be *office_second floor.ptd*.

> **NOTE:** *There is only one exception to this naming rule. When you are in the default model, the file name is the design file name with the .ptd extension.*

Associating solutions with different models makes it convenient to have various setups, such as different models with different lighting, with different levels of detail, or even different rooms of a house. By default, each of these models will use different work files for particle tracing solutions.

NOTE: *If Use Alternate Workfile is enabled, the alternate file name is used for particle tracing work files without modification.*

NOTE: *To use particle tracing solutions that were computed with earlier software versions, for non-default models, enable Use Alternate Workfile in the Advanced Settings interface of the Particle Tracing dialog box and enter the name of the DGN file. Alternatively, you can rename the files in the Particle Tracing working directory (MS_PTDIR) from the relevant DGN file name to DGNfilename_modelname.*

✔ Exercise 10-13: Save a particle traced solution to disk

1   Continuing in *simple interior PT.dgn*, in the Particle Tracing dialog box, select File > Save Solution.

NOTE: *You also can right-click in the Render tool dialog box icon tool bar and select Save Solution from the pop-up menu.*

2   In the Save Rendering Database dialog box, select a directory and file name.

Because you are working in the default model, by default the rendering database is given a name using the DGN file and the extension *.ptd*.

3   Click OK.

Loading a particle traced database from disk

Your current particle trace database remains on disk unless you clear it. If you have previously saved the particle trace solution to disk, you can reload it later and render any view.

✔ Exercise 10-14: Retrieve a particle traced database and render other views

1   Continuing in *simple interior PT.dgn*, in the Render tool dialog box, click Clear current rendering solution.

An Alert box asks if you are sure that you want to clear the current particle tracing solution.

| How Particle Tracing works | **347**

2 Click OK.

Notice, in the Rendering tool dialog box, that Display current solution (in any view) now is disabled.

3 In the Particle Tracing dialog box, select File > Load Solution.

Alternatively, right-click in the Render tool icon bar and select Load Solution.

4 In the Load Rendering Database dialog box, select the database that you created in the previous exercise.

5 In the Render tool settings, select Display Current Solution.

6 Enter a data point in View 2.

The view is rendered, using the loaded particle tracing solution.

7 Apply the saved view *other* to View 4.

This saved view provides a different camera setup to render with the retrieved solution.

8 Enter a data point in View 4 to particle trace the view with the current solution.

NOTE: *The view is rendered using the loaded particle tracing solution. Since this view differs from the original view, some additional meshing will likely occur since the option on Meshing was set to Visible Surfaces Only. Further meshing is possible since the hit point file and the mesh files are still on your hard drive. If this option had not been checked, a complete solution would be available and no further meshing would be required.*

Another view of scene particle traced with retrieved solution.

9 Apply the saved view *caustic* to view 2.

This saved view provides a view farther back where caustic effects can be seen when rendered with the retrieved solution.

| Chapter 10: Interior Spaces and Global Illumination |

10. Enter a data point in View 2 to particle trace the view with the current solution.

   A little more meshing will take place to render this view.

   Since additional meshing was required to render the additional views, the solution is now more complete than when previously loaded. You can save this more complete solution or turn off Visible Surfaces Only and let the lighting solution continue to mesh all remaining elements.

Caustic effect caused by highly specular finish on chair arm. Sunlight entering the window is reflected off this surface onto the ceiling.

NOTE: *To avoid unpredictable results, it is highly recommended that a particle traced solution be loaded only into the model from which it was originally saved.*

11. Turn off Visible Surfaces Only in the Particle Tracing dialog box.

   The action causes the Continue After Reset button to appear in the Render dialog box where it was grayed out before.

12. Click on the Continue After Reset button in the Render dialog box and enter a data point in any view to complete meshing of remaining elements.

   The progress view will display progress of the meshing phase. The additional meshing may take a few minutes to finish.

| IES Lighting |

13 From the Particle Tracing dialog box, select File > Save Solution to save the complete solution to disk.

Interrupting/continuing the process

You can interrupt the processing of a particle traced view by entering a Reset. When you do this, the Continue After Reset icon becomes active. Clicking this icon lets you continue the process from where it was stopped. This applies even after you have exited and restarted MicroStation.

> **NOTE:** *If Visible surfaces only is enabled and processing is aborted after the shooting phase was complete, Display current solution is enabled and can be used to continue the solution. As the view is rendered, any unmeshed surfaces are meshed as they are displayed.*

If Visible surfaces only is not enabled or processing is aborted during the shooting phase, the solution can be continued by clicking the Continue After Reset icon.

IES LIGHTING

MicroStation's advanced photorealistic rendering options—ray tracing, radiosity, and particle tracing—let you produce lifelike images of models from within MicroStation. This includes the option of working with industry-standard lighting values.

Lighting Considerations for Photorealism

When you are working with radiosity solving or particle tracing, you still can use standard light source cells to provide the illumination. Both processes, however, use the lumens value multiplied by the intensity value to determine the brightness of the light source. Thus, you can set the correct Lumens value for the light source and then use the Intensity setting like a dimmer switch to quickly change its brightness as needed. For Ray Tracing, the Lumens setting is ignored, unless Real World Lighting is enabled, but when ray tracing a Radiosity, or Particle Traced solution the Lumens value always is considered.

Where correct lighting effects are required, it is recommended that you work with Illuminating Engineering Society (IES) lighting data files. For accurate lighting in rendered images, MicroStation supports the use of

IES lighting files for both radiosity solving and particle traced solutions, as well as for ray tracing when Real World Lighting is enabled. IES data files are available for download from most lighting manufacturers. They apply the correct values to the source lighting cells for the rendering modes that support IES lighting. In addition, they define the photometric web to correctly display the spread of the light from a light source, which in turn results in more natural-looking rendered images. The photometric web is a three-dimensional representation of how the light spreads out from a light fixture and takes into account the physical shape and reflective properties of the lamp and the fixture.

In the next exercise, you will use the particle trace rendering technique to render an interior scene illuminated by two source lights, both of which use IES data files. The IES data is used to determine the lumens value and also the photometric characteristics for each light source.

Exercise 10-15: View an IES lighting photometric web and its data file

1. Open *simple interior IES.dgn*.

2. In the Rendering Tools tool box, select the Define Light tool with the following settings:

   Mode: Modify
   Method: Edit Light

3. Select the first Point light in the light list.

4. Click the Show IES Data icon (down arrow at the bottom left of the Define Light dialog box).

5. Set the following:

   IES Data: Enabled
   Show Webs: Enabled

   The 3D photometric web for the selected light appears in all open views. This web shows how the light is distributed from the

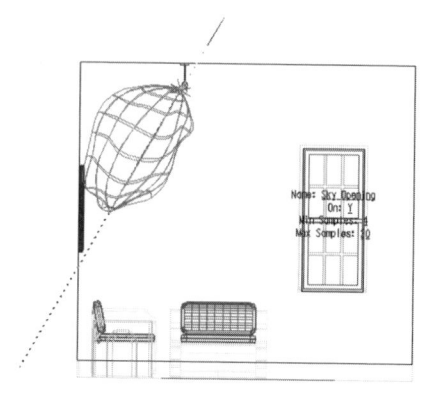

   Photometric web displayed.

| IES Lighting |

light source. The light sprays out like water would spray from a sprinkler nozzle.

6 In the IES Data section, enable Show IES Detailed Text.

An IES Lighting dialog box opens, displaying the IES data for the selected light source. It is this information that controls the IES light source in the model.

7 Close the IES Lighting dialog box.

This model contains two ceiling-mounted light fixtures modeled using data from the lighting manufacturer Ardron Mackie, using the correct IES photometric data files for the fixture, which were downloaded from their web site.

✔ **Exercise 10-16: Render with IES lighting**

1 Continuing in *simple interior IES.dgn*, apply the saved view IES Shot to View 2.

2 Select the Render tool with the following setting:

Render Mode: Particle Trace

3 Click the magnifying glass icon to open the Particle Tracing settings dialog box and check, or set, the following:

Action: Create new solution
Particles: Use 5 Million Particles
Meshing: Turn on Visible Surfaces only

4 Enter a data point in View 2.

The view is rendered with 5 million particles, but the recorded hits are over 30 million as the particles are bounced around the room before they are dissipated. These figures can be checked in the Message Center.

Using IES data files can provide you with an accurate representa-

Scene particle traced with 5 million particles using IES lights.

tion of the lighting based on the photometric web, even without a model for the fixture.

As you can see in the image at left, even with the light fixture level turned off, the light's direction is focused by the IES photometric data. The lumens or brightness is also controlled by the IES data file.

NOTE: *When using IES photometrics, you should place lights as point lights rather than use directional lights such as spot or area lights.*

IES lights without light fixtures.

Lighting Solution Considerations

With radiosity or particle tracing, you can obtain very photorealistic lighting solutions of models. Radiosity allows you to obtain realistic results quickly, but uses more memory than particle tracing and is better suited to small projects. Particle tracing can be used for large models, but at the expense of hard disk space. In addition, particle tracing can produce caustics, lighting effects caused by light reflected off surfaces or refracted through transparent objects.

Whether using particle tracing or radiosity, you can make minor modifications to a model to overcome light leaks and shadow leaks. These anomalies are caused by the meshing elements that receive shadows or light extending beyond these areas into visible areas.

Ultimately, you could shoot enough particles to overcome the light leaks and shadow leaks, but you could also make modifications to the model to achieve the results you want in far less time.

In the image at left, the light leak occurring around the right window does not occur in the left window. The simple fix for this problem is to make sure the wall containing the opening has a thickness that prevents the light from hitting the edges of the opening.

Shadow leaks can be prevented by making sure geometry does not extend under the shadow object. In the case of the shadow leak above the baseboard be-

Scene with light leak and shadow leaks.

| IES Lighting | 353

low the right window, the wall extends below the baseboard. The baseboard shadow is not a problem under the left window since the wall element does not extend below the baseboard geometry. In the image below, you can see the differences in the modeling for the wall on the left (no shadow or light leaks), and that on the right, where shadow and light leaks were evident.

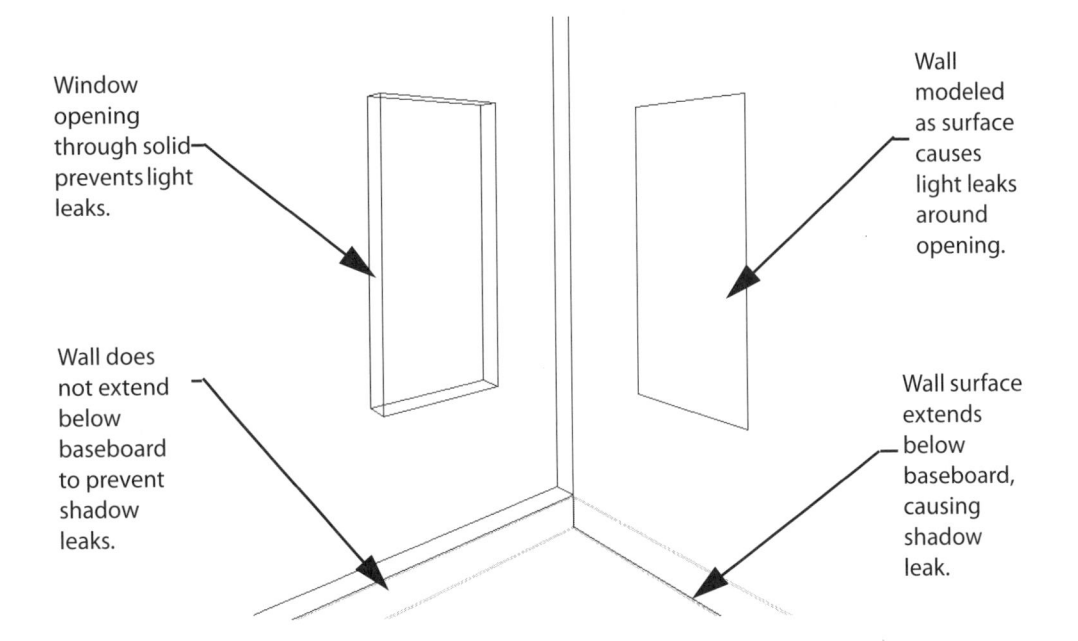

Window opening through solid prevents light leaks.

Wall does not extend below baseboard to prevent shadow leaks.

Wall modeled as surface causes light leaks around opening.

Wall surface extends below baseboard, causing shadow leak.

In the image at right, the right picture has a shadow-like halo around the frame which does not exist around the picture on the left. The solution here is to remove or cut the wall element so that no wall elements extend behind the picture.

Shadow leak appears around the picture on the right.

NOTE: *To prevent shadow leaks from insignificant geometry, you could apply a non-shadow-casting material. For instance, instead of cutting a hole in the wall behind the pictures, it might make more sense to turn off Shadow*

Casting for the picture material. The same could be said for the baseboard material in the example, since the shadows from these lend nothing to the scene and only cause the shadow leaks.

Review Questions

1 What are the two global illumination methods used by MicroStation?

2 In the literature of physics, what is defined as the total power leaving a point on a surface, per unit area on the surface?

3 Particle tracing includes effects such as light reflected off mirrors or focused through a lens. What are these called?

4 Particle tracing can be considered a lighting _____ rather than a rendering process.

5 Particle tracing occurs in two distinct phases. What are they?

6 Will you have a complete particle traced solution after a view is rendered if Visible Surfaces Only is checked?

7 Where correct lighting effects are required, what type of lighting data files are recommended?

8 What terms are used to denote anomalies caused by the meshing elements that receive shadows or light extending beyond these areas into visible areas?

Chapter Summary

In this chapter, you worked with MicroStation's most advanced rendering options, particle tracing and radiosity. You learned that both options produce global lighting solutions that then may be rendered to produce photorealistic images.

11 Photomatching

Photomatching is the process of adjusting the view camera to match the perspective of a photograph, or rendered image. This is done by matching points in the photograph to the equivalent points in your 3D design. Using photomatching, you can create a rendered image of your design overlaying existing conditions (in the photograph).

MicroStation's Photomatch tool lets you quickly and precisely match geometry in a 3D model to an existing photograph.

MATCH DESIGN GEOMETRY TO A RASTER REFERENCE

To get the best results on the first try, you need to set up a camera view that closely matches that of the photograph. This camera view does not need to be matched perfectly, but should be somewhat close. This will make it easier to choose and match points in the 3D model to those in the photograph. By matching known points in the design to equivalent points in the photograph, the system refines the camera view to accurately match the perspective of the photograph.

Once this step has been completed, the view can be rendered to display the design geometry merged with the existing conditions.

356 | Chapter 11: Photomatching |

Scanned photograph of existing conditions.

After photomatching the design geometry to the photograph, the view is ray traced to produce the combined image at right.

✔ Exercise 11-1: Set up the initial camera view size

1. Open *phmatch.dgn*.

   The file has been saved with Top and Front views displaying elements representing the existing buildings. These elements, on level *existing house,* will be used to align a camera view to a photograph. Once matched, the existing house level will be turned off, and the levels containing the proposed building addition geometry will be turned on for display.

2. Select Utilities > Image > Display.

3. In the Display Image dialog box, select *IMG0017.JPG* from the course *Textures* folder. Enable the Preview option and note the size of the image.

   This information helps you match the view's aspect ratio to the image.

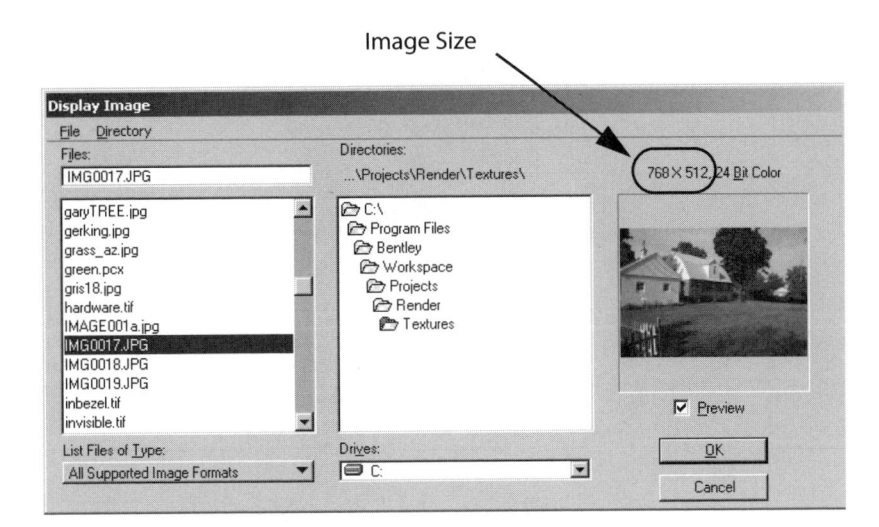

| Match Design Geometry to a Raster Reference | 357

Image Size

4   After noting the image size, you can click the Cancel button to close the dialog box

5   In the Rendering Tools tool box, select View Size tool.

6   Enter a data point in View 3.

7   Set the following in the tool settings:

Maintain View Parameters: Enabled
Proportional Resize: Disabled
X: 768
Y: 512

8   Enter a data point in View 3 to apply these values and resize the view.

The view is resized to 768 pixels x 512 pixels, which may be too large to display properly in the MicroStation application window. However, once you have established the proper aspect ratio (768 x 512), you can use View Size again, this time enabling Proportional Resize to maintain the aspect ratio. Once enabled, you can set either the X or Y value and the view size ratio will remain intact.

9   Close the Image Display

Next, you will attach a background image for View 3.

Exercise 11-2: Attach a background image to the resized view

1. Continuing in *phmatch.dgn*, select Settings > Design File.
2. In the Design File Settings dialog box, select the Views category.
3. Set View to 3, enable Background Image, and click the magnifying glass.

   The Select Background Image dialog box opens.

4. In the Select Background Image dialog box, navigate to the course *Textures* directory and select the file *IMG0017.JPG*.
5. Click OK in the Select Background Image dialog box.
6. Click OK in the DGN File Settings dialog box to accept the settings and close it.

As you can see, the geometry is not even close to being aligned with the background image. You need to first use the camera tools to get a rough alignment between the geometry and the photograph. Later you will use the Photo Matching tool to precisely match the perspective of the model to that of the image.

Background image with geometry in isometric view.

Exercise 11-3: Use the camera tools to align the geometry to the photograph

1. Continuing in *phmatch.dgn*, in the Rendering Tools tool box, select the Define Camera tool.
2. Enter a data point in View 3.

   This turns on the camera for View 3.

3. In the Define Camera tool dialog box, set the following:

Projection: Three Point
Continuous View Updates: On
Display View Cone: On

4 Fit Views 1 and 4.

This fits the views, including the camera cone.

5 Use the camera controls to manipulate the camera target point, eye point, and so on, to roughly match the geometry to the equivalent points in the photograph. This will put your view camera in a position similar to the one used to take the photograph that you are trying to match.

The initial alignment can be very rough. You do not need to spend much time trying to align the background to the geometry. You could even skip this procedure, placing the camera approximately where the photo was taken from and the camera target in a position roughly where it would have been in the original photo.

A rough approximation to match the geometry to the background image.

6 In the View Attributes dialog box (Settings > View Attributes), turn off Background for View 3, to turn off the display of the Background image.

NOTE: *In cases where you do not have known image points modeled in 3D model space, it is possible to achieve a suitable match using the previous procedure, although this method can be time-consuming.*

Your model now is ready to use the Photomatch tool to precisely match the geometry to a background photograph.

MAKING ADJUSTMENTS WITH THE PHOTOMATCH TOOL

With the view roughly lined up with the image, you can now use Photomatch to make the fine adjustments to the camera view so the design file geometry accurately matches the photograph.

✔ **Exercise 11-4: Use Photomatch**

1. Continuing in **phmatch.dgn**, enable AccuSnap.

2. In the Rendering Tools tool box, select the Photomatch tool.

   You are prompted to Select View For Photomatch.

3. Enter a data point in View 3.

4. In the Select Photomatch Image dialog box, select *IMG0017.JPG* and click OK.

   The image is attached to View 3 as a raster reference, and you are prompted to enter a design file point.

   NOTE: *In the next few steps you will be selecting design file match points, snapping first to the geometry, accepting, and then matching corresponding points to the photo.*

5. In View 3, snap to the apex of the left building's roof line, and accept with a data point.

   You are now prompted to enter an image point. There may be a slight hesitation as the magnifier loads and displays a magnified portion of View 3 with cursor lines showing the pointer location. As you move the pointer, the image in the magnifier updates to keep the lines at the pointer location. By default, the magnification is set at 2.0. If required, you can change this value.

6. In View 3, move the pointer to the apex of the roof on the left building in the photograph, using the magnifier as a guide, and enter a data point.

   When you have entered the second point, you will notice small squares at the respective points in both the raster image and the design geometry, joined by a line. These may be hard to see, depending on the colors in the raster image. They provide a visual indication of the points that you have defined previously.

   NOTE: *If you know the camera focal length used to obtain the original photograph—for instance, 28 mm—you can enter 28 in the Lock Focal length field and enable this lock in the Photomatch tool settings. MicroStation will attempt the match using this value. If for some reason a match cannot be made using the provided focal length, the*

Making Adjustments with the Photomatch Tool

1. Snap to the design geometry at the apex.

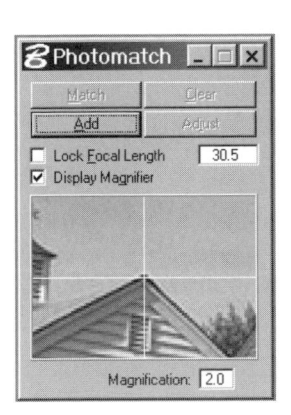

2. Use the Magnifier to locate the equivalent point on the photo background.

box will be disabled after the match is made, meaning a different focal length had to be used.

7 Using the figure below as a guide, snap to point 2 in the design and match it to point 2 on the raster image.

8 Snap to points 3 through 5, in turn, matching them to the equivalent points on the raster image.

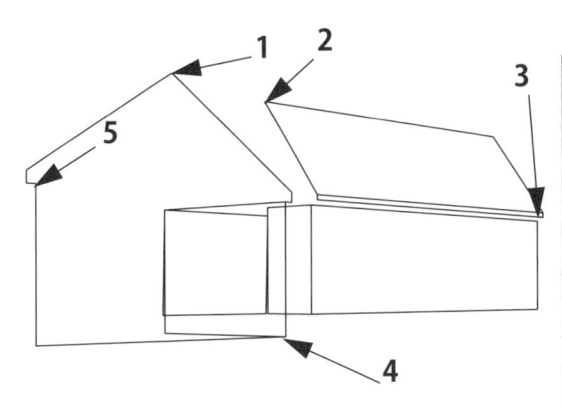

After placing the third point, notice that the Match button becomes active. This indicates that you have placed enough points for the system to attempt to match the geometry to the photograph.

NOTE: *If you select an incorrect point during placement, click Adjust, identify the point, and relocate it. When you finish adjusting the point, click Add to continue adding points.*

9 Click Match.

View 3 updates with the view camera adjusted to show the points as defined.

If the geometry still does not match exactly, you can add extra points to further refine the match. As you do this, you can try matching any point in the image.

NOTE: *If the camera view is too far removed from the original camera view, you will get an error message stating that fact. When this happens, go back to the Define Camera tool and try to make the geometry match the image more closely before using Photomatch.*

DISPLAYING THE PROPOSED GEOMETRY

Now that you have the design geometry of the existing buildings matching the background photograph, you can turn on the proposed design geometry (and turn off the existing). The design has been saved with the Solar Lighting values set to match the time that the original photograph was taken. This ensures that shadows cast by the design elements will look natural.

Exercise 11-5: Display the proposed geometry and render the view

1 Continuing in **phmatch.dgn**, in View 3, turn off the level *existing house* and turn on all other levels.

2 Select Render with the following tool setting:

Render Mode: Ray Trace

3 Enter a data point in View 3.

| Displaying the Proposed Geometry |

View 3 updates with the proposed geometry being ray traced over the existing photo.

NOTE: *When photo-matching, you often need to use a photo editing application to get the most realistic results. In the above right image, you can clearly see that the fence in the foreground is clipped by the deck in the model. You can use an image editing application to copy the fence, and even the shadows, from the original photograph and add these to the saved rendering.*

Finished image edited with foreground and shadows added.

NOTE: *Match points should be spread out both horizontally and vertically. If points are all distributed in a narrow horizontal band across the image, then the Photomatch tool may be unable to successfully compute the camera settings.*

In the following additional exercises, you can practice using the Photomatch tool. In the next exercise, you can skip the process of getting initial alignment by using a background image. The design file has been saved with an approximate camera location that will allow you to make the match using just the Photomatch tool.

✔ **Exercise 11-6: Photomatch model 1**

1 Open **phmatch1.dgn**.

2 Use the Photomatch tool to attach the image *IMG0018.JPG* to View 3. Select a minimum of three design file and image points to align the design file with the raster image file.

| Chapter 11: Photomatching |

3 Turn off the existing geometry, turn on the new geometry and then render the view.

Remember that if you are not satisfied with your results you can detach the raster reference and undo the view manipulations. Just start the process over using the Photomatch tool.

✔ **Exercise 11-7: Photomatch model 2**

1 Open *phmatch2.dgn*.

2 Using the same steps as in the previous Photomatch exercise, match the geometry to *IMG0019.JPG*.

PHOTOMATCH USING A CIVIL ENGINEERING EXAMPLE

You can use photomatching for both small and large projects. In the next exercise you will be using a civil data set and matching a model of a proposed road widening with a photo taken from the existing roadway. (Data set for this exercise courtesy of South Carolina DOT Roadway Design.)

In the previous photomatching exercises, a 3D wireframe design was created as part of the existing structure. This was used to match the photo to the design geometry. In this next exercise, the existing condition is represented by several surveyed points in the 3D model. These points were surveyed in the field, and then added to the 3D design as weighted points matching the surveyed x-y-z coordinates.

✔ **Exercise 11-8: Photomatch survey points**

1 Open *phmatch_civil.dgn*.

This model of terrain geometry has several weighted points, representing survey data taking in the field. View 2 is a camera view clearly showing the points, which you will use to match corresponding geometry in a photograph of the existing site conditions.

2 Check that AccuSnap is enabled.

| Photomatch Using a Civil Engineering Example | 365

AccuSnap will make it easy to pick the surveyed points in the design file.

NOTE: *AccuSnap can be toggled on and off using the AccuDraw shortcut J, while the focus is in the AccuDraw window.*

3 In the Rendering Tools tool box, select the Photomatch tool.

You are prompted to Select View for Photomatch.

4 Enter a data point in View 2 to select this view for photomatching.

The Select Photomatch Image dialog box opens.

5 In the course *Textures* directory, select the file *phmatch_civil.jpg*.

The photo is displayed in View 2, and you can clearly see that the weighted blue points representing the bottoms and tops of the power poles are not aligned. The weighted green points representing the traffic cones on the roadway also are not aligned.

You are prompted to enter a design file point.

Photomatch image with geometry overlaid.

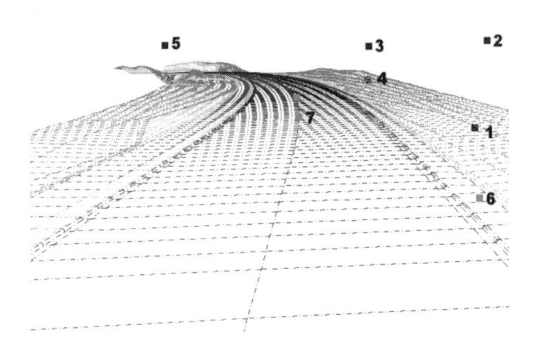

Reference wireframe image and photo showing the points to be matched.

6 Move your screen pointer to the lower right, blue-weighted point (point 1 in the above reference wireframe) and, when AccuSnap snaps to it, accept with a data point.

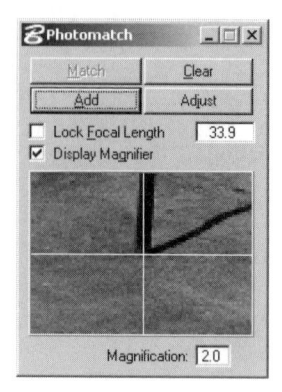

The Photomatch dialog becomes active, displaying a magnified view of the photo without the design file geometry, making it easier to select the appropriate image point.

7   Move the pointer to the bottom of the first power pole on the right of the image (point 1 in the reference photograph) and accept with a data point.

    Note the rubber band between the two points depicting where the design file point eventually will be aligned to match the photo.

8   Snap to the blue weighted point located above the previous point (point 2), and enter a data point.

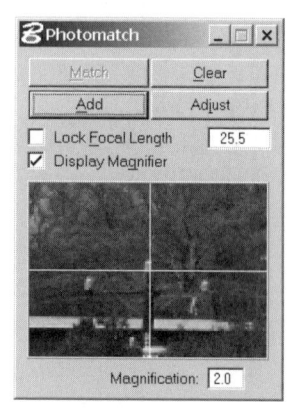

9   Using the Photomatch magnified view to guide you, move the pointer to the top of the same power pole (point 2 in reference photo) and enter a data point.

10 There are two blue points (3 and 4 in the reference wireframe) to the left of the previous two. Snap to the top point (3) and accept with a data point.

11 Move the pointer to the corresponding image point for the top of this power pole and enter a data point.

12 Snap to the lower point (4) and accept with a data point.

13 Move the pointer to the bottom of this pole in the image, using the magnified window, and enter a data point at the base of the pole on the right, as shown below.

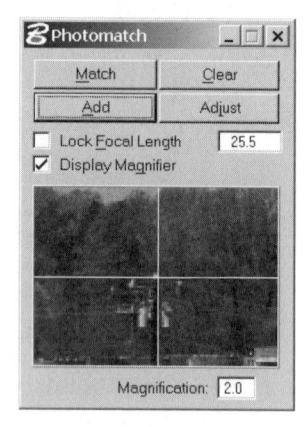

Magnified view matching bottom of power pole location 1.

The second point at the top of the pole.

The top of the second pole.

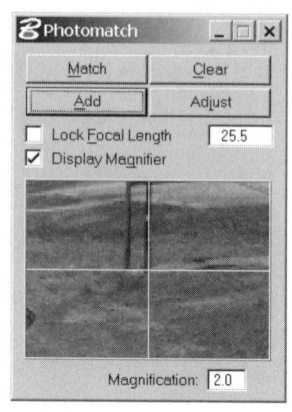

The bottom of the second pole.

| Photomatch Using a Civil Engineering Example | 367

14 Snap to the blue point at the left of the view (point 5) and accept with a data point.

15 Using the magnified view, move the pointer to the top of the corresponding pole in the photo and enter a data point.

This pole is located to the right of the building on the left side of the road. It is a little difficult to spot, but you should be able to make use of the Photomatch magnify feature as you move your cursor over this area of the image.

16 In the Photomatch dialog box, click the Match button.

After matching, traffic cones are not matched to survey data.

Survey point traffic cone

Traffic cone location

The camera location and perspective are modified to achieve a photo-match. The five points you picked appear to be matched, but the cones are a little off. You can fine-tune the match by adding these additional survey points and matching again.

✔ Exercise 11-9: Fine-tune the photomatch by adding additional points

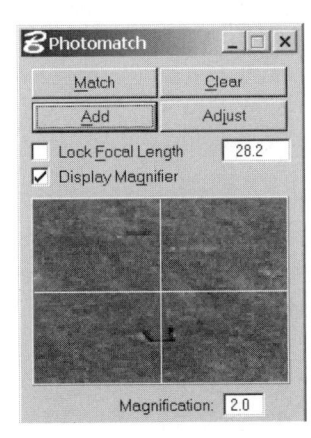

1 Continuing in *phmatch_civil.dgn*, in the Photomatch tool dialog box, click the Add button.

2 Snap to the green point at the lower right in the view (point 6) and accept with a data point,

3 Move the pointer to the top of the traffic cone on the lower right side of the photo in the grass area and enter a data point.

The top of the traffic cone grass area.

| Chapter 11: Photomatching |

Looking at the model, in View 2, notice two more green points in the middle of the roadway. Either could be matched to the photo but, for this exercise, you will use the lower one of the two (point 7).

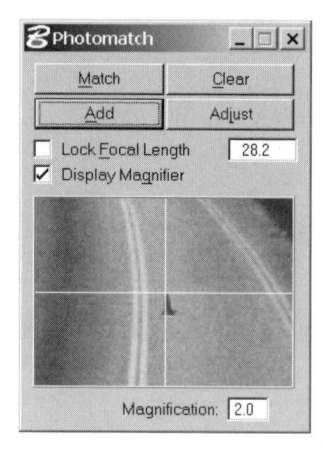

4   Snap to the lower green point (7), in the middle of the roadway, and accept with a data point.

   There are three cones in the middle of the roadway in the photo you are matching. This point corresponds to the top of middle cone.

5   Using the magnified view to guide you, move the pointer to the top of the middle cone and enter a data point.

6   In the Photomatch tool dialog box, click the Match button to modify the camera location and perspective.

Magnified view of cone being matched.

Notice that now the cone survey points match those in the photo and the image is perfectly matched.

Final Photomatch Render

Now that you have the proposed roadway model matched to the existing photo, you can render the scene. To make the area more visually appealing, several new trees are to be planted along both sides of this new stretch of roadway. The trees already have been placed on a separate level and are ArchVision RPC files.

| Photomatch Using a Civil Engineering Example |

✔ Exercise 11-10: Ray trace the final civil photomatch

1. Continuing in *phmatch_civil.dgn*, make RPC the active level.

   The RPC files are displayed in all views.

2. Look at the shadow from the power poles in the existing photograph and make a mental note of their direction.

3. Select the Render tool with the following setting:

   Render Mode: Ray Trace

4. Enter a data point in View 2.

   The view is ray traced, and you can see the shadows from the RPC trees are in a different direction from those of the existing power poles.

   It is important to try and match the time of day so the shadows match those in the photograph. By looking at the shadows in the photo, you can get a rough idea of the solar direction. Enter this by locking the Solar Direction Vector and entering the Azimuth Angle and Altitude Angle.

✔ Exercise 11-11: Modify the Solar lighting to match the photograph

1. Continuing in *phmatch_civil.dgn*, select the Global Lighting tool.

2. In the Global Lighting dialog, turn on the Lock setting for the Solar Direction Vector to use Azimuth Angle and Altitude Angle rather than the location and time of day.

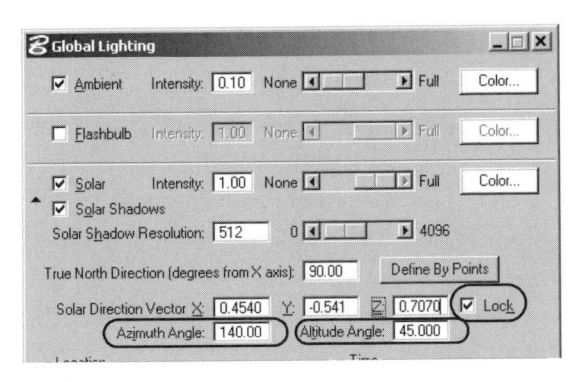

3. Enter the following values:

   Azimuth Angle: 140
   Altitude Angle: 45

4. Ray trace View 2, creating a new solution.

   The view is ray traced, and the direction of the shadows from the RPC trees now more closely matches that in the existing photograph.

Final render with RPC trees and people.

Review Questions

1. What is the displayed background image when you use the Photomatch tool?

2. Approximating a photomatch using only camera manipulations requires you to size the view to match the _____ _____ of the photo.

3. What does the Lock Focal Length do if the specified lens cannot be used?

4. How do you correct a misplaced photomatch point?

5. How would you add foreground images back into the rendered image?

6. How should your match points be spread out?

7. When using the Photomatch tool, you snap to the geometry and enter a data point. What do you do at the matching image point?

8. Why is it important in Global Lighting to try and match the time of day?

Chapter Summary

In this chapter, you learned how to use MicroStation's Photomatch tool. You saw how to set up the initial camera view, and then how to adjust the view to match the perspective of the photograph. You saw that this procedure lets you render your design over the existing photograph to see how the finished project will look.

12   Generating Output

This chapter teaches you how to save images to disk and how to use multiple networked systems to render a single high-resolution image to disk. You will see how to save Virtual Reality (VR) panorama images, as well as Image Objects, or IMOBs. You also will learn how to create scripts for batch rendering using Save Image Multiple. This routine lets you save image files, including panoramas, from several DGN files and multiple views, using rendering setups and saved views.

You will learn how to add 3D content to an Adobe PDF file by enabling Plot to 3D in the Print dialog box.

SAVING IMAGES TO DISK

While much of your visualization work will be rendered and displayed on the computer screen, MicroStation supports many different image file formats for saving to disk. The rendering engine lets you save your image to any of the supported raster file types. Saving images to disk in this way lets you quickly recall them later for viewing or printing. This saves minutes, or even hours, that could be spent waiting for an antialias ray traced image to appear on the screen.

✔ Exercise 12-1: Save an image file to disk

1 Open *BC1.dgn*.

This DGN file has Views 5 and 6 set up as camera views for rendering.

2 Select Utilities > Image > Save.

3 In the Save Image dialog box, set View to 5.

4 From the Format option menu, select JPEG (JFIF).

There are many image file formats to choose from. However, the most commonly used raster formats are JPEG, TIFF, Targa, and BMP.

One of the most common compressed image file formats, JPEG, stands for **J**oint **P**hotographic **E**xperts **G**roup. While there is always some loss in quality when using this format, generally it requires the least amount of disk space.

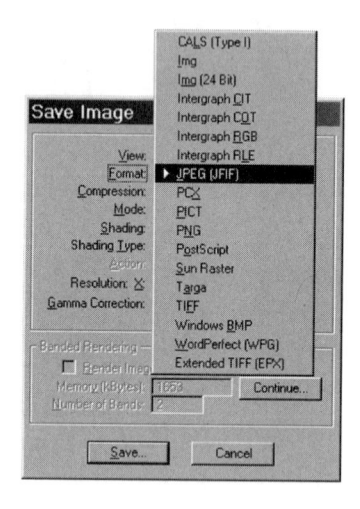

5 From the Compression option menu, select Minimum Loss.

Options are Minimum, Low, Medium and High Loss, with Minimum Loss offering the best quality.

6 From the Mode option menu, select 24 Bit Color.

24-bit color is 16.7 million colors, often referred to as *true color*, and the limit that the human eye can discern.

NOTE: *You can save images in 32 Bit Color (RGB Alpha) in either Targa or Tiff format. The 32-bit color option stores the image as 24- bit color and contains an additional 8-bit (256 color) alpha channel used to contain masking information. With this mode, you can save an image and add a sky background with an image editor later, since the mask information is stored with the image.*

7 Via the remaining option menus, set the following:

Shading: RayTrace
Shading Type: Antialias
Action: Create New Solution

When the Shading option is Ray Trace, Radiosity, or Particle Trace, choose the required action from the Action option menu.

8 In the Resolution field, enter an X value of 600.

The Y value will change appropriately in order to maintain the current view aspect ratio. Defaults are calculated according to the aspect ratio of the selected view (its height relative to its width). Changing either the X or Y value automatically changes the other.

NOTE: *In the Gamma Correction field, you can change the value from the default that appears. Higher values will lighten the image, while lower values will darken it.*

9 Click Save.

The Save Image As dialog box appears. By default, the image file is given the same name as the design file, but with a suffix matching the format (for example, *.jpg*, *.tif* or *.rgb*).

10 Click OK.

Rendering commences and the image file is saved. You can monitor the progress via the status fields at the bottom of the MicroStation window.

11 When the image file is created, select Utilities > Image > Display and open the image you just created.

BANDED RENDERING

This option, in the Save Image dialog box, automatically divides an image into strips, or bands, during the rendering process. These bands are saved as files on your hard drive until all bands are completed. They then are assembled into a complete image when the final band is finished. By dividing the process into smaller jobs, less memory is used than normally would be required to render the entire image to disk. Dividing the image into bands also makes it possible to use multiple systems to render a single image to disk.

To use banded rendering, you must save the image in a 24-bit format. This is limited to BMP, Intergraph RGB, Targa, or TIFF. The JPEG format will not work, since the compression algorithm requires the entire image to be evaluated in order to determine the compression. Since only partial bands would be available during the process, the ability to save to JPEG is disabled for banded rendering.

Creating a Rendered Image Using the Banded Method

In the next exercise, you will use banded rendering to conserve memory during the image saving process.

✔ **Exercise 12-2: Save an image in bands**

1. Continuing in *BC1.dgn*, select Utilities > Image > Save.

2. In the Save Image dialog box, set the following:

   View: 5
   Format: TIFF
   Resolution: X: 1024
   Mode: 24 Bit Color
   Shading Type: Antialias
   Action: Ray trace current solution
   Resolution: X: 1024
   Gamma Correction: 1.00

3. Turn on Render Image in Bands.

4. Set the Number of Bands to 16.

   Memory in kBytes will be adjusted automatically.

   You could alternatively set the memory, and the number of bands would be calculated based on memory.

5. Click Save to save the image to a file.

6. In the Save Image As dialog box, click OK to start the process.

As the image is processed, notice that the status bar reports the band that currently is being rendered, such as "Rendering band 2 of 20," as well as the estimated time to complete the band. In an office with net-

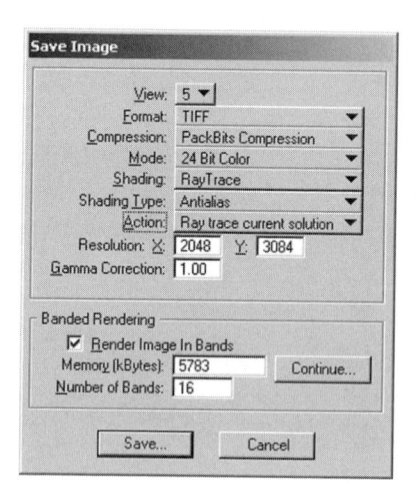

| Banded Rendering |

worked computers, you could speed up the process by using multiple systems to render the image. While this current image is processing, continue with the following section and exercise to see how you can use multiple sessions of MicroStation to process a single image.

Using Multiple Computers to Compute a Single Image

Using banded image creation lets you use multiple systems to network render a single image. By breaking the processing into bands, each system can render a portion of the image. The system that finishes the final band will then assemble the finished image into a single file.

In the exercise that follows, you will simulate a network rendering job by running two instances of MicroStation on the same computer. Normally you would open the design file from another computer or multiple computers on your network to take advantage of their CPUs. The procedure used in the exercise, however, is identical to the procedure you would use on a dual or multiprocessor computer or on the new generation of dual-core processors to fully utilize their additional processors.

✔ Exercise 12-3: Network distributed image creation

1   With the initial instance of MicroStation running, and creating the saved image from the previous exercise, launch another instance of MicroStation.

NOTE: *Depending on the amount of time and speed of your computer, it is possible that the first instance of MicroStation has already completed the rendering job. In that case start the process over and set the resolution X value to something higher—for example, 1600.*

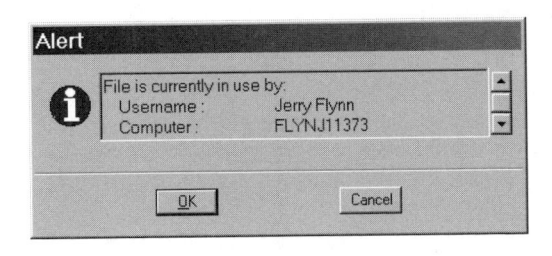

2   Open **BC1.dgn** in this second instance.

An Alert box opens, notifying you that the file is currently in use and asking whether you want to open it in read-only mode.

3   Click OK to open the file read-only.

4   Select Utilities > Image > Save.

5 In the Save Image dialog box, Banded Rendering section, click Continue.

6 In the Continue Banded Rendering dialog box, browse to the folder where the TIFF file from the previous exercise is being saved.

7 Select the file, *BC1.bnd*, and click OK or just double-click on the BND file.

The Save Image dialog box appears with grayed out entries as these are picked up by the BND file.

8 Click the Save button in the Save Image dialog box to start the rendering process.

This starts the rendering process with the second instance of MicroStation.

Once the last band is computed, the image will be assembled and you can display the final result.

NOTE: *Don't be alarmed if you see a message "Error creating image file." Only one processor can stitch all the bands together and make the image file. The machine or processor that finishes last will create the assembled image.*

Requirements for banded rendering over a network

When using multiple systems to compute a single image over a network, the design file must be in a shared folder, or drive. In addition, the textures, patterns, bump maps, and palette files must be visible to all systems in order for networked systems to render the same design file. One sure way not to miss anything is to have the textures, palette, and material files in the folder with the design file, as MicroStation will always look there for these files.

Benefits of using banded rendering

In addition to being able to process an image using multiple systems, banded rendering has additional benefits, such as:

- Lower memory requirements. This is especially true when rendering high-resolution images.

- Rendering interrupt. You can stop the rendering process and then restart the job later. For instance, if you wanted to render a

| Creating Panoramas | 377

job overnight, but you find in the morning that it did not finish, you can simply Reset. The rendering will stop and the current incomplete band will be deleted. You then can restart the job at the end of the day using the Continue option.

- Restart. In the event of a power outage or crash, you will need to manually delete the 0-byte band file or files being worked on at the time of failure. Then you can just restart by using the Continue option.

CREATING PANORAMAS

Imagine being able to look at your rendered model in real time and dynamically pan around it with antialiased ray traced or particle traced results. You can do this by saving images as a panorama.

MicroStation provides the ability to create panorama files that can be viewed using third-party applications, such as Apple Computer's QuickTime player. Such players let you interactively view the panorama image by changing the initial viewpoint from which the image is viewed. Additionally, when a complete QuickTime application installation is detected, further options are available during the panorama creation process. These include:

- Saving panorama output to a QuickTime VR file (.*mov* extension).

- Additional panorama types for creating Image Object panoramas.

To start the panorama image creation process, select Utilities > Image > Save Panorama, which opens the Save Panorama dialog box.

This dialog box provides options for generating standard panoramas:

- *Cube* — Creates images that let you view forward, backward, left, right, up, and down.

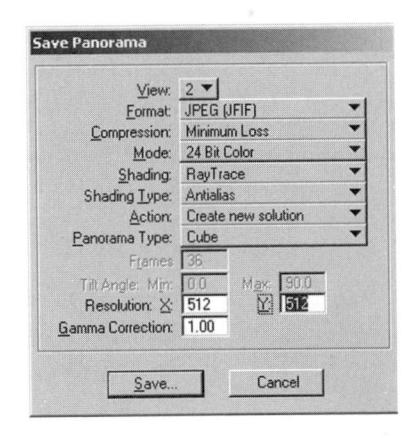

- ▶ *Cylinder* — Creates images that you view in the horizontal direction only.

When the full version of QuickTime is installed, additional options are made available in the Save Panorama dialog box:

- ▶ *Object - Sphere* — Creates images that let you view the target object from any direction.

- ▶ *Object - Top Hemisphere* — Creates images that let you view the target object from any position from horizontal to directly above.

- ▶ *Object - Circle* — Creates images that let you view the target object from a fixed altitude.

- ▶ *Object - Custom* — Lets you specify the minimum and maximum altitudes for viewing the target object.

In each of the QuickTime panorama types, the camera will revolve 360° around the target object. The number of frames created at each altitude is set by the Frames field in the Save Panorama dialog box.

QuickTime requirements

In order to use the advanced QuickTime VR functionality, a complete QuickTime installation must be loaded. To ensure this, during the installation of QuickTime, make sure you select Custom installation and install *all* of the components listed. A no-cost version of QuickTime can be obtained from the Apple Computer web site located at:

http://www.apple.com/quicktime/download/standalone
Select Operating System **Win 98/Me/2000/XP**

When installing QuickTime, choose Custom Installation (as shown in the image on the next page).

After choosing Custom, click Next to go to the Select Components dialog box.

Click Select All, then Next, to continue with the installation.

In order for Save Panorama to be able to use the QuickTime VR formats, the libraries *QTJavaNative.dll* and *QuickTime.qts* must be present in the *windows system32* folder. Both of these critical files are installed as part of the full QuickTime application installation process.

QuickTime Installer: Choose Installation Type.

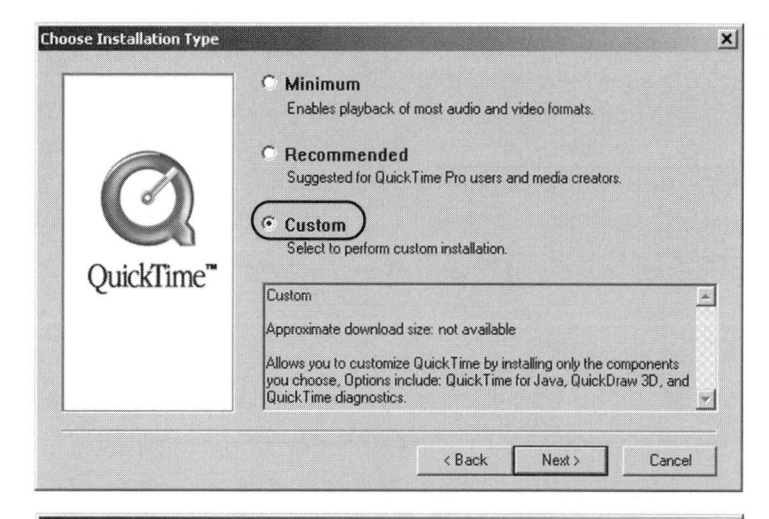

QuickTime Select Components.

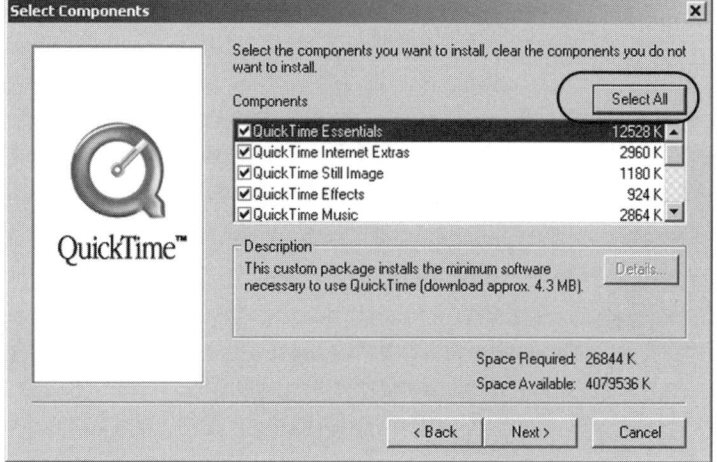

NOTE: *If the QuickTime setup program does not let you install QuickTime for Java, it may be because the Java 2 Runtime Environment cannot be found on your computer. In this situation, you should exit from the QuickTime setup and install the Java 2 Runtime Environment. Java 2 Runtime Environment can be obtained from the Sun Microsystems web site location:*

http://java.sun.com/j2se/1.3/jre/download-windows.html.

Follow the instructions to download and install the Java 2 Runtime Environment, Standard Edition. Once this has been installed, the QuickTime setup program will let you install QuickTime for Java.

Using Alternate QuickTime Video Codecs

QuickTime uses a data codec (short for compress-decompress) to compress image data written to the QuickTime VR movie files. This codec determines the data format used to store each image. The codec that is selected is the one that matches the format that you select for the output image. The following output formats have a matching codec:

- JPEG
- TGA
- PNG
- BMP
- TIFF

If you select a file format that is not in this list, the TIFF codec will be used by default. You can override the codec selection by setting the configuration variable MS_QTVR_CODEC_TYPE to *jpeg*, *tga*, *png*, *bmp*, or *tiff*. When set, the codec defined by this variable is used, regardless of the selected output format. Changes that you make to the configuration variable MS_QTVR_CODEC_TYPE take effect immediately. You do not have to restart MicroStation.

In the next exercise, you will be setting up a camera vantage point and creating a cubic panorama. With the cube type panorama, you can achieve a truly immersive VR effect. The cube panorama will be rendered as six faces of a box, with the camera being inside. The six images, or pictures, taken during the process will be shot using a camera lens angle of 90°.

✔ Exercise 12-4: Save a panorama image file

1. Open **hotel_room.dgn**.
2. Apply the saved view *pano* to View 5.

   This saved view has the eye point in the middle of the room.
3. Open the Particle Tracing Settings dialog box (Settings > Rendering > Particle Tracing).
4. Select File > Load Solution.

| Creating Panoramas | 381

5 In the Load Rendering Database dialog box, select *hotel_room.ptd* from the list of files.

This will load a previously solved lighting solution for the current design file.

6 Open the Save Panorama dialog box (Utilities > Image > Save Panorama).

7 In the Save Panorama dialog box, set the following:

View: 5
Format: TIFF
Compression: PackBits Compression
Mode: 24 Bit Color
Shading: Particle Trace
Shading Type: Antialias
Action: Display current solution
Panorama Type: Cube
Resolution X: 512
Gamma Correction: 1.7

8 Click Save.

9 In the Save Panorama As dialog box, set List Files of Type to QuickTime VR[*.mov].

10 Click OK to start the panorama image save process.

For a panorama to be created, a camera must be enabled in the view from which you are creating the panorama. The view you choose, therefore, automatically will be converted to a camera view if one does not currently exist. To achieve the best results, you should set up a camera view prior to creating the panorama and place the eye point toward the center of the room, rather than in a corner.

NOTE: *Creating a panorama from the corner of a room will result in a distorted image during the view pan operation.*

Viewing the Panorama

Once the panorama image has been created, you can view it by double-clicking on the resulting *.mov* file located in the output folder. Provided

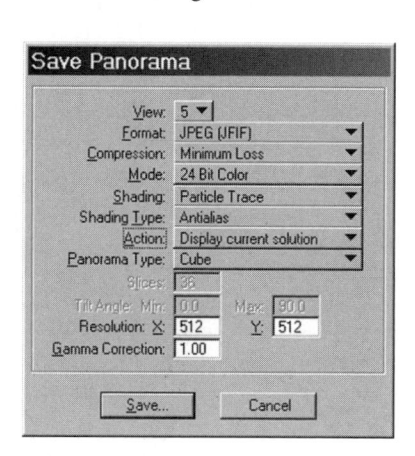

| Chapter 12: Generating Output |

QuickTime was properly installed, you will be able to dynamically pan around the view using the QuickTime Movie Player.

✔ Exercise 12-5: View the saved panorama

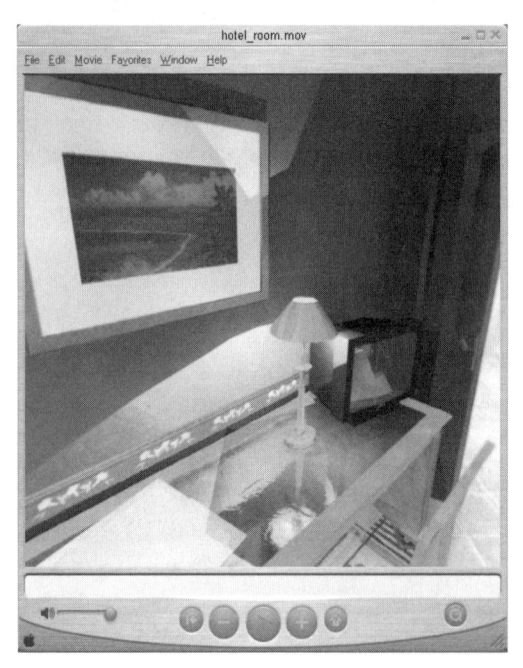

1   Open Windows Explorer.

2   Navigate to the output folder and double-click on **hotel_room.mov** to launch the QuickTime Movie Player.

3   Dynamically pan within the cubic panorama by clicking and dragging the pointer in the image area of the QuickTime movie player.

4   Hold the <Ctrl> key to zoom out or the <Shift> key to zoom in.

IMAGE OBJECTS

Essentially, the image object (IMOB) is the inverse of the panorama, where the camera's target remains fixed and the camera is rotated around the target image. This creates a series of images that, when viewed dynamically, provides you with a virtual object.

NOTE: *It is a good idea to try to center your camera target point on the object you are trying to show. If the target is off center too much, the manipulated IMOB will have obvious shift from side to side when manipulated in a QuickTime movie player.*

Image Objects (IMOBs) can be saved in the following types:

▶ ***Object-Circle*** — The camera is rotated around the target from a fixed altitude, creating a circular view.

| Image Objects | **383**

- ▶ *Object - Top Hemisphere* — The camera is rotated horizontally and up around the target object, creating a hemispherical view of the object.

- ▶ *Object - Sphere* — The camera is rotated horizontally as well as up and down, creating a spherical view to the object.

- ▶ *Object - Custom* — Similar to Top Hemisphere and Sphere except that you can specify the vertical angle at which the camera is rotated.

Creating an Image Object Panorama

In the following exercise, which assumes that QuickTime is installed on your system, you will create an image object of a small home. The type will be Object-Top Hemisphere, meaning the camera will rotate horizontally around the object taking pictures at specified degree intervals, the default being 10°. After making a complete revolution of 360°, the camera will be raised above the horizon by 10° and another set of images will be taken. As this progress takes place, the camera path sweeps a dome or hemisphere around the target object.

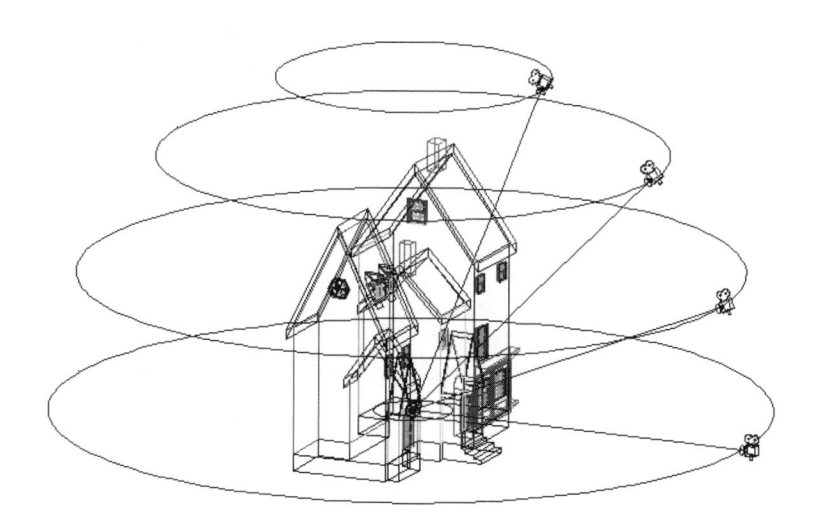

Typical camera paths to create a Top-Hemisphere IMOB.

✔ Exercise 12-6: Save an image object

1 Open model *Pan_01*, in DGN file *village home.dgn*.

2 Open View 4.

3 Select Utilities > Image > Save Panorama.

> **NOTE:** *You must have a camera enabled in the target view to save an Object Panorama.*

4 In the Save Panorama dialog box, set the following parameters:

View: 4
Format: JPEG
Compression: Minimum Loss
Mode: 24 Bit Color
Shading: RayTrace
Shading Type: Antialias
Action: Create new solution
Panorama Type: Object -Top Hemisphere
Frames: 36

This defines the frames to make one revolution of your camera around the object. The camera will make 10 revolutions beginning at 0 and rotating up through 90°. The total number of frames will actually be 360.

Changing Frames to 64 would create 64 images per revolution, or 360/64 = 5.625° / frame. The vertical motion would also be divided into 5.65° increments, so 90/5.625 = 16 — but since you start at 0, this is actually 17 revolutions. Therefore, setting Frames to 64, the total frames in a top hemisphere works out to be 64 x 17 = 1088.

Resolution X: 400
Gamma Correction: 1.5 (setting the gamma correction to your current display gamma would be even better)

5 Click Save.

6 In the Save Panorama As dialog box, click OK to save the file with the name of the DGN file, but with a *.mov* suffix.

The create panorama image process begins. It will create a QuickTime MOV file containing 360 images. Each image is a different camera vantage point looking at the model and camera target point. The image data will be saved to the file *village home.mov*.

7 Select the finished IMOB file *village home.mov* in the course *output* folder.

QuickTime opens and loads the selected file.

8 With the pointer in the QuickTime player window, click and drag to rotate the image about the object.

SAVING MULTIPLE IMAGES

In addition to saving single image files, you can set up your system to save a series of images. This is especially useful for automatically creating and saving rendered images and panoramas during the hours when your system normally is not in use. To do this, you first create a script that contains the names of the files and models to be rendered, along with the view number or the saved view to be used. A Save Multiple Image script can even recall a rendering setup that could change the time of day, background, or any other rendering setting, saved in the rendering setup file.

Once this script is written and executed, MicroStation will open the model in the design file, load the appropriate rendering setups or saved views, and then render the desired images to any of the supported raster formats. In addition, you can set the resolution and choose from any of the rendering or hidden line options.

NOTE: *When rendering multiple images from several different models or design files, you should set up saved views in each model or design file. You can also use rendering setup files to change a variety of rendering settings, such as global lighting settings, general settings for fog, or even to turn the background image on or off in the target view.*

In the following exercise, you will use the Save Multiple Images dialog box to create a script file containing a list of rendering commands to create images or panoramas to disk.

✓ Exercise 12-7: Save multiple images

1 Continuing in model *Pan_01*, select Utilities > Image > Save Multiple.

The Save Multiple Images dialog box opens.

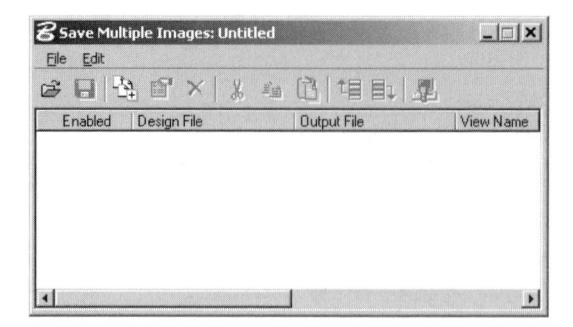

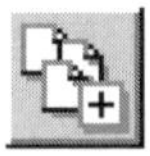

| Chapter 12: Generating Output |

2 In the Save Multiple Images dialog box, click the New Entry icon.

A new entry, which is highlighted, is added to the Save Multiple Images dialog box and the Edit Script Entry dialog box opens. This dialog box lets you adjust the settings for the highlighted script entry.

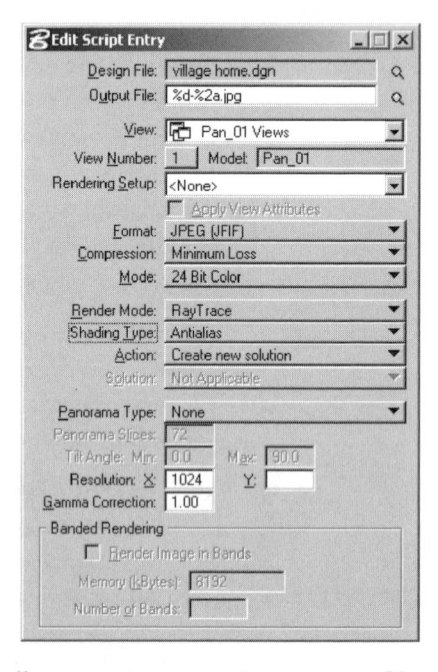

NOTE: *From the Edit Script Entry dialog box, you can choose the design file you wish to render. By default, when you first create a new entry it will assume the current model in the current file. The output file name uses a default macro that defines the design file name and a number that is automatically incremented to prevent accidentally overwriting an existing image file from the same model/DGN file.*

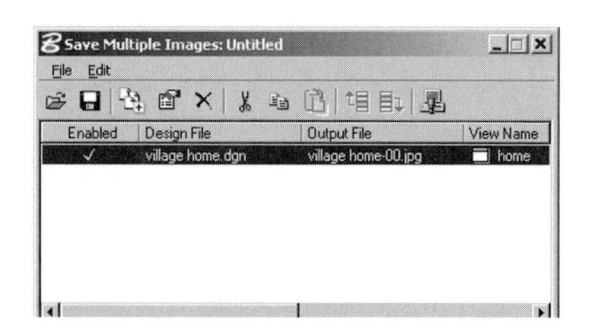

Save Multiple Images with new entry.

| Saving Multiple Images | **387**

3 In the Edit Script Entry dialog box, set the following:

View: home
View Number: 4
Format: TIFF
Render Mode: Ray Trace
Shading Type: Antialias
Action: Create new solution
Resolution X: 1024
Gamma Correction: 1.7

These changes are made to the entry.

4 In the Save Multiple Images dialog box, click the New Entry icon.

Another entry is added. A second *village home.dgn* entry is added to the Save Multiple Images dialog. Notice that the output file name increments by one. The initial settings are a copy of the settings for the previous entry, so you will need to change only a few parameters.

5 With the second entry highlighted in the Save Multiple Images dialog box, use the Edit Script Entry dialog box to set the following:

View: imob
Format: JPEG
Action: Ray trace current solution
Panorama Type: Object -Top hemisphere
Panorama Slices: 72
Resolution X: 512

6 Click on the first entry in the Save Multiple Images dialog box. Notice the Edit Script Entry dialog box settings change to match those settings for the first entry you made.

7 In the Save Multiple Images dialog box, click the New Entry icon.

A third entry for *village home.dgn* is added to the list of entries in the Save Multiple Images dialog box. Because the first entry was highlighted, the new entry takes its default settings from this entry.

You will modify this new entry to save an image from another DGN file.

8 In the Edit Script Entry dialog box, click the Browse for design file icon to the right of the Design File name field.

The Select File to Render dialog box opens.

9 Select *cool home.dgn* from the list of files and click OK.

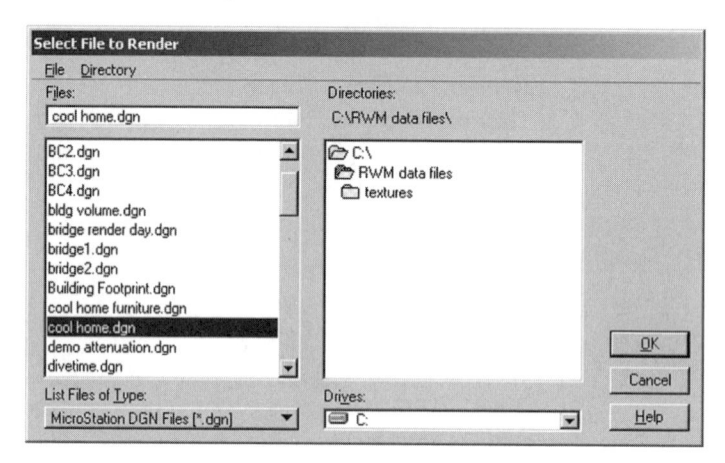

The Edit Script Entry and the Save Multiple Images dialog boxes both update to reflect the Design File change.

10 In the Edit Script Entry dialog box, change the following settings to:

View: main
Action: Create New Solution
Resolution Y: 1500

Looking at the Save Multiple image dialog box, as you can see the *cool home.dgn* entry is located between the two *village home.dgn* entries. In the second of the *village home* entries, you selected the option to render the current solution, which assumes you have a good solution already in memory.

The current scenario would switch from *village home.dgn* to *cool home.dgn* for the second image. This would delete the solution created when rendering the first item in the list.

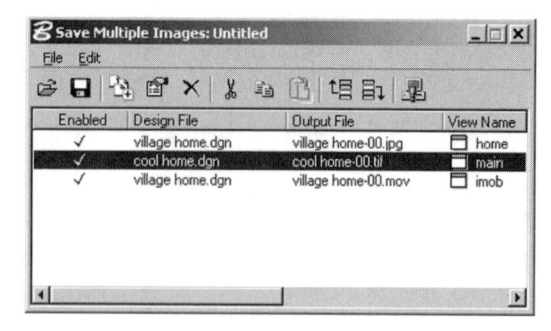

To fix this potential problem, you need to move the *cool home* entry either to the top or the bottom of the current list.

✔ **Exercise 12-8: Finalize the list and execute the script**

1 Continuing in model *Pan_01*, in the Save Multiple Images dialog box, select the *cool home.dgn* entry.

2 Click the Move Down icon, to move the entry down in the list.

3 In the Save Multiple Images dialog box, choose File > Save As.

4 The Save Script As dialog box opens, with the default name *village home.scr* displayed.

5 Change the name to *my script.scr*.

6 Click OK to save the script.

NOTE: *By now you may be starting to realize the potential of the Save Multiple Images utility and how your computer can be kept very busy rendering images and panoramas from multiple design files overnight and on weekends. Now that you have created and saved your script, you can open it later to add more entries, or to edit your current entries. When you have time, you can execute the saved script.*

7 (Optional) In the Save Multiple Images dialog, click the Execute Script icon to run the script and render the images and panorama.

3D CONTENT IN PDF FILES

With the release of Adobe® Reader® 7.0, Adobe's PDF format supports the embedding of 3D content within documents. In MicroStation, the creation of PDF documents with 3D content is similar to printing a standard 2D document.

Where 3D content is included, it will contain any visualization data and settings that already exist within the design file, such as lights, materials, texture maps, and animation or camera movement (flythroughs) that were created using the Animation Producer. Additionally, saved views are included in the 3D content.

Any 3D content within a PDF document is stored in "Universal 3D" (U3D) format. This format was introduced by the 3D Industry Forum *(http://www.3dif.org/)* as a means for transferring three-dimensional data from CAD systems to mainstream applications such as marketing, training, sales, technical support, and customer service. MicroStation lets you export geometry directly to U3D, or to seamlessly create PDF documents with embedded U3D objects.

Adding 3D Content from Design Models

From a 3D design model, you can add 3D content to a PDF file simply by enabling the Plot to 3D setting in the Print dialog box.

3D Plotting Options

Settings that control the 3D content are found in the 3D Plotting Options dialog box (Settings > 3D Plotting, in the Print dialog box). These settings, which are saved in the user preference file, are retained between sessions.

Animation in 3D content

Animation scripts created with MicroStation's Animation Producer (Utilities > Render > Animation) can be used to specify geometry or camera motion that can be exported to U3D and viewed dynamically within the PDF document. When a model is saved to U3D, either the default script (a file with same name as the design file but with a *.msa* extension) or the script currently loaded in the animator is used to specify the U3D animation. In Adobe Reader, the animation can be started or paused by selecting the 3D object and then selecting the Start Animation or Pause Animation buttons from the tool bar.

Creating 3D content in PDF

To demonstrate this feature, in the next exercise you will create a PDF file that contains 3D content. The data set that you will use also includes an animation script for a simple fly-around of a building. The animation script is provided for you to see this functionality when creating the PDF file. Details on the creation of the animation, however, are beyond the scope of this book.

✔ **Exercise 12-9: 3D in PDF from a design model**

1 Open the design file *BC4.dgn*.

2 From the MicroStation main menu, choose File > Print to open the Print dialog box.

| 3D Content in PDF Files |

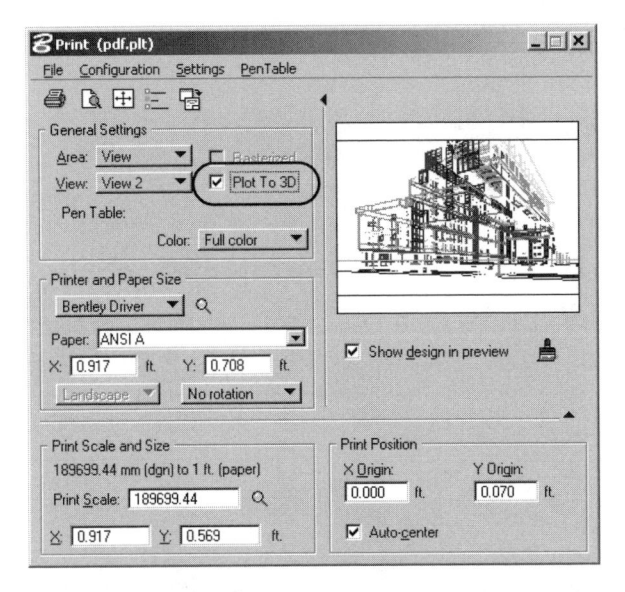

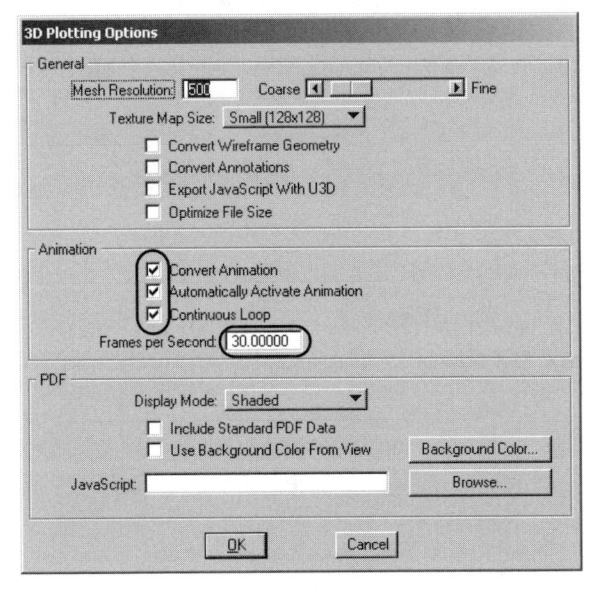

3 Set the Printer to Bentley Driver, and select *pdf.plt* as the printer driver.

4 In the Print dialog box, turn on Plot To 3D.

5 In the Print dialog box choose Settings > 3D Plotting.

The 3D Plotting Options dialog box opens.

6 In the 3D Plotting Options dialog box set the following options:

Convert Animation: On
Automatically Activate Animation: On
Continuous Loop: On
Frames per Second: 30

7 Click OK in the 3D Plotting Options dialog box.

8 In the Print dialog box, click the Print icon or select File > Print.

The Save Print As dialog box opens.

9 Set the Directory in Save Print As dialog box to *c:* .

10 Click OK to save the *BC4.pdf* file to your hard drive.

A progress bar appears at the bottom of the MicroStation window, indicating the percentage of completion. Once the PDF is finished, you will see the message "Finished Creating Print" at the bottom of the screen.

NOTE: *The 3D content in the Adobe PDF file will be displayed using smooth shading. For best results, you may need to adjust your materials to look good using a smooth shading routine. For instance, a* glass material that looks great ray traced may appear too transparent when smooth rendered.

NOTE: *The design file used for this exercise has an associated Animator script, and the animation will play back on startup from Adobe Acrobat Reader 7.*

Interacting with 3D Content in Adobe Reader

In order to open the PDF file generated in MicroStation, it is necessary to download and install Adobe Acrobat® 7.0 (or later version, if available). Currently, you can download the software from *http://www.adobe.com/products/acrobat/readstep2.html*.

Once a PDF document containing 3D content is created from MicroStation, it can be opened with Adobe® Reader® 7.0 in the same manner as a standard PDF file. Inside the PDF file, clicking on a 3D object will activate a tool bar with a set of tools for navigating within the scene. The standard Adobe Reader tools (Rotate, Navigate, Zoom, and Pan) are documented in the Adobe Reader Help. Saved Views are available from the Views menu entries.

✔ **Exercise 12-10: View PDF with 3D content in Acrobat 7.0**

1 Open the newly created **BC4.PDF** with Adobe Acrobat 7.0

   Adobe Acrobat 7.0 will automatically play the animation upon opening the file, since you selected this option in the 3D Plotting Options dialog box.

2 Click the Pause button to stop the animation.

   Notice the pause button changes now to a play button. Clicking it again restarts the animation.

   NOTE: *You can change to a MicroStation saved view by clicking on the small down arrow, on the right side of the navigation tools, and selecting a saved view from the list.*

3 Click the down arrow to open the Saved View list and select Fountain.

4 Click in the image window.

   The view changes to a close-up view of the fountain.

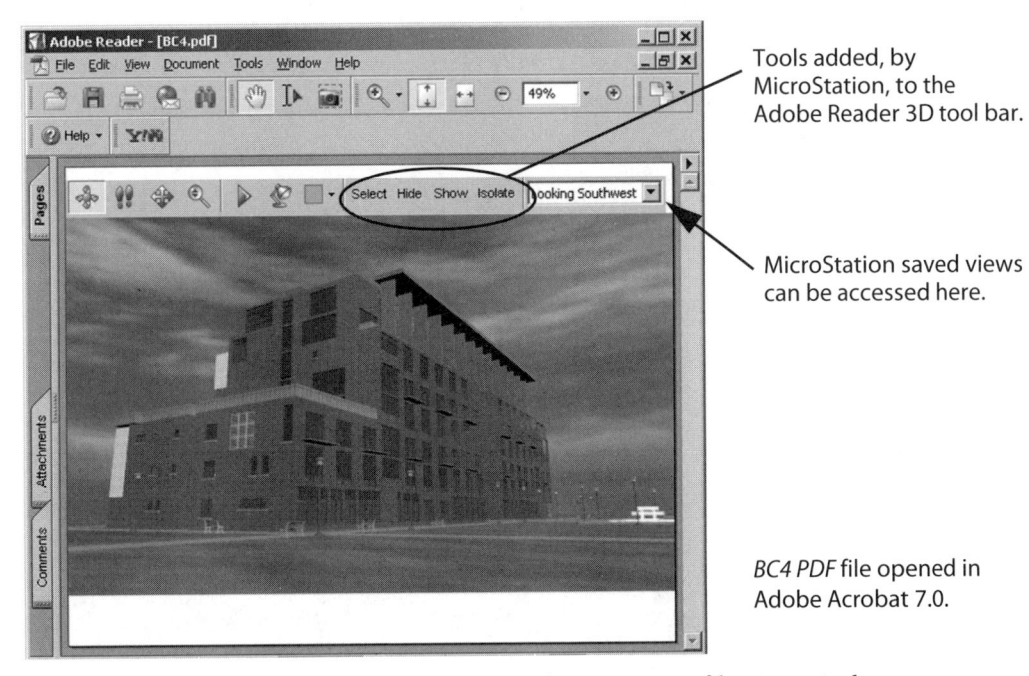

| 3D Content in PDF Files | 393

Tools added, by MicroStation, to the Adobe Reader 3D tool bar.

MicroStation saved views can be accessed here.

BC4 PDF file opened in Adobe Acrobat 7.0.

5 Right-click anywhere in the open PDF file view window.

An option menu for navigation and viewing displays.

6 Select Scene Illustrated and click in the view area to change the display mode.

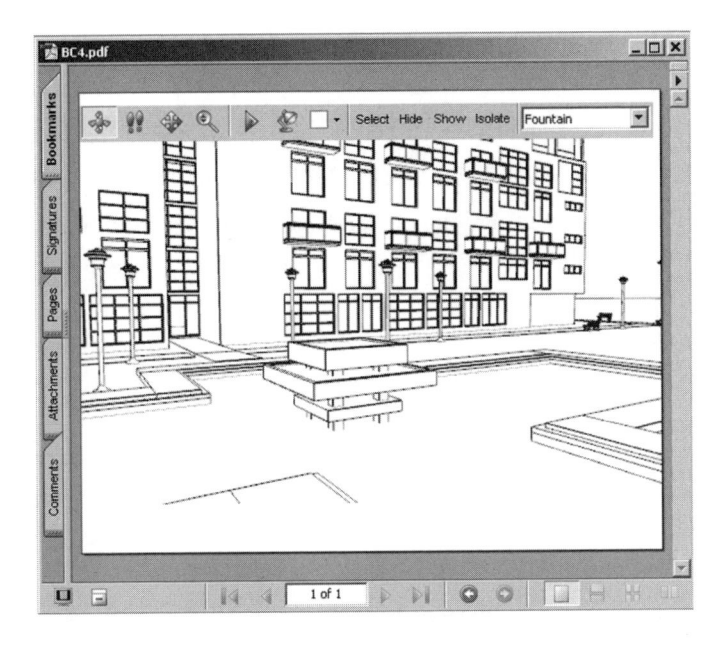

Scene Illustrated view mode for saved view Fountain.

NOTE: *You can play the animation in any of the display modes, but the shaded mode usually plays more smoothly than the illustrated modes.*

7 Again, right-click anywhere in the open PDF file view window.

8 Select Scene Shaded Illustrated and click in the view area to change the display mode.

Scene Shaded Illustrated.

3D Content Tool Bar in Adobe Reader 7.0

When a MicroStation PDF file that contains 3D content is opened in Adobe Reader, the following items are added to the standard Adobe Reader 3D tools: Select, Hide, Show, and Isolate.

Select

This lets you select geometry in the 3D view by clicking on it. You can add to an existing selection by holding down the <Shift> key while selecting further geometry.

Selected geometry can be set to a different display mode from the overall scene display via the Select <display options> entries in the right-

3D Content in PDF Files

click context menu, or used as targets for the Show, Hide, and Isolate tools.

You can select geometry by element, level, material, or model. This is controlled by the Select <method> options in the right-click context menu.

To select geometry in the 3D view:

1 If necessary, move the pointer into the 3D view to display the tool bar.

2 Click Select.

3 Click on the geometry that you want to select.

4 (Optional) To add other geometry to the selection, hold down the <Shift> key and click on the geometry.

Hide

This lets you remove selected geometry from the display in the 3D view.

To hide geometry from the 3D view:

1 Use the select tool to select geometry that you do not want to see in the 3D view.

2 In the tool bar, click Hide.

3 Click in the 3D view window to accept.

Show

This lets you display all geometry in the 3D view, including that which you have previously hidden.

To show all geometry in the 3D view:

1 Click Show in the 3D tool bar.

2 Click in the 3D view to accept.

Isolate

This lets you remove from display all geometry other than the current selection.

To isolate geometry in the 3D view:

1. Use the select tool to select the geometry that you want to see in the 3D view.

2. In the tool bar, click Isolate.

Items Added to the Right-Click Menu

When a MicroStation PDF file that contains 3D content is opened in Adobe Reader, the following items are added to the context <right-click> menu: Scene Display Modes, Select Display Modes, Select Methods.

Scene Display Modes

These control the display modes for the 3D scene. Options are the same as those available in the 3D Plotting Options dialog box. The initial display mode is controlled by the Display Mode setting in that dialog box. After selecting the required display mode, clicking in the 3D view changes the display to the selected mode.

To set the Display mode of 3D content:

1. Right-click in the 3D view.

2. From the pop-up menu, select from Scene <Shaded/Illustration/Shaded Illustration/Transparent>.

3. Click in the 3D view to accept the selected scene display mode.

Select Display Modes

These control how geometry that you select will display, or highlight. Options are the same as those available in the 3D Plotting Options dialog box. Any geometry that is selected displays in the chosen display mode. Typically, you would set the Select display mode to something other than the Scene display mode, so that you can discern the selected geometry.

To set the Select display mode:

1. Right-click in the 3D view.

2. From the pop-up menu, choose from Select <Shaded/Illustration/Shaded Illustration/Transparent>.

Select Methods

These control the method for selecting geometry in the scene. Options for selecting geometry are Element, Level, Material, or Model. Selecting by Material will select any geometry with the same material as the selected object. Selecting by Model will select the entire model (or reference file) as the clicked object.

To set the Select method mode:

1 Right-click in the 3D view.

2 From the pop-up menu, choose from Select <Element/By Level/By Material/By Model>.

Review Questions

1 What does JPEG stand for?

2 What is "true color"?

3 What additional information can be stored in 32-bit color (RGB Alpha) images?

4 What must be enabled to use more than one CPU to render a single image to disk?

5 How does a cube panorama differ from a cylinder panorama?

6 What is a panorama object?

7 Name at least three types of panorama objects.

8 When saving an image to disk, a higher number in the Gamma Correction field has what effect on the resulting image?

9 What is the file format used to store 3D content in an Adobe PDF file?

Chapter Summary

In this chapter, you have learned several ways to generate output. You have learned how to render an image file on your hard drive, and how to utilize the banded rendering option to use multiple CPUs to render a single image. You learned how to render output to VR Panoramas or

Image Objects (IMOBs). Using the Save Multiple Images utility, you learned to create custom scripts that you can run overnight or over weekends. You learned that you can use this utility to save multiple images or panoramas, from multiple design files/models, in the rendering mode of your choice. Finishing the chapter, you learned how to print 3D content from MicroStation to an Adobe PDF file and how to display the file in Adobe® Reader® 7.0.

Appendix: Rendering Glossary

This glossary defines visualization terms used with MicroStation.

adaptive subdivision Process within radiosity solving that dynamically subdivides a surface element mesh along shadow boundaries, resulting in more accurate and detailed shading.

aliasing Source of several common computer graphics artifacts such as jagged lines, missing objects, and jerky motion in animation. In signal processing terms, aliasing is caused by the undersampling of a signal, resulting in some high-frequency components of the signal assuming the alias (or false identity) of the low frequency components, and mixing together in such a way that they can no longer be distinguished properly.

ambient light Imaginary light that is presumed to strike every point on a surface with equal intensity. Used to approximate the large-scale effects of diffuse inter-reflections, a phenomenon not usually accounted for by most lighting methods. Ambient light should be turned off when using particle tracing or radiosity solving, both of which take into account the diffuse reflection of light between surfaces.

antialiasing Special rendering processing to remove or limit the appearance of aliasing artifacts in an image or an animation sequence. *See also* sample.

area light source Light source created from a MicroStation shape element. This type of light source casts softer, more natural shadows than a Point light source.

camera Imaginary entity that specifies a scene's viewing position, orientation, and perspective. *See also* animation camera.

caustics	Lighting effects caused by light reflected off surfaces, or refracted through transparent objects.
color bleeding	Shading effect observable in particle traced and radiosity solutions caused by diffuse inter-reflections between surfaces. For example, a colored wall often reflects a small amount of its color onto an adjoining white wall.
diffuse inter-reflection	Global process of light transport among all the surfaces in an environment, based on a series of diffuse reflections between surfaces. This is the process that is simulated in radiosity solving.
diffuse reflection	Type of reflection that sends light in all directions with equal energy. Diffuse reflection is said to be "view-independent." *See also* specular reflection.
dolly (camera)	To move the view cone while keeping the camera and target points in the same positions relative to each other — that is, without changing their orientation.
dolly (light source)	To move a directional light source and its target point such that they remain in the same positions relative to each other — that is, without changing their orientation.
element	For radiosity solving, a triangular subdivision of a patch. Light energy is "shot" from a single patch to each of the elements of the other surfaces.
element mesh	For radiosity solving, the set of elements composing a surface.
elevate	To move the view cone linearly in a vertical direction.
environment cube	Imaginary cube surrounding the entire design, on which images are applied as environment maps.
environment map	Image file representing the projection of a 3D environment onto a 2D surface from a specific point of view. A set of these files can be applied to the six faces of the environment cube that surrounds a design (or environment). An environment map is not directly visible in the view, but is seen only when reflected or transmitted by surfaces in the model to which material characteristics are applied.
Fresnel effects	Effects of the angle of view on the reflectivity and transparency of a surface. For example, a window appears more reflective than transparent when viewed at a sharp angle.

frustum	Geometric shape used to describe the viewing volume in computer graphics, where the viewing plane sits at the top of a truncated pyramid that extends into the 3D environment.
global lighting	Shading of a surface that takes into account both direct lighting and some indirect lighting, such as reflections and refractions. Ray tracing, radiosity solving, and particle tracing account for global lighting, but in different ways. Also refers to the Ambient, Flashbulb, and Solar light settings that are grouped in the Global Lighting settings box.
highlight	Brightly lit area on a surface caused by a specular reflection.
illumination	Specification of lighting on a surface.
image point	In photomatching, a known point on the photograph or rendered image that correlates to a monument point in the computer model.
image script	Text file (*.scr*) containing entries that define the names of design files, views, output filenames and formats, and rendering options for batch rendering.
intermediate image	Rendered image showing an intermediate result of a radiosity solving process. Constant shading is typically used to render the image to decrease processing time.
interpolation	Method by which an animation parameter smoothly varies from one state to another. Also refers to the blending of adjacent pixels of a texture map for smoother rendered images.
jittering	Antialiasing technique in which samples are taken in a non-uniform manner which efficiently approximates a Poisson distribution. This distribution is particularly effective in eliminating regular-pattern artifacts, such as jagged edges, from a rendered image.
local lighting	Shading of the surface that accounts for direct lighting only — that is, lighting directly attributed to light sources. Phong shading is an example of a rendering method that is based on local lighting.
lumens	Units in which the brightness of light sources is expressed. Lumens are the photometric equivalent of watts, but only account for energy in the visible part of the electromagnetic spectrum. If a light source's Intensity setting is 1.0, then its Lumens setting closely approximates lumens. In other words, if you set the Intensity to 0.5 and Lumens is 800, the brightness would be reduced to about 400 lumens.
mip mapping	*See* multilevel texture interpolation.

monument point	In photomatching, a known point in the model whose corresponding image point is visible.
multilevel texture interpolation	Texture mapping option for phong and ray traced rendering that provides less noisy images and smoother animations by pre-filtering the texture into a series of progressive lower resolution images, and then smoothly interpolating between them. In an image rendered with this option, repetitive patterns fade to constant as the distance from the camera increases.
pan	To manipulate the view cone by revolving either the camera about the target (horizontally or vertically), or vice-versa.
particle tracing	Global lighting method that computes a view-independent solution that includes all lighting effects such as color bleeding, and specular light effects including reflections, refractions, and caustics.
patch	For radiosity solving, a subdivision of a surface that "shoots" light energy to each of the triangular elements of other surfaces. Each patch is subdivided into one or more elements.
photomatching	Process of matching a model's viewing perspective to that of a photograph or rendered background image, which is attached to the model as a reference raster file. The expected result is a composite image in which the model is superimposed on the background image with correct positioning and orientation.
Poisson distribution	Random set of points with the property that no two points are closer together than a given fixed distance. This distribution is expensive to compute, but is generally regarded as the optimal sampling pattern for computer graphics. Jittering is commonly used to generate a point set that approximates a Poisson distribution, but with significantly less computation.
procedural bump map	Special type of bump map that dynamically calls a procedural texture function to compute a perturbed surface normal rather than performing a lookup into a stored image.
procedural pattern map	Special type of pattern map that dynamically calls a procedural texture function to compute pixel color rather than performing a lookup into a stored image.

procedural texture	Function that takes either a 2D texture coordinate or a 3D world coordinate as input and returns a texture value (either a color for a pattern map or a normal for a bump map). The function can perform anything from a simple lookup into a standard texture map to a very complex calculation. When a solid to which a 3D procedural texture is applied is rendered, the solid appears to be sculpted from the specified pattern rather than wrapped with the pattern.
radiosity	Total power (light energy per unit time) per unit area leaving a point on a surface. *See also* radiosity solving.
radiosity database	*See* rendering database.
radiosity solution	3D view-independent lighting solution calculated using radiosity solving.
radiosity solving	Global lighting method that accurately calculates the distribution of light energy in an environment by accounting for both direct lighting and diffuse inter-reflections. Radiosity solving is particularly useful for handling effects such as color bleeding and indirect lighting.
ray tracing	Photorealistic rendering method in which the global lighting of an environment is computed by simulating the reflection and refraction of light rays (recursively), using the principles of geometric optics. The output of ray tracing is a 2D view-dependent image. Ray tracing accurately depicts reflections, refractions, and semi-transparent materials.
rendering database	Data structure containing the geometry and settings that are constructed in memory during preprocessing for ray tracing, radiosity solving, or particle tracing. The rendering database is kept in memory, automatically, when repeatedly rendering the same design.
roll	Rotate the camera about the view z-axis.
sample	In radiosity solving, the process of examining a point on the current light source or shooting patch. The computation time increases roughly one-for-one with the number of samples. In antialiasing, the process of examining part of a pixel. Samples are combined into a final pixel value. The number of samples and the threshold at which sampling stops are adjustable settings.
shot	In radiosity solving, the process of transporting light energy from a single patch to each of the elements of the other surfaces.

specular reflection	Type of reflection that sends light primarily in a single outgoing direction related to a single incoming direction by the principles of geometric optics, resulting in either a mirror-like reflection or a glossy highlight. Specular reflection is said to be view-dependent.
terminator	Line separating light and dark on curved surfaces, most noticeable when an object is illuminated by a single light source.
texture map	Stored image used for texture mapping.
texture mapping	Process of applying detail to a surface without explicitly modeling it as part of the geometry of the surface. This process can be either a standard lookup into an image texture map or a function call to compute a value algorithmically. The resulting value can be used either as a pixel color value (as in a pattern map) or as a perturbed surface normal (as in a bump map).
uniform sampling	Regular distribution of samples, equally spaced in all dimensions.
view cone	Dynamically displayed indication of view extents that is used to set up the camera.
view-dependent lighting	Global lighting of a 3D environment that varies from image to image as the position of the view is changed, primarily because of specular reflections or refractions of visible surfaces.
view-independent lighting	Global lighting of a 3D environment that remains constant from image to image as the position of the view is changed, thereby allowing for reuse, which significantly shortens the rendering time of subsequent images.
viewing pyramid	*See* view cone.

Index

Numerics
3 point rotation 10–13
3D content in PDF files
   3D plotting options 390
   3D toolbar 394–395
   adding from design models 390–392
   animation 390
   creating 390–392
   description 389
   display mode, setting 396
   format 389
   Hide tool 395
   hiding geometry 395
   Isolate tool 395
   isolating geometry 395
   right-click menu 396
   Scene Display Modes option 396
   Select display mode, setting 396
   Select Display Modes option 396
   Select Methods option 397
   Select tool 394
   selecting geometry 394, 397
   Show tool 395
   showing geometry 395
   U3D (Universal 3D) format 389
   viewing in Adobe Reader 392–394
3D design cube, definition 2
3D plotting options 390
3D space, definition 1
3D toolbar 394–395
3D views 3–5

A
active depth 6, 15
Active View setting 74
adapt to brightness 125
adaptive subdivision 324
Add Sky Light...
   adding sky light 294–296
   description 157
   shadows 160
adjust mesh, rendering setting 129–130
advanced rendering, rendering setting 129
ambient lighting
   adjusting 147
   and materials 148–150
   description 147
animation in 3D 390
antialiasing settings
   contrast threshold 127
   depth of field 128
   f-stop 128
   jitter samples 128
   quality 126
   ray tracing 126–129
   rendering 104
Approximate Ground Reflection... 159
ArchVision Rich Photorealistic Content files. *See* RPC files
area light
   creating 185–187
   description 170
   shadows 187

Index

assigning materials by level and color 194-197, 213-215, 226, 246-251
attaching materials
  as attributes 217-221
  directly to elements 197-198
  to solids 202-204, 245
attenuation 187-189

B

Back view 3
background
  photomatching 357
  photorealism 298-300
  rendering setting 114
  sky, with
    environment mapping 306-311
    sky cylinders 302-306
  transparent 233-235
banded rendering
  benefits of 376
  description 373
  network distributed image creation 375-377
  rendering an image 374
  with multiple computers 375-377
Basic Mode tool 74
blending texture with base color 240
Bottom view 3
brightness 333
bump maps
  dynamic map adjust 251-253
  photorealism 96, 241-244
  rendering setting 116
Bump option 229

C

calculation time and accuracy 325
Camera Action options
  Dolly 65-67
  Dolly/Elevate 63-65
  Lens Focal Length 67-70
  Lens View Angle 70-71
  Pan 53-57
  Pan Horizontal 57-59
  Pan Vertical 59-61
  Pan/Dolly 71-74

Roll Camera 61-63
summary of 49
camera actions
  See also navigate camera
  dollying
    description 65-67
    with elevation 63-65
    with panning 71-74
  elevating 63-65
  lens focal length, changing 67-70
  lens view angle, changing 70-71
  options, summary of 49
  panning
    definition 53-57
    horizontally 57-59
    vertically 59-61
    with dollying 71-74
  pointer movement 50
  precision settings 52
  rolling 61-63
  tilting 61-63
Camera Settings tool 31-36
camera, rendering setting 114
cameras
  See also Define Camera tool
  Camera Settings tool 31-36
  Change View Perspective tool 28-30
  navigation. *See* navigate camera
  perspective, changing 28-30
  view cone
    color coding 44
    handles 45, 46
    locating the eye point 46
    modifying the eye point 45
    moving 47
    orientation 42
  view projections
    changing 37
    one point 39
    parallel 38
    three point 41
    two point 40
    types of 37
  views
    rendering setup 36
    selecting 49

setting up 31-36, 42
walking through models. *See* navigate camera
Change View Perspective tool 28-30
clip back, front, and volume, rendering setting 115
clip mask 18-22
Clip Mask tool 15, 18-22
clip volume 18-22
Clip Volume tool 15, 18-22
cloud texture 262-265
color coding, view cone 44
color keys
  adding to gradient maps 268
  changing in gradient maps 268
  deleting from gradient maps 268
  repositioning in gradient maps 268
Color option 228
color table 191, 193
Constant mode 86-88
constructions, rendering setting 115
Content Manager 271
contrast 333
contrast threshold, antialiasing 127
cube panoramas 377
cylinder panoramas 377

D

daytime lighting
  light ring 296-298
  setup 291-293
  sky light 294-296
  solar cluster 296-298
Define Camera tool
  camera action settings 51
  Camera Orientation setting 52
  Camera Position setting 52
  Controlled Movement setting 53
  description 36
  Display Depths setting 53
  precision settings 52
  view cone orientation 42-49
  View Information setting 53
Define Light tool, settings 165

| Index | 407

Degrees setting 74
delayed display, rendering setting 115
depth cueing, rendering setting 117–121
depth of field, antialiasing 128
Diffuse option 228
Display Active Depth tool 15–18
display depth 15, 16
display phase 342
Display View Cone setting 74
display volume. *See* view volume
display, rendering setting 116
displayset, rendering setting 115
displaysets 22
distance cueing 112, 113, 116
Distance setting 74
distant light
   adding sky light 174
   description 168
   placing 172–173
   reducing intensity 179
Dolly option 65–67, 81
Dolly/Elevate option 63–65
dollying the camera
   description 65–67
   walking 81
   with elevation 63–65
   with panning 71–74
dusk lighting 312
dynamic map adjust 251–253
dynamic view rotation 8

E

Edit RPC tool 277–278
editing, RPCs 277–278
Efficiency option 228
elevating the camera 63–65
elevation draping
   assigning elevation drape material 288
   creating elevation drape material 287
   description 286
   getting material map information 286
   pattern mapping 225
environment maps
   photorealism 93

reflective or transparent elements 123
rendering setting 133–136
sky background 306–311
exterior lighting. *See* lighting, exterior
eye point 45, 46
eye rays 90

F

facet smoothing
   attaching to a DTM 284–285
   elevation draping
      assigning elevation drape material 288
      creating elevation drape material 287
      description 286
      getting material map information 286
   purpose of 283
   surface normals 281–283
falloff 187–189
far density, rendering setting 112
Filled Hidden Line routine 84–86
filled polygon display 86
Finish option 229
flashbulb lighting
   adjusting 151
   description 151
   hot spots 151
   ray tracing 152
Float option 80
floating the camera 80
Fly option 79
flying the camera 79
fog 117–121, 300–302
Fresnel effects 124, 137
Front view 3
frustum 138
f-stop, antialiasing 128

G

gamma correction 83
Glide option 80
gliding the camera 80
global lighting
   See also lighting; lso source lighting

Add Sky Light...
   adding sky light 294–296
   description 157
   shadows 160
Ambient
   adjusting 147
   and materials 148–150
   description 147
Approximate Ground Reflection... 159
daytime
   adding sky light 294–296
   light ring 161–163, 296–298
   setup 291–293
   sky light 294–296
   solar cluster 296–298
Flashbulb
   adjusting 151
   description 151
   hot spots 151
   ray tracing 152
Light Ring 161–163, 296–298
nighttime
   dusk 312
   particle traced rendering 317–319
   setup 315–317
   sunset 311
   twilight 315
sky lighting 157, 160
Solar
   configuring 155
   description 153
   enabling 155
   settings 153
Solar Cluster 161–163, 296–298
Solar lighting, shadows 153, 156, 159
types of 146
gradient maps
   adding color keys 268
   changing color keys 268
   deleting color keys 268
   inspecting settings 267, 270
   linear gradient 265
   radial gradients 265, 269–271
   repositioning color keys 268
   types of 265

Index

working with 265
graphics acceleration, rendering setting 117

H
handles, view cone 45, 46
Hidden Line routine 84–86
Hide tool 395
hiding 3D geometry 395

I
IES lighting 349–352, 352–353
ignore open elements and text, rendering setting 111
illumination. *See* lighting
IMOBs (image objects)
    creating a panorama 383–385
    description 382
    saving 384–385
    types of 382
interior lighting. *See* lighting, interior
interpolate textures, rendering setting 109
interrupting particle tracing 349
Isolate tool 395
isolating 3D geometry 395
Isometric view 3

J
jitter samples, antialiasing 128

K
keyboard 75

L
Left view 3
Lens Focal Length option 67–70
lens focal length, changing 67–70
Lens View Angle option 70–71
lens view angle, changing 70–71
Light Ring 161–163, 296–298
lighting
    See also global lighting; source lighting
    adapt to brightness 125
    atmospheric effects. *See* sky lighting
    display contrast 125

exterior scenes, brightening. *See* light ring; sky lighting; solar cluster
ground reflection 159
real world 125
sunlight. *See* distant light; solar lighting
lighting, exterior
    daytime
        adding sky light 294–296
        light ring 296–298
        setup 291–293
        sky light 294–296
        solar cluster 296–298
    nighttime
        dusk 312
        particle traced rendering 317–319
        setup 315–317
        sunset 311
        twilight 315
lighting, interior
    IES lighting 349–352, 352–353
    particle tracing
        description 335–341
        disk space requirements 342
        display phase 342
        interrupting 349
        loading solutions 346
        mesh detail 344
        meshing settings 343–345
        minimum mesh spacing 345
        particle shooting phase 341
        saving solutions 345
        smoothness 343
    radiosity
        adaptive subdivision 324
        adjusting settings 329–331
        and lighting 322
        and sky openings 326
        brightness 333
        calculation time and accuracy 325
        contrast 333
        description 321
        elements 323–324
        generating solutions 323–325, 327, 332
        loading solutions 334

        patches 323–324
        ray trace direct illumination 331
        saving solutions 333
linear gradients 265
log rendering statistics, rendering setting 112

M
Material Editor
    adjusting material properties 222
    Advanced Mode 227, 228
    assigning materials by level and color 213–215, 226, 246–251
    attaching materials
        as attributes 217–221
        to solids 245
    bump mapping 241–244, 251–253
    creating materials 221–225
    elevation drape pattern mapping 225
    parametric pattern mapping 225
    pattern mapping
        dynamic map adjust 251–253
        modes 225
        on materials 223
    photorealistic materials, creating
        blending texture with base color 240
        bump mapping 241–244
        exercises 235–240
        from existing materials 230–233
        transparent background 233–235
    planar pattern mapping 225
    previewing materials 225
    recovering missing materials 217–221
    removing materials 216
    renaming default materials 222
    tour of 211
material files 191

| Index | 409

Material option 228
materials
    adjusting properties 222
    assigning by level and color 194–197, 213–215, 226, 246–251
    attaching
        as attributes 217–221
        directly to elements 197–198
        to solids 202–204, 245
    bump mapping
        creating photorealistic materials 241–244
        dynamic map adjust 251–253
    changing element color 196
    color table
        attaching 193
        rendering with 191
    creating 221–225
    elevation drape pattern mapping 225
    gradient maps
        adding color keys 268
        changing color keys 268
        deleting color keys 268
        inspecting settings 267, 270
        linear gradient 265
        radial gradients 265, 269–271
        repositioning color keys 268
        types of 265
        working with 265
    material files 191
    modifying 198
    naming 208
    palette files 191
    parametric pattern mapping 225
    pattern mapping
        dynamic map adjust 251–253
        elevation drape 225
        modes 225
        on materials 223
        parametric 225
        planar 225
    photorealistic, creating
        blending texture with base color 240
        bump mapping 241–244
        exercises 235–240
        from existing materials 230–233
        transparent background 233–235
    planar pattern mapping 225
    previewing 225
    procedural textures
        cloud texture 262–265
        description 255
        modifying 258
        selecting 256–258
        wood texture 260–262
    Query Material tool 198
    recovering missing 217–221
    removing 199–201, 216
    renaming 222
    render ready cells 204–208
    RPC files
        Content Manager 271
        description 271
        Edit RPC tool 277–278
        editing 277–278
        Place RPC tool 272–276
        placing 272–276
        RPC toolbox 271
mesh detail 344
mesh spacing, minimum 345
meshing settings 343–345
MicroStation color table. *See* color table
MicroStation Material Editor. *See* Material Editor
missing materials, recovering 217–221
Mode setting 74
Mouse Control setting 74
mouse, camera navigation 74, 76–78
multilevel texture interpolation, rendering setting 109

N

navigate camera
    See also camera actions
    active view, setting 74
    Basic/Advanced mode, setting 74
    default angle of movement 74
    default keys 75
    default movement distance 74
    dollying 81
    floating 80
    flying 79
    forward/back
        along current camera angle 79
        at current height 81
        at current plane 80
        in camera plane 80
    gliding 80
    left/right
        along current camera angle 79
        at current height 81
        in camera plane 79, 80
        in design plane 80
        walking 80
    mouse movement 74, 76–78
    sliding 79
    swiveling 80
    tilt about camera axes 81
    turning about
        camera axes 79
        design axes 80
    up/down in
        camera plane 79
        design plane 80
    view cone, displaying 74
    walking 80
Navigate Camera control
    Active View setting 74
    advanced mode
        Dolly option 81
        Float option 80
        Fly option 79
        Glide option 80
        Slide option 79
        Swivel option 80
        Tilt option 81
        Turn option 79
        Walk option 80
    Basic Mode tool 74
    default keys 75
    Degrees setting 74
    description 74
    Display View Cone setting 74
    Distance setting 74
    Mode setting 74
    Mouse Control setting 74

mouse movement 76–78
Show Settings 74
near density, rendering setting 112
near distance, rendering setting 112
nighttime
  dusk 312
  particle traced rendering 317–319
  setup 315–317
  sunset 311
  twilight 315

O

one point view projections 39
opening MicroStation 1
output
  3D content in PDF files
    3D plotting options 390
    3D toolbar 394–395
    adding from design models 390–392
    animation 390
    creating 390–392
    description 389
    display mode, setting 396
    format 389
    Hide tool 395
    hiding geometry 395
    Isolate tool 395
    isolating geometry 395
    right-click menu 396
    Scene Display Modes option 396
    Select display mode, setting 396
    Select Display Modes option 396
    Select Methods option 397
    Select tool 394
    selecting geometry 394, 397
    Show tool 395
    showing geometry 395
    U3D (Universal 3D) format 389
    viewing in Adobe Reader 392–394
  banded rendering
    benefits of 376

description 373
network distributed image creation 375–377
rendering an image 374
with multiple computers 375–377
IMOBs (image objects)
  creating a panorama 383–385
  description 382
  saving 384–385
  types of 382
panoramas
  cube 377
  cylinder 377
  description 377
  QuickTime codecs 380
  QuickTime requirements 378–379
  saving 380
  viewing 381
saving an image to disk 371–373
saving multiple images to disk 385–388

P

palette files 191
Palette option 228
Pan Horizontal option 57–59
Pan option 53–57
Pan Vertical option 59–61
Pan/Dolly option 71–74
panning the camera
  definition 53–57
  horizontally 57–59
  vertically 59–61
  with dollying 71–74
panoramas
  cube 377
  cylinder 377
  description 377
  from IMOBs (image objects) 383–385
  QuickTime codecs 380
  QuickTime requirements 378–379
  saving 380
sky background
  with environment mapping 306–311

with sky cylinders 302–306
viewing 381
parallel view projections 38
parametric pattern mapping 225
particle shooting phase 341
particle tracing
  description 335–341
  disk space requirements 342
  display phase 342
  interrupting 349
  loading solutions 346
  mesh detail 344
  meshing settings 343–345
  minimum mesh spacing 345
  particle shooting phase 341
  saving solutions 345
  smoothness 343
patches 323–324
pattern mapping
  dynamic map adjust 251–253
  elevation drape 225
  modes 225
  on materials 223
  parametric 225
  planar 225
patterns, rendering setting 116
perspective
  changing 28–30
  matching. *See* photomatching
Phong mode 86–88
phong rendering 90, 105–109
Photomatch tool
  displaying proposed geometry 362–364
  example 364–368
  final render 368
  using 359–362
photomatching
  adjustments with Photomatch
    displaying proposed geometry 362–364
    example 364–368
    final render 368
    using Photomatch 359–362
  aligning geometry to photo 358
  attaching a background image 357
  camera view size, setting 356
  design geometry to raster reference 355–359

Index

photorealism
    background images 298–300
    bump map material 96
    description 89
    environment maps 93
    eye rays 90
    fog 300–302
    gamma correction 83
    IES lighting 349–352
    panoramic sky background
        with environment mapping 306–311
        with sky cylinders 302–306
    primary rays 90
    ray tracing
        bump map material 96
        description 89
        environment maps 93
        eye rays 90
        primary rays 90
        reflections 97
        rendering options 95
        settings 91
        using 92
        visible environment 98
    reflections 97
    rendering
        gamma correction 83
        workflow 91
    rendering options 95
    settings 91
    sky background
        with environment mapping 306–311
        with sky cylinders 302–306
    sky cylinders 302–306
    using 92
    visible environment 98
    visible environment maps 307–311
    workflow 91

photorealistic materials, creating
    blending texture with base color 240
    bump mapping 241–244
    exercises 235–240
    from existing materials 230–233
    transparent background 233–235

Place RPC tool 272–276
placing
    lights
        distant light 172–173
        editing placed lights 184
        point light 177–178
        spot light 180–183
    RPCs 272–276
planar pattern mapping 225
point light 169, 177–178
pointer movement, camera 50
previewing materials 225
primary rays 90
procedural textures
    cloud texture 262–265
    description 255
    modifying 258
    selecting 256–258
    wood texture 260–262
projections. *See* view projections

Q

Query Material tool 198
quick display 124

R

radial gradients 265, 269–271
radiosity
    adaptive subdivision 324
    adjusting settings 329–331
    and lighting 322
    and sky openings 326
    brightness 333
    calculation time and accuracy 325
    contrast 333
    description 321
    elements 323–324
    generating solutions 323–325, 327, 332
    loading solutions 334
    patches 323–324
    ray trace direct illumination 331
    saving solutions 333
ray trace direct illumination 331
ray tracing
    adjusting settings 131
    Fresnel effects 137
    photorealism
        bump map material 96

description 89
environment maps 93
eye rays 90
primary rays 90
reflections 97
rendering options 95
settings 91
using 92
visible environment 98
previewing 124
render all objects 138–139
Ray Tracing dialog box
    adapt to brightness 125
    antialiasing 126–129
    display contrast 125
    environment mapping 123
    Fresnel effects 124
    quick display 124
    real world lighting 125
    reflections 122
    render all objects 125
    shadows 122
    transparency 123
    visible environment 123
realistic photographs. *See* photorealism
Reflect option 229
reflections
    enabling 132
    photorealism 97
    ray tracing 122
Refract option 229
relative axes 13
render all objects 125, 138–139
render ready cells 204–208
rendering
    banded
        benefits of 376
        description 373
        network distributed image creation 375–377
        rendering an image 374
        with multiple computers 375–377
    Constant mode 86–88
    distance cueing 113
    modes 86–88
    Phong mode 86–88
    photorealism
        gamma correction 83

Index

workflow 91
shaded image renderers 86–88
Smooth mode 86–88
statistics, logging 112
Stereo 3D 99
variable shading 86–88
rendering settings
  adjust mesh 129–130
  advanced rendering 129
  antialiasing 104
  background 114
  bump maps 116
  camera 114
  clip back, front, and volume 115
  constructions 115
  delayed display 115
  depth cueing 117–121
  display 116
  displayset 115
  distance cueing 112, 116
  environment mapping 133–136
  far density 112
  fog 117–121
  graphics acceleration 117
  ignore open elements and text 111
  interpolate textures 109
  log rendering statistics 112
  multilevel texture interpolation 109
  near density 112
  near distance 112
  patterns 116
  phong shadows 105–109
  ray tracing 131
  Ray Tracing dialog box
    adapt to brightness 125
    antialiasing 126–129
    display contrast 125
    environment mapping 123
    Fresnel effects 124
    quick display 124
    real world lighting 125
    reflections 122
    render all objects 125
    shadows 122
    transparency 123
    visible environment 123

reflections, enabling 132
rendering view attributes 115–117
shadows 116
shadows, enabling 132
solar shadow resolution 105
stroke tolerance 100–103
transparency
  enabling 132
  increasing 133
  rendering view attribute 116
view attributes 114
view number 115
visible environment 136
Rendering Setup dialog box
  Apply 141
  Auto Apply To View 141
  Auto Load From View 141
  Delete 141
  description 139
  File Menu 141
  rendering setup
    creating 141
    exporting 142
    importing 142
  Save As 141
  Setup Name 141
  View 141
Rendering Tools toolbox, tool summary 24
rendering view attributes, rendering setting 115–117
Right Isometric view 3
Right view 3
Roll Camera option 61–63
rolling the camera 61–63
Rotate View tool 6
rotating views
  by 3 points 10–13
  centering active depth 6
  Front 5
  relative axes 13
  relative to view or drawing 13
  Rotate View tool 6
  standard view orientations 7
  with dynamics 8
RPC files
  Content Manager 271
  description 271
  Edit RPC tool 277–278

editing 277–278
Place RPC tool 272–276
placing 272–276
RPC toolbox 271

S

Scene Display Modes option 396
Select display mode, setting 396
Select Display Modes option 396
Select Methods option 397
Select tool 394
selecting 3D geometry 394, 397
Set Active Depth tool 15–18
Set Display Depth tool 15–18
shaded image renderers 86–88
shadows
  Add Sky Light... 157
  ambient light 147
  area light 187
  enabling 132
  flashbulb light 151
  ray tracing 122
  rendering 116
  sky light 158, 160
  solar lighting 153, 156, 159
  solar shadow resolution 105
Show Display Depth tool 15–18
Show Settings 74
Show tool 395
showing 3D geometry 395
sky background
  with environment mapping 306–311
  with sky cylinders 302–306
sky cylinders 302–306
sky lighting
  daytime lighting 294–296
  description 157
  shadows 160
sky opening
  and radiosity 326
  creating 174–177
  description 170
Slide option 79
sliding the camera 79
Smooth mode 86–88
smoothness 343
Solar Cluster 161–163, 296–298
solar lighting
  configuring 155

description 153
enabling 155
settings 153
shadows 153, 156, 159
solar shadow resolution, rendering setting 105
solids, attaching materials 202–204
source lighting
  area light
    creating 185–187
    description 170
    shadows 187
  attenuation 187–189
  Define Light tool, settings 165
  description 163–165
  diffuse lighting. *See* area light
  distant light
    adding sky light 174
    description 168
    placing 172–173
    reducing intensity 179
    softening shadows 296–298
  falloff 187–189
  flashlight. *See* spot light
  light bulb light. *See* point light
  placing lights
    distant light 172–173
    editing placed lights 184
    point light 177–178
    spot 180–183
    spot light 180–183
  point light 169, 177–178
  sky opening 170, 174–177
  sources 171
  spot light 170, 180–183
  sunlight 168
    See also distant light; solar lighting
  types of 163
Specular option 228
spot light 170, 180–183
standard view orientations 7
standard views 3–5
starting MicroStation 1
Stereo 3D 99
stroke tolerance, rendering setting 100–103
sunlight simulation 168
sunset lighting 311
surface normals 281–283
Swivel option 80
swiveling the camera 80

T
terminator 129
textures. *See* materials; procedural textures
three point view projections 41
Tilt option 81
tilting the camera 61–63, 81
Top view 3
Translucency option 228
transparency
  backgrounds 233–235
  enabling 132
  increasing 133
  phong rendering 90
  ray tracing 123
  rendering view attribute 116
Transparency option 229
Turn option 79
twilight lighting 315
two point view projections 40

U
U3D (Universal 3D) format 389

V
variable shading 86–88
view attributes, rendering setting 114
view cone
  color coding 44
  displaying 74
  handles 45, 46
  locating the eye point 46
  modifying the eye point 45
  moving 47
  orientation 42
View Control toolbox
  active depth 15–18
  Clip Mask tool 15, 18–22
  Clip Volume tool 15, 18–22
  Display Active Depth tool 15–18
  display depth 15–18
  displaysets 22
  Set Active Depth tool 15–18
  Set Display Depth tool 15–18
  Show Display Depth tool 15–18
  tool summary 15
view number, rendering setting 115
view orientations, standard 7
view projections
  changing 37
  one point 39
  parallel 38
  three point 41
  two point 40
  types of 37
view rotation. *See* rotating views
view volume
  clip mask 18–22
  clip volume 18–22
  definition 13
  limiting 18–22
views
  rendering setup 36
  selecting 49
  setting up 31–36, 42
visible environment
  maps 307–311
  photorealism 98
  ray tracing 123
  rendering setting 136
volume. *See* view volume

W
Walk option 80
walking the camera 80
wireframe routines 84–86
Wiremesh routine 84–86
wood texture 260–262

END USER LICENSE AGREEMENT FOR BENTLEY SOFTWARE

IMPORTANT – READ CAREFULLY: This End-User License Agreement ("EULA") is a legal agreement between you (either an individual or a single entity) and Bentley Systems, Incorporated ("Bentley") for the Bentley software and associated documentation that accompanies this EULA, which includes the associated media and Bentley internet-based services ("Software").

YOU AGREE TO BE BOUND BY THE TERMS OF THIS EULA BY DOWNLOADING, INSTALLING, COPYING, OR OTHERWISE ACCESSING OR USING THE SOFTWARE. YOUR ACCEPTANCE OF ALL OF THE TERMS AND CONDITIONS OF THIS EULA IS A CONDITION TO THE GRANT OF LICENSE BELOW. THIS EULA, AS MAY BE MODIFIED BY ANY APPLICABLE SIGNED WRITTEN AGREEMENT BETWEEN YOU AND BENTLEY, REPRESENTS THE ENTIRE SET OF TERMS AND CONDITIONS GOVERNING YOUR USE OF THE SOFTWARE AND SUPERSEDES ALL PRIOR OR CONTEMPORANEOUS ORAL OR WRITTEN COMMUNICATIONS, PROPOSALS AND PRESENTATIONS WITH RESPECT TO THE SOFTWARE OR THE SUBJECT MATTER OF THE EULA.

If this agreement is translated into a language other than English and there is a conflict of terms between the English and the other language, the English version will control. You should keep a copy of this EULA for your records. The latest version of this EULA appears in its entirety on *http://www.bentley.com/legal/eula_en.txt*. Bentley may update or amend the EULA at any time without notice to you; however, the form of EULA in effect at the time of the Software acquisition will apply.

1. **CERTAIN DEFINITIONS.**
    1.1. **"Academic Related Use"** means the use of designated Software in object code form solely for internal classroom instruction or research of your teaching staff and/or students matriculated in a degree program and not to include student use in a paid employment setting or any other use prohibited under this EULA.
    1.2. **"Academic Software"** means Software that is identified as "Academic Edition" or "Academic License" (or words of similar meaning).
    1.3. **"CAL"** means client access license.
    1.4. **"Device"** means a single personal computer, workstation, terminal, hand held computer, pager, telephone, personal digital assistant, Server or other electronic device used by a User.
    1.5. **"External User"** means any individual (not an organization) who is not: (i) one of your full-time, part-time or temporary employees; or (ii) agency temporary personnel or an independent contractor on assignment at your place of business or work-site.
    1.6. **"License Key"** means the document furnished to you by Bentley in electronic or such other format, as determined in Bentley's sole discretion, that sets forth a unique serial number for the Software and authorizes use of the Software.
    1.7. **"Production Use"** means use of the Software in object code form by a single User or a Device, as applicable, solely for internal production purposes in support of one Site.
    1.8. **"Site"** means the discrete geographic location where you first install or use the Software.
    1.9. **"Time Clocks"** means any time clocks, copy-protection mechanisms, or other security devices embedded in the Software which may deactivate the Software after expiration of any applicable subscription or termed license period.
    1.10. **"User"** means any individual or entity that is not an External User.
2. **GRANT OF LICENSE.** As and for so long as you comply with all of the terms of this EULA, Bentley grants you the right to (a) install and use one copy of the Software for Production Use in the country where the Software is first obtained and (b) use the documentation that accompanies the Software for internal, non-commercial reference purposes only.
3. **RESERVED RIGHTS.** You acknowledge and agree that the Software is a proprietary product of Bentley or its suppliers, distributors and unrelated third parties ("Suppliers") protected by copyright and other applicable intellectual property laws and treaty provisions. You further acknowledge and agree that the entire right, title and interest in and to

the Software including associated intellectual property rights, shall remain with Bentley or its Suppliers. This license grant may be made by Bentley on behalf of Suppliers as third party beneficiaries of the license rights provided herein. Bentley retains all rights not expressly granted to you in this EULA. **THE SOFTWARE IS LICENSED NOT SOLD.**

4. **REGISTRATION.** You acknowledge that registration or activation may be required in order for you to utilize the full benefits of the Software.

5. **NO RENTAL OR COMMERCIAL HOSTING.** Software is licensed for Production Use only. You may not rent, lease, lend or provide commercial hosting services with the Software. You may also not use the Software to provide fee or transaction based services. Contact Bentley for the availability of alternate pricing if you desire to use the Software in such fashion.

6. **NO "MULTIPLEXING" OR POOLING.** Use of software or hardware that reduces the number of electronic devices directly monitored or managed by the Software or directly accessing or utilizing the Software (sometimes called "multiplexing" or "pooling" software or hardware) does not reduce the number of licenses required; the number of licenses required would equal the number of distinct inputs to the multiplexing or pooling hardware/software "front end."

7. **LIMITATIONS ON REVERSE ENGINEERING.** You may not decode, reverse engineer, reverse assemble, reverse compile, or otherwise translate the Software except and only to the extent that such activity is expressly permitted by applicable law notwithstanding this limitation. To the extent that you are expressly permitted by law to undertake any of the activities listed in the previous sentence, you will not exercise those rights until you have provided Bentley with thirty (30) days prior written notice of your intent to exercise such rights.

8. **DATA CAPTURE AND USE.** You agree that Bentley may collect and utilize technical information gathered as part of Software support services that may be provided to you. Data capture in this form will only be used to improve Bentley's products and/or provide customized services to you and will not be disclosed or disseminated to third parties except in an aggregated form.

9. **ARCHIVAL COPY.** You may make one copy of the Software on media appropriate for your single Device for the express purpose of backup in the event that the Software media is damaged or destroyed, provided that you reproduce and include on the backup copy all the information appearing on the original labels.

10. **RESTRICTIONS ON CERTAIN SOFTWARE.** Software identified as demo, evaluation, BDN, Beta or "NFR" (or "Not for Resale" or with words of similar meaning) may not be sold, bartered or otherwise transferred. Such Software may not be used for any purpose other than your testing or evaluation unless specified otherwise pursuant to a separate agreement signed by both you and Bentley.

11. **ACADEMIC SOFTWARE.** For Academic Software, Bentley hereby grants you a non-exclusive right and license to use in object code form such Academic Software for Academic Related Use only. You may not sell, barter or otherwise transfer Academic Software. **Special Note Applicable to Academic Software:** If you have covered the Academic Software subject to this EULA pursuant to a valid BEN SELECT Agreement (or successor agreement) with Bentley then you may be entitled to additional and incremental licensing benefits to those set forth in this EULA by virtue of that relationship. In the event that Academic Software is no longer covered by a valid BEN SELECT agreement due to termination of the BEN SELECT agreement or any other reason, then you will lose those incremental benefits, and your license rights will only be as set forth in this EULA.

12. **TIME CLOCKS.** Bentley's default licensing term is perpetual unless otherwise specifically identified for the Software licensed. If you have licensed the Software subject to this EULA for a term shorter than a perpetual license, you acknowledge that the Software may be delivered to you with embedded Time Clocks. You agree that Time Clocks are not considered a defect of the Software and you release Bentley from any and all claims, however characterized, arising from or related to Time Clocks or their operation.

13. **TRANSFER.** *Internal.* You may transfer the Software and the EULA to a different Device at the same Site, provided you completely remove the Software from all prior Devices. You may also make a one-time transfer of a CAL to another of your Users or Devices located at the same Site. In order to accomplish these transfers you may need to contact Bentley. *External.* You may not transfer the Software and license granted under this EULA, or a CAL, to a third party without Bentley's prior written consent. If such consent is obtained, you may permanently transfer the Software and the license granted under this EULA, or the CAL, provided you transfer the Software and all and media to such third party, and you do not retain any copies. The recipient of such transfer must agree to all terms and conditions of the EULA. Any purported sublicense, assignment, transfer or encumbrance is void without Bentley's prior consent.

14. **UPGRADES.** You may not use any Software identified as an upgrade unless you are properly licensed to use Software which Bentley has identified as being eligible for an upgrade. After installing an upgrade, you may use the original Software product that was eligible for an upgrade provided that at any one time you use *only* the upgraded Software or the prior Software version subject to the upgrade.

15. **NO EXTENSION OF CAPABILITIES.** You may develop your own applications that interoperate or integrate with the Software. Bentley prices its Software, among other factors, based on capabilities that we expose to you. You may not extend the Software to enable or unlock capabilities of the Software not specifically identified by Bentley as forming part of the specified end user functionality.

16. **SEPARATION OF COMPONENTS.** The Software is licensed as a single product. Component parts of the Software may not be separated and installed or used on multiple Devices.

17. **TERMINATION.** If you breach the terms and conditions of this EULA, Bentley may terminate this EULA without prejudicing any of its other rights. In such event you must destroy and remove all copies of the Software from your Device(s). Sections 1, 3, 13, 20, 21, 23, 25, 26, 27, 28 and 29 specifically survive termination.

18. **NO AUTOMATED USE.** A license for the Software may not be shared or used concurrently on different Devices, nor to support multiple User or operational requests as indicated above. As a result, you may not use the Software in an automated, unattended, non-interactive server application or component (including ASP) where: (i) multiple User requests from different Users are queued for processing; or (ii) multiple requests from one User are queued for processing but acting against content created or edited by other Users. Examples which would violate this Section 18 include but are not limited to use as a plot server, file translator, print server or other applications using or employing similar methods.

19. **LIMITED WARRANTY.** Except for Software which is identified as no-charge, free, demo, evaluation, BDN, Beta or NFR, which is provided to you "AS-IS" and specifically without warranty of any kind, for sixty (60) days from the date of first installation (the "Warranty Period"), Bentley warrants that (i) the Software will perform substantially in accordance with the functional specifications in the documentation which accompanies the Software; and (ii) the media on which the Software is distributed meets generally accepted industry standards. It is understood that neither Bentley nor its Suppliers are responsible for your use of the Software or the results from such use. It is further understood that there may be errors or omissions in the information contained in the Software, that the information contained in the Software may not be current or complete and that defects in hardware or software may prevent you from gaining access to the Software. This limited warranty is offered by Bentley alone, and is not extended to any software code that may be contributed to the Software by our Suppliers. Any supplements or updates to the Software (including but not limited to fixes, work in progress builds, or subsequent updates) provided to you after the expiration of the Limited Warranty period above are not covered by any warranty or condition, express, implied or statutory.

20. **DISCLAIMER.** THE FOREGOING LIMITED WARRANTY STATES THE SOLE AND EXCLUSIVE REMEDIES FOR BENTLEY'S OR ITS SUPPLIER'S BREACH OF WARRANTY. EXCEPT FOR THE LIMITED WARRANTY AND TO THE MAXIMUM EXTENT PERMITTED BY APPLICABLE LAW, BENTLEY AND ITS SUPPLIERS PROVIDE THE SOFTWARE *AS IS AND WITH ALL FAULTS*, AND TO THE MAXIMUM EXTENT PERMITTED BY APPLICABLE LAW IN YOUR JURISDICTION, BENTLEY AND ITS SUPPLIERS DISCLAIM ANY AND ALL OTHER WARRANTIES, FOR ITSELF AND FOR ALL SUPPLIERS, EITHER STATUTORY, EXPRESSED OR IMPLIED, INCLUDING, WITHOUT LIMITATION, WARRANTIES OF GOOD TITLE, WARRANTIES AGAINST INFRINGEMENT, AND THE IMPLIED WARRANTIES OF MERCHANTABILITY AND FITNESS FOR A PARTICULAR PURPOSE. THIS LIMITED WARRANTY GIVES YOU SPECIFIC RIGHTS; YOU MAY HAVE OTHER RIGHTS, WHICH VARY AMONG JURISDICTIONS.

21. **HIGH RISK ACTIVITIES.** The Software is not fault tolerant and is not designed, manufactured or intended for use or resale as control equipment in hazardous environments requiring fail-safe performance, such as in the operation of nuclear facilities, aircraft navigation or communication systems, air traffic control, direct life support machines, or weapons systems, in which the failure of the Software could lead directly to death, personal injury, or severe physical or environmental damage ("High Risk Activities"). Accordingly, Bentley and its Suppliers specifically disclaim any express or implied warranty of fitness for High Risk Activities.

22. **END USER REMEDIES.** If a defect in the Software appears that constitutes a breach of the above Limited Warranty, Bentley shall, at its sole option, repair the Software, refund the price you paid for the Software or replace the defective item(s), provided that: (i) you notify Bentley of the defect during the Warranty Period; (ii) the Software is not modified, changed, or altered by anyone other than Bentley, unless authorized by Bentley in writing; (iii) your computer equipment is in good operating order and the Software is installed in an officially supported environment; and (iv) the

non-conformity is not caused by a third party or by you, your agents, employees or contractors. Repaired, corrected, or replaced Software shall be covered by this limited warranty for the period remaining under the warranty covered by the original Software, or if longer, for thirty (30) days after the date: (a) of installation by you of the repaired or replaced Software, or (b) Bentley advised you how to operate the Software so as to achieve the functionality described in the documentation. YOU AGREE THAT THE FOREGOING CONSTITUTES YOUR SOLE AND EXCLUSIVE REMEDY FOR BREACH BY BENTLEY OF THE LIMITED WARRANTY MADE IN THIS EULA. Outside the United States, neither these remedies nor any product support services offered by Bentley are available without proof that you acquired the accompanying copy of the Software from an authorized source outside the United States.

23. **LIMITATION OF LIABILITY**. Regardless of whether any remedy set forth herein fails of its essential purpose by law, in no event will Bentley or its Suppliers be liable for indirect, special, incidental, economic or consequential damages, regardless of the nature of the claim, including without limitation lost profits, costs of delay, interruption of business, loss of use, costs of lost or damaged data or documentation or liabilities to third parties arising from any source, even if Bentley has been advised of the possibility of such damages. In no event shall the liability of Bentley or its Suppliers exceed the amount paid by you (in the currency used to purchase) for the Software. Some jurisdictions do not allow the exclusion or limitation of implied warranties or limitation of liability for incidental or consequential damages, so the above limitation or exclusion may not apply to you. THE PROVISIONS OF THIS EULA ALLOCATE THE RISKS BETWEEN BENTLEY AND YOU. BENTLEY'S PRICING REFLECTS THIS ALLOCATION OF RISK AND THE LIMITATION OF LIABILITY SPECIFIED HEREIN.

24. **STATUTORY CONSUMER RIGHTS**. Nothing in this EULA is meant to contravene statutory rights that consumers may have pursuant to local law.

25. **EXPORT CONTROLS**. The Software has been manufactured or developed in the United States of America and accordingly may be subject to U.S. export control laws, regulations and requirements. Regardless of any disclosure made by you to Bentley of an ultimate destination of the Software, you must not export or transfer, whether directly or indirectly, the Software, or any portion thereof, or any system containing such Software or portion thereof, to anyone outside the United States (including further export if you took delivery of the Software outside the United States) without first complying strictly and fully with all export controls that may be imposed on the Software by the United States Government or any country or organization of nations within whose jurisdiction you use the Software. The countries subject to restriction by action of the United States Government are subject to change, and it is your responsibility to comply with the United States Government requirements as they may be amended from time to time. You shall indemnify, defend and hold Bentley harmless for any breach of your obligations pursuant to this Section.

26. **U.S. GOVERNMENT RESTRICTED RIGHTS.** If the Software is acquired for or on behalf of the United States of America, its agencies and/or instrumentalities ("U.S. Government"), it is provided with restricted rights. The Software and accompanying documentation are "commercial computer software" and "commercial computer software documentation," respectively, pursuant to 48 C.F.R. 12.212 and 227.7202, and "restricted computer software" pursuant to 48 C.F.R. 52.227-19(a), as applicable. Use, modification, reproduction, release, performance, display or disclosure of the Software and accompanying documentation by the U.S. Government are subject to restrictions as set forth in this Agreement and pursuant to 48 C.F.R. 12.212, 52.227-19, 227.7202, and 1852.227-86, as applicable. Contractor/Manufacturer is Bentley Systems, Incorporated, 685 Stockton Drive, Exton, PA 19341-0678.

27. **GOVERNING LAW.** This EULA will be governed by and construed in accordance with the substantive laws in force in the Commonwealth of Pennsylvania. The state courts located in Chester County, Pennsylvania and the federal courts located in Philadelphia, Pennsylvania shall have exclusive jurisdiction over all disputes relating to this Agreement. To the maximum extent permitted by applicable law, the parties agree that the provisions of the United Nations Convention on Contracts for the International Sale of Goods, as amended, and of the Uniform Computer Information Transactions Act, as it may have been or hereafter may be in effect in any jurisdiction shall not apply to this Agreement.

28. **SEVERABILITY.** The provisions of this EULA shall be deemed to be separable and the invalidity of any provision hereof shall not affect the validity of the remainder of this Agreement.

29. **NOTICES.** Please send all notices under this EULA to Bentley Systems, Incorporated, Attn: General Counsel, 685 Stockton Drive, Exton, PA 19341-0678.

30. **QUESTIONS.** Should you have any questions regarding this EULA, please contact the Bentley subsidiary serving your country, or write to: Bentley Systems, Incorporated, Legal Department, 685 Stockton Drive, Exton, PA 19341-0678.

31. **RE-DISTRIBUTION OF BENTLEY® VIEW™.** If you are interested in re-distributing Bentley View either internally or externally to your organization, please complete the online Bentley View Distribution Agreement found at: *http://www.bentley.com/bentleyview/redistribute.html*.